Book of the Disappeared

ETHNIC CONFLICT: STUDIES IN NATIONALITY, RACE, AND CULTURE

Series Editors: Daniel Rothbart and Karina V. Korostelina

TITLES IN THE SERIES

Book of the Disappeared:
The Quest for Transnational Justice
Jennifer Heath and Ashraf Zahedi, Editors

First Nationalism Then Identity:
On Bosnian Muslims and Their Bosniak Identity
Mirsad Kriještorac

Torture, Humiliate, Kill: Inside the Bosnian Serb Camp System
Hikmet Karčić

BOOK OF THE DISAPPEARED

The Quest for Transnational Justice

Jennifer Heath and Ashraf Zahedi, Editors

University of Michigan Press
Ann Arbor

Published in the United States of America by the
University of Michigan Press
Manufactured in the United States of America
Printed on acid-free paper
First published May 2023

A CIP catalog record for this book is available from the British Library.

Library of Congress Cataloging-in-Publication data has been applied for.

ISBN 978-0-472-07593-5 (hardcover : alk. paper)
ISBN 978-0-472-05593-7 (paper : alk. paper)
ISBN 978-0-472-90325-2 (open access ebook)

DOI: https://doi.org/10.3998/11953892

Library of Congress Control Number: 2023932730

An electronic version of this book is freely available, thanks in part to the support of libraries
working with Knowledge Unlatched (KU). KU is a collaborative initiative designed to make
high quality books Open Access for the public good. More information about the initiative
and links to the Open Access version can be found at www.knowledgeunlatched.org.

The University of Michigan Press's open access publishing program is made possible
thanks to additional funding from the University of Michigan Office of the Provost and the
generous support of contributing libraries.

Cover art courtesy of Stephen Parlato.

To the victims and their survivors

Contents

Digital materials related to this title can be found on the Fulcrum platform via the following citable URL: https://doi.org/10.3998/mpub.11953892

Just as it is necessary to rob your enemies of their humanity, so you have to find a way of relinquishing responsibility of the evil you are about to commit. You must define yourself as a victim. It follows that you, in committing murder, even genocide, are merely acting in self-defense. It is the victim who is responsible.

—Jonathan Sachs

Now we will count to twelve
and we will all keep still
for once on the face of the Earth,
let's not speak in any language;
let's stop for a second,
and not move our arms so much.
. . .
If we were not so single-minded
about keeping our lives moving,
and for once could do nothing,
perhaps a huge silence
might interrupt this sadness
of never understanding ourselves
and of threatening ourselves with
death.
Now I'll count up to twelve
and you keep quiet, and I will go.

—excerpt: "Keeping Quiet"
Pablo Neruda

Acknowledgments

We would both like to express our gratitude to Elizabeth Demers, Mary Hashman, and Haley Winkle of the University of Michigan Press for their enthusiasm and kindness. And to our marvelous contributors and artists for their amazing generosity and superb talents. Working with them has been pleasurable and enlightening.

• • •

I thank my late husband, Jack Collom, for the indominable spirit that saw me through so many projects. I only wish he were here to celebrate the completion of this one. To my children, Sarah, Scott, Matt, and Robin, and my stepson, Chris, *compañeros* all along the way. To the dear friends who have held my hand through thick and thin, advised me, encouraged me, and wined and dined me—gratitude is insufficient. Essentially, I thank Ashraf Zahedi for the incredible work she did to kickstart this book while I was out of commission, and for her infinite patience and compassion.

—Jennifer Heath

My deep gratitude to Ashok Mehta for believing in this book and whole-heartedly supporting me through the course of its completion.

Also, I would like to thank Mary Hegland and Ed Petrillo for their enthusiastic support for the book.

—Ashraf Zahed

Artworks

Stephen Parlato
Cover: *The Cave of Forgotten Dreams*
Pinned collage, 40″ x 60″
2022
Courtesy of the artist
©Stephen Parlato

Chitra Ganesh and Mariam Ghani
From *Index of the Disappeared*
Detail: "Intro to an Index"
Work on paper, dimensions vary
2004–present
Courtesy of the artists
©Chitra Ganesh and Mariam Ghani

Sama Alshaibi
From *Between Two Rivers*
Details: "Razor Wire" and "To Eat Bread"
Digital archival prints, limited editions 5+ 1AP, 20″ x 30″
2008–2009 and 2016
Courtesy of the artist
©Sama Alshaibi

Nancy Maron
Abu Ghraib
Acrylic on canvas, 18″ x 14″
2007
Photo by Paul Gillis, Artwork Photography
Courtesy of the artist
©Nancy Maron

Helen Zughaib
From *Do Not Forget Us, La Tanssana*
Shirts, permanent ink, wood hangers, dimensions vary
2020
Photo by © Graham Snodgrass
Courtesy of the artist
©Helen Zughaib

Yassi Golshani
From *The Eyes*
Papier mâché from Iranian newspapers, dimensions vary
1997–2000
Courtesy of the artist
©Yassi Golshani

Leang Seckon
The Elephant and the Pond of Blood
Mixed media and collage on canvas, 79″ x 59″
2013
Courtesy of the artist and Rossi & Rossi, Ltd.
©Leang Seckon

Melvin Edwards
From *Lynch Fragments*
"Memory of Winter"
Welded steel, 13″ x 6 5/8″ x 8 5/8″
1996
"Jom Time"
Welded steel, 11 6/8 x 8 1/2″ x 7 2/8″
1998
Courtesy of the artist and Alexander Gray Associates,
New York; Stephen Friedman Gallery, London.

©Melvin Edwards / Artists Rights Society (ARS), New York.

Jonathan Herrera Soto

In Between/Underneath (Entremedio/Por Debajo)
Stencil prints with mud (unfired clay, water, sawdust, charcoal, ink), 25″ x 40″ each print (72′ x 24′ total installation)
2018–2019
Courtesy of the artist
©Jonathan Herrera Soto

Morgan C. Page

Stolen
Digital illustration printed on archival cold-press paper with archival pigments, dimensions vary
2021
Courtesy of the artist and Supporting Indigenous Sisters: An International Print Exchange, Midwestern State University
©Morgan C. Page

Introduction

Jennifer Heath and Ashraf Zahedi

"Bring his body to me," said Hatidza Hren, a Bosnian Muslim searching for her husband.
    "I will recognize his bones."

Enforced disappearances and genocide are as ancient as the inventions of governments and armies. And despite human evolution, these crimes against humanity continue with no notable suspension anywhere on Earth. Human progress has not taken us far enough: we can visit the moon, but somehow, we cannot curb our cruelty toward one another. Although States and individuals occasionally express outrage, too often, official backs are turned, attention spans diminished.

Book of the Disappeared aims to expose some of these crimes, concentrating primarily on those committed in the twentieth century, now into the twenty-first, and sadly likely to continue ad infinitum. With growing tensions, many related to climate change—which is intensifying conflicts already facing the world, with stressors such as poverty and political instability magnified by increased droughts, floods, or heat waves—the chances of our living peaceably are dangerously reduced, yet ever more urgent.

For those and other reasons, we decided to assemble this book to explore violations and quests for justice. In partnership with eminent, insightful scholars, practitioners, and artists—all performing groundbreaking work—we wish to help elucidate and confront the roles and inactions that have empowered perpetrators, as well as amplify, wherever possible, the voices of survivors, whose testimonies, in the words of Richard Hovannisian, "may be as valuable as official dispatches and reports. It is in such versions especially that the human element becomes manifest, affording insight not found in documents."[1]

This book does not claim to be definitive, nor could we cover every region where crimes occur. We attempt to provide a basic overview, addressing the plights of women and children, discussing methods of investigation, detection, and retribution, ways in which movements network and build on each other's experience, and the psychology that enables ruthless offenses. We hope *Book of the Disappeared*—like others that engage similarly—may become a crucial contribution.

We are currently experiencing (not uniquely through history) a rise in authoritarian regimes and nationalism that exploits ethnic and racial animosity and builds power for a corrupt few. The world is trapped in yet another age of strongmen, contemporary despots[2] and their cronies in Europe, Russia, Asia, Africa, Latin America, and the United States, despite the U.S. Bill of Rights, adopted in 1791. Among the first acts of any totalitarian system are to erode essential human rights such as due process, free speech, and independent journalism, which United Nations Secretary General António Guterres has called a global "media extinction event." The increasing intolerance of governments toward a free press—censorship, arrests, and murders of journalists—might be considered another form of enforced disappearance.[3]

Origins of Human Rights: A Brief History

Human rights are regarded as the foundation of social justice and the protection of human dignity.

The earliest known concept of human rights is typically associated with the writings of the Greek philosopher Aristotle (384–322 BCE). In *Nicomachean Ethics*, he supported the existence of a natural moral order, which, he wrote, "has the same validity everywhere."[4] Roman Stoics Cicero (106–43 BCE) and Seneca the Younger (c. 4 BCE–65 CE) expressed an analogous idea, arguing that "morality originated in the rational will of god." Having a shared relationship with god, the Stoics believed humans have a duty to obey god's will. Although varied in their expressions, most world religions share beliefs in the existence of a universal moral community—love, compassion, and forgiveness—guided by the divine.[5] But as we've experienced across the millennia, ordinary humans pay surprisingly little attention to the dictates of their faiths, instead twisting spirituality into politics.

Blatant examples of corrupt spiritual "guidance" might comprise Pope Pius XII, an anti-Semitic Nazi sympathizer; pro-military, anti-Muslim Buddhist leaders in Burma/Myanmar, such as the monk Ashin Wirathu; the cruel, misogynist, Jihadist Wahabi leaders in Saudi Arabia, whose vicious doctrine informs the Taliban in Afghanistan; the merciless, misguided Islamic State in Iraq, Syria, and throughout much of the Middle East; or Russian Orthodox Patriarch Kirill, a virulent proponent of the invasion of Ukraine and the massacre of its people.[6] Militant religious radicals have existed across time, from Buddhists to Christians, Hindus, Jews, and more.

By contrast, political activists of faith—Mohandas Karamchand (Mahatma) Gandhi, Archbishop Óscar Arnulfo Romero y Galdámez, Reverend Martin Luther King, Jr., Archbishop Desmond Tutu, Sister Helen Prejean, Jewish Voice for Peace, and the Poor People's Campaign: A National Call for Moral Revival, to name only a *very* few obvious, but necessary, examples—have long supported grassroots movements for peace and human rights against tyranny, disappearance, genocide, inequality, poverty, and social injustice of all varieties.[7]

Documents asserting individual rights, such as the Magna Carta (1215) and the English Bill of Rights (1689) are precursors of today's human rights documents. English philosopher John Locke upheld in his 1688 *Two Treatises of Government*[8] that individuals possess natural rights, regardless of politics, and that these natural rights evolved from natural law. In the eighteenth century, amid his myriad writings, German philosopher Immanuel Kant championed dignity, equality, and moral autonomy within what he deemed to be humans' unique capacity to exercise reason. Locke and Kant have come to be associated with principles of the Enlightenment.

Ideals such as natural rights, moral autonomy, human dignity, and equality provided a normative bedrock for attempts to reconstituting political systems, for overthrowing formerly despotic regimes and seeking to replace them with forms of political authority capable of protecting and promoting these new emancipatory ideals. These ideals effected significant, even revolutionary, political upheavals through the eighteenth century, enshrined in such documents as the United States Declaration of Independence (1776) and the French National Assembly's Declaration of the Rights of Man and the Citizen (1789).[9]

But there was no universally agreed upon definition of human rights until the United Nations Declaration of Human Rights, which, in December 1948, provided the legal framework for violations to be addressed. The extermination of as many as fifteen million people by Nazi Germany—six million Jews, as well as Sinti and Romani,[10] homosexuals, and persons with disabilities—as an explicit State policy propelled the endeavor by shocked governments to create a UN Charter.[11] It was signed in June 1945 in order to bolster international peace and answer a call for standards that would protect citizens from abuses by their governments and hold nations responsible.

Transnational Quests for Justice

In this book, contributors have used both "transnational" and "transitional." In many ways, they are interchangeable. We have subtitled this book *The Quest for Transnational Justice*, because transnational justice expands beyond national boundaries, focusing on broad aspects of human rights violations. Transitional justice, an aspect of transnational justice, considers the issues faced by countries moving from a period of conflict and mass atrocities to post-conflict reconciliation. With this volume, it is our desire to assist in bridging those struggles from the fundamentally essential local to the global.

Across the years, the United Nations has adopted additional resolutions to cover different aspects of human rights, such as the Convention on the Prevention and Punishment of the Crime of Genocide (1951),[12] the International Covenant on Civil and Political Rights (1976),[13] and the International Convention for the Protection of All Persons from Enforced Disappearance (2010).[14] These instruments have provided the legal foundation for the transnational quest for justice.

However, the promotion of these rights and their collective applications are not possible without the necessary work of human rights advocates around the world. Their advocacy has become a movement, largely facilitated by independent organizations such as the International Federation of Human Rights (Paris, 1927),[15] Amnesty International (London, 1961),[16] and Human Rights Watch (New York, 1978),[17] as well as many other non-governmental organizations and religious groups.[18] They maintain strong ties to local, regional, and national organizations across the globe. Their work is profoundly important, particularly in countries where domestic human rights associations have not been permitted to operate. With the advent of the internet, some advocates living under repressive regimes have managed to bypass government censorship and forge transnational alliances. Thus, they've set in motion forces to expose crimes against humanity and hold offenders accountable.

Vital—indeed central—among these are family activisms such as *Las Madres de la Plaza de Mayo* (the Mothers of the Plaza de Mayo), who—along with their confederates, the original *Abuelas* (Grandmothers) of the Plaza de Mayo—fashioned the first major human rights group in 1977, in Buenos Aires, Argentina, during the 1974 to 1983 *Guerra sucia*, or Dirty War. The association initially formed to demand the identification of the approximately thirty thousand *desaparecidos* (disappeared), including their own unarmed, non-combatant children or grandchildren, many of whom were stolen as infants and given for adoption to members of the junta.[19] The Abuelas have set up a national genetic data bank so that kidnapped children can find their actual parents or learn their true origins in absence of family.

The Madres have also worked to determine the culprits of crimes against humanity, promoting their trials and sentencings. The highly successful Abuelas and Madres have inspired other mothers and family members, such as *Cumartesi Anneleri/Cumartesi İnsanları*, who gather each Saturday in Istanbul, Turkey, and *Madaran-e Khavaran*, the Mothers of Khavaran, in Tehran, Iran, the sole advocacy group operating inside that country.[20]

The Mothers and Grandmothers of Argentina's Plaza de Mayo, Ariel E. Dulitzky writes, as well as "the Vicariate of Solidarity in Chile, FEDEFAM—the first international federation of families of disappeared persons—and many organizations in every country have created new strategies on disappearances. Their work serves as models in other parts of the world."

In our opening chapter, "Latin America's Contributions to the Development of Institutional Responses to Enforced Disappearances," Dulitzky documents how efforts to bring perpetrators to justice, to guarantee the right to truth, to provide reparations, and memorialize the practice of enforced disappearance began in Latin America. Dulitzky, a leading expert in the inter-American human rights system, illustrates how it was in Latin America that most responses to disappearances emerged, were advanced, and consolidated.

To uncover and identify the disappeared, forensic teams in Argentina, Peru, Guatemala, and Chile established specialized services that led the search for the remains of the disappeared in Latin America and other parts of the world. But the practice, Soren Blau writes in "Our Resilient Bodies: The Role of Forensic Science and Medicine in Restoring the Disappeared to History," has naturally come with ethical, legal, social, and political challenges. Blau, Senior Forensic Anthropologist at Australia's Victorian Institute of Forensic Medicine, provides this book with a deep history of the use and valuable contributions of forensic science and medicine in the context of humanitarian and criminal investigation.

The Cold War, the War on Terror, and the ICPPED

Ironically, since the end of World War II, more countries around the world have drawn on enforced disappearance as a way of dealing with opponents. The magnitude of cases has required clear delineation and legal structures by which perpetrators could be prosecuted.

The term "disappearance" is most often associated with abduction. However, the United Nations definition is broader and more encompassing. The International Convention for the Protection of all Persons from Enforced Disappearance (ICPPED), founded in 2007, and entered into force in 2010, states

> for the purpose of this Convention, "enforced disappearance" is considered to be the arrest, detention, abduction, or any other form of deprivation of liberty by agents of the State or by persons or groups of persons acting with the authorization, support, or acquiescence of the State, followed by a refusal to acknowledge the deprivation of liberty or by concealment of the fate or whereabouts of the disappeared person, which place such a person outside the protection of the law.[21]

Among one hundred and ninety-five countries in the world, only sixty-two have ratified the ICPPED, including all Latin American and most Northern and Western European nations. The superpowers—the United States, Russia, and China—which have veto power in the UN Security Council, have not signed the convention.[22] Their non-committal has naturally emboldened perpetrators of enforced disappearances and genocides.

Dirk Adriaensens is a member of the executive committee of the B*Russells* Tribunal, an activist thinktank and peace organization based in Brussels, Belgium, and part of the Bertrand Russell Tribunal.[23] In "Iraq: Enforced Disappearance as a Tool of War," Adriaensens notes that Iraq has been a member of the ICPPED since its inception, the twentieth country to implement its ratification. Iraq's own Missing Campaign claims the numbers of disappeared persons is one million. But other sources, Adriaensens says, suggest that as many as four million remain unaccounted for. Between the Iran-Iraq War in 1980, the 1991 First Gulf War led by the United States, and the U.S.-led operation in 2003, Iraq may face the highest number of missing people on Earth.

Essentially a post–World War II rivalry between the United States and its allies against the Union of Soviet Socialist Republics (USSR)—allied powerfully with the People's Republic of China—the Cold War (1945–1991), was the most significant conflict shaping the century: a market-led economy, with or without democracy, versus a State-controlled, political, socioeconomic system. The Korean War (1950–1953, ending without an armistice), the protracted Vietnam War (1955–1975), and the war in Afghanistan that effectively began in 1979 with the Soviet invasion, are manifestations of the Cold War, which drew upon the social and political construction of their enemies and thus legitimized their punishment and potential elimination.

The Cold War provided a doctrine through which adversaries of the U.S. government and its allies were labeled as communists or Maoists and were therefore subjected to detention, disappearances, and executions. In 1953, Julius and Ethel Rosenberg became the only U.S. citizens to be put to death during peacetime, convicted of conspiracy to commit espionage.[24] In 1954, during what was known as the Second Red Scare (the first took place in 1917–1920),[25] U.S. President Dwight Eisenhower signed the Communist Control Act outlawing the Communist Party of the United States and criminalizing membership in or support for it. Likewise, in China and the USSR, favoring democracy and capitalism were regarded as treason.[26] Through its declared and undeclared wars, proxy wars, and coup d'états, the Cold War undermined the paths to home-grown democracies circling the planet from Guatemala to Iran.[27] It ended with the dissolution of the USSR in 1991, yet anti-communist dogma continues to be used against perceived foes of the State.

The Cold War has continued in various guises, from the overthrow of "hostile" governments to spy-versus-spy pranks, and internet hacking. But in February 2022, the Cold War began to heat up with the Russian invasion of Ukraine by strongman/dictator Vladimir V. Putin,[28] and a new(ish) version, as of this writing, is fomenting between the U.S., China, and Taiwan.

The War on Terror was invented by the George W. Bush administration (2001–2009) to advance United States National Security Policy in the aftermath of the September 11, 2001, airborne attacks on the United States when nearly three thousand people died. The heightened sense of nationalism and political anxiety set the stage for public support. On October 7, 2001, a U.S.-led coalition invaded Afghanistan to wage war on the ruling Taliban as punishment for harboring Osama bin Laden, a Saudi extremist who lead a group calling itself al-Qaeda, which claimed responsibility for the 9/11 attacks.[29] Shortly after the fall of the Taliban, the United States largely abandoned Afghanistan's promised reconstruction—certainly as many Afghans saw it—to invade Iraq in 2003 on false pretenses, waging a War on Terror against its ruler, Saddam Hussein, but in fact, to gain power over Iraq's oil.[30]

Afghanistan and Egypt are among the sites to which the U.S. Central Intelligence Agency (CIA) have kidnapped and delivered suspected "terrorists." In "Extraordinary Rendition: A Human Rights Analysis," David Weissbrodt, late professor of law at the University of Minnesota, describes in dramatic detail innocent lives ruined by government-sponsored abduction and extrajudicial transfer of persons from one country to another to circumvent laws on interrogation, detention, extradition, and/or torture. It is, Weissbrodt writes, "a hybrid human rights violation," not only of the Office of the United Nations High Commissioner for Human Rights (OHCHR) and the ICPPED, but also the Convention against Torture and Other Cruel, Inhuman, or Degrading Treatment or Punishment, and the Universal Declaration of Human Rights. Extraordinary renditions have accelerated since 9/11, bolstering the U.S. government's efforts in its ostensible, and open-ended, War on Terror.[31]

While Afghanistan was an extraordinary rendition destination,[32] it also has an extraordinary history of war, disappearances, and genocide. In 2013, the *New York Times* reported a Dutch exposé that gave the names and details of nearly five thousand victims buried alive by bulldozers in the fields around Kabul's Pul-e Charkhi Prison. The victims were arrested, tortured, and murdered by the Afghan Communist government in 1978 and 1979, shortly before the Soviet invasion.[33]

"Lives in Limbo: Afghanistan's Epidemic of Disappearances," by Dallas Mazoori—who coordinated the Afghanistan Independent Human Rights Commission's Conflict Mapping project—and Stefan Schmitt—who helped found the Afghan Forensic Science Organization—outline the country's forty years of armed conflict, widespread arrests, and secret detentions, all outside any legal protection. Mazoori and Schmitt examine the impact on families and communities as tens of thousands of Afghans have been disappeared and suffered summary executions by State and non-State agents.

Disappearances have become a key feature of the Syrian conflict, which began in 2011. In "Vanishing Nation: Enforced Disappearance in Syria," Sareta Ashraph and Nicolette Waldman reveal how tens of thousands of Syrians have disappeared—mostly young men who have dematerialized after arrests or abduction from or on their way to their homes, universities, and workplaces. Ashraph—who heads the Office of Field Investigations at the UN Investigative Team to Promote Accountability for Crimes Committed by Daesh/ISIL (UNITAD)—and Waldman—a Middle East North Africa researcher for Amnesty International—trace the initial use of disappearance by Syrian President Bashar al-Assad's government during the unrest against demonstrators, political activists, human rights defenders, media workers, doctors, and humanitarian aid workers. Disappearance in Syria, much like Iraq or Afghanistan and elsewhere, is a ubiquitous weapon against anyone suspected of disloyalty. The sweeping and increasing rise in Syrian disappearances, Ashraph and Waldman note, speak to the near impossibility of securing justice and lasting peace.

The politics of the Cold War and the War on Terror have greatly impacted countries covered in this book—Iran, Cambodia, Afghanistan, and Latin American nations, as well as others. Their devastation, their curse, endures, stalking helpless people through time like golems or ghosts. Likewise, the War on Terror continues to shape the political destinies of Afghanistan, Iraq, Syria, and elsewhere around the world.

Genocide

The destruction of Carthage (now in Tunisia) may be the first recorded incitement of genocide during the three Punic Wars (264–146 BCE) that killed 145,000 people out of a population of between 200,000 and 400,000. The destruction of Carthage, historian Ben Kiernan writes, "set a precedent for genocide."[34] Other genocides followed everywhere, although there was no name for them. Nor was there a label for the slaughter of Indigenous peoples in their millions throughout the Americas, beginning in 1492, with the landing of Christopher Columbus; or for the butchery that continues into the present of African Americans originally brought in chains to North American shores in 1619.

In 1944, Raphael Lemkin, a Polish Jewish émigré, at last coined a word for the annihilation of members of a group. *Genocide* combines the Greek *genos* (race, tribe) with *cide* (killing). After much debate about the definition of genocide, in 1948, the international community adopted the UN Convention on the Prevention and Punishment of Genocide (CPPCG), which entered into force in 1951. It describes genocide as

> any of the following acts committed with intent to destroy, in whole or in part, a national, ethnical, racial or religious group, as such: (a) Killing members of the group; (b) Causing serious bodily or mental harm to members of the group; (c) Deliberately inflicting on the group conditions of life calculated to bring about its physical destruction in whole or in part; (d) Imposing measures intended to prevent births within the group; (e) Forcibly transferring children of the group to another group.[35]

The charter does not include political groups. Yet "politicide" can also be regarded as genocide, for instance, the rounding up of communists during the Dirty War, or the wholesale, deliberate murders of aid workers and journalists. Nor does it address gendered genocide.[36]

Both genocide and enforced disappearance are carried out systematically. Both have specific targets, whether of ethnic, religious, racial, linguistic, cultural, or political groups.[37] Both utilize extrajudicial killings and arbitrary deprivation of the right to life. There can be no ceiling on the numbers victimized in acts of enforced disappearance or genocide.

Genocides generally take place in full view and with the active or tacit support of the citizens of a given country or members of a group who stand to benefit materially or ideologically, whereas enforced disappearances usually take place in secret, without much public participation. Often, only family members or neighbors are witness to the arrest or kidnapping and subsequent disappearance of the targeted person. Nevertheless, genocide frequently results in disappearance. Bodies disposed of and never again seen by their communities. One such event was the 2014 kidnapping of forty-three male students from the Ayotzinapa Rural Teachers' College, murdered then disappeared in Iguala, Guerrero, México.[38]

The first known genocide of the twentieth century took place in colonial Southwest Africa (present-day Namibia), in lands inhabited by the Herero and Nama peoples and occupied by the German Empire, the Second Reich, whose troops were headed by General Lothar von Trotha. In 1904, von Trotha issued a deadly eviction notice to the Herero and Nama. They were forced into the forbidding Omaheke Desert. Captured men were massacred, and women and children were left to die of starvation, dehydration, and exhaustion. Trapped, surrounded by soldiers, the desert became a concentration camp where as many as seventy thousand died. Survivors were tortured, lived in unsanitary conditions, suffered malnutrition, used for medical experiments, and exploited as slave labor. In 2015, the German government admitted to the genocide, but would not agree to reparations. In 2021, they outlined an offer of more than $1.34 billion (€1.1 billion) in development aid to the Namibian government. Many descendants of the Herero and Nama believe their people, not the Namibian government, should negotiate directly with the Germans.[39]

The ethnic cleansing of Armenia, beginning in 1915, is considered the second genocide of the twentieth century.[40] The Armenian Holocaust, as it is often referred to, was a carefully calculated attack by the Ottoman Empire that eliminated most of the Armenian population of Anatolia and historical West Armenia. Men and boys were shot, while women and children were mustered and marched into the uninhabitable Syrian desert. When the brutality finally ended in 1923, approximately 1,500,000 Armenians were disappeared, starved to death, executed, kidnapped, or exiled.[41] To this day, the Turkish government denies responsibility or that a genocide ever took place. To speak of it is a crime. In 2021, Joe Biden became the first U.S. president to recognize the mass killings of Armenians by the Ottoman Empire as a genocide.[42]

The third and most horrendous twentieth-century genocide was perpetrated by the Nazi Third Reich—described briefly above and referred to in various chapters of this book. The Holocaust—the *Shoah* in Hebrew—drove the formation of the United Nations and its Declaration of Human Rights. It is said that concentration camps, inspired by von Trotha to imprison the Herero and Nama people, and the Turkish techniques of forced deportations of Armenians, crammed into cattle cars, as well as the incineration of hundreds trapped in caves, were adopted by the Nazis.[43]

A short, insufficient list of other genocide victims in modern times would include Vietnamese, Aboriginal Australians, Kashmiris, Bangladeshis, East Timorese, Sudanese in the Nuba Mountains and Darfur, Yazidis, Chinese Uyghurs, Tigrayans in Ethiopia, and shamefully more.

The uncovering of mass graves tells many diverse tales, notwithstanding those of discarded infants discovered in Ireland and interred First Nations school children in unmarked pits found in Canada.[44] Forensic teams have exhumed burial sites in Rwanda, Former Yugoslavia, Kashmir, Indonesia, and the U.S. state of Texas. Bodies, as Soren Blau notes, can be concealed in rivers, warehouses, fields, wells, even latrines, with others yet to be unveiled.

In "Politics of Silence and Denial: 1988 Enforced Disappearances and

Executions in Iran," this book's co-editor Ashraf Zahedi, provides a thorough analysis of the 1988 executions that killed more than ten thousand people, most of whom were tossed unceremoniously into mass graves or whose bodies simply disappeared. Zahedi poignantly describes some of the suffering and heartbreak that occurs when the mourning and death rituals of survivors are impaired.[45]

Akila Radhakrishnan and Elena Sarver—president and a legal advisor at the Global Justice Center, respectively—unpack the ongoing campaign of violence against Rohingya Muslims in Burma (now Myanmar, renamed in 1989 by the ruling junta). The persecution has continued for decades and includes specifically designed gender crimes against women and girls, from outright killings to gang rape, torture, and the imposition of cruel methods to prevent births. "Genocide of the Rohingya" focuses critically on how these crimes have affected a traumatized community.

Rape is without a doubt an act of genocide, and therefore also an element of cultural genocide. Catherine MacKinnon put it this way

[G]enocidal rape is particular. . . . This is rape as an official policy of war in a genocidal campaign for political control. That means not only a policy of the pleasure of male power unleashed, which happens all the time in so-called peace; not only a policy to defile, torture, humiliate, degrade, and demoralize the other side which happens all the time in war. . . . It is specifically rape under orders . . . under control. It is also rape unto death, rape as massacre, rape to kill . . . an instrument of forced exile . . . rape as spectacle . . . to drive a wedge through a community, to shatter a society, to destroy a people.[46]

In "The Legacy of Wartime Rape in Bosnia and Herzegovina," Edina Bećirević and Majda Halilović speak in astute and discerning detail to rape as a weapon of the 1992–1995 war in Bosnia and Herzegovina. It was used on at least twenty thousand women, many of whom, Bećirević—professor of Security Studies at the University of Sarajevo—and Halilović—head researcher of the Atlantic Initiative-Center for Security and Justice in Bosnia and Herzegovina—tell us, were held captive and tortured, and some deliberately impregnated to make Serb babies. Throughout, there were methodical rape campaigns. Populations were terrorized, "cleansed." It was not only Bosniak (Muslim) or Bosnian Croat women who were victimized, but Serb women as well. Several thousand men were also victims of rape.[47] And then there is the silence, the reticence, even refusal, of women to speak of the degradations perpetrated upon them.

In 2014, ISIS—Islamic State—attacked the Sinjar region of northern Iraq. Their target: the Yazidi, an Indigenous, often-persecuted, pre-Zoroastrian religious group that ISIS reviles as pagans. Islamic State is also called *Daesh* by Kurds and many mainstream media and world leaders. They are insulted by the term, an acronym in Arabic meaning "to trample and crush" or "a bigot who imposes his views on others."

During the Sinjar invasion, thousands of Yazidi men, women, and children were captured. Those who had escaped, were rescued, or, most often, sold back to their families, returned to their trampled and nearly crushed communities and relayed tales of almost unimaginable atrocities, including the genocide of about ten thousand men and older boys, the indoctrination and forced recruitment of younger boys, and the enslavement and torture of about six thousand women and girls, who were repeatedly raped, traded, or sold.

When ISIS was driven from southeastern Syria in early 2019, many Yazidi women and their children were taken to halfway houses. The mothers were permitted by Yazidi elders to return home but had to leave their children behind. The elders would not accept them, declaring that the children "would destroy the Yazidi community. . . . The fathers of these children killed the parents of these survivors," Yazidi religious authority Baba Sheikh Ali Elyas told the *New York Times*, "How can we accept them?"

The women who wish to keep their children are now forced to choose between returning to their parents, siblings, and neighbors or cutting ties to rejoin their sons and daughters who now reside in Syrian or Kurdish orphanages.[48]

Amrita Kapur's "The Impact of Enforced Disappearance on Women" tackles government responses to enforced disappearances as they relate to women. Kapur—an expert with Switzerland's Geneva Centre for Security Sector Governance—looks specifically at victims in Nepal and Lebanon and examines surveys from thirty-one countries to help design programs to address the issues facing women who may be shoved into the workforce, often in exploitative conditions, who suffer uncertain legal status restricting their access to assets held in male relatives' names or experience reduced social status and interfamilial harassment. Some may themselves be targeted for enforced disappearance, and, in addition, face torture, abuse, and sexual violence.

Trauma, Trials, and Tribunals

Kapur also notes that transitional justice measures have typically focused on bodily harm and men's experiences. She reviews administrative mechanisms to resolve the ambiguous status of wives of the disappeared (sometimes called "half widows"), gender-sensitive approaches to exhumations and reburials, reparations, designing memorialization, criminal justice, and reform measures that adequately consider women's differentiated experiences.[49]

In "The Khmer Rouge Bureaucrats: Counting the Missing," James A. Tyner, professor of Geography at Kent State University, ties the legal proceedings of the Extraordinary Chambers in the Courts of Cambodia, better known as the "Khmer Rouge Tribunal," to Hannah Arendt's famous "banality of evil."[50] The first trial, Case 001, convened four years after its establishment and, in 2007, Kaing Guek Eav (alias "Duch"), commandant of the 5–21 security center was formally charged with crimes against humanity and grave breaches of the 1949 Geneva Convention. Under the administrative supervision of Duch, upwards of fifteen thousand men, women, and children were arrested, detained, and executed, a genocide that forms one component of the broader Cambodian genocide, which resulted in the deaths of approximately 1.7 million people between 1975 and 1979. Tyner considers these events from the standpoint of bureaucratic accounting, provides insight into implications for remembrance among survivors, and reveals some of the intersections between enforced disappearance and genocide.

"Retributive or Restorative Justice: Gacaca Courts' Contribution to Transitional Justice and Reconciliation in Post-Genocide Rwanda," by Hilmi M. Zawati, Chair of Montreal's Centre for International Accountability and Justice, explores a 1994 genocide that took approximately eight hundred thousand Tutsi and moderate Hutu lives, and the failures and successes of a national reconciliation process called the Genocide Law of 1996, which hosted, among others, community-based Gacaca courts to restore justice and mend Rwanda's torn society. Gacaca's foundation was truth-telling and public apology, intended to eradicate the culture of impunity. It was meant to provide an alternative to failed modern models of justice.

In "MIA: Disappearing Political Analysis in Transnational Justice," Vasuki Nesiah—a professor of Human Rights and International Law at New York University's Gallatin School—analyzes the dominant history of the field of transitional justice, which has grown exponentially on many fronts, consolidating, maturing, and becoming institutionalized within the

United Nations and organizations globally. It has produced truth commissions, reparations programs, and prosecutorial initiatives, which have become, Nesiah writes, especially significant as to how the field uses historical memory. The absorption and assimilation of historical memory in the practice of transitional justice, she says, requires examination and caution.

"To the victor belong the spoils," and among the victor's loot are claims about history, recounting it in his favor, while victims are silenced, their stories conveniently disappeared.

Kayhan Irani—an Emmy-award winning writer and cultural activist—embraces what she calls "counter-storytelling" as "a mechanism to weather," and even overcome, the pain of injustice and the victor's version of history. The work of creating a "mnemonic community" to affirm the reality of experience often comes most effectively through the arts, rather than the formalities (and bureaucracies) of transitional/transnational systems. In "Story as Portal: Healing, Regeneration, and Possibility after Genocide," she describes the work of a Guatemalan theater collective, *Grupo Sotz'il*, that confronts the centuries-old suffering of the Maya people, most recently with the carnage of Maya civilians by the U.S.-backed Guatemalan military, which began in 1965 and continues in various forms to this day. Indigenous Maya youth recreate and reclaim ancestral music, dance, and embodied storytelling as a means not only to maintain their cultural traditions, but to renew the community's struggle for political autonomy and self-determination in the twenty-first century.

Arts of Resistance

The arts have always been crucial in presenting information to the public about crimes against humanity and providing strength and support to societies in transition. In their roles as human rights advocates, artists (of all disciplines) can be historians or documentarians and are natural rebels against oppression.

With each generation, artists have sought, individually or collectively, to shed light on injustice—from enforced disappearance to genocide, war, civil rights, climate change, and other desecrations. Their work and lives have been shaped as much by the "real" world as by the art world and they bring to bear the power of the arts to foster awareness and bring about change. Some have been severely punished for their resistance. Examples from the many: Armenian painter Panos Terlemezian—active during the repressive regime of nineteenth-century Sultan Abdulhamid II and the genocide of 1915—spent his early life imprisoned and in exile; poet/playwright Federico Garcia Lorca died in 1936 at the hands of nationalists during the Spanish Civil War (his exhumed, unmarked grave is thought to have been discovered in 2017); in the 1960s, left-leaning musicians and dancers were arrested, killed, or disappeared under the rule of Indonesian dictator Suharto (r. 1968–1998); Chilean poet/musician Victor Jara was tortured and murdered during the dictatorship of Augusto Pinochet (r. 1973–1981); during the first reign of the Taliban in Afghanistan (1996-2001), musicians were forced to hide their instruments and today, they and visual artists are again under threat of severe punishment for pursuing their artforms; young artists in the MENA (Middle East and North Africa) region were subjected to immense penalties, including death, during the Arab uprisings which began in 2010; and, in 2011, dissident artist Ai Weiwei was arrested by the Chinese authorities and held without charges for eighty-one days. Artists all over the world have been and continue to be at risk when they dare challenge tyranny.

Cadres of contemporary artists are examining and attempting to expose human rights abuses. The artists whose works are scattered throughout this book represent a fraction of those whose art articulates crimes against humanity. They include Chitra Ganesh and Mariam Ghani, with an excerpt from their vast collaboration, *Index of the Disappeared*; Sama Alshaibi, who looks at the plight of Iraqi women with "Razor Wire" and "To Eat Bread," bextracted from her larger photographic project, *Between Two Rivers*; Nancy Maron's painting, *Abu Ghraib*, expresses her horror at the scandalous abuse that took place in that notorious Iraqi prison; Helen Zughaib's detail from her installation *Do Not Forget Us, La Tanssana*, relates the story of a Syrian prisoner tasked with assuring his fellow detainees that their names would not be lost; Yassi Golshani's *The Eyes*, is a detail from a massive project of the same name largely about societal self-censorship constructed from Iranian newspapers; Leang Seckon's painting *The Elephant and the Pond of Blood* recalls a Cambodian phrase describing the bloody killing fields of the 1970s; Melvin Edwards's "Memory of Winter" and "Jom Time" are only two works from his *Lynch Fragments*, a decades-long project (beginning in the 1960s) that explores social justice, issues of identity, and political awareness; the detail from Jonathan Herrera Soto's installation *In Between/ Underneath (Entremedio/Por Debajo)* memorializes two hundred journalists murdered in México; and Morgan C. Page's print, *Stolen*, considers the numerous Indigenous Canadian women and girls who have been murdered or gone missing and whose cases are by and large ignored by authorities.

The texts accompanying all these artists' images include their own statements describing the work's raison d'être, and where appropriate, we have added a few facts that relate to the work itself thereby briefly unfolding topics or occurrences that, regrettably, could not appear in this book in full. We have placed some of the artwork in relation to the chapters they proceed or follow, but not always. None are meant to "illustrate" the chapters, but to stand alone as testimonies of their own.

The artists' full biographies are featured alongside those of our chapter contributors at the end of this book.

The Roots of Group Violence

We close this book with "The Psychology of Bystanders, Perpetrators, and Heroic Helpers," by Ervin Staub. In this abridged version of his renowned longer essay,[51] the Founding Director of the Psychology of Peace and Violence doctoral program at the University of Massachusetts, Amherst, asks what leads groups of people or governments to perpetuate genocide, mass killings, or disappearances. What are the characteristics and psychological processes of individuals and societies that contribute to such group violence? What are their motives and how do they arise and intensify? How do inhibitions decline? Staub focuses on the psychology and role of both perpetrators and bystanders who can influence events, while individuals, groups, or nations frequently remain passive. And what of would-be saviors, "heroic helpers," who endanger their own lives trying to protect intended victims?

Transnational human rights advocacy networks have turned the ideal of human rights into something of a universal norm and have influenced change in the behaviors of some States. In 2010, families of the disappeared, along with their allies, successfully lobbied the United Nations to hold a day of remembrance on August 30 as International Day of the Victims of Enforced Disappearance, still observed. It is a wonderful gesture. But it does not go far enough.

The questions Staub poses must be confronted and posited to as many people as possible. Much more public education is needed in institutions throughout the globe, with more consciousness-raising in schools, places of worship, through the arts, and wherever else possible to deliver knowledge of the causes and ramifications of enforced disappearance and genocide and to make clear that it is each human being's responsibility to root it out and to prevent it as best we can in peace and compassion.[52]

Our hope is that this book will become an educational tool and valuable component of the human rights movement and that it will play its part in strengthening transnational justice.

Notes

Epigraph from Elizabeth Neuffer, "Mass Graves," *Nieman Reports: The Nieman Foundation for Journalism at Harvard University* 53, no. 2 (Summer 1999): 9. https://niemanreports.org/wp-content/uploads/2014/04/99summer.pdf. Elizabeth Neuffer (June 15, 1956–May 9, 2003) was an American journalist who specialized in covering war crimes, human rights abuses, and post-conflict societies. She died at the age of forty-six in a car accident while covering the Iraq War.

1. As quoted in Samuel Totten and William S. Parsons, *Centuries of Genocide: Essays and Eyewitness Accounts*, 4th ed. (New York: Routledge, 2009), 6.

2. As of this writing, in Spring 2022, self-styled strongman leaders—Vladimir Putin of Russia, Recep Tayyip Erdoğan of Turkey, Xi Jinping of China, Narendra Modi of India, former President of the United States Donald Trump, Jair Bolsonaro of Brazil, and even Nobel Peace Prize winner Abiy Ahmed of Ethiopia—are among those charting the most dangerous global political course of our era. See Gideon Rachman, *The Age of the Strongman: How the Cult Leader Threatens Democracy Around the World* (New York: The Other Press, 2022).

3. The Committee to Protect Journalists lists six critical threats to press freedom: legal intimidation and retaliation, denial of access, government threats, physical violence, harassment, and declining financial viability of local news. https://protectpressfreedom.org/threats/#threats

In 2021, the Norwegian Nobel Committee awarded the Peace Prize to Maria Ressa—co-founder of *Rappler*, a digital media company for investigative journalism in the Philippines—and Dmitry Muratov—a founder of the independent Moscow-based newspaper *Novaya Gazeta*,—"for their efforts to safeguard freedom of expression, which is a precondition for democracy and lasting peace. Ms. Ressa and Mr. Muratov are receiving the Peace Prize for their courageous fight for freedom of expression. . . . They are representatives of all journalists who stand up for this ideal in a world in which democracy and freedom of the press face increasingly adverse conditions." *Rappler* and its staff have been continually harassed and arrested. Since 2000, seven reporters for *Novaya Gazeta* have been assassinated. In March 2022, thanks to repeated threats from the Russian government and the paper's opposition to the Ukraine invasion, *Novaya Gazeta* suspended its print activities and a month later launched *Novaya Gazeta Europa* from Riga, Latvia, to avoid censorship. In May 2022, Vox, reported 23 journalists of various nationalities have died in the Russian-Ukraine war. https://www.voanews.com/a/media-group-at-least-23-journalists-killed-in-ukraine-war/6558137.html

4. Aristotle, *Nicomachean Ethics* (Oxford: Oxford University Press, 2009).

5. Throughout much of history, people acquired rights and responsibilities as members of a family, Indigenous nations, religion, class, community, or State. All societies, whether in oral or written tradition, have had systems of propriety and rules for tending to the wellbeing of their members. The Hindu Vedas, the Baby-

lonian Code of Hammurabi, the Hebrew and Christian Bibles, the Qur'an, and the Analects of Confucius are among the oldest written sources addressing questions of duty, rights, and responsibilities. Inca and Aztec codes of conduct and justice and an Iroquois Constitution (said to have inspired the U.S. Constitution) were Native American sources that existed long before the invasion and conquest of the Americas. See Harold Coward, *Human Rights and the World's Major Religions*, annotated ed. (Westport, CT: Praeger Publishers, 2005).

6. A few references include Tom Heneghan, "Pope Pius XII, Accused of Silence During the Holocaust, Knew Jews Were Being Killed, Researcher Says," *Washington Post*, April 29, 2020. https://www.washingtonpost.com/history/2020/04/29/vatican-pope-pius-records-holocaust/; "Wirathu: Myanmar Military Releases Firebrand Buddhist Monk," *BBC*, September 7, 2021. https://www.bbc.com/news/world-asia-58471535#:~:text=Myanmar's%20military%20junta%20has%20released,in%20a%20February%20military%20cou; Ahmed Rashid, *Taliban: The Story of the Afghan Warlords* (New York: Palgrave McMillan, 2001), Mohamed Rabie, "The Rise of Islamic Fundamentalism," ResearchGate, March 2021. https://www.researchgate.net/publication/350189555_The_Rise_of_Islamic_Fundamentalism; John Chryssavgis, "The Unholy Ideology Driving both Putin and Patriarch Kirill in the Russian-Ukraine War," *America, The Jesuit Review*, March 21, 2022. https://www.americamagazine.org/faith/2022/03/21/ukraine-russia-war-putin-church-242632?gclid=CjwKCAjwx46TBhBhEiwArA_DjKq5zEy-C03Ho4uhhjmSbKgJr5TPI__JfArusA6toLp8feHK1pDapLxoCFbYQAvD_BwE. See also Omer Bartov and Phyllis Mack, eds. *In God's Name: Genocide and Religion in the Twentieth Century* (New York: Berghahn Books, 2001); and Steven Leonard Jacobs and Marc L. Sherman, eds. *Confronting Genocide: Judaism, Christianity, Islam* (Plymouth, UK: Lexington Books, 2009).

7. A few references include "8 Books on Mahatma Gandhi every Indian Should Read." *Times of India*, October 1, 2019. https://timesofindia.indiatimes.com/life-style/books/features/8-books-on-mahatma-gandhi-every-indian-should-read/photostory/71393566.cms; University of Notre Dame, Kellogg Institute for International Studies, "Biography: Archbishop Óscar Romero." https://kellogg.nd.edu/archbishop-oscar-romero; and Genevieve Jordon Laskey, "Celebrate the Feast of Saint Óscar Romero," Catholic Relief Services, September 2018. https://www.crs.org/resource-center/commemorating-saint-oscar-romero?gclid=CjwKCAjwx46TBhBhEiwArA_DjAlNIgLP0N4TAJwr8qAf3WBAN_Iw5kSijS33aSF-lU85ppLKWLoa9VxoCHMAQAvD_BwE; Clayborne Carson, ed., *The Autobiography of Martin Luther King, Jr.* (Brentwood, TN: Warner Books, 2001); Mary L. G. Theroux, "Remembering Desmond M. Tutu," Independent Institute, January 5, 2022. https://blog.independent.org/2022/01/05/remembering-desmond-tutu/?gclid=CjwKCAjwx46TBhBhEiwArA_DjCSi-HcjYwHJo4sergSb11V-DOlbHvIKU_03x37ESQKzzW_Ps5BenxoCIgwQAvD_BwE; Helen Prejean, *River of Fire: My Spiritual Journey* (New York: Random House, 2019); Jewish Voice for Peace, https://www.jewishvoiceforpeace.org; the Poor People's Campaign was organized in response to a call by Rev. Martin Luther King Jr. for a "revolution of values" and is organized by, among others, Bishop William J. Barber, and Rev. Dr. Nancy Petty, https://www.poorpeoplescampaign.org/. For further examples, see, for instance, Guthrie Graves-Fitsimmons and Maggie Siddiqi, "21 Faith Leaders

to Watch in 2021," Center for American Progress, May 20, 2021. https://www.americanprogress.org/article/21-faith-leaders-watch-2021/; Graves-Fitzsimmons and Siddiqi, "22 Faith Leaders to Watch in 2022," Center for American Progress, March 31, 2020. https://www.americanprogress.org/article/22-faith-leaders-to-watch-in-2022/; and "Religious Leaders and Activists," Georgetown University, Berkeley Center for Religion, Peace and World Affairs. https://berkleycenter.georgetown.edu/religious-leaders-and-activists

8. John Locke, *Two Treatises of Government* (Cambridge: Cambridge University Press, 1988).

9. James Fieser and Bradley Dowden, eds., *Internet Encyclopedia of Philosophy*. https://iep.utm.edu/eds/

10. The word "gypsies," commonly used to describe the Sinti and Roma people, is now understood to be pejorative.

11. To read the original United Nations Charter, the founding document of the UN, visit: https://www.un.org/en/about-us/un-charter

12. https://www.un.org/en/genocideprevention/documents/atrocity-crimes/Doc.1_Convention%20on%20the%20Prevention%20and%20Punishment%20of%20the%20Crime%20of%20Genocide.pdf

13. https://www.ohchr.org/en/professionalinterest/pages/ccpr.aspx

14. https://www.ohchr.org/en/hrbodies/ced/pages/conventionced.aspx

15. https://www.fidh.org/en/

16. https://www.amnesty.org/en/

17. https://www.hrw.org/

18. Aryeh Neier, *The International Human Rights Movement: A History* (Princeton: Princeton University Press, 2013).

19. See Rita Arditti, *Searching for Life: The Grandmothers of Plaza de Mayo and the Disappeared Children of Argentina* (Berkeley: University of California Press, 1999). The practice in Argentina of killing parents and stealing their infants was made famous in the 1985 film, *La historia oficial* (*The Official Story*), directed by Luis Puenzo and written by Puenzo and Aida Bortnik. The theft of children is all too usual. An earlier, parallel tragedy took place with Christian Armenian children whose parents were killed in the 1915–1923 genocide and who were deposited in Muslim Turkish homes. In the slave-holding era of the United States, it was common for hunters to steal Black children to sell. In the nineteenth century, Indigenous children in South Africa, Australia, the United States, and Canada were forcibly installed in boarding schools without their parents' consent. Other examples abound, from persistent sex trafficking of children to Operation Babylift in 1975 South Vietnam, to Guatemalan adoption scams, to U.S. child separation policies against migration. Several organizations have formed to investigate these crimes: The International Commission on Missing Persons, the International Centre for Missing & Exploited Children (ICMEC), the National Center for Missing & Exploited Children in the US, Missing People in the UK, Child Focus in Belgium, and The Smile of the Child in Greece.

20. Losif Kovras, *Grassroots Activism and the Evolution of Transitional Justice: The Families of the Disappeared* (Cambridge: Cambridge University Press, 2017).

21. https://www.ohchr.org/en/hrbodies/ced/pages/conventionced.aspx

22. United Nations Treaty Collection. https://treaties.un.org/

23. For a complete history and description of the Russell Tribunal, also known as the International War Crimes Tribunal, see https://en.wikipedia.org/wiki/Russell_Tribunal

24. Much has been written about the Rosenbergs. It is generally acknowledged that Ethel was innocent of all charges (and the only woman in the United States sentenced to death for any crime other than murder). Julius is recognized to have passed military information to the Soviets, although none of it involved treasured atomic secrets. Their trial was flawed with multiple miscarriages of justice. They left two children, Michael and Robert Meeropol, who wrote *We Are Your Sons: The Legacy of Julius and Ethel Rosenberg* (New York: Houghton Mifflin, 1975). Other volumes include a novel by E. L. Doctorow, *The Book of Daniel* (New York: Random House, 1971) and a history by Anne Sebba, *Ethel Rosenberg: An American Tragedy* (New York: St. Martin's Press, 2021).

25. The First Red Scare was brought on by widespread fear of Bolshevism, anarchism, and the 1917 Russian Revolution. The period comprised labor strikes and bombings, suppression of radical organizations, illegal searches and seizures, race riots, anti-immigrant nativism, convictions under the United States Espionage and Seditions acts, and deportations of citizens. Among the victims were anarchist Italian immigrants Nicola Sacco and Bartolomeo Vanzetti, arrested in 1920, and tried on trumped-up charges of robbery and murder, then executed in 1927. Of interest: Bruce Watson, *Sacco and Vanzetti: The Men, the Murders, and the Judgment of Mankind* (New York: Viking, 2007).

The Second Red Scare began immediately after World War II with fears about the perceived threat posed by Communists in the United States during the Cold War. In 1938, the U.S. House of Representatives formed the House Un-American Activities (HUAC) whose investigations focused on exposing Communists working inside the federal government, within universities, and the Hollywood film industry. Notorious among the investigators was U.S. Senator Joseph McCarthy of Wisconsin, who used hearsay and intimidation to establish his own political power. See for instance Ellen Schrecker, *Many Are the Crimes: McCarthyism in America* (New York: Little Brown and Company, 1998).

26. Paul R. Haerle, "Constitutional Law: Federal Anti-Subversive Legislation: The Communist Control act of 1954," *Michigan Law Review* 53, no. 8 (1955): 1153–65. In 1973, a federal district court in Arizona determined the act was unconstitutional, although the U.S. Supreme Court has not yet ruled on its constitutionality. No administration has tried to enforce it. The provisions of the act outlawing the U.S. Communist Party have not been repealed, and it continues to exist.

27. After centuries of strife and tyranny, Guatemala deposed its U.S.–backed dictator, Jorge Ubico, in a popular uprising. Juan José Arévalo won the country's first democratically free election in 1945. He was followed in 1950 by Jacobo Árbenz Guzmán, who was overthrown in 1954 by a CIA coup in collaboration with the United Fruit Company, whereupon a military junta resumed power. Piero Gleijeses, *Shattered Hope: The Guatemalan Revolution and the United States, 1944–1954* (Princeton, NJ: Princeton University Press. 1992).

In 1951, Iran's democratically elected prime minister, Mohammad Mossadegh, nationalized the country's oil industry, then under control of the British Anglo-Persian Oil Company. In 1953, the CIA and Britain's Secret Intelligence Service

(MI6) carried out a coup d'état removing Mossadegh from power. The National Security Archive, "CIA Confirms Role in 1953 Iran Coup," *National Security Archive Briefing Book*, no. 4, 435, August 19, 2013. https://nsarchive2.gwu.edu/ NSAEBB/NSAEBB435/

28. There is speculation, and that is all it can be, that Putin watched the United States invade countries such as Iraq on righteous pretenses such as delivering democracy and felt he could also invade sovereign nations based on his own pretenses. His 2014 Crimean and 2022 Ukrainian adventures hinge on an imperialist, revisionist history claiming that he is returning those countries their Soviet origins, because they were entirely created by the Russian Empire. For an interesting analysis, see Isaac Chotiner, "Vladimir Putin's Revisionist History of Russia and Ukraine," *The New Yorker*, February 23, 2022. https://www.newyorker.com/ news/q-and-a/vladimir-putins-revisionist-history-of-russia-and-ukraine. For background on early (1823) U.S. imperialist ambitions and claims to international proprietorship, see Howard Zinn, *A People's History of the United States* (New York: Harper & Row, 1980).

29. In 1979, Osama bin Laden joined *Mujahidin* forces in Pakistan fighting against the Soviet Union in Afghanistan. Along with the United States, under National Security Advisor Zbigniew Brzezinski, bin Laden helped to fund the Mujahidin, funneling arms, money, and fighters from the Arab world into Afghanistan. Julie Lowenstein, *US Foreign Policy and the Soviet-Afghan War: A Revisionist History* (senior essay, Yale University, 2016), 16 https://elischolar.library.yale.edu/ cgi/viewcontent.cgi?article=1045&context=applebaum_award. In 1988, bin Laden formed Al-Qaeda and shifted his base to Sudan. After returning to Afghanistan in 1996, he declared war against the United States, initiating a series of attacks, notably the 1998 U.S. Embassy bombings in Dar es Salaam, Tanzania, and Nairobi, Kenya. In 2011, bin Laden was killed by U.S. Navy SEALs in Abbottabad, Pakistan. The SEALs were going house-to-house on the fabrication of offering polio vaccines. *Medical News Today* speculates that this covert operation has contributed to Pakistani fears of receiving vaccinations against COVID-19. https://www.medicalnewstoday. com/articles/how-a-covert-cia-operation-led-to-vaccine-hesitancy-in-pakistan

30. The United States falsely claimed that Iraqi leader Saddam Hussein was developing weapons of mass destruction. For more about this and the War on Iraq, see a report from the Council on Foreign Relations: https://www.cfr. org/timeline/iraq-war. There is much interesting and sad reading about the desertion of and fumbling in Afghanistan by the United States, but to begin with, see: Ahsan I. Butt, "The Afghan War: A Failure Made in the USA," *Al Jazeera*, December 23, 2019. https://www.aljazeera.com/opinions/2019/12/23/ the-afghan-war-a-failure-made-in-the-usa

In August 2021, after nearly twenty years of occupation, the United States abruptly left Afghanistan, leaving the Taliban in charge. Among many news and other reports, see Thomas Gibbons-Neff, "In Afghanistan, an Unceremonious End and a Shrouded Beginning," New York Times, August 30, 2021, updated October 5, 2021. https://www.nytimes.com/2021/08/30/world/asia/us-withdrawal-afghanistan-kabul.html

31. Music is among many methods of torture, despite a ban by the United Nations and the European Court of Human Rights. Incessant loud music played to

prisoners causes intense discomfort, and has long-term psychological effects, leaving no visible physical traces. The technique is thought to have been devised in the 1950s and 1960s by the Soviets and has gone on to be used in Guantanamo and at Abu Ghraib prisons. Yet communal noise, novelist-playwright Elias Canetti (1905–1994) wrote, is also fundamental to the unity of a bloodthirsty crowd. See Kelsey McKinney. "How the CIA Used Music to 'Break' Detainees." *Vox*, December 11, 2014. https://www.vox.com/2014/12/11/7375961/cia-torture-music. In 2015, the American Civil Liberties Union on behalf of former detainees held in secret CIA prisons, sued psychologists James Mitchell and Bruce Jessen who were paid more than $80 million by the CIA to develop "enhanced interrogation" techniques, a.k.a. torture, such as waterboarding. The lawsuit was settled in 2017. See Laurence Alison and Emily Alison, "Revenge versus Rapport: Interrogation, Terrorism, and Torture," *American Psychologist* 72, no. 3 (2017): 266–77.

32. On April 13, 2021, President Joe Biden announced the withdrawal of U.S. troops from Afghanistan by September 11, 2021, therefore, he said, ending "the forever war." Ultimately, the evacuation took place on August 30, 2021, but on July 6, 2021, the *Guardian* reported that all U.S. troops had left the notorious Bagram Airfield surreptitiously in the dark of night, "leaving about 5,000 mostly Taliban prisoners." The report did not specify whether any of those deserted prisoners had been victims of "extraordinary rendition." Emma Graham-Harrison and Peter Beaumont, "Afghan Anger Over US's Sudden, Silent Bagram Departure," *Guardian*, July 6, 2021. https://www.theguardian.com/world/2021/jul/06/afghan-anger-over-uss-sudden-silent-bagram-departure

33. Rod Norland, "Old Atrocities, Now Official, Galvanize Afghanistan," *New York Times*, September 30, 2013. https://www.nytimes.com/2013/10/01/world/middleeast/release-of-decades-old-death-lists-stirs-anger-and-grief-in-afghanistan.html. Norland writes that "So many people were buried alive by bulldozers in the barren fields around the Pul-e Charkhi Prison . . . that guilty soldiers later said it was like an earthquake as their victims tried to claw their way out."

34. Ben Kiernan, "The First Genocide: Carthage, 146 BC," *Diogenes* 51, no. 3 (2004): 29–39; Kiernan, *Blood and Soil* (New Haven: Yale University Press, 2007), 264, 60.

35. *United Nations Convention on the Prevention and Punishment of the Crime of Genocide*, Article II: https://www.un.org/en/genocideprevention/documents/atrocity-crimes/Doc.1_Convention%20on%20the%20Prevention%20and%20Punishment%20of%20the%20Crime%20of%20Genocide.pdf

36. Gendered genocide has not yet found its way into the UN Convention on the Prevention and Punishment of Genocide (CPPCG) but may soon be added: https://www.researchgate.net/publication/256058549_Gendered_Genocide_The_Socially_Destructive_Process_of_Genocidal_Rape_Killing_and_Displacement_in_Darfur. An inclusion of gendered genocide must surely comprise the murders of LGBTQ+ people, which have been ongoing worldwide since at least the Christianizing of the Roman Empire in 324 CE: https://en.wikipedia.org/wiki/Violence_against_LGBT_people

37. Jeremy Sarkin and Grazyna Baranowska, "Why Enforced Disappearances Are Perpetrated Against Groups as State Policy: Overlaps and Interconnections Between Disappearance and Genocide," *Catolica Law Review* 11, no. 3 (2018), 11–50.

38. Most of the students' bodies have not been found, although burned bone fragments of three of them have been identified. "México's 43 missing students: Experts slam 'falsified' inquiry," *Al Jazeera*, March 29, 2022. https://www.aljazeera.com/news/2022/3/29/falsified-experts-slam-mexican-probe-of-42-missing-students. In August 2022, an official inquiry in México reported that the kidnappings were a "'crime of the State' involving every layer of government." Oscar Lopez. "México says disappearance of 43 students was a 'crime of the State." *New York Times*, August 20, 2022. Internationally renowned artist Ai Weiwei, whose work is deeply concerned with human rights, took on the tragic affair in 2019, creating colorful Lego portraits of each missing student that were displayed in México City. "43 Disappeared Mexican Students Remembered in Ai Weiwei Exhibit," *Voice of America*, April 19, 2019. https://www.voanews.com/a/disappeared-mexican-students-remembered-in-ai-weiwei-exhibit/4882715.html. In 2020, Ai produced and directed *Vivos*, a documentary featuring interviews with the students' families and an exploration of the inadequate official investigation. It premiered at the Sundance Film Festival. Ari Shapiro, "Ai Weiwei Takes On 43 Missing Mexicans in 'Vivos' Documentary," *National Public Radio*, January 29, 2020. https://www.npr.org/2020/01/29/800938097/ai-weiwei-takes-on-43-missing-mexicans-in-vivos-documentary#:~:text=Ai%20Weiwei%20Takes%20On%2043,In%20'Vivos'%20Documentary%20%3A%20NPR&text=Press-,Ai%20Weiwei%20Takes%20On%2043%20Missing%20Mexicans%20In%20'Vivos'%20Documentary,speaks%20with%20NPR's%20Ari%20Shapiro

39. Casper Erichsen and David Olusoga, *The Kaiser's Holocaust: Germany's Forgotten Genocide and the Colonial Roots of Nazism* (London: Faber & Faber, 2011); David Adetayo Olusoga, director/producer, *Namibia: Genocide and the Second Reich*, BBC, 2005, YouTube video, 58:37.https://www.youtube.com/watch?v=Rbon6HqzjEI; "Why Germany's Apology for Its 1904–1908 Genocide in Namibia Does Not Go Far Enough," *Democracy Now!*, June 11, 2021. https://www.democracynow.org/2021/6/11/namibia_german_apology_reparations

40. For a thorough, profound history of the Armenian genocide, see, among other sources, J. Michael Hagopian, writer, director, producer, *The Witnesses Trilogy*: "Voices from the Lake" (2000); "Germany and the Secret Genocide" (2003); and "The River Ran Red" (2009) (Encino, CA: The Armenian Film Foundation). http://www.armenianfilm.org/drupal/

41. The Armenian genocide of 1915–1923 was not the first premeditated attack by the Turkish government on the Armenian people. Earlier massacres occurred in 1894–1896 and again in 1909, which left ten thousand to thirty thousand victims and was, according to Vahakn N. Dadrian, "one of the most gruesome and savage bloodbaths ever recorded." Vahakn N. Dadrian, *The History of the Armenian Genocide: Ethnic Conflict from the Balkans to Anatolia to the Caucasus* (Oxford: Berghahn Books, 2003). See also "Armenian Survivors Project," notably an interview between Alternative Radio founder/director David Barsamian and his mother Araxie Barsamian. *Alternative Radio*, dates vary. https://www.alternativeradio.org/collections/armenian-survivors-project/

42. Benjamin Din, "Biden Recognizes Armenian genocide," *Politico*, April 24, 2021.

43. Elizabeth R. Baer, *The Genocidal Gaze: From German Southwest Africa to the Third Reich* (Detroit: Wayne State University Press, 2017).

44. James Grierson, "Mass Grave of Babies and Children Found at Tuam Care Home in Ireland," *Guardian*, March 3, 2017. https://www.theguardian.com/world/2017/mar/03/mass-grave-of-babies-and-children-found-at-tuam-orphanage-in-ireland; Ian Austen, "'Horrible History: Mass Grave Reported in Canada," *New York Times*, May 28, 2021. https://www.nytimes.com/2021/05/28/world/canada/kamloops-mass-grave-residential-schools.html; see also https://www.nytimes.com/2021/07/05/world/canada/Indigenous-residential-schools-photos.html?searchResultPosition=4https://www.nytimes.com/2021/05/28/world/canada/kamloops-mass-grave-residential-schools.html

45. See Barbara Preitler, *Grief and Disappearance: Psychological Interventions* (Thousand Oaks, CA: Sage Publications, 2015).

46. Catharine A. MacKinnon, "Rape, Geocide, and Women's Human Rights," *Harvard Journal of Law and Gender* 17, no. 5 (1994).

47. See Hilmi M. Zawati, "Impunity or Immunity: Wartime Male Rape and Sexual Torture As a Crime Against Humanity," *Torture* 17, no. 1 (2007): 27–47.

48. Special thanks to Sareta Ashraph and Dirk Adriaensens for information based on their expertise about the plight of the Yazidi. See Dana Taib Menmy, "'We Do Not Accept Those Children: Yazidis Forbid ISIL Offspring," *Al Jazeera*, March 24, 2021. https://www.aljazeera.com/features/2021/3/24/wrenching-choice-yazidi-mothers-to-choose-children-or-community; Jane Arraf, "ISIS Forced Them into Sexual Slavery: Finally, They've Reunited with Their Children," *New York Times*, May 28, 2021; and Kate Denereaz, "'Still Going Through Hell': The Search for Yazidi Seven Years On," Global Development, August 3, 2021.

49. War crimes are not only committed by men. In their book and subsequent essay, Jessica Trisko Darden and Izabela Steflja propose that many women war criminals "go unnoticed because their participation in exceptional wartime violence challenges deeply held assumptions about war and about women . . . [who have been] historically enshrined as innocent civilians in both policy and the population imagination. . . . This tendency has been reinforced by the passage of United Nations Security Council Resolution 132, which states that women and children are the vast majority of those adversely affected by armed conflict . . . such statements, though undoubtedly true, neglect the fact that women have played key roles in perpetrating war crimes and crimes against humanity." Jessica Trisko Darden and Izabela Steflja, *Women as War Criminals: Gender, Agency, and Justice* (Redwood City, CA: Stanford University Press, 2020) and Darden and Steflja, "When Women Commit War Crimes," War on the Rocks and the Texas National Security Review, October 28, 2020. https://warontherocks.com/2020/10/when-women-commit-war-crimes/

50. Hannah Arendt, *Eichmann in Jerusalem: A Report on the Banality of Evil* (New York: Penguin, 1964), 109.

51. "The Psychology of Bystanders, Perpetrators, and Heroic Helpers," here abridged by Ashraf Zahedi and Jennifer Heath with permission from the author Ervin Staub, was originally published by L. S. Newman and R. Erber, eds., *What Social Psychology Can Tell Us About the Holocaust: Understanding Perpetrator Behavior* (New York: Oxford University Press, 2002).

52. In Europe, the United States, and elsewhere, we are experiencing a resurgence of anti-Semitism, by and large from white Christian fundamentalist supremacists. See "Rise in Anti-Semitism, White Supremacy Exacerbated by Pandemic, Secretary-General Warns at Holocaust Remembrance Service, Calling for End to Attacks on Truth." United Nations Press Release, January 25, 2021. https://press.un.org/en/2021/sgsm20553.doc.htm; Michelle Boorstein, "White-supremacist propaganda remained high in the United States in 2021, new ADL report says." Washington Post, March 3, 2022. Also, of interest, Bernard Harrison. *The Resurgence of Anti-Semitism: Jews, Israel, and Liberal Opinion.* (Lanham, MD: Rowman and Littlefield, 2006).

Index of the Disappeared

Chitra Ganesh and Mariam Ghani

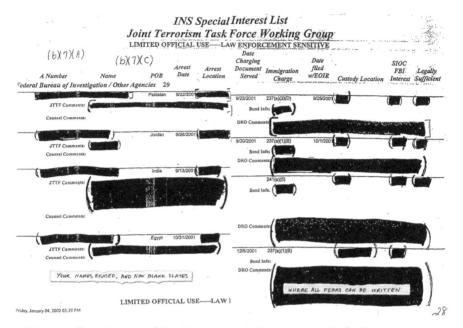

Excerpt from *Index of the Disappeared*, "Intro to an Index"

Index of the Disappeared is a collaboration, ongoing since 2004, between artists Chitra Ganesh and Mariam Ghani. The *Index* is both a physical archive of post-9/11 disappearances and a mobile platform for public dialogue.

As an archive, *Index of the Disappeared* foregrounds the difficult histories of immigrant, "Other," and dissenting communities in the United States since 9/11, as well as the effects of United States military and intelligence interventions around the world. Through official documents, secondary literature, and personal narratives, the *Index* archive traces the ways in which censorship and data blackouts are part of a broader shift to secrecy that allows for disappearances, deportations, renditions, and detentions on an unprecedented scale. The *Index* collection is built on the work of others actively engaged in political and legal challenges to the policies we track, and draws on radical archival, legal, and activist traditions to select, group, and arrange information. While the *Index* has become quite staggeringly comprehensive over the years, covering everything from black sites to Bagram, corporate surveillance to contract translators, Pelican Bay to the

Pentagon Papers (and much, much more), the point of the *Index* is not to collect everything relevant that is released into the public domain, but to sort through masses of information to retrieve and preserve small bits of significance, and then to make the connections that allow others to understand that significance.

—Chitra Ganesh and Mariam Ghani

Latin America's Contributions to the Development of Institutional Responses to Enforced Disappearances

Ariel E. Dulitzky

Historically, many consider Hitler's "Night and Fog" (*Nacht und Nebel*) decree of December 7, 1941, which ordered the secret detention and removal of political activists and resistance leaders, as the origin of modern enforced disappearances.[1] In 1946, the International Military Tribunal of Nuremberg executed German Field Marshal Wilhelm Keitel for this practice and the subsequent American Military Tribunal of Nuremberg in the *Justice* case, convicted the main lawyers of the Nazi regime for, among other things, administering the Night and Fog decree.[2]

Today, the term "enforced disappearance" encompasses many different situations, everything from kidnappings by drug cartels in México,[3] to the detention in "black holes" of alleged persons involved in terrorism by the United States Central Intelligence Agency (CIA).[4] The term "enforced disappearances" can refer to persons detained in political prison camps in North Korea,[5] those who disappeared in Bosnia during the war in Former Yugoslavia,[6] or those abducted by the death squads in El Salvador during the civil war.[7] Some insist on the danger of overusing the term, highlighting the need for a definition that addresses only the cases of disappearance similar to those that took place in Latin America in the 1970s.[8]

Yet enforced disappearance includes diverse forms of State repression. There are distinct reasons for this criminal practice and a multiplicity of political, economic, and psychosocial effects on the victims, as well as on the communities and societies where this technique of terror takes place.[9] This chapter embraces the premise that the "Latin American" definition has become a yardstick for many forms of enforced disappearance practices. Regardless of whether governments target their victims selectively and systematically, whether victims are individuals, ethnic or religious groups, or rural populations. The Latin American experience helped to create an international framework, flexible enough to travel from one continent to another, through different eras, and to adapt to diverse places, causes, and needs.

Until the tragic events of Latin America in the 1970s, the issue of disappearance was not a matter of concern, conceptualization, or national or international judicial responses.[10] Indeed, the term "disappeared," or *desaparecido*, to describe victims is a Latin American invention.[11] As Argentinean human rights defense attorney, Emilio Mignone, put it bluntly, the methodical practice of enforced disappearances in Latin America "is the maximum contribution to the history of the human cruelty."[12]

In 1988, The Inter-American Court of Human Rights (the Court) gave its first judgment on a case of enforced disappearance

> Disappearances are not new in the history of human rights violations. However, their systematic and repeated nature and their use not only for causing certain individuals to disappear, either briefly or permanently, but also as a means of creating a general state of anguish, insecurity, and fear, is a recent phenomenon. Although this practice exists virtually worldwide, it has occurred with exceptional intensity in Latin America in the last few years.[13]

Thus, not surprisingly, the evolution of the very concept of enforced disappearance and the main concerns surrounding those disappearances are grounded in narratives emanating from Latin America. In the late 1970s and early 1980s, the focus of human rights advocates had been on the immediate safety of the disappeared. As victims remained unaccounted for during the next three decades, the lack of access to meaningful legal recourse became central and the emphasis on impunity and unknown truths came to define enforced disappearances.[14]

For better or worse, the region has always been at the forefront of the use of or combat against this policy and technique of terror.[15] Latin America developed the most effective responses to overcome enforced disappearances. New types of resistance and hope go hand in hand with the demands of truth, justice, reparation, and memory. Latin American countries learned from each other[16] and served as models for other regions in confronting enforced disappearances.[17]

This chapter is not a historical, political, sociological, anthropological, or legal study about disappearances in Latin America, although it recognizes that all those approaches are needed to comprehensively study, understand, and respond to them. It summarizes the relationship between enforced disappearances and Latin America,[18] and speculates on the consequences of this relationship for other regions in the world.

The Practice of Enforced Disappearances in Latin America

In 1983, the Latin American Federation of Associations for Relatives of the Detained Disappeared (FEDEFAM) held that there were more than ninety thousand disappeared persons. In 2010, fifty-one thousand disappeared were reported in Colombia. In México, although there is reliable official data as of 2014, the total number of missing persons or those not localized was 24,812 (not all were enforced disappearances). In 2015, cases of disappearance in Peru, according to the Single Registry of Victims, amounted to 8,661, although it is believed that the figure is actually much higher.[19] These disappearances in many Latin American countries were fundamentally part of a systematic practice of human rights violations as described in 1977 by the Inter-American Commission on Human Rights (IACHR):

> some governments continue to refuse to provide information on the fate of persons kidnapped from their homes, places of work, ports or airports or in public thoroughfares, by non-uniformed, heavily armed individuals, traveling in unmarked vehicles and acting with such security and impunity that they are assumed to be forces invested with some authority. The truth is that until now, all the remedies provided for under domestic law, and the innumerable efforts made by family members, friends, institutions, agencies, and by this Commission itself, to find out what has happened to victims of such procedures have been fruitless.[20]

Indigenous peoples, community, political and union leaders, students, academics, members of religious communities, military or paramilitary agents (those suspected of collaborating with the enemy), and members of armed opposition groups[21] are among those forcibly disappeared.[22] Most of those who disappeared were not immediately killed, but were tortured in secret detention centers, then executed. Their bodies were thrown into rivers or the sea or mutilated and discarded at roadsides, buried in unmarked graves, or cremated.[23] Few have ever been found.[24] Although the majority of those disappeared were men, a large number of women have also gone missing.[25] There were also disappearances in the form of the appropriation of children and changes of their biological identities.[26]

As José Zalaquett Daher—the Chilean lawyer renowned for his work in the defense of human rights during the de facto regime that governed Chile under General Augusto Pinochet (1973–1990)—writes, in most Latin American countries, enforced disappearances were part of "a carefully organized method in order to exterminate opponents considered dangerous and to avoid answering for their deeds."[27] The practice was frequently a joint effort between various States, as archetypally represented by Operation Condor, in which security and intelligence forces, mainly from Chile, Argentina, Brazil, Uruguay, and Paraguay, worked together to repress, kill, and dispose of people designated as "subversive elements," even beyond the borders of the States themselves. Operation Condor coordinated clandestine "security forces and military and intelligence services" and was supported by the CIA.[28]

Enforced disappearances continue to occur in high numbers in countries such as El Salvador, Colombia, and México, and in isolated incidents elsewhere, including Chile and Argentina.[29] In some Latin American countries, particularly in México, disappearances occur in other than political contexts, carried out by organized crime groups and drug cartels.[30] Among other things, these events raise the issue of whether State participation is required to qualify a disappearance as enforced.[31] However, there are encouraging signs. In the context of the "war against terrorism," after the September 11, 2001 attack on the United States, the CIA's "extraordinary rendition" program has been nothing less than the use of enforced disappearance, in which suspects are kidnapped and shipped in silence and anonymity to prisons outside the United States, such as Egypt or Afghanistan.[32] To date, no Latin American country has cooperated with or assisted the CIA in disappearing people through extraordinary rendition.[33]

Unfortunately, disappearances have become a global phenomenon. Since its inception in 1980, the Working Group on Enforced or Involuntary Disappearances has reported 59,212 cases to 110 States. The number of cases under active consideration stands at 46,490 in ninety-five States.[34] However, while the systematic use of enforced disappearances practiced during the Latin American dictatorships of the 1960s and 1970s and the civil wars of the 1980s has remained in the world's collective memory, it also created a model for understanding a particular form of State violence.

Latin America's Role in the International Response to Enforced Disappearances

Until the events in Latin America, enforced disappearances were not properly or even minimally considered or conceptualized. The first international reactions date from the mid-1970s, largely because of the work of Latin Americans in response to the region's needs.[35]

The reactions of the Organization of American States (OAS) and the United Nations to Latin American disappearances laid the groundwork for the international response. While the IACHR denounced disappearances as early as 1974, undoubtedly, its most important contributions are its visit to Argentina and the subsequent report in 1979 and 1980.[36] The Commission's report was the first comprehensive intergovernmental description and understanding of enforced disappearances. Although it was not the first to address the issue of disappearance, in 1983, the OAS General Assembly became the first regional international institution to declare that the practice of enforced disappearances constitutes a crime against humanity.[37]

The Latin American situation motivated the UN to start dealing with the issue.[38] The first reactions occurred in 1978 with a statement of the UN General Assembly proposed by Colombia.[39] In 1979, the General Assembly entrusted the Commission on Human Rights to consider enforced disappearances. A Working Group on Chile made an unprecedented mission to the country in 1978. In 1979, after dissolving the Working Group, the Commission on Human Rights appointed two experts to study the fates of disappeared persons in Chile.[40]

Latin America's influence on the international response to disappearance continued with the establishment in 1980 of the Working Group on Enforced on Involuntary Disappearance (Working Group), the first specialized human rights mechanism within the UN. The Working Group was created largely in response to disappearances in Argentina and Chile, thanks to the work of mainly Latin American victims, despite fierce resistance from the Argentine dictator, General Jorge Rafael Videla (r. 1976–1981) and his government.[41] Not surprisingly, out of thirteen countries considered during the Working Group's first year, eight were Latin American—Argentina, Bolivia, Brazil, El Salvador, Guatemala, México,

Nicaragua, Peru, and Uruguay. The Working Group's first two visits were to Latin America (Bolivia in 1984 and Peru in 1985).[42]

Contributions to the Development of International Law

In the 1970s and early 1980s, the international community lacked a universally accepted definition to distinguish enforced disappearances from other violations. Influenced and (sometimes) led by Latin Americans, Amnesty International, the Working Group and the IACHR carried out essential analysis, which also concentrated on establishing legal principles to prevent, investigate, and punish those responsible, as well as to frame the rights of disappeared persons and their family members.[43]

Latin American organizations and countries have driven the progressive development of international law in the fight against enforced disappearances.[44] Since the early 1980s, FEDEFAM and other Latin American organizations have promoted the adoption of legal instruments to deal with this crime.[45] In 1992, the UN General Assembly adopted the Declaration on the Protection of All Persons from Enforced Disappearance.[46] In 1994, the OAS adopted the Inter-American Convention on Forced Disappearance of Persons, the first international legally binding document on this topic.[47] The region was also at the forefront of the process leading to the International Convention for the Protection of All Persons from Enforced Disappearance, adopted by the UN in 2006.[48] In addition, Latin American initiatives led to the inclusion in the Declaration, the Inter-American Convention, the International Convention, and the Convention on the Child of specific rules on disappeared and abducted children and the right to identity.[49]

Latin American countries and civil society organizations also contributed to the creation in 1998 of the International Criminal Court[50] and pushed for the inclusion of enforced disappearance as one of the international crimes over which the court has jurisdiction and for the specific content of the elements of the crime of enforced disappearances.[51] The Court has opened an investigation into Venezuela and Colombia, including cases of disappearances, and several organizations have requested an investigation into disappearances in México.[52] While not all these international norms coincide with the definition of enforced disappearance, the rights of the victims and the individual or State responsibilities, all those instruments respond to the Latin American model or where the results of leading Latin American efforts.

The original development of international jurisprudence on enforced disappearances also rested almost exclusively on Latin American cases. The first case decided by the UN Human Rights Committee (the Committee) regarded the disappearance of an Uruguayan, Eduardo Bleier, and the rights of his family.[53] The Committee on Enforced Disappearances (CED) issued its decisions on the urgency procedure (article 30 of the Convention) and conducted its first visit to México. The first individual case decided by CED was on Argentina.[54] Moreover, case law on the disappearance and abduction of children developed almost exclusively around Latin American cases.[55]

The conceptualization of enforced disappearances as a complex form of human rights violations and correlative State duties are due largely to the Inter-American Court.[56] Since its first three cases, the Court has developed a comprehensive, progressive doctrine on enforced disappearances.[57] It contributed to

- the understanding of the continuous nature of the crime;
- the right to know the truth about the fate or whereabouts of the victim;
- the right to know the scope and beneficiaries of reparations;
- the right to justice and the inapplicability of amnesty laws and statutes of limitations;
- the concept of "victim," encompassing the disappeared person and family members;
- presumptions of violations of rights in cases of enforced disappearances;
- specific evidentiary standards and the shifting of the burden of proof; and
- the understanding that the prohibition of enforced disappearance is an *erga omnes* (opposable to all) norm.[58]

These essential contributions made by the Inter-American system to respond to disappearances in Latin America had worldwide influence and were crucial in developing international case law around enforced disappearances while enforced disappearances also influenced the nature of the Inter-American system.[59]

National Latin American Responses to Enforced Disappearances

Uneven domestic efforts to develop policies dealing with enforced disappearances accompanied the international responses. Although most measures adopted have been clearly insufficient—Latin America led the effort and laid the foundation.[60]

The Legislative Response

Several Latin American constitutions specifically refer to enforced disappearance, thus leading the way to adopting national legislation against it.[61] A number of criminal codes include an autonomous crime of enforced disappearance.[62] Nevertheless, the inclusion of such a crime does not necessarily mean that its definition is compatible with international instruments or that it is required or has contributed to the punishment of those responsible for the crime.[63] In 2017, México approved the first law in the world to regulate all aspects related to enforced disappearances.[64]

Given the legal uncertainty that remains for the disappeared and his or her family members, Latin American countries, almost exclusively, have adopted a specific declaration of absence due to enforced disappearance.[65] Very few countries in other regions in the world have such legislative and constitutional frameworks to deal with and refer to enforced disappearances. An important exception is the Philippines Republic Act of 2012, a very comprehensive law. Other relevant exceptions could be the law establishing the Office of Missing Persons in Sri Lanka, the Laws on Missing Persons from Kosovo, Bosnia and Herzegovina, and Croatia. However, most of these laws are about "missing persons" and not enforced disappearances.[66] These legal provisions are important as recent studies demonstrate that the existence of a national law against crimes against humanity (including enforced disappearances) double the likelihood of initiating prosecution and increase the chances of successful convictions.[67]

The Response in Terms of Justice

Latin America is the one region where significant numbers of countries have made inroads into prosecuting officials for enforced disappearances and other acts that constitute international crimes in national courts. The number of indictments and trials is impressive. Across the region, convictions include five former heads of state and a number of high-ranking military, police, and civilian officials. No other region in the world can match Latin America's progress in this area.[68]

Argentina and Chile are the vanguard, with hundreds processed and convicted.[69] Other impressive advances include court-convicted heads of state, such as Alberto Fujimori (r. 1990–2000) in Peru and Juan María Bordaberry (r. 1973–1976) in Uruguay, in part for their responsibilities for enforced disappearances.[70] In Guatemala, courts tried and convicted Efrain Rios Montt (r. 1982–1983) for genocide, including enforced disappearances, although his conviction was later partially annulled. In Colombia, though there are pockets of impunity and sometimes grave relapses, there have nevertheless been a few important advances.[71] All these efforts have created a rich, unique Latin American case law on enforced disappearances.[72] The advances have not been easy and have provoked strong political, ethical, and legal debates on the viability of justice and the proper balance between truth and justice.[73] Yet there is still a long way to go in countries like México, Brazil, Honduras, or Paraguay.[74]

On a parallel yet somehow contradictory track, in the past, the region has adopted laws providing amnesty for those who commit enforced disappearance (or laws with similar effects). In a first wave, most national courts ratified the constitutionality of such laws.[75] In response, Latin American organizations turned to international bodies and the Inter-American system led to the development of jurisprudence, ruling that amnesty laws were not acceptable in enforced disappearance cases.[76] Additional steps were taken to keep judicial proceedings open in spite of amnesty laws, this time through Latin American judges, who developed extremely important jurisprudential theories, such as the continuous nature of the crime of enforced disappearance, to avoid the application of statutes of limitation or to overcome some of the effects of amnesty laws.[77]

Until recently, in many Latin American countries—with exceptions such as Brazil—the discussion has moved from the idea of total impunity to the issue of how to prosecute criminals in enforced disappearance cases. The new issues ranged from prosecuting increasingly complex and sensitive kinds of crimes to organizing trials involving multiple defendants and victims, to reaching behind the triggermen to arrive at the high-ranking military and civilian official, as well as financial and political figures who were complicit.[78] One Argentinian court convicted a priest for his participation in enforced disappearances and another convicted several judges for their complicity in such cases.[79] Additionally, a final set of issues arises from post-conviction dilemmas related to alternatives to imprisonment and the role of sentencing.[80] However, today the region is seeing some setbacks such as the reinstatement of the pardon of former Peruvian President Alberto Fujimori.[81]

Alongside these efforts, Latin America also pursued justice for victims in foreign courts. Examples range from the use of the Alien Torts Claim Act in the United States to the invocation of universal jurisdiction in the famous case of former Chilean President Augusto Pinochet (r. 1974–1990) and the conviction of former Argentine naval officer, Adolfo Scilingo, both in Spain.[82] Latin American lawyers led some of these efforts, contributing to the development of case law on universal jurisdiction and the State's responsibility in prosecuting enforced disappearances in third countries (e.g., Scilingo was tried in Spain for the disappearances he committed in Argentina). Lawyers included Carlos Slepoy, an Argentinian attorney residing in Madrid, and others with strong connections to Latin America, such as Manuel Olle, Joan Garces, Ana María Chávez de Seropaj, and Gregorio Dionis.[83] As in Spain, courts in Italy, Sweden, France, Switzerland, Belgium, and Germany also heard cases of enforced disappearances in Latin America.[84]

These generated or consolidated the cascade effect, also called the Pinochet Effect, that is, the opening and reopening of human rights trials.[85] Nevertheless, these trials abroad cannot obscure the processes that already existed in Latin America.[86] In a parallel process, some Latin American judges support the efforts to obtain justice in cases of enforced disappearances that occurred in other countries and are exercising universal jurisdiction for grave human rights violations including enforced disappearances.[87] Of particular importance are the decisions of the Mexican Supreme Court authorizing the extradition of Argentinian ex-naval officer Ricardo Miguel Cavallo to Spain and the Chilean Supreme Court's authorization for the extradition of Fujimori back to Peru. By contrast, however, in 2007, the Constitutional Court of Guatemala rejected the request for arrest and extradition of Guatemalan military including Rios Montt accused of genocide before the Spanish courts.[88]

All these efforts for justice and responses at national, transnational, and international levels transformed the view that many Latin Americans had of judges. During the dictatorships and civil wars, judges sided with the government perpetrators of disappearances, methodically rejecting attempts to find justice through habeas corpus.[89] Now, however, as executive and legislative branches collaborate with political parties, ignoring the demands of victims, judges often confront political powers that question their decisions. Judges, lawyers, and victims are taking leading roles in dismantling these political alliances.[90] This new situation creates fresh doubts and tensions.

The Response Regarding the Truth

The Latin American experience has shaped an understanding about the victimization of the families of the disappeared and as holders of the right to know the truth, as well as the legal, ethical, moral, and political reasons for seeking the truth. The Inter-American system made key contributions to the legal meaning of this right and duty.[91] Latin American courts and tribunals have expressly reaffirmed the right to the truth in cases of enforced disappearances.[92]

Other countries and regions, such as South Africa, copied, transformed, and adopted the initiatives taken since the 1980s. Latin America's methods appealed to truth commissions to underscore the practice of enforced disappearances. Truth commissions as strategies for accountability came to international attention in the 1980s and early 1990s, and, since then, almost all countries in the region have formed truth commissions to explore enforced disappearances.[93]

To uncover and identify the disappeared, strong search techniques and genetic capabilities were established with forensic teams like those in Argentina, Peru, and Guatemala or, as in Chile, formed specialized services for forensic medicine.[94] Those forensic teams led the search for the remains of the disappeared in Latin America and in other parts of the world. Africa and Asia have been slower to initiate large-scale missing persons projects and they still lack strong capacity in forensic science and the array practiced is limited.[95] Forensics were not used at all prior to Latin America's initiation. Those efforts came with ethical, legal, social, and political challenges, such as the protection of privacy, the idea that searching for the disappeared would reopen past wounds, the tensions between the needs of criminal investigations and the humanitarian approaches to the identification of remains, to mention a few.[96]

Latin America, more than any other region, also adopted national search plans, national commissions for search and/or identity of disappeared persons.[97] In recovery and identification of the missing, the Western Balkans probably made more progress with the disappeared than Latin America. The International Commission on Missing Persons indicates that a successful combination of civil society engagement, institutional development, and scientific innovation has made it possible to account for more than 70 percent of the missing from the conflict in Bosnia and Herzegovina.[98]

The laws of access to information that proliferated in Latin America stipulate that information on human rights violations, including enforced disappearances, cannot be restricted.[99] Some Latin American countries enlisted regulators, such as Guatemala's Human Rights Ombudsman, to search for the disappeared.[100]

In Argentina there were *juicios por la verdad* (trials for the truth) whose purpose was "not judgement and condemnation of criminals accused of serious human rights violations, but, rather, via establishment and clarification of facts, knowledge of the victim's fate, coupled with legal recognition of the factual truth."[101]

These efforts, particularly those of the Latin American truth commissions, have been essential to avoid denial or revisionist theories and to dismiss such theories.[102] However, despite all these initiatives, most forcibly disappeared bodies are never found, and their fates never revealed.[103]

The Response on Reparations and Memory

Latin America also made enormous contributions on the right and scope of reparations for victims of enforced disappearances. The Court has advanced impressive and innovative jurisprudence on the subject. Several countries, such as Argentina, Brazil, Chile, Peru, Guatemala, and Colombia, to a greater or lesser extent, granted reparations or designed plans for reparations with varying degrees of implementation and success. Reparations ordered by the Court have not always produced the desired results and have not been free of implementation problems.[104] This process brought debates about a broader perspective of reparations beyond financial aspects, mostly initiated in Latin America, then expanded to other regions. Some discussions include

- gender approaches;
- the possibilities of administrative reparations programs;
- the non-applicability of statutes of limitation on reparations;
- memory as part of reparations;
- the distinctions between reparations and university public social spending policies;
- individual and collective reparations; and
- reparations from a cultural perspective.[105]

The region also pioneered development of important programs and standards for mental health care for the relatives of the disappeared.[106] Latin America also made significant contributions to State and civil society initiatives related to memory. There has been important work in the field of museums and memory spaces in recovering places symbolic to the disappearances and the construction of memorials. There is also remarkable production on the theme of memory in cinema, literature, and photography, among other art forms.[107] There are also important Latin American steps in the systemization, declassification, access, digitization, and reconstruction of archives with documents on disappearances.[108] There is also progress in developing a legal right to memory. Here, the Court (although with many theoretical and practical gaps) is also contributing to the understanding of memory for enforced disappearances.[109]

Sadly, these efforts have not been applied in some other areas of the world. A Report of the Working Group on Enforced or Involuntary Disappearances on its mission to Sri Lanka expressed concern that there is no government supported memorial built for the victims of enforced disappearances and the Working Group's report on its mission in Turkey indicated that, in light of political reluctance to come to terms with past enforced disappearances, as those perpetrated against Kurds in the 1990s, it is not unexpected to note the absence of official memorial sites or remembrance places.[110]

Latin American contribution to the Human Rights Movement

Latin America has forged the work of human rights at national, regional, and international levels based on its reaction to enforced disappearances. Investigation, reform, and mobilizations have had an impact on international organizations and human rights movements in other countries.[111]

The famous *Madres de la Plaza de Mayo* (Mothers and Grandmothers of the Plaza de Mayo) in Buenos Aires, the Vicariate of Solidarity in Chile, FEDEFAM—the first international federation of families of disappeared persons—and many organizations in every country have created new strategies on disappearances.[112] Their work serves as models in other parts of the world (not only about issues of enforced disappearances). At least two decades later, multiple organizations in other regions, where disappearances had existed long before, are now following the Latin American human rights example. These include the Euro-Méditerranéenne Fédération Contre Les Disparitions Forcées, the Asian Federation against Disappearances, and the International Coalition against Enforced Disappearances, newly established in 2000.[113] The Saturday Mothers in Istanbul who hold their vigils each week at noon, fashioned themselves after the Mothers of the Plaza de Mayo, who began their protests in 1977.[114]

Indeed, it is impossible to conceive of the human rights movement today without analyzing its origins and consolidation during the 1970s, 1980s, and 1990s in Latin America, mainly in response to enforced disappearances.[115] Latin American women play a leading, central, and crucial role at the forefront of the struggle for justice. Azucena Villaflor, whose son disappeared in 1976, was one of the founders of the Mothers of the Plaza de Mayo and was herself disappeared in 1977. In México, Rosario Ibarra de Piedra, whose son disappeared in 1975, is the director of *Comité Eureka*. Mamá Angelica Mendoza, whose son was kidnapped and disappeared in 1983, joined other women to form the National Association of Families of the Kidnapped, Detained and Disappeared of Peru. She was its leader until her death in 2017. In Colombia, Yanette Bautista, whose sister disappeared in 1987, is director of the Nydia Erika Bautista Foundation. In Chile, Sola Sierra Henríquez, whose husband disappeared in 1976, was the first president of the *Agrupación de Familiares de Detenidos Desaparecidos*. Bertha Oliva de Nativi, whose husband disappeared in 1981, founded the *Comité de Familiares de Desaparecidos de Honduras*. Aura Elena Farfán, whose brother disappeared in 1984, directs the Association of Relatives of Detained and Disappeared of Guatemala.[116]

Is the Latin American Model Valid for Other Regions?

Latin America influenced the development of enforced disappearances as an international concern and a specific complex human rights violation as well as the responses. Thus, there is an obvious question: does this model provide an appropriate global and universal framework for addressing State violence that in Latin America is called enforced disappearance? The answer is yes.

One of the main lessons from Latin America is that the model is flexible and comprehensive enough to accommodate differences in the practice of enforced disappearances and the responses to it.[117] Despite many commonalities, enforced disappearances are contextualized forms of violence.[118] The model allows for looking at enforced disappearances in its many forms, such as those carried out predominantly in urban areas against middle-class professionals, as happened in Argentina; or those which occurred on a massive scale in rural areas and during authoritarian regimes such as Fujimori's in Peru; or against Indigenous people in Guatemala; or those that occurred within civil wars as in El Salvador; or under military dictatorships like that of Uruguay.[119] The model has also allowed dealing with isolated enforced disappearances in democratic contexts.

The framework is broad, encompassing disappearances carried out exclusively or mainly by the armed forces (such as in the Southern Cone of Argentina and Chile in the 1970s) to those practiced by private or non-State actors with the cooperation, tolerance, or acquiescence of the State (like many that happened in Colombia and currently occur in México). In addition, the framework is sufficiently flexible to understand enforced disappearances in the context of the doctrine of national security, the fight against terrorism, and combating drug trafficking or organized crime. It also allows for the inclusion of enforced disappearances practiced as part of systematic plans and crimes against humanity (such as those conducted by Operation Condor), as acts within a practice of genocide (as in Guatemala) or as mere isolated incidents (such as disappearances in the Dominican Republic).

Latin American experiences demonstrate the validity of the basic principles of truth, justice, reparations, memory, and guarantees of non-repetition, while taking a contextualized perspective that suits local needs and realities, from international truth commissions as in El Salvador, mixed national and international comissions as in Guatemala, or purely national ones in the rest of the region to truth commissions limited to dealing exclusively with enforced disappearances (as in Argentina) or commissions with broad mandates (as in Peru). In Asia, for example, Sri Lanka so far has chosen to create inquiry commissions rather than truth commissions.[120]

The responses to enforced disappearances need to pay attention to global and universal principles, as well as to local realities on the ground and to local and micro perspectives and needs. The phenomenon of disappearances finds its roots in the political structure of the society in which they occur.[121] Thus, it is important to be attentive to the different contexts, manifestations, spatial, and temporal patterns, as well as to local and regional dynamics of enforced disappearances in different parts of the world.[122] In terms of justice, the paths, progress, and setbacks have been different throughout Latin America.[123]

Anthropologists such as Sally E. Merry and Richard Wilson insist on the processes of domestication or the explanation of local uses and resignifications of university human rights concepts, in our case enforced disappearances. Merry and Wilson explain the dynamics and diversity of social actors participating in the translations from global or universal practices and perceptions to the local spaces. In these processes, attention should be paid to the victims' subjectivity, perpetrators, origins, causes, and consequences of violence, its meaning, and the social mobilization generated.[124] That is precisely this article's application. As Francisco Ferrandiz explains, there is a process of "legal download" in the use of the concept of enforced disappearance in the Spanish context. This refers to the many ways, modalities, and channels international law is transferred and translated to national or local contexts.[125] Ferrandiz describes the need to understand the historical, sociological, legal, or even symbolic differences and parallels of particular forms of repression and the type of violence they generate, the bureaucracies of silence and death they trigger. However, it is perfectly legitimate to integrate these historical experiences, with all their particularities, with the international legal concept of enforced disappearance. The opposite would be to argue that the only legitimate possibility of applying the concept of enforced disappearances is to the social context in which it took the first steps of its classification and jurisprudence. That is the Latin American context. Of course, that means that one must recognize the historical and political contexts and short-, medium-, and long-term social, legal, and political responses that each disappearance generates.[126] As Adam Rosenblatt explained in relation to the use of the terms "disappearances" and "missing persons," both are

> context-dependent and often highly unstable in nature. . . . In colloquial English usage, "missing person" conjures up associations of runaways, kidnappings, and others unfortunately affected by everyday incidents, whether criminal or not. . . . "The disappeared" . . . calls to mind authoritarian regimes, political programs of extermination, and the language of human rights reports. In practice, however, these two kinds of events can occur simultaneously in one geographical setting. For example, people living under oppressive regimes can go missing for ordinary reasons, and those same regimes can try to cover up their programs of disappearance by claiming that their victims have actually run off with lovers or gone into involuntary exile, and so on. However, at the end of the day, a distinction between missing and disappeared exists and the contexts in which disappearances take place influences those distinctions with missing persons.[127]

This article proposes to understand the Latin American model and influence on enforced disappearances as a normative transnational/international framework that operates under unique cultural and political logics, necessarily conditioned by local particularities and meanings. It recognizes how national or even regional processes absorb and influence international human rights approaches.[128] Socioeconomic, political, cultural, and even religious conditions determine the ways in which repressive practices develop and how people respond to them. For example, the power held by perpetrators during political transitions or victims' profiles or their ability to mobilize are essential for understanding the dynamics in transitional justice processes. The same is true whether disappearances occur within the same country when the victims are remote, isolated, or marginalized, or whether, conversely, they reside in urban centers or are middle class.[129] However, the approach insists that the rights to truth, justice, reparation, and memory and guarantees of non-repetition of victims adequately addressed, recognizing the need to consider each situation on its own merits and particularities in order to develop tailored policies accordingly.

The basic right to know the truth about the fate or whereabouts of a disappeared person required this contextualized approach, considering the family situation and careful assessment of the cultural, religious, and social contexts.[130] This is also valid for memorialization or burials, exhumations, and identification. The concept of victim-centered approaches to enforced disappearances and victims' participation, on which international standards insist, require one to understand that the victim's needs are highly context-specific, local, emotional, psychological, and spiritual constructs.[131]

By contextualizing the practice of enforced disappearances, it is easier to understand some of the differences between Latin America and other regions and to highlight the similarities. One can understand why, unlike Latin America, Southeast Asian nations did not support the creation of the International Criminal Court or the inclusion of the crime of enforced disappearance in the Rome Statute. As explained in this article, Latin America uniquely and unlike other regions has placed a strong emphasis on criminal accountability and the criminalization of the practice of enforced disappearance both domestically and internationally.[132] It is understandable that enforced disappearances affect women differently, as, for instance, Jeevasuthan Subramaniam and her co-writers describe in "Implications of enforced disappearances on women-headed families in the northern province, Sri Lanka," explaining how cultural, ethnic, and social context influenced the identification of the wives of disappeared, the so-called half-widows,[133] or why broader definitions of disappearances, including non-State actors are used more often in certain parts of Asia.[134] Similarly, it helps to recognize the differences in healing processes. In Timor-Leste (East Timor), some families do not want DNA tests and burial rituals are possible even without the body or remains of the disappeared person, something that does not happen in Latin America.[135] Underreporting of disappearances is more pronounced in Africa or Asia than in Latin America, because the consent of the family to present cases to the Working Group is required.

And in places like North Korea, international laws, and even research are unenforceable.[136]

The contextualized approach to enforced disappearances also allows understanding that both the practice and response are temporal processes that evolve over time and that different regions do not follow the same paths.[137] The evolution of crime and resistance is also determined geographically within countries themselves.[138]

Conclusion

Understanding Latin America is important, considering the place it has held in discussions about enforced disappearances on a global scale. As this article tries to demonstrate, Latin America has played a prominent role, as a source of innovation and protagonism, both in developing and perfecting this heinous crime and in constructing national, transnational, regional, and international responses. Of course, Latin America has not always been the leader or pioneer. In 2004, Bosnia and Herzegovina adopted the first law on missing persons, while a 1981 agreement between the Greek and Turkish Cypriot communities under the auspices of the United Nations created the first specialized body to search for disappeared people.[139]

Revisiting the relationship between Latin America and enforced disappearances serves another important aspect. It challenges the idea that the global south is the place where abuses are committed and the global north where ideas and strategies on how to confront them emerge. The scholar Paolo Carozza wrote

> [Even] among human rights enthusiasts and activists, Latin America has long been regarded as the object of human rights concerns more than a contributor to human rights thinking. Or rather, its "contributions" have been perceived almost exclusively in negative terms. For example, the creativity of its repressive regimes in fashioning new forms of abuse, like the "disappearance," provoked the governments and human rights organizations of Europe and North America to come up with new norms and institutions to address problems. . . . But the affirmative dimensions of human rights in Latin America, instead, have much more often been seen to be tarnished and inferior copies of grand, rich European ideas.[140]

The purpose of this chapter is, in part, to highlight the immense contributions Latin America has made against enforced disappearances and to the human rights movement. However, despite the resemblances and generalizations, there are profound dissimilarities between diverse historical moments in which the disappearances occur, between methodologies or between sub-regions (with marked differences between disappearances in the Southern Cone and Central America). Many of the advances, developments, or "wins" have not happened uniformly. Chile and Argentina are at the positive end of the continuum, although moving at different speeds and vicissitudes, while other countries, like Honduras, are making less progress.[141] Others, like Guatemala and Peru have had both improvements and regressions. In still other countries, such as Colombia, progress coexists with the continuation of enforced disappearances. In countries like México, progress on disappearances has been extremely limited and the situation has worsened.[142]

While eliminating political opponents has long been a strategy of those in power throughout the world, the Latin American story, and its ability to capture international attention has forever left its imprint on international law defining enforced disappearances. The need to frame a distinct legal norm, and the content of that normative prohibition against enforced disappearance are deeply connected to the narrative that emerged from Latin America. The international norms outlawing, preventing, and punishing the use of enforced disappearance might never have existed but for the Latin American experience. Its narrative provided the urgency for the international community to address the crime through its own distinct frame, as a separate violation that was more than the sum of its criminal parts. The human stories that emanated from Latin America demanded an international call for action.[143]

Although Latin America's change from a system of enforced disappearance to one that deals with the crime more effectively is still fragile, uneven, and incomplete, it is nevertheless remarkable. The region's experience provides essential and inspirational lessons on the ability of civil society networks—especially family members, human rights advocates, and the professionals allied with them—to change law, policy, and political consensus through creativity and perseverance.[144]

As enforced disappearances continue and are globalized, societies that now face the same challenges are equipped with intellectual resources, policy, and activism models that can be readily employed, without having to invent them from scratch, as Latin America did.[145] The challenge is how to continue adapting and contextualizing the model to other regions, realities, and needs.

Notes

1. The author wishes to thank Jennifer Heath for her assistance in preparing and doing an amazing editing of this paper. Thanks to Federico Andreu, Gabriella Citroni, Cath Collins, Lucrecia Molina Theissen, and Wilder Tyler who commented on an earlier and different Spanish version of this article.

2. See the "Proceedings of the International Military Tribunal sitting at Nuremberg," in *Trial of German Major War Criminals*, vol. 3 (London: United Nations War Crimes Commission, 1950); and *Trials of War Criminals Before the Nuremberg Military Tribunals under Control Council Law No. 10* (Washington, DC: U.S. Government Publishing Office, 1949–1953).

3. Open Society, Justice Initiative Program, *Undeniable Atrocities, Confronting Crimes Against Humanity in Mexico* (New York: Open Society Foundations, 2016). https://www.opensocietyfoundations.org/sites/default/files/undenialble-atrocities-2nd-edition-20160808.pdf

4. See, e.g., Edmund Clark and Crofton Black, "The Appearance of Disappearance: The CIA's Secret Black Sites," *Financial Times*, March 17, 2016. https://www.ft.com/content/90796270-ebc3-11e5-888e-2eadd5fbc4a4

5. United Nations, Human Rights Council, *Report of the Detailed Findings of the Commission of Inquiry on Human Rights in the Democratic People's Republic of Korea*, February 7, 2014, A/HRC/25/CRP.1.

6. For example, Trial International, *Bosnia and Herzegovina: ECHR Denies Justice To Victims Of Enforced Disappearances And Arbitrary Executions*, July 22, 2014. https://trialinternational.org/latest-post/bosnia-and-herzegovina-echr-denies-justice-to-victims-of-enforced-disappearances-and-arbitrary-executions/

7. Belisario Betancourt, Reinaldo Figueredo Planchart, Thomas Buergenthal, "From Madness to Hope: The Twelve-Year War in El Salvador," *Report of the Commission on the Truth for El Salvador* (New York: United Nations, 1993).

8. Gabriel Gatti, "'Lo nuestro, como en Argentina': Humanitarian Reason and the Latin Americanization of Victimhood in Spain," *Journal of Latin American Cultural Studies* 25, no. 1 (2016): 147–65. http://dx.doi.org/10.1080/13569325.2016.1143352

9. Jonah Rubin, *Aproximación al concepto de desaparecido: reflexiones sobre El Salvador y España* (Ciudad de México: Alteridades, 2015).

10. José Zalaquett, "The Emergence of 'Disappearances' As a Normative Issue in Walling," in Carrie Spiderman, Susan Waltz, eds., *Human Rights: From Practice to Policy* (Ann Arbor: University of Michigan, 2011), 9. http://deepblue.lib.umich.edu/handle/2027.42/89426

11. Zalaquett, "The Emergence of 'Disappearances,'" 9.

12. Emilio Fermín Mignone, et al., *Repressive Strategy of the Military Dictatorship: The Doctrine of Global Parallelism* (Buenos Aires: Ediciones Colihue, 2006), 3–39.

13. "Velásquez Rodríguez v. Honduras," *Inter-American Court*, Judgment of July 29, 1988, (Merits), para. 149.

14. Barbara A. Frey, "Los Desaparecidos: The Latin American Experience as a Narrative Framework for the International Norm against Forced Disappearances," *Hispanic Issues Series* (2009): 69. http://hdl.handle.net/11299/182852

15. Molina Theissen and Ana Lucrecia, "The Forced Disappearance of Persons in Latin America," *Ko'aga Rone'eta*, Series 7 (1998).

16. José Zalaquett, introduction to the English edition of the *Report of the National Truth and Reconciliation Commission of Chile*, 9. Http://www.cdh.uchile.cl/media/publicaciones/pdf/18/61.pdf; original title: *Introduction to the English Edition of the Report of the Chilean National Commission on Truth and Reconciliation*, Center for Civil and Human Rights, Notre Dame Law School (Notre Dame:Notre Dame University Press, 1993).

17. Martin Scheinin, et al., *Joint Study Prepared by Mr. Martin Scheinin, Special Rapporteur on the Promotion and Protection of Human Rights and Fundamental Freedoms in the Fight Against Terrorism, Mr. Manfred Nowak, Special Rapporteur on Torture and other Cruel, Inhuman or Degrading Treatment or Punishment; the Working Group on Arbitrary Detention, Represented by Its Vice-President, Mr Shaheen Sardar Ali; and the Working Group on Enforced or Involuntary Disappearances, Represented by its President, Mr. Jeremy Sarkin*, A/HRC/13/42, para. 5.

18. Most of this article's references will be from Chile and Argentina, which have led, experienced, exported, and shared both the development of enforced disappearances as a systematic practice and responses to them.

19. See http://elpais.com/diario/1983/02/11/internacional/413766003_850215.html; http://lawg.org/storage/documents/Colombia/RompiendoElSilencio.pdf; and http://aristeguinoticias.com/0309/mexico/25-mil-desaparecidos-en-mexico-reconoce-segob-la-mayoria-en-tamaulipas/

20. *Annual Report of the Inter-American Commission on Human Rights*, 1977, section II.

21. "Case of Bámaca Velásquez v. Guatemala," *Inter-American Court of Human Rights*, Sentence of November 25, 2000, (Merits), series C no. 70.

22. As it was described in Guatemala, "*Informe de la Comisión para el Esclarecimiento Histórico*," MEMORIA DEL SILENCIO, *Conclusiones y Recomendaciones*, para. 89, (*Memorias del Silencio*).

23. Eric Stover and Rachel Shigekane, "The Missing in the Aftermath of War: When Do the Needs of Victims' Families and International War Crimes Tribunals Clash?" *Revue Internationale De La Croix-Rouge/International Review of the Red Cross* 84, no. 848 (2002): 845–866 at 849.

24. Committee on Enforced Disappearances, *Concluding Observations on the Report Submitted by Paraguay Under Article 29, Paragraph 1 of the Convention*, CED/C/PRY/CO/1, para. 34.

25. See, for example, *Fundación Nydia Erika Bautista para los Derechos Humanos, Desapariciones forzadas de Mujeres en Colombia, Un estudio de casos del conflicto armado: 1985–2015.* http://www.hchr.org.co/player/internalvideo/DesaparicionDeMujeresEnColombiaIMP.pdf

26. As documented by the truth commissions of Argentina, Guatemala, and El Salvador, "Memoria del Silencio," in *Informe CONADEP Nunca Más* vol. 2 (1984), para. 451ff; and Comisión de la Verdad, "De la locura a la esperanza: La guerra de 12 años en El Salvador," *San Salvador: Editorial Arcoíris* (1993): 118.

27. Zalaquett, *Introduction*, 3.

28. Ariel C. Armony, *Argentina, the United States, and the Anti-Communist Crusade in Central America, 1977–1984*, vol. 26 (Athens, OH: Ohio University Press, 1997).

29. See for example, U.S. State Department, *2020, Country Reports on Human*

Rights Practices: El Salvador, 2021, HUMAN RIGHTS Watch, The War in Catatumbo. Abuses by Armed Groups Against Civilians Including Venezuelan Exiles in Northeastern Colombia, (2019) or *Amnistía Internacional, México: Justice on Trial: Failures in criminal investigations of femicides preceded by disappearance in the State of Mexico,* 2021, and for example in Chile, Centro de Derechos Humanos, Universidad Diego Portales, *Informe Anual sobre Derechos Humanos en Chile 2009,* at 130 and 325 or in Argentina, Committee on Enforced Disappearances, Consideration of reports of States Parties under article 29 of the Convention, Reports of States parties under article 29, paragraph 1, of the Convention that are due in 2012, CED/C/ARG/1, para. 14.

30. Committee on Enforced Disappearances, *Concluding Observations on the Report Submitted by Mexico Under Article 29, Paragraph 1 of the Convention,* CED/C/MEX/CO/1, para. 10.

31. Rainer Huhle, "Non-State Actors of Enforced Disappearance and the UN Convention for the Protection of All Persons from Enforced Disappearance," in *HumanitäresVölkerrecht—Informationsschriften / Journal of International Law of Peace and Armed Conflict* 1 (2013): 21–26.

32. Margaret Satterthwaite, "Extraordinary Rendition on Disappearances in the War on Terror," *Gonzaga Journal* 10 (2006): 70, 72. See also, chapter 4 in this volume, "Extraordinary Rendition: A Human Rights Analysis," by David Weissbrodt.

33. United States Senate Select Committee on Intelligence, *Committee Study of the Central Intelligence Agency's Detention and Interrogation Program, Foreword by Senate Select Committee on Intelligence Chairman Dianne Feinstein, Findings and Conclusions, Executive Summary*; and Open Society, Justice Initiative, *Globalizing Torture: CIA Secret Detention and Extraordinary Rendition* (2013), 61–118, listing fifty-four governments that participated in the CIA program. None of those from Latin America.

34. *Report of the Working Group on Enforced or Involuntary Disappearances,* August 4, 2021, A/HRC/48/57.

35. Wilder Tayler, "Background to the Elaboration of the Draft International Convention for the Protection of All Persons from Forced Disappearance," *The Review/International Commission of Jurists* 62–63 (2001): 65.

36. IACHR, *Report on the Situation of Human Rights in Argentina,* OEA/Ser.L/V/II.49, doc. 19, April 11, 1980, Original: Spanish.

37. OAS, *General Assembly,* AG/RES. 666 (XIII-0/83), November 18, 1983.

38. For a brief explanation of the UN concern with enforced disappearances prior to 1980, see "Question of Human Rights of all Persons Subjected to Any Form of Detention of Imprisonment, In Particular Question of Missing and Disappeared Persons," *Report of the Working Group on Enforced or Involuntary Disappearances,* E/CN.4/1435, January 26, 1981, Original: English/Spanish, para. 13–25.

39. UN General Assembly, Resolution 33/173, December 20, 1978. There are some references since 1975, resolution 3450 (XXX), on Cyprus; and Resolution 3448 (XXX), both on December 9, 1975, on Chile. However, in the English version, they refer to "persons unaccounted for." The term "disappeared" first appears in resolution 32/118.

40. Reed Brody and Felipe Gonzalez, "*Nunca Más*: An Analysis of International Instruments on Disappearances," *Human Rights Quarterly* 19, no. 2 (1997): 365–405.

41. Iain Guest, *Behind the Disappearances: Argentina's Dirty War Against Human Rights and the United Nations* (Philadelphia: University of Pennsylvania Press, 1990).

42. Nigel S. Rodley, "United Nations Action Procedures Against 'Disappearances,' Summary or Arbitrary Executions, and Torture," *Human Rights Quarterly* 8, no. 4 (1986): 708.

43. Amnesty International USA, 1980; and Howard M. Kleinman, "Disappearances in Latin America: A Human Rights Perspective," *NYU Journal of International Law and Politics* 19 (1986): 1033.

44. Patricio Rice, "La Fédération Latino-Américaine des Organisations de Familles de Détenus Disparus et le Projet de Convention," in Olivier de Frouville and Emmanuel Decaux, eds., *La Convention internationale pour la protection de toutes les personnes contre les dispaitions forcées* (Bruxelles: Bruylant, coll. « Droit et Justice», 2009), 235, 37.

45. For the different initiatives see, Wilder Taylor, "Background to the Elaboration of the Draft International Convention for the Protection of All Persons from Forced Disappearance," *International Court of Justice Review* 62 (2001): 65.

46. *Declaration on the Protection of All Persons from Enforced Disappearance*, adopted by the United Nations General Assembly, A/RES/47/133, December 18, 1992. See Brody and Gonzales, "*Nunca Más*."

47. Inter-American Convention, *Inter-American Convention on Forced Disappearance of Persons*, adopted on June 9, 1994. See Brody and Gonzales, "*Nunca Más*."

48. Olivier de Frouville, "The Committee on Enforced Disappearances," in *The United Nations and Human Rights: A Critical Appraisal*, vol 3., 2nd ed., ed. by Philip Alston et al. (Oxford: Oxford University Press, forthcoming).

49. *Declaration*, article 20; *Inter-American Convention*, article 12; *International Convention*, article 25; and *Convention on the Rights of the Child*, 1989, article 8.

50. José A. Guevara and Tarciso Dal Maso, *La Corte Penal International: Una Visión Iberoamericana* (México: Ed. Porrua, 2005).

51. Brigitte Suhr, "*La desaparición forzada de personas en el Estatuto de Roma y los Elementos de los Crímenes*," in José Guevara and Mariana Valdés Riveroll, eds., *La Corte Penal Internacional: ensayos para la ratificación e implementación de su estatuto.* (Universidad Iberoamericana and Secretario de Relacions Exteriors, 2002), 61.

52. Jocelyn Courtney. "Enforced Disappearances in Colombia: A Plea for Synergy Between the Courts," *International Criminal Law Review* 10, no. 5 (2010): 679–711; International Federation of Human Rights, "México Coahuila: Ongoing Crimes Against Humanity," *Communication to the International Criminal Court*, https://www.fidh.org/IMG/pdf/angmexico_coahuila_ongoing_crimes_against_humanity_fidh-final_a_revisar-1.pdf; "ICC Prosecutor, Mr. Karim A. A. Khan QC, Opens an Investigation into the Situation in Venezuela and Concludes Memorandum of Understanding with the Government," press release, November 5, 2021. https://www.icc-cpi.int/Pages/item.aspx?name=pr1625

53. "Eduardo Bleier v. Uruguay," Communication no. R.7/30, UN doc. supp. no. 40 (A/37/40) at 130, 1982.

54. "Press Conference following the visit of the Committee on Enforced Disappearances to Mexico," November 26, 2021. https://www.ohchr.org/en/statements/2021/11/press-conference-following-visit-committee-enforced-disappearances-mexico; and Committee on Enforced Disappearances, *Views Approved by*

the Committee Under Article 31 of the Convention for Communication, no. 1/2013, CED/C/10/D/1/2013.

55. See IACHR Annual Report Informe Annual 1986–1987, *A Study About the Situation of Minor Children of Disappeared Persons Who Were Separated from Their Parents and Who Are Claimed by Members of Their Legitimate Families, Inter-Am. Ct. H.R., Case of Molina Theissen*, Sentence of May 4, 2004, series C 106; and Committee on Human Rights, *Darwinia Rosa Mónaco de Gallicchio v. Argentina*, Comunication no. 400/1990, UN doc. CCPR/C/53/D/400/1990, 1995.

56. For example, "Case of Godínez Cruz v. Honduras," Merit, sentence of January 20, 1989, para. 158.

57. Cecilia Medina, "*Los 40 años de la Convención Americana sobre Derechos Humanos a la luz de cierta jurisprudencia de la Corte Interamericana*," *Anuario de Derechos Humano* vol. 18 (Santiago, Chile: Brill, 2009).

58. Gabriella Citroni. "The Contribution of the Inter-American Court of Human Rights and Other International Human Rights Bodies to the Struggle against Enforced Disappearance," in Ruiz-Chiriboga Haeck and Burbano Herrera, eds., *The Inter-American Court of Human Rights: Theory and Practice, Present and Future* (Cambridge: Intersentia, 2015), 379–403.

59. Ophelia Claude, "A Comparative Approach to Enforced Disappearances in the Inter-American Court of Human Rights and the European Court of Human Rights Jurisprudence," *Intercultural Human Rights Law Review* 5 (2010): 407; and Cecilia Medina, *The American Convention on Human Rights, Crucial Rights and their Theory and Practice*, 2nd ed., (Cambridge: Intersentia, 2016), 63.

60. José Zalaquett, "*Procesos de Transición a la Democracia y Políticas de Derechos Humanos en América Latina*," in IIDH, *Presente y Futuro de los Derechos Humanos*, 1998, summarizing the cases of Argentina, Chile, Uruguay, and El Salvador. Available at https://www.rindhca.org/en/actualidad/videos-indh/los-derechos-humanos-pasado-presente-y-futuro; Kathryn Sikkink. *From Pariah States to Global Protagonist: Argentina and the Struggle for International Human Rights* on behalf of the Center for Latin American Studies at the University of Miami (Cambridge: Cambridge University Press, 2008), 1–29.

61. Constitution of the Plurinational State of Bolivia (article 15, IV and 114.1); Political Constitution of Colombia (article 12); Constitution of the Republic of Ecuador (articles 66.3.c.; 80; 120.3 and 129.3); Constitution of the United Mexican States (articles 29 and 73.XXI.a); National Constitution of Paraguay (article 5) and Constitution of the Bolivarian Republic of Venezuela (article 45 and Third Transitional Provision). By Law 24.820 Argentina gave constitutional status to the Inter-American Convention on Forced Disappearance of Persons.

62. *Report of the Working Group on Enforced or Involuntary Disappearances—Addendum—Best practices on Enforced Disappearances in Domestic Criminal Legislation*, A/HRC/16/48/Add.3.

63. See for example, *Report of the Working Group on Enforced of Involuntary Disappearances Addendum Mission to Mexico*, A/HRC/19/58/Add.2, para. 13; and Committee on Enforced Disappearances, *Concluding Observations on the Report Submitted by Uruguay Under Article 29, Paragraph 1 of the Convention, Adopted by the Committee at Its Fourth Session, April 8–19, 2013*, para. 11; and *Observations on the Report Sub-*

mitted by Paraguay under Article 29, Paragraph 1 of the Convention, paras. 13 and 17, and Inter-American Court of Human Rights, *Case of Gómez Palomino*, para. 92ff.

64. *Ley General En Materia De Desaparición Forzada De Personas, Desaparición Cometida Por Particulares Y Del Sistema Nacional De Búsqueda De Personas*. In 2016, Peru adopted a law on search of disappeared persons, *Ley N° 30470 o Ley de búsqueda de personas desaparecidas durante el período de violencia 1980–2000*. http://www.elperuano.com.pe/NormasElperuano/2016/06/22/1395654-1.html

65. "General Comment on the Right to Recognition as a Person Before the Law in the Context of Enforced Disappearances," para. 2, in *Report of the Working Group on Enforced or Involuntary Disappearances*, A/HRC/19/58, 2011. Also, Peru, law no. 28.413; Argentina, law no. 24.321; Brazil, law no. 9.140/95; Chile, law no. 20377; Colombia, law no. 1531; México, article 21 of the General Law on Victims, and Uruguay law no. 17.894. See also, in México, the respective laws of the states of Coahuila, Chihuahua and Queretaro.

66. An important exception is the Philippines Republic Act 10535, *Anti-Enforced or Involuntary Disappearance Act of 2012*. http://www.officialgazette.gov.ph/2012/12/21/republic-act-no-10353/

67. Mark Berlin and Geoff Dancy, "The Difference Law Makes: Domestic Atrocity Laws and Human Rights Prosecutions," Law and Society Review, 51, no. 3 (2017): 532–66.

68. Naomi Roht-Arriaza, "After Amnesties are Gone: Latin American National Courts and the new Contours of the Fight Against Impunity," *Human Rights Quarterly* 37, no. 2 (2015): 341–82, at 342.

69. For example, Catalina Smulovitz, *The Past is Never Dead: Accountability and Justice for Past Human Rights Violations in Argentina*, in Mónica Serrano and Vesselin Popovski, eds., *After Oppression: Transitional Justice in Latin America and Eastern Europe* (Tokyo, New York, Paris: United Nations University Press, 2012); and Catherine Collins, "Chile a más de dos décadas de justicia de transición," *Política. Revista de Ciencia Política* 51, no. 2 (2013): 78–79.

70. Ronald Gamarra, *Juzgar a un jefe de Estado: lecciones del proceso al expresidente Alberto Fujimori por delitos contra los derechos humanos* (Lima: Coordinadora Nacional de Derechos Humanos, 2010).

71. Open Society Justice Initiative, *Judging A Dictator: The Trial of Guatemala's Ríos Montt* (November 2013); and Hernando Salazar, *Primer general condenado por desaparición forzada en Colombia* (Bogotá: *BBC Mundo*, April 29, 2011). http://www.bbc.com/mundo/noticias/2011/04/110429_colombia_condena_general_corte_suprema_fp

72. Due Process of Law Foundation, *Digesto de Jurisprudencia Latinoamérica sobre crímenes de Derecho Internacional* (Institute for Peace, Washington, DC, 2000).

73. For earlier debates see José Zalaquett, "Confronting Human Rights Violations Committed by Former Governments: Applicable Principles and Political Constraints," *Hamline Law Review* 13 (1990): 623, 628; Juan E. Méndez, "Accountability for Past Abuses," *Human Rights Quarterly* 19, (1997): 255, 256; Carlos Nino, "The Duty to Punish Past Abuses of Human Rights Put into Context: The Case of Argentina," *Yale Law Journal* 100: 2619; and Jaime Malamud-Goti, "Transitional Governments in the Breach: Why Punish State Criminals?" 12 *Human Rights Quarterly* 12: 1.

74. See, for example, Committee on Enforced Disappearances, *Concluding Observations on the Report Submitted by Paraguay Under Article 29, Para. 1, of the Convention*, CED/C/PRY/CO/1, para. 17.

75. See Supreme Court of Chile, *Decision on Appeal of Inapplicability of Decree Law 2191*, August 24, 1996; Supreme Court of Justice of the Nation of Argentina, *Proceedings Instituted under Decree 280/84 of the National Executive Camps, Ramón Juan Alberto and Others*, Decision 310:1162, June 22, 1987; Sentence-97/21–98 Constitutional Chamber, May 2, 1988, *D., J.; M., N.; M., F.; M., O.; B., J. Complaint. Unconstitutional Law 15.848. Arts. 1, 2, 3 y 4*, F. n° 112/ 87, May 2, 1988; and *Decision of July 14, 1995, of the Tenth Criminal Chamber of the Superior Court of Lima, Peru*. The most recent example of this trend is the decision of the Supreme Federal Court of Brazil on April 28, 2010, Accusation of breach of fundamental precept n° 153.

76. The first IACHR cases were on Argentina, Uruguay, and El Salvador in 1992 and several years later, the Court with the case of Barrios Altos IACHR, Report 26/92. Case 10.287. Las Hojas Massacre. El Salvador. September 24, 1992; Informe 28/92. Cases 10.147, 10.181, 10.240, 10.262, 10.309 and 10.311. Argentina. October 2, 1992; Report 29/92. Cases 10.029, 10.036, 10.145, 10.305, 10.372, 10.373 and 10.375, Uruguay, October 2, 1992. Inter-Am. Ct. H.R. Case of Barrios Altos v. Peru. Merits. Sentence of March 14, 2001. Series C No. 75, para. 41ff.

77. *Resolución de la Corte de Constitucionalidad de fecha 7 de julio de 2009, Expediente* No. 926–2008. Constitutional Court of Peru, Sentence of December 9, 2004, File No. 2798–04-HC/TC, Case of Gabriel Orlando Vera Navarrete; Supreme Court of Argentina, Sentence de August 24, 2004, cause A.533.XXXVIII, Arancibia Clavel, Enrique Lautaro, et al. *s/ homicidio calificado y asociación ilícita* -Cause No. 259-; Constitutional Court of Bolivia, Sentence of November 12, 2001, Case of José Carlos Trujillo; Supreme Court of Chile, Pleno, Sentence of August 8, 2000, Case for removal of immunity of Pinochet; Constitutional Court of Colombia, Sentence C-580/02, of July 3, 2002; Supreme Court of Justice of the Nation of México, Thesis: P./J. 87/2004; Supreme Court of Uruguay, Sentence of April 17, 2002, Case of Gavasso and Supreme Court of Venezuela, Sentence of August 10, 2007, Exp. No. 06-1656, Appeal Case Review—Marco Antonio.

78. Roht-Arriaza, "After Amnesties are Gone."

79. See Trial International, "Christian Von Wernich." https://trialinternational.org/latest-post/christian-von-wernich/; and TELESUR, "28 Ex-Officials of Argentina's Military Dictatorship Sentenced." http://www.telesurtv.net/english/news/In-Landmark-Ruling-28-Former-Officials-of-Argentinas-Military-Dictatorship-Sentenced-20170726-0039.html

80. Roht-Arriaza, "After Amnesties are Gone."

81. Associated Press, "Peru Court Orders Ex-President Fujimori Freed From Prison," NPR, March 18, 2022. https://www.npr.org/2022/03/18/1087442224/peru-court-orders-ex-president-fujimori-freed-from-prison

82. Initiated in cases of disappearances, such as "Argentina Forti v. Suarez-Mason," *U.S. Circuit Court for the Northern District of California*, 694 F. Supp 707, 1988. Another case of enforced disappearance in Latin America is "Xuncax v. Gramajo" *U.S. District Court for Massachusetts*, 886 F. Suat 162, 1995. And see also, "Daimler AG v. Bauman," 134 S. Ct. 746, 761–62, 2014, (rejecting a claim on

corporate complicity in forced disappearances of persons in Argentina during the dictatorship); and Manuel Marraco, "*La Audiencia Nacional condena a Scilingo a 640 años de cárcel por delitos de lesa humanidad*," *El Mundo*, April 20, 2005.

83. See Naomi Roht-Arriaza, "After Amnesties are Gone," 8ff, 208ff. *Human Rights Quarterly* 37, no. 2 (May 2015).

84. See Redress, *Universal Jurisdiction in Europe: Criminal Prosecutions in Europe Since 1990 for War Crimes, Crimes Against Humanity, Torture, and Genocide*, 1999. https://redress.org/wp-content/uploads/2018/01/G.-June-1999-Universal-Jurisdiction-in-Europe.pdf

85. See Ellen Lutz and Kathryn Sikkink, "The Justice Cascade: The Evolution and Impact of Foreign Human Rights Trials in Latin America," *Chicago Journal of International Law* 2, no. 1, art. 3 (2001); and Naomi Roht-Arriaza, *The Pinochet Effect: Transnational Justice in the Age of Human Rights* (Philadelphia: University of Pennsylvania Press, 2005).

86. David Pion-Berlin. "The Pinochet Case and Human Rights Progress in Chile: Was Europe a Catalyst, Cause or Inconsequential?" *Journal of Latin American Studies* 36 (2004): 479–505; and Juan Guzmán Tapia, "*En el borde del mundo: memorias del juez que procesó a Pinochet*," *Editorial Anagrama* 70 (2005).

87. Javier Chinchón, *El tratamiento judicial de los crímenes de la Guerra Civil y el franquismo en España: una visión de conjunto desde el derecho internacional*, no. 67 (Bilbao, Spain: Universidad de Deusto, 2012), 91.

88. Rosales Herrera and Eduardo Alfonso, *El juicio del siglo: Augusto Pinochet frente al derecho y la política internacional* (México: Plaza y Valdés, 2007); Javier Dondé-Matute. "International Criminal Law Before the Supreme Court of México," *International Criminal Law Review* 10, no. 4 (2010): 572–75, at 571.

89. *Buenos Aires Herald*, "Landmark, Human Rights Convictions for Former Judges," July 28, 2017. http://www.buenosairesherald.com/article/226413/landmark-human-rights-convictions-for-former-judges

90. Javier Couso, Alexandra Huneeus, and Rachel Sieder, *Cultures Of Legality: Judicialization and Political Activism in Latin America* (Cambridge: Cambridge University Press, 2010).

91. IACHR, "The Right to Truth in the Americas," OEA/Ser.L/V/II.152 Doc. 2, 2014.

92. Peru, Judgment of March 18, 2004, File No. 2488–2002-HC/TC Piura, Case Genaro Villegas Namuche; Colombia, Constitutional Court, see, e.g., Judgment T-249/03, 2003 and Supreme Court of Justice, Criminal Chamber, Decision on appeal, of July 11, 2007, Case Orlando César Caballero Montalvo, *Tribunal Superior de Antioquia*; El Salvador, Supreme Court of Justice, Constitutional Chamber, Judgment 665–2010 of February 5, 2014, Argentina, Supreme Court of Justice, Urteaga Facundo Raul C/ Estado Nacional—*Estado Mayor Conjunto de La FFAA S/Amparo Ley* 16986 and México, Second Chamber, Supreme Court of Justice, Amparo en Revisión 934/2016, 29 March, 2017.

93. Priscilla B. Hayner, *Unspeakable Truths: Facing the Challenge of Truth Commissions*, vol. 21 (Oxfordshire: Routledge, 2002); Naomi Roht-Arriaza, "Truth Commissions and Amnesties in Latin America: The Second Generation," *American Society of International Law* 92 (1998): 313–15.

94. See Silvia Dutrénit Bielous, *"Los Equipos de Antropología Forense en América Latina: Coadyuvantes en el Camino de la Verdad y la Justicia,"* 1 *Publicación de la Red Universitaria sobre Derechos Humanos y Democratización para América Latina*, year 2, n° 3, April 2012, Buenos Aires, Argentina.

95. Stover, "The Missing in the Aftermath of War," 850.

96. Victor B. Penchaszadeh, "Ethical, Legal, and Social Issues in Restoring Genetic Identity after Forced Disappearance and Suppression of Identity in Argentina," *Journal of Community Genetics* 6, no. 3 (2015): 207–13.

97. Veronica Hinestroza et al., *Comisiones de búsqueda en América Latina. Una apuesta extraordinaria por la integralidad en la investigación de las desapariciones*, 2021. https://www.identificacionhumana.mx/comisiones-de-busqueda-en-america-latina/; see also the National Commission for the Search of children who disappeared during the internal armed conflict in El Salvador and Argentina, National Commission for the Right to Identity, see Disposition 1328/92 of the Human Rights Under-Secretariat of the Interior Ministry, Resolution 1392/98 of the Ministry of Interior and Law 25.457.

98. See International Commission on Missing Persons, *Missing Persons from the Armed Conflict of the 1990s: A Stocktaking*. https://www.icmp.int/wp-content/uploads/2014/12/StocktakingReport_ENG_web.pdf

99. Inter-American Commission on Human Rights, *Office of the Special Rapporteur for Freedom of Expression, The Right to Access to Public Information in the Americas: Inter-American Standards and Comparison of Legal Frameworks*, 2012, para. 355.

100. *Código de Procedimientos Penales de Guatemala*, article 467.2.a.

101. Sévane Garibian, "Ghosts Also Die: Resisting Disappearance through the 'Right to the Truth' and the *Juicios por la Verdad* in Argentina," *Journal of International Criminal Justice* 12, no. 3 (2014): 515–38.

102. Martin Imbleau, "Initial Truth Establishment by Transitional Bodies and the Fight Against Denial," in William A. Schabas and Shane Darcy, eds., *Truth Commissions and Courts: The Tension Between Criminal Justice and the Search for Truth*, vol. 15, no. 1–2 (Berlin, Heidelberg: Springer, 2007).

103. Elizabeth Lira, *"Chile, Desaparición Forzada: 1973–2015,"* in Miguel Giusti, Gustavo Gutierrez, Elizabeth Salmón, eds., *La Verdad nos Hace Libres. Sobre las relaciones entre Filosofía, Derechos Humanos, Religión y Universidad* (Lima, Perú: Fondo Editorial, Universidad Catolica de Perú, 2015), 550.

104. Claudia Nash Rojas and David Valeska, *Las Reparaciones ante la Corte Interamericana de Derechos Humanos (1988–2007)* (Santiago, Chile: Universidad de Chile, Facultad de Derecho, Centro de Derechos Humanos, 2009).

105. Pablo De Greiff, *The Handbook of Reparations*, (Oxford: Oxford University Press, 2006); Ruth Rubio-Marín, ed., *The Gender of Reparations: Unsettling Sexual Hierarchies While Redressing Human Rights Violations* (Cambridge, England: Cambridge University Press, 2009).

106. M. Brinton Lykes and Ramsay Liem, "Human Rights and Mental Health in the United States: Lessons from Latin America," *Journal of Social Issues* 46 (1990): 151, 159; *Consenso mundial de principios y normas mínimas sobre trabajo psicosocial en procesos de búsqueda e investigaciones forenses para casos de desapariciones forzadas, ejecuciones arbitrarias o extrajudiciales*, (a work which emerged and was developed fundamentally from a Latin American initiative). http://cooperaciocatalana.gencat.

cat/web/.content/continguts/02serveis/05publicacions/04informes_estudis_guies/ consens_mundial/normas_minimas.pdf

107. See *Sitios de la Memoria en América Latina*, http://www.sitiosdememoria. org; and, for example, the poem *"Desaparecidos,"* by Mario Benedetti (Uruguay) or *"Los escogidos,"* by Patricia Nieto (Colombia). See also, Jorge Ladino Bayona Gaitán, *"El arte de la desaparición forzada en dos novelas colombianas,"* *Espéculo: Revista de Estudios Literarios* 46 (2010): 62; Lancelot Cowie, *"Los desaparecidos y la represión de estado en la narrativa argentina actual,"* *Revista del CESLA*, 16 (2013): 195–205. In Ecuador, the documentary *Con mi corazón en Yambo*, about the disappearance of the Restrepo brothers during the 1984–1988 period of León Febres-Cordero de María Fernanda Restrepo Arismendi or *NN: Sin identidad* by Héctor Gálvez in Perú. Also, *Verena Berger*, *"La búsqueda del pasado desde la ausencia: Argentina y la reconstrucción de la memoria de los desaparecidos en el cine de los hijos,"* *Edición digital a partir de Quaderns de Cine: Cine i memòria històrica* 3 (2008): 23–36. https://www. researchgate.net/profile/Verena-Berger-2/publication/268254428_La_busqueda_ del_pasado_desde_la_ausencia_Argentina_y_la_reconstruccion_de_la_memoria_ de_los_desaparecidos_en_el_cine_de_los_hijos/links/54fadac10cf23e66f0332001/ La-busqueda-del-pasado-desde-la-ausencia-Argentina-y-la-reconstruccion-de-la-memoria-de-los-desaparecidos-en-el-cine-de-los-hijos.pdf; María Noela Ibáñez. *"El ojo que espía por las grietas del pasado. Una aproximación al estudio sobre el tratamiento de la memoria y la historia reciente en el cine argentino (1983–2009),"* *Passagens. Revista Internacional de História Política e Cultura Jurídica* 4, no. 3 (2012): 384–400. https://www.academia.edu/32339327/El_ojo_que-esp%C3%ADa_por_las_orietas_del_pasad_0_pdf; in photography, see the work of Gustavo Germano, Ausencias on Argentina and Brazil in http://www.gustavogermano.com/, or in Peru the photographic work de Ricardo Wiesse on the execution and disappearance of students from the University of La Cantuta http://www.micromuseo.org.pe/publicaciones/itinerarios/itinerarios6.html; Ana Longoni, *"Fotos y siluetas: dos estrategias en la representación de los desaparecidos,"* comp. by Emilio Crenzel, *Los desaparecidos en la Argentina. Memorias, representaciones e ideas (1983–2008)* (2010): 35–57; María Elena Rodríguez Sánchez, *"La fotografía y la representación de la memoria de las víctimas de desaparición en Colombia,"* *Revista Sans Soleil* 4 (2012): 216–23. https:// www.academia.edu/32339327/El_ojo_que_esp%C3%ADa_por_las_grietas_del_ pasado_pdf; Diego A. Mazorra, *Fotografía Y Memoria: Imágenes Y Lugares En La Fotografía De Los Desaparecidos En Colombia* [Photography and memory: Images and places in the photography of the missing people in Colombia] (Universidad Externado de Columbia: Revista Comunicación, 2010).

108. For example, Alfredo Boccia Paz, Rosa Palau, and Osvaldo Salerno, *Paraguay: Los Archivos dl Terror, Los Papeles que Resignificaron la Memoria del Stronismo* (Asunción, Paraguay: Centro de Documentación y Archivo para la Defensa de los Derechos Humanos, 2007); or Kirsten Weld. *Paper Cadavers: The Archives of Dictatorship in Guatemala* (Durham, NC: Duke University Press, 2014).

109. *See, for example, Catalina Uprimny Salazar, "La memoria en la Ley de Víctimas de Colombia: derecho y deber," Anuario de Derechos Humanos 8 (2012).*

110. See *Report of the Working Group on Enforced or Involuntary Disappearances Addendum Mission to Chile*, A/HRC/22/45/Add.1, January 29, 2013, para. 49–50; *Report of the Working Group on Enforced or Involuntary Disappearances on Its mis-*

sion to Peru, A/HRC/33/51/Add.3, July 8, 2016, para. 63–66; *Report of the Working Group on Enforced or Involuntary Disappearance, Addendum Mission to Argentina*, A/HRC/10/9/Add.1, January 5, 2009, para. 65; *Report of the Working Group on Enforced or Involuntary Disappearances on Its Mission to Sri Lanka*, A/HRC/33/51/Add.2, 64; and *Report of the Working Group on Enforced or Involuntary Disappearances on Its Mission to Turkey*, A/HRC/33/51/Add.1, 51. For examples of memory work in Chile, see Steve J. Stern, *Remembering Pinochet's Chile* (Durham, NC: Duke University Press, 2004); Elizabeth Jelin, *Los trabajos de la Memoria* (Madrid, Spain: Siglo XXI editors, 2002).

111. See, for example, Elizabeth Jelin, *"La política de la memoria: El movimiento de derechos humanos y la construcción democrática en la Argentina,"* in *Juicio, castigos y memoria: Derechos humanos y justicia en la política argentina*, (Buenos Aires: Nueva Visión, 1995); and Kathryn Sikkink and Margaret Keck, *Activists Beyond Borders: Advocacy Networks in International Politics* (Ithaca: Cornell University Press, 1998).

112. At the risk of leaving crucial organizations unmentioned, see, for example, Association of Relatives of the Disappeared and Victims of Human Rights Violations (AFADEM), México; Relatives of the Disappeared and Detained for Political Reasons, Argentina; Association of Relatives of Disappeared Detainees (AFDD), Chile; ASOFAM, Bolivia; Association of Relatives of Disappeared Detainees (ASFADDES), Colombia; Committee of Relatives of Detained—Disappeared of Honduras (COFADEH); CODEFAM, El Salvador; Mutual Support Group (GAM), Guatemala; Mothers and Relatives of the Disappeared, Uruguay; Torture Never Again, Brazil; National Association of Families of the Kidnapped, Detained and Disappeared of Peru (Anfasep).

113. See *Historie de la FEMED* at http://www.disparitions-euromed.org/

114. Americas Watch, *The Vicaría de la Solidaridad in Chile, An Americas Watch Report*, December 1987, at 3, 7; and Manuel Bastías Saavedra, *Sociedad civil en dictadura: relaciones transnacionales, organizaciones y socialización política en Chile (1973–1993)* (Santiago, Chile: Ediciones Universidad Alberto Hurtado, 2013); Gülsüm Baydar and Berfin İvegen, "Territories, Identities, and Thresholds: The Saturday Mothers Phenomenon in İstanbul," *Signs: Journal of Women in Culture and Society* 31, no. 3 (2006): 689–715.

115. Sikkink and Keck, *Activists Beyond Borders*.

116. Ronald Gamarra, the Mothers of ANFASEP, *Rosario: Memoria indómita*, directed by Shula Eremberg (2013) (http://derechoshumanos.pe/2008/09/a-las-madres-de-anfasep/); see *Yanette Bautista: 27 años de lucha* at http://www.pazconmujeres.org/pg.php?pa=3&id=1bd45f2925d82a0143d123b59fcafa9c&t=Yanette%20 Bautista:%2027%20a%F1os%20de%20lucha) for Sola Sierra Henríquez, see http://www.educarchile.cl/ech/pro/app/detalle?GUID=04dd8ea8-d673-474e-bd7c-2da8584102ac&ID=137092&FMT=519; for Villaflor see http://www.pagina12.com.ar/diario/elpais/subnotas/60225-19937-2005-12-09.html. For de Nativi, see http://www.1325mujerestejiendolapaz.org/otrsem_bertha.html); for Farfán, see *The Time* http://time.com/3822942/aura-elena-farfan-2015-time-100/) For women in other Latin American countries see, for example, Raquel Andrea Vera Salerno and Rosa M. Palau Aguilar, *Luchadoras de Ayer en la Dictadura. Luchadoras de Hoy en Democracia* and *Rago, Margareth, A coragem feminina da verdade: mulheres na ditadura militar no*

Brasil, at 523, both in Assy, Bethania; Melo, Carolina de Campos; Dornelles, João Ricardo; Gomez, José Maria (Org.), *Direitos Humanos, justiça, verdade e memória*, (Rio de Janeiro: Lumen Juris, 2012).

117. Radhika Coomaraswamy makes the same argument on the general framework and local adaptations of international law of human rights in general in Radhika Coomaraswamy, "Women and Children: The Cutting Edge of International Law," *American University International Law Review* 30 (2015): 50–51, 62.

118. See similarly, in relation to genocide, Susanne Karstedt, "Contextualizing Mass Atrocity Crimes: Moving Toward a Relational Approach," *Annual Review of Law and Social Science* 9 (2013): 383–404.

119. For the list of professions and occupations of those who disappeared in Argentina in Proyecto Desaparecidos, *Listas de Detenidos-Desaparecidos y Asesinados en Argentina*, http://www.desaparecidos.org/arg/victimas/listas/#profe; for rural Peru and Fujimori, see *Comisión de la Verdad y la Reconciliación, Informe Final*, http://www.cverdad.org.pe/ifinal/index.php; for Guatemala, see Pinzón González and Mónica Esmeralda, "Psychosocial Perspectives on the Enforced Disappearance of Indigenous Peoples in Guatemala in Missing Persons," in Derek Congram, ed., *Multidisciplinary Perspectives on the Disappeared* (Toronto: Canadian Scholar's Press, 2016). Esmeralda's chapter explains the particular impact of "enforced disappearances in an indigenous community in Guatemala"; for El Salvador, see *From Madness to Hope: The 12-Year War in El Salvador: Report of the Commission on the Truth for El Salvador*, https://www.usip.org/sites/default/files/file/ElSalvador-Report.pdf; for Colombia see, *Inter-American Commission on Human Rights, Truth, Justice and Reparation: Fourth Report on Human Rights Situation in Colombia*, http://www.oas.org/en/iachr/reports/pdfs/Colombia-Truth-Justice-Reparation.pdf; for Uruguay, see *Informe de Madres y Familiares de Desaparecidos, A Todos Ellos*. https://desaparecidos.org.uy/wp-content/uploads/2015/07/A-todos-ellos_.pdf

120. Wasana Punyasena, "The Façade of Accountability: Disappearances in Sri Lanka," *Boston College Third World Law Journal* 23 (2003): 115.

121. Sylvia Karl, "Rehumanizing the Disappeared: Spaces of Memory in México and the Liminality of Transitional Justice," *American Quarterly* 66, no. 3 (2014): 727–48, 733; and Howard M. Kleinman, "Disappearances in Latin America: A Human Rights Perspective," *NYU Journal of International Law and Politics* 19 (1986–1987): 1033–42.

122. Shaery Yazdi-Roschanack, "The Local Politics of the Lebanese Disappeared," *Middle East Report* 262 (2012): 2–5 (explaining the phenomenon of enforced disappearances carried out by Syrian forces in Lebanon and the dynamic of the relatives' efforts to find their loved ones in Syria and Lebanon); and Caroline L. Payne and M. Rodwan Abouharb, "The International Covenant on Civil and Political Rights and the Strategic Shift to Forced Disappearance," *Journal of Human Rights* 15, no. 2 (2016), 163–88 (arguing that increased international scrutiny could move their repressive techniques from extrajudicial executions to enforced disappearances as they are more difficult to prove). See also, Due Process of Law Foundation, *Victims Unsilenced: The Inter-American Human Rights System and Transitional Justice in Latin America*, 2007. http://www.dplf.org/en/resources/inter-american-system-transitional-justice-0

123. See for example, Francesca Lessa, et al., "Persistent or Eroding Impunity?

The Divergent Effects of Legal Challenges to Amnesty Laws for Past Human Rights Violations," *Israel Law Review* 47, no. 1 (2014): 105–31.

124. Sally E. Merry. "Transnational Human Rights and Local Activism: Mapping the Middle," *American Anthropologist* 108, no. 1: 38–51. Richard A. Wilson, "Afterword to 'Anthropology and Human Rights in a New Key': The Social Life of Human Rights," *American Anthropologist* 108, no. 1: 77–83.

125. Fernando Ferrándiz, "*De las fosas comunes a los derechos humanos: El descubrimiento de las desapariciones forzadas en la España contemporánea,*" *Revista de antropología social* 19 (2010): 163.

126. Ferrándiz, "*De las fosas comunes a los derechos humanos,*" 175, 177.

127. Adam Rosenblatt, "Missing Persons: Multidisciplinary Perspectives on the Disappeared," in Derek Congram, ed., *Human Rights Quarterly* 39 no. 3 (2017): 758–763, 760.

128. See particularly the works of Sally Engle Merry and Mark Goodale, eds., *The Practice of Human Rights: Tracking Law Between the Global and the Local* (Cambridge: Cambridge University Press, 2007); and "Vernacularization in Action: Using Global Women's Human Rights Locally" 9, no. 4, Special Issue of *Global Networks*, co-ed. by Peggy Levitt. (2009).

129. IACHR, *Justice and Social Inclusion: The Challenges of Democracy in Guatemala*, OEA/Ser.L/V/II.118, doc. 5 rev. 1, December 29, 2003, Original: Spanish (explaining how justice and reparation efforts in Guatemala are less effective in the case of indigenous peoples due to structural racism among other factors).

130. Jay D. Aronson, "The Strengths and Limitations of South Africa's Search for Apartheid-Era Missing Persons," *International Journal of Transitional Justice* 5, no. 2 (2011): 262–81, at 271 (explaining that the Missing Persons Task Team in South Africa only investigates cases that are explicitly "political" in nature).

131. See Margaret Blaauw and Virpi Lähteenmäk, "Denial and Silence or Acknowledgement and Disclosure," *International Review of the Red Cross* 84, no. 848 (2002): 767–84; and *Report of the Working Group on Enforced or Involuntary Disappearances on its mission to Sri Lanka*, A/HRC/33/51/Add.2, para. 70.

132. Lasse Schuldt, "Southeast Asian Hesitation: ASEAN Countries and the International Criminal Court," *German Law Journal* 16 (2015): 75.

133. Jeevasuthan Subramaniam, Nur Mohammad Majumder, Zulkarnain A. Hatta, and Abul Fozol Muhammod Zakaria, "Implications of Enforced Disappearances on Women-Headed Families in the Northern Province, Sri Lanka," *International Journal of Humanities and Social Science* 4, no. 4 (2014): 236–43.

134. *Report of the Working Group on Enforced or Involuntary Disappearances Addendum Mission to Nepal*, December 6–14, 2004, para. 25 (describing those disappearances are carried out both by the State and by insurgents).

135. Naomi Kinsella and Soren Blau, "Searching for Conflict Related Missing Persons in Timor-Leste: Technical, Political, and Cultural Considerations," *Stability: International Journal of Security and Development* 2, no. 1 (2013).

136. See for example, Fred Ross, III and Jae Chun Won, "North Korean Kidnappers: A Response to Illegal Abductions by the Democratic People's Republic of Korea before the Working Group on Enforced and Involuntary Disappearances," *Regent Journal of International Law* 9 (2012): 277.

137. Alberto L. Zuppi, "Swinging Back and Forth Between Impunity and Impeachment: The Struggle for Justice in Latin America and the International Criminal Court," *Pace International Law Review* 19 (2007): 195.

138. "Question Of The Human Rights Of All Persons Subjected To Any Form Of Detention Or Imprisonment, In Particular: Question Of Enforced Or Involuntary Disappearances," *Report of the Working Group on Enforced or Involuntary Disappearances Addendum Report on the Visit to Peru by Two Members of the Working Group on Enforced or Involuntary Disappearances* E/CN.4/1986/18/Add.1, June 17–22, 1985, para. 35–61 (explaining how enforced disappearances took place in Ayacucho and describing the socio-economic context and different actors in that part of Peru).

139. Tilman Blumenstock, "Legal Protection of the Missing and Their Relatives: The Example of Bosnia and Herzegovina," *Leiden Journal of International Law* 19, no. 3 (2006): 773–93; and Grażyna Baranowska, "Shedding Light on the Fate of the Disappeared?" *Committee on Missing Persons in Cyprus, International Journal of Rule of Law, Transitional Justice and Human Rights* Year 3, Vol. 3, (Sarajevo 2012). http://ssrn.com/abstract=2216767

140. Paola Carozza, "From Conquest to Constitutions: Retrieving a Latin American Tradition of the Idea of Human Rights,'" *Human Rights Quarterly* 25 (2003): 281–300, at 283.

141. Emily Braid and Naomi Roht-Arriaza, "De Facto and De jure Amnesty Laws," *Amnesty in the Age of Human Rights Accountability: Comparative and International Perspectives* 182 (2012).

142. *Report of the Working Group on Enforced or Involuntary Disappearances Addendum Mission to Mexico*, December 20, 2011, A/HRC/19/58/Add.2.

143. Frey, "*Los Desaparecidos*," 52.

144. Roht-Arriaza, "After Amnesties are Gone," 343.

145. Kathryn Sikkink and Carrie Booth Walling, "Argentina's Contribution to Global Trends in Transnational Justice," Naomi Roht-Arriaza and Javier Mariezcurrena, eds., *Transitional Justice in the Twenty-first Century: Beyond Truth and Justice* (New York: Cambridge University Press, 2006), 301.

TWO

The Impact of Enforced Disappearances on Women

Amrita Kapur

This chapter, adapted from a 2015 global study conducted by the International Center for Transitional Justice, identifies the impacts of and government responses to enforced disappearances on women. Informed by primary research, including interviews with women victims in Nepal and Lebanon, the chapter surveys experiences from thirty-one countries to identify how transitional justice initiatives can better respond to women's needs and experiences related to enforced disappearances.

The 2006 International Convention for the Protection of All Persons from Enforced Disappearance identifies both the disappeared and their family members as victims of enforced disappearance. This has important consequences for women, who comprise the minority of the disappeared, but most family members who suffer exacerbated social, economic, and psychological disadvantages because of the loss of a male family member who is often a breadwinner.

While enforced disappearance has been a primary focus of transitional justice mechanisms, its impact on women is not always effectively acknowledged or addressed. Accordingly, the first section of the chapter describes the gendered impacts both for women who are disappeared and female family members of the disappeared. The second section explores how truth-seeking initiatives have or have not accurately captured the scope of women's experiences and violations when investigating enforced disappearances. The third section surveys the range of material and symbolic reparations and relief measures able to address the range of consequences experienced by women in the wake of disappearances. Key aspects include recognizing family members as victims eligible for reparations and ensuring access to reparations is not dependent on a declaration of death. The fourth section describes the scope of criminal justice responses.

Women, in their roles as mothers and wives of the disappeared, activists, advocates for truth, and representatives of communities, are key to the success of transitional justice mechanisms seeking to provide truth, justice, and accountability for enforced disappearances. This chapter explores important lessons that have been learned across time and contexts, and from different transitional justice mechanisms, about how to address enforced disappearance in a gender-sensitive manner.

Gender Differences in the Disappeared

Although no exact figures exist, according to the United Nations Working Group on Enforced or Involuntary Disappearances (UNWGEID), most reported cases of disappearances are of men.[1] In certain circumstances there may be a problem of under-reporting or under-recording of women's disappearances. Women victims are most often targeted because of their real or perceived opposition to repressive regimes or as a form of punishment for challenging gender norms by participating in the public sphere. Women who work with victims or who are engaged in searching for truth about the disappeared are especially at risk.

Women who disappear face similar forms of torture, ill-treatment, and abuse as men. However, they face a higher risk of sexual violence and gendered forms of abuse, such as "humiliation and abuse around biological functions such as menstruation and childbirth."[2] Disappeared women have been subjected to rape, beatings, and electric shocks (Guatemala); repeated rape that led to hemorrhage (Argentina)[3]; and gang rape, sometimes repeatedly (Morocco).[4] In many countries, relationships with children and maternal instincts have been used to psychologically torture women detainees and their families by forcing them to witness the torture of those they care about, including infants suffering from hunger, heat, and cold. Pregnant women and their unborn children face enormous risks while in detention, including the risk that one or both will be executed after birth.[5]

Women Relatives of the Disappeared

Wives, mothers, and daughters of disappeared men also suffer diverse, lasting consequences and often human rights violations. Gender inequalities steeped in tradition, race, culture, religion, and class often mean that these social, legal, economic, and psychological consequences will differ to those experienced by men. Women experience more severe poverty and victimization when the disappeared is the family's main or even sole breadwinner and may be forced into low-paying, insecure jobs, often far away from their family. This in turn increases their risk of exploitation[6] and jeopardizes their children's well-being and education. Women who can avoid extreme poverty often do so at the cost of educating and providing adequate healthcare for their children,[7] and forgoing their own educations.[8] In Uganda, some families of the disappeared married off girl children as a means of economic survival.[9]

The precarious legal status of the disappeared often results in the inability of their wives to access bank accounts, social services, or retain ownership of assets. Women relatives are also adversely affected by discriminatory laws in some countries that make it difficult for women to own land, homes, and other forms of property or to transfer assets into their name. For example, in Lebanon, authorities require large sums of money to transfer land into the name of a wife or child of the disappeared, which often means family assets (such as homes) remain unsettled, and cars go unused.[10]

Often the only way for family members to access frozen funds and property is to declare a missing husband, son, or father dead. However, this may only be possible after time has passed, and family members are reluctant to do this, sometimes because of guilt, trauma, or fear about both the disappearance and being seen to have abandoned the search.[11] Women face economic hardships within the constraints of traditional gender roles.

Wives often remain in the homes of their in-laws, where they may be seen as, and consider themselves, an economic burden. This hardship is compounded when women pay for costs associated with searching for information about the whereabouts and fate of a disappeared loved one. Extortionists, blackmailers, and con artists, seeing an opportunity to profit from a family's desperate need for information, often prey on vulnerable relatives of the disappeared.[12]

Social and Physical Impact

Family problems, or "intra-familial harassment," due to increased economic burdens after an enforced disappearance are widely documented around the world.[13] Women may be blamed for the disappearance, ostracized for financially burdening the family, and condemned for challenging social norms if they actively seek the truth and advocate for the rights of the disappeared. Inevitably, these difficulties compound the emotional and psychological trauma stemming from the uncertain fate of their relative.

Women and girls are also more prone to being victimized as a result of losing a loved one to enforced disappearance. In many cultures, without the protective presence of a father or husband, women and girls are at higher risk of abuse and sexual violence, including from male family members. In Guatemala, some female relatives of the disappeared were targeted for "selective rapes" by the military.[14] Members of the *Madres de la Plaza de Mayo* (Mothers of the Plaza de Mayo) in Argentina have been subjected to a wide range of violence and harassment. Three founding members of the Madres—Azucena Villaflor, Esther Careaga, and María Eugenia Bianco—were disappeared in December 1977, immediately after the Madres published a newspaper advertisement listing the names of their disappeared children.

Wives of the disappeared also face unique social challenges linked to personal, familial, and societal pressure to conform to the traditional role of either a widow or a wife. Women in Kashmir have coined the term "half widows" to capture their plight.[15] Similarly, in Nepal, married women have a higher social status and are more visible by wearing bangles and *sindhur* (red powder in the hair). Widows are expected to remove these symbols, resulting in the loss of privileges and "a social death."[16]

Wives of the disappeared face judgment, questions, and pressure about remarriage.

For some groups, such as the Marionites in Lebanon[17] and high-caste Nepalese, remarriage is strictly forbidden. Among lower-caste Nepalese and other patrilocal cultures, as in Kashmir and Sri Lanka, women who remarry bring stigma to their in-laws. Enforced disappearances also require women to make difficult choices around childcare and child custody. Mothers in patrilocal cultures who decide to elope or remarry are expected to leave their children with their in-laws.[18]

In many cultures, disappearances can also have a spiritual impact, particularly when the spirit world is understood to be as real and important as the physical world. In some cultures, the spirits are only appeased when certain rituals are conducted, especially those associated with the recovery of remains or the performance of burial rites. Where this is not possible, spirits of the disappeared may be perceived as haunting families and communities if proper burial rituals have not been performed, causing sickness in the family or even the death of livestock.[19]

Psychological Impact

Enforced disappearances negatively affect women's mental health. Commonly reported symptoms include nightmares, anxiety, depression, guilt, anger, numbing of emotions, avoidance, constant alertness, and disturbed sleep.[20] For many women, the stress of a disappearance is also expressed somatically as high blood pressure, chronic tiredness, and chronic pain.[21] While some early researchers linked the psychological challenges faced by families of the disappeared to post-traumatic stress disorder (PTSD), a more appropriate description is that women and other family members are dealing with "ambiguous loss."[22] The ambiguous loss model recognizes that the source of stress for families of the disappeared is external and ongoing, differing greatly from PTSD, which stems from discrete earlier traumatic experiences. Others have framed the psychological impact of enforced disappearances as frozen, interrupted, or complicated grief because of the inability to mourn or perform grieving rituals that would allow them to move on with their lives.[23]

Women as Advocates and Seekers of Truth and Justice

Despite economic hardships, social stigma, and mental health challenges, many transform their lives after a disappearance to assume roles as activists and community and movement leaders. This may prompt new ways of thinking about the social roles of women.[24]

The Madres de la Plaza de Mayo is the best-known example of women using their roles as mothers to create new models of activism in the wake of disappearances.[25] The Madres have become a model for human rights movements around the world, specifically those struggling against disappearances. Some organizations have followed the Madres' tactics very closely, including in Kashmir, Istanbul, Jerusalem, Tehran, and Tiananmen.[26]

Truth

For most relatives of the disappeared, the need to obtain the truth about what happened is a top priority. To do this, most mechanisms—in the form of truth commissions or omissions of inquiry—conduct investigations, gather archival evidence, and collect testimony from victims, survivors, and witnesses. Their findings are generally published in final reports.

A gendered approach to truth-seeking initiatives has evolved over time. While early truth commissions, such as in Chile and Argentina, adopted a gender-neutral approach, later commissions in South Africa, Guatemala, and Peru took some steps to include a gender perspective in their work. Further, truth commissions in Morocco and Timor-Leste (East Timor) explicitly included gender in their mandates. However, significant challenges remain in properly revealing the gender-related aspects of enforced disappearances.

A common gender critique of truth-seeking initiatives is that they focus too narrowly on bodily harm, at the expense of social and economic harms, and because the majority of the disappeared are men, the focus is therefore mainly on men's experiences.[27] Given the risk that disappearances of women are under-reported, investigation and research units should incorporate a gender-sensitive approach in their work.

Reporting on Disappeared Women

Despite the lack of gender-focused investigations, most truth commissions have reported to some extent on disappearances of women. In the final reports of truth commissions in Chile, Guatemala, and Argentina the experiences of female disappeared-detainees are integrated into the general accounts of conditions at secret detention centers but often limitedly. The Argentine report includes an account of the rape of a woman detainee that resulted in a hemorrhage—not to highlight sexual violence against female detainees, but rather to draw attention to abysmal medical treatment available in detention centers.[28] One exception to the tendency of most reports to generalize about cases of female detainees is the reporting on pregnant disappeared women, who received specific attention in several reports, suggesting that the treatment of women drew attention because of their role as mothers and child bearers.[29]

Gathering the Stories of Women Victims

While family associations and activist groups working on the issue of enforced disappearances have played a key role in broader outreach to ensure that as many stories as possible are collected, truth commissions often face challenges in accessing women, especially rural and Indigenous women who live far from statement-taking centers and do not speak dominant languages.

Truth commissions and other transitional justice mechanisms need to provide encouragement for women's participation and create a suitable space for them to speak about their own victimization and the impact of enforced disappearance on their own lives.[30] Commission outreach strategies to women's groups, the media, and disappearance organizations should include awareness raising and interviewing techniques.[31] To encourage women to speak out, gender-sensitive interview questionnaires must be developed, along with training for interviewers on how to respectfully prompt women about their own experiences. Commission staff must also be trained to take a gender-sensitive approach at public hearings and to provide safe spaces (such as women-only hearings) for female survivors.

Given the limited resources of truth commissions, locally driven, women-led truth-telling processes after their closure are also important. Timor-Leste has had some success in this, with groups of victims (men and women) actively constructing their own histories through local memory practices that appear to be a "more valuable coping mechanism than public testimony."[32]

Lack of Gender Analysis About Women Victims in Final Reports

Truth commission final reports have thus far at best partially analyzed the experiences of women partners of the disappeared. Early truth commissions lacked any gender analysis. For example, although the final report of the South African Truth and Reconciliation Commission (TRC) devotes an entire chapter to disappearances, the only specific reference to women is made in the TRC's recommendation that special attention be given to women facing difficulties as single heads of household.[33]

There is a more nuanced analysis in the Peruvian report, which might be a model for future commissions. The report analyzes certain patterns beyond just sexual violence through a gender lens, and that women suffered victimization to a different—and greater—degree than others.[34]

Exhumations and Reburials

Exhumations and reburials can be powerful forms of truth and reparation for families of the disappeared. If done properly, they can provide many benefits for women, such as clarifying the fate of their loved ones, lifting the burden of the search, allowing burial and grieving rituals to be performed and providing evidence to hold perpetrators accountable. Such rituals may also assist women to privately and publicly deal with the psychological impact of frozen grief and ambiguous loss and rehabilitate their social status and restore the social fabric of communities.

Exhumations have been conducted in most countries where transitional justice mechanisms have occurred, including Argentina, Brazil, Chile, Colombia, El Salvador, Ghana, Guatemala, México, Morocco, Paraguay, Peru, South Africa, and Uruguay. In most Latin American countries, families have advocated for them before, during, and after a truth commission or inquiry.[35]

Using a gender perspective does not mean prioritizing the exhumation of women but considering the gender of the person to be exhumed in the examination of remains, including looking for evidence of gender-based violence. Preliminary research suggests that there is, at best, limited psychosocial accompaniment during exhumations for women and survivors in most parts of the world, although the exhumation process is rife with potential sources of trauma.[36] The working document on the International Minimum Standards for Psychosocial Work in Exhumations sets out "psychosocial accompaniment" as the model for survivor support whereby individual victims, families, and communities are supported and involved throughout all stages of the investigation and exhumation process.[37] Guatemala has become a model of best practice, with six institutions providing long-term psychosocial accompaniment to family members at all stages of the process.[38]

Reparations and Relief

The diverse and complex social, economic, psychological, and cultural consequences of enforced disappearance on women require a comprehensive reparative response. This may take different forms, such as monetary compensation, psychosocial support services, healthcare, educational benefits, and housing.

At the outset, it is important to acknowledge that no amount of money can ever bring back a person who was disappeared or "repair the irrep-arable,"[39] thus material reparations will be largely symbolic in nature. Nonetheless, they still offer practical benefits to women, including easing some of the economic hardship resulting from the loss of a relative who may be the family breadwinner, reducing the guilt associated with being an economic burden on in-laws, and offsetting costs for searching for the disappeared. Unfortunately, the gap between recommendations and actual implementation is immense.

Reparations, Truth, and Justice

Financial reparations for disappearances have been met with controversy and resistance from many women. Some see reparations as "blood money" or an attempt by the State to buy their silence, especially when the govern-ment is seen to be doing little to seek the truth or promote justice.

Given that reparations programs in Argentina in the mid-1990s were implemented by the same administration that supported amnesty and had pardoned military officers found guilty of enforced disappearances and other human rights violations, Hebe de Bonafini, a leader of the Madres of the Plaza de Mayo, compared taking its money with prostitution.[40] In Nepal, wives have expressed concern that payments were designed to dis-tract from the search for the truth about their husbands.[41] While these examples all deal with financial reparations, similar concerns could arise in accepting other forms of reparations without any matching truth or accountability effort by the State.

Linking reparations to broader truth and justice initiatives importantly ensures that more women victims of enforced disappearance will receive—and accept—reparations. It will also encourage women to participate and have confidence in reparations programs, leading to a more coherent and successful transitional justice process. By acknowledging women relatives as direct victims, reparation programs are better able to respond to the psy-chological, social, and economic consequences for women that, although less visible, are equally challenging.

Trading Death Declarations for Reparations

Some reparation and relief programs only provide financial compensation to relatives of deceased persons. For example, Morocco defines beneficiaries as "successors (spouse, children, parents) of victims who *died* during enforced disappearance."[42] In Nepal, the Interim Relief Program (IRP) initially granted lump-sum awards of twenty-five thousand Nepalese rupees (NR) to the next-of-kin of the disappeared that were only 25 percent of the amount awarded to the next-of-kin of the deceased (one hundred thousand NRs).[43] With widespread poverty and social pressure from in-laws who perceived some wives of the disappeared as economic burdens, this placed many women in a difficult position of having to decide whether to declare their husband dead in order to receive higher compensation. In 2009, the IRP amended its policy to equalize next-of-kin awards for the disappeared and deceased.

However, by then, some of the disappeared had already been declared dead by their loved ones, in part to access benefits.

Transitional justice approaches should not require women to trade declarations of death for reparations. Doing so forces them to make an unacceptable decision that can have long-term social and psychological consequences, especially for those who feel that declaring a loved one dead is tantamount to "killing" them.[44] Declaring a death may also seem to impede or remove the State's incentive to investigate, sending a message that women must choose between reparations and truth.

Recognizing Partnerships

Although reparation and relief programs have generally recognized partnerships that go beyond legalistic concepts of matrimony,[45] some evidence of conservative notions of marriage and family remain. No reparations program has acknowledged same-sex unions, thereby denying compensation to female partners of disappeared women (and male partners of disappeared men). Common-law partners also faced unequal treatment in some countries. In Brazil, common-law partners were given lower priority than spouses. As a result, they were only able to receive financial payments if the spouse had died or was absent.

In South Africa, where multiple partnerships are legally recognized and widespread, there was a lack of clarity surrounding policy and practice. When a man left behind a wife and a domestic partner, formally only the wife benefited from reparations; however, there is also evidence that "girlfriends" were accommodated in practice.[46] Argentina adopted an egalitarian approach: if the disappeared man had a spouse and a common-law partner they shared the pension equally.[47] In Peru, where there are many de facto unions and many of the disappeared had two partners, the Truth and Reconciliation Commission recommended that reparations be paid to all claimants who could prove dependency.[48] While reparation programs have demonstrated the ability to flexibly and progressively accommodate a wide array of partnerships, more work needs to be done to ensure that no legitimate female partner is excluded.

Acknowledging Harms to Girl Children

Children of the disappeared have been recognized as beneficiaries by most reparations programs. There is, however, no distinction made between girl and boy children or recognition of the gendered impact of disappearances on children. In Argentina, children are at the top of the priority order for lump-sum awards. In other countries, payments are made to the surviving parent with the assumption that they will share it equitably with their children. This distribution policy may place girl children of the disappeared at risk where deep-rooted cultural beliefs and societal attitudes favor expenditure on boy children.

Some countries have taken steps to provide a greater number of children of the disappeared with access to educational benefits. In Chile, children can access educational benefits until the age of thirty-five.[49] In Argentina, they are entitled to pensions until the age of twenty-five or until they receive a university degree.[50] Reparation programs need to develop policies that overcome the gendered impact of enforced disappearances and structural disadvantages faced by many girl children victims. This requires, for example, reviewing distribution methods (notably "apportioning") that earmark equitable payments specifically for each child and creating scholarship programs specifically for girls and young women victims.

Recognizing and Addressing Harms to Mothers of the Disappeared

In most countries, there is no differentiation between mothers and fathers, with little acknowledgement of the gendered impact of disappearances, the additional harms that many mothers face, and their additional vulnerabilities in certain contexts. As mentioned previously, many have become tireless activists, appearing at the forefront of the search for the disappeared and as leaders of advocacy campaigns and organizations. Yet these mothers are not treated as priority beneficiaries by most reparation programs.

Although countries such as Brazil, Guatemala, and South Africa have set aside the rights of inheritance to include parents, mothers are often prioritized near the bottom for disbursement. In Chile and Peru, where awards are apportioned, parents receive a smaller share. These policies may give the impression that reparation programs perceive mothers (and fathers) to be less affected by disappearances than children and partners, or at least that they have less-significant reparation needs.[51]

As exceptions, Chile and Peru affirm the unique role of mothers and older women. Under Law 19.980, the Chilean reparations program specifically assigns awards to mothers; fathers are only able to access awards in the case of the mother's death or absence.[52] In Peru, the Truth and Reconciliation Commission recommended a pension equivalent to one-half of the minimum salary for women victims over the age of fifty as "a form of acknowledgement for the mothers who had fought over so many years for truth and justice."[53] Thus, reparations programs should consider the gendered impact of disappearances on mothers when developing their policies.

The Burden of Proving a Secret Crime

To access reparations and relief in some countries, women must first prove that an enforced disappearance took place. Given the secretive nature of the crime, it can be incredibly difficult to find any evidence or witnesses, particularly when mass atrocities have occurred and there are many missing persons. Women victims may face additional challenges in establishing that a disappearance occurred, given their lower rates of literacy and decreased access to public services compared to men.

Further, women, particularly wives and partners, face the additional burden of having to establish their relationship with the disappeared to access reparations and relief. This entails providing certificates of marriage or proof of common-law partnerships, pushing women into the public sphere, sometimes for the first time, which can involve negative social consequences and discrimination. Reparations programs, therefore, need to streamline procedures to reduce the burden on women.

In Nepal, women had to fill out lengthy forms to access relief from the IRP and obtain written confirmation from public and political party officials that the missing person was both absent and had been a member of a political organization. This forced women into public roles and interaction with male officials—spaces from which they were normally excluded, which proved particularly challenging.

In Morocco, the Equity and Reconciliation Commission (IER) came under heavy criticism for its inability to resolve cases of enforced disappearance. Compounding the ill effects for victims, the reparations program that emerged from the truth-seeking process only provided benefits to families of the disappeared who were found to be deceased.[54] The South African TRC's investigative team was also unable to clarify cases submitted by families who believed that their loved ones had been disappeared during the apartheid era. The TRC chose not to confer victim status on those with unresolved enforced disappearances out of concern that declaring the missing person as dead would close the door to future investigations. This lack of victim status resulted in family members being ineligible for reparations.[55] It also put relatives in a double bind: they could appeal to the TRC to declare their loved one a victim (thus declaring him or her deceased) or hope that the government would fulfil its promise to implement the TRC's recommendation to set up a unit to conduct ongoing investigations.

The reparations program set up by Morocco's Equality and Reconciliation Program provides examples of positive innovations for gender-sensitive payment of reparations for women affected by enforced disappearance. Although the IER failed to disclose the criteria it used for calculating award amounts, it did aim to take an affirmative action approach regarding women.[56] It broke from *Sharia* inheritance law[57] (which favors male heirs) in the apportioning of payments and promoted equal payment for both sexes: 40 percent for the spouse, whether man or woman; 10 percent for each parent; and 40 percent distributed equally among the descendants of both sexes.[58] This is a very significant development, especially for a majority Muslim country.

Disbursing Money to Women

Most reparation and relief programs distribute payments in the form of lump-sum awards, which many victims prefer, as it is sometimes harder to trust in or imagine the effectiveness of smaller installment payments over time.[59] With lower rates of financial literacy and access to banking institutions, women face increased challenges in procuring payouts. Female relatives of the disappeared may be at even greater risk because of intrafamilial tensions and the ambiguous legal nature of the disappeared. Preliminary research from South Africa found that many female grantees (for all types of human rights violations) requested that reparation payments be paid into the accounts of their male relatives or authority figures, giving them less control over how money was used.[60] Women affected by enforced disappearance may be even more likely to cede or lose control of payouts to in-laws and male authority figures if they have been made to feel like an economic burden on their family. Women may also feel more daunted in dealing with banking institutions after being refused access to frozen bank accounts of the disappeared.

The IRP in Nepal highlights some of the complications that arise when gender issues are not considered while distributing lump-sum awards. Some women reported that authorities (without consultation) parceled out benefits meant entirely for wives of the disappeared to in-laws and children to resolve family disputes. In other cases, authorities collaborated with wives who felt bound by tradition to share their benefits with others.[61] In both instances, authorities undermined the autonomy of these women and infringed on their right to reparation.

The South African TRC adopted a gendered approach to distribution to ensure financial compensation made it into the hands of women beneficiaries for whom it was intended. The TRC required beneficiaries to have a bank account to receive reparations and assisted women in opening one. They also facilitated access to identity documents required to open bank accounts.[62] While not specifically targeted at women affected by enforced disappearance, these actions certainly benefited them.

Further, in many countries, mothers, daughters, and partners of the disappeared have advocated for a wide range of services as reparations. For example, victims in Guatemala qualified for not only lump-sum awards, but also psychosocial support services and housing. In Peru, educational and healthcare benefits were offered to victims in addition to monetary compensation.[63]

Death Certificates and Declarations of Disappearance

Several transitional justice mechanisms have taken steps to address the ambiguous legal status of the disappeared, and its consequences. Commissions in South Africa and Morocco implemented policies to grant or accelerate access to death certificates. While this may be helpful to women who are ready to declare their loved one as dead, it is harmful when presented as the only solution.

The creation of a special legal status for the disappeared has been widely welcomed by victims. Argentina pioneered the concept in 1994, enacting legislation that set out a new legal status for the disappeared, which described them as "absent by enforced disappearance,"[64] without mentioning the possible death of the victim or a presumed date of death. Relatives applying for the status are only required to establish the date of detention/deprivation of liberty and the last time there was news of the victim.[65] This legal status has provided a wide array of practical benefits, particularly to women, including access to frozen bank accounts, property transfer/ownership, and the ability to formalize new partnerships. It also contributes to repairing the social impact of enforced disappearance on wives and partners by publicly acknowledging their loss and officially providing them with a status that transcends the traditional roles of either widow or wife.

Peru established a new legal category of "absence by reason of forced disappearance" in 2004. Like Argentina, Peru's legislation enabled women to access social security benefits, inherit, hold title on property, and formalize new relationships. Although this legislation is undoubtedly a step forward, there are still challenges in its implementation. The process is complex and requires legal assistance. Also, it is not sufficiently accessible, particularly for families living in rural areas.[66] Such geographical barriers have a greater effect on women than men, because of economic and structural inequalities leading to lower levels of (legal) literacy among women.

Building on these experiences, the Chilean government under Michele Bachelet enacted similar legislation in 2009.[67] The declaration of disappearance confers benefits such as allowing relatives of the disappeared to inherit wealth and assets without a death certificate and spouses to dissolve marriages without divorce papers, if desired.[68] Chile's law also expressly recognizes that such a declaration has no effect on criminal investigations or the eventual application of statutes of limitation for criminal prosecutions. Many Chilean women have welcomed this move.

Reparation and relief programs should offer women relatives both the option of obtaining declarations of enforced disappearance and procuring a death certificate, to fully guarantee their rights. Further, programs should simplify their procedures to make them more accessible to women, particularly disadvantaged women.

Memorialization and Other Forms of Symbolic Reparations

Since 1990, transitional justice mechanisms have recommended a wide range of symbolic reparations for human rights violations. These include erecting monuments, issuing apologies, establishing commemorative days, renaming buildings or streets, and converting prisons into museums or sites of conscience.

Monuments to disappeared persons and survivors have been erected in several countries, including Argentina, Bosnia, Chile, Indian-controlled Kashmir, the Philippines, Switzerland, Sri Lanka, and Uruguay. In some cases, monuments were constructed with government support in connection with a transitional justice process, while in other countries they were the result of family- or civil society-led initiatives.

There are currently two annual international commemorations for the disappeared. The International Day of the Disappeared, on August 30, was initiated by the Latin American Federation of Associations of Families of the Detained-Disappeared (FEDEFAM) to publicize the plight of the disappeared on an annual basis. The origins of the International Week of the Disappeared, commemorated during the last week of May, are less well known, but are also attributed to FEDEFAM. National days of remembrance for all victims of human rights violations, including disappearances, have been established in Chile (April 9), Peru (August 28), and Sri Lanka (October 27).

Some countries have opted to create public parks—or convert and dedicate existing sites—in honor of the disappeared. The Garden of the Disappeared in Geneva was established in 2000 to honor those who have disappeared around the world. Many consider Argentina's Plaza de Mayo as a memorial not only to the disappeared but also to the Madres. In some countries, notorious detention centers or prisons where disappearances occurred have been transformed into sites of remembrance; the Villa Grimaldi Peace Park in Chile and the Navy Petty-Officers School of Mechanics (ESMA) in Argentina are two well-known examples.

Rituals for the disappeared take a wide array of forms, reflecting the religious and cultural practices of the cultures and societies where they take place. Examples include candlelight vigils, prayer sessions, cleansing rituals, and tree-planting ceremonies. They can occur at the private, family, community, or national level. Many are broadly linked to raising awareness around the disappeared while others are more personal and may be designed to honor a specific person. The lines between the past and the present—and between protest and commemoration—can be blurry at these events: a candlelight vigil to remember a loved one may evolve into a demonstration calling for investigations, while a speech calling for exhumations may also become a moving tribute to the heroism of a disappeared activist.

Gender Issues in Memorializing the Disappeared

While memorialization projects have multiple and overlapping potential benefits for women affected by enforced disappearance, they also run the risk of marginalizing, misrepresenting, or retraumatizing them. Reburials and grieving rituals can be powerful ways for women to privately and publicly deal with the psychological impact of frozen grief and ambiguous loss. They may also play a role in assisting women victims to rehabilitate their social status and restore the social fabric of communities.

Consultation with women and other family members about the design and form of symbolic reparations is crucial. In some countries, governments and communities have attempted to erect memorials in cemeteries or monuments that resemble or serve the function of tombstones, but many women have rejected these because they see them as another example of the State trying to prematurely bring closure to cases of enforced disappearance without proper investigations. Others may find tombstones inappropriate because they continue to hope that their loved ones will be found alive. In Nepal, many communities have erected "Martyrs' Gates" inscribed with the names of Maoist rebels who died in the struggle (1996-2006). Many women reported wanting to remove the names of their missing loved ones from the gates to emphasize that they were disappeared, and not dead.[69] Clearly, women must be consulted so that memorials meet their needs.

Some researchers contend that women prefer "living memorials," such as gardens, community centers, and even roads, over "dead memorials," such as statues, obelisks, and arches.[70] There is certainly evidence of this in Latin America, where the Madres and other family associations have prioritized the establishment of archives, oral history projects, and cultural centers that focus on documentation and raising awareness about enforced disappearance and human rights. These types of reparative initiatives may more accurately capture the ongoing impact of the crime of enforced disappearance and provide an avenue for women to continue their search for the truth. Ultimately, the content, structure, and format of symbolic reparations initiatives for enforced disappearance should be decided by victims.

Further, victimization of women and their involvement in conflict is often overshadowed in the conceptualization and design of memorialization projects. The fact that women experience the bulk of ongoing victimization emanating from enforced disappearance, including poverty, family conflict, and psychological trauma, outside the public sphere also leads to the invisibility of their suffering. Moreover, the housing of disappearance memorials within former detention centers may further entrench the public/private, male/female divide, highlighting the more public physical acts of an enforced disappearance, such as torture and detention, and privileging the narrative of men as victims of enforced disappearance.

In Argentina, ESMA, a former detention center, has been transformed into a museum and cultural center, providing detailed information on disappearances during the Dirty War. The testimony of female detainees is displayed alongside that of their male counterparts throughout the center. At the same time, the former maternity ward focuses only on the experiences of pregnant detainees and their children. A monument in front of the building also commemorates women detainees. Similarly, Chile's Villa Grimaldi, a former detention center transformed into a peace park, provides detailed descriptions and oral history.

Acknowledging Women's Agency

While some symbolic reparations initiatives represent women as passive or disengaged victims,[71] fortunately, this does not appear to be the norm with memorials and sites of conscience for the disappeared. More research into the depiction of women at disappearance sites is needed, but an initial survey suggests that women are often depicted as activists and agents of change. One example is the Flame of Courage monument in the Philippines.[72] Unveiled on July 13, 1994, it depicts a mother carrying a torch, accompanied by a young child holding a photo of his disappeared father. Standing tall and gazing firmly ahead, the figure of the woman is clearly one of strength, determination, and action.

Although more abstract, the *Mujeres en la Memoria* (Women in Memory) monument in Santiago de Chile goes beyond portraying women as passive victims of enforced disappearance.[73] Initially envisioned in 1992 as a memorial to the seventy-two women who disappeared and one-hundred-and-eighteen who were executed under the dictatorship, the conceptualization of the monument evolved to depict the activism of female victims of political repression in Chile and abroad. Erected in 2006, the glass structure is meant to evoke posters of the disappeared and candlelight vigils, which became symbols of the struggle for truth and justice in Chile. The monument serves as both a remembrance of those lost and a testament to the activism of women. While exploring the strength of women, some disappearance memorials and sites of conscience also reflect on women's use of traditional gender roles in their mobilization and activism. Consultation is key to ensuring that women's experiences are reflected appropriately.

Criminal Justice

Criminal convictions contribute to non-recurrence of violations and help toward reestablishing the rule of law in societies emerging from conflict and repression. They serve long-term, broad societal benefits while offering an appropriate remedy to surviving relatives. Presently there is little, if any, literature on the gender dimensions of enforced disappearance in legal cases. As a high proportion of the disappeared are men, women relatives frequently become the main advocates for justice, including through prosecuting those responsible for disappearances.

Best practice includes considering the crime of enforced disappearance as "continuous," meaning that the crime continues from the date of the disappearance until determination of the fate of the victim. The language used should not assume the death of the victim, but rather acknowledge that he or she is absent due to enforced disappearance. In jurisdictions where the criminal code contains no specific crime of enforced disappearance, prosecutors can pursue charges of kidnapping, abuse of power, torture (if there is relevant evidence available), and murder, particularly if the remains of the victim are found. There may be other associated crimes committed by authorities in relation to denials of detention or, even, the survival of the disappeared. In the case of disappeared pregnant women, these crimes may include forced abortion, kidnapping, murder of the children, and identity substitution.

In legal systems where victims may be parties to criminal proceedings, such as in civil law countries, authorities must take steps to ensure the basic rights of women complainants. This includes providing access to legal representation and public records, examining evidence and challenging its admissibility or relevance where victim interests are concerned, ensuring access to hearings and the entire process, and giving victims the ability to make opening and closing statements and initiate special proceedings.

Important support measures include a comprehensive outreach process that ensures victims are aware of their rights, with a focus on the poor, illiterate, ethnic or social minorities, and those living in rural or remote communities. Women tend to be over-represented in many of these groups.

The failure to consider the specific needs of victims who participate in criminal trials risks further or additional traumatization and undermines the integrity of proceedings and, ultimately, the likelihood of convictions. These factors apply with equal force to prosecutions for enforced disappearances, where witnesses are likely to be female relatives. Valuable protective measures, when more effective methods are not available, include ensuring the anonymity of victims at all stages of proceedings. This can be achieved through voice distortion, testimony via video link, or the use of screens in courtrooms.

The relationship between criminal prosecutions and enforced disappearances has been addressed several times by the Inter-American Court of Human Rights. Initially, the court refused to consider the alleged violation of a right to a fair trial under article 8(1) of the American Convention on Human Rights (the "American Convention")[74] brought by family members of victims of enforced disappearance. It limited the application to the rights of defendants in criminal trials.[75] Then in 1997 the court recognized that article 8(1) also includes respecting the "accusing party's" procedural rights in the criminal trial.[76] Soon after, and in subsequent cases, the court held that article 8(1) extends to include the right of victims' relatives to judicial guarantees and specifically to a criminal investigation to identify and, when possible, prosecute and punish those responsible.[77]

More recently, the court has found that fulfilling the duty to guarantee surviving human rights victims' right to know the truth in cases of enforced disappearance requires criminal trials to determine the circumstances of the crime and the responsible perpetrators.[78] In general, the gender dimensions of prosecuting such cases do not seem to have been explicitly considered.

Conclusions

The important gender dimensions of enforced disappearance encompass women who are disappeared and women who are victims through their familial ties to the disappeared. In both cases, gender roles and inequalities steeped in tradition, race, culture, religion, and class mean that women's experiences differ from those of men.

Women may be disappeared because of their relationship to men, but also because they take on activist roles, which in some cases attracts additional negative attention by challenging gender norms that inhibit women's political participation. Further, while women may be less likely to be disappeared, they are more likely to experience direct human rights violations when disappeared because of their subordinate status and social vulnerability. Compared to men, their treatment while disappeared is far more likely to include various forms of sexual assault and the exploitation of maternal relationships.

Female relatives of the disappeared suffer devastating social, economic, and psychological consequences because of the loss of male family members who tend to earn more, be more literate, and have greater access to justice. Despite this, or because of this, many women victims become activists, presenting themselves as wives and mothers searching for the truth about the disappeared. Combined with the necessity to enter the public sphere in search of work, sometimes for the first time, this increases women's civic participation and may contribute to transforming their social status and roles in positive ways.

While truth-seeking initiatives are becoming increasingly gender-sensitive, challenges remain, such as counteracting the under-reporting of disappeared women and identifying traits of women who may be more likely to be disappeared. Understanding the gender dimensions of accessing and interviewing survivors to increase the likelihood of full disclosure, including about sexual violence, is critical for a comprehensive record of truth.

This, in turn, is likely to extend gender-sensitive reporting of human rights violations inflicted on women beyond the former focus on pregnancy-related violations in truth commission reports. Exhumations and reburials can provide both truth and reparative relief for family members of the disappeared, particularly if accompanied by psychosocial support, which must become standard practice. If those conducting such operations understand this, they are more likely to consult and involve family members. Compensation as well as legal, administrative, and symbolic reparations will be more effective if they are understood not to preclude or obstruct the search for truth.

Family members of the disappeared must be regarded as primary beneficiaries of reparations, consistent with the internationally accepted definition of a victim of enforced disappearance. For women who experience additional human rights violations when searching for the disappeared, unresolved questions remain about which violations give rise to a right to reparation. To avoid compounding the trauma experienced by family members, access to benefits should not be contingent on declaring the disappeared person deceased. In addition, experience shows that the creation of a special legal status for the disappeared can provide a range of practical benefits to families of the disappeared, such as access to bank accounts and pensions as well as the transfer of ownership of property.

Reparations initiatives need to acknowledge several other gender dynamics to ensure that those who are most vulnerable receive benefits. These include minimizing the disadvantages faced by women who are not a victim's sole partner; girl children who are less likely to be able to access education than their male counterparts; and mothers and older women who, despite likely enduring additional suffering in their search for truth, may be treated as less of a victim than wives or children.

Ensuring gender equality in access to reparations is as important as the substance of reparations. It requires gender-sensitive approaches to outreach; procedural rules that do not rely on literacy or proof of the enforced disappearance; removing gender bias in pre-existing laws; and overcoming gender blindness to women's access to, and capacity to control, finances.

Similarly, symbolic reparations that have meaning and value for affected communities are contingent on consultations with family members. Their involvement enhances the prospect that memorials will appropriately recognize disappeared women alongside men and acknowledge women's agency, activism, and multiplicity of roles, including in the search for the truth.

Many of the gender-specific considerations of prosecuting the crime of enforced disappearance extend to the generalized flaws of criminal justice systems' treatment of victims, particularly women victims. Broader gender inequalities mean issues of witness protection, psychosocial support, and the risk of more traumatization and stigma all disproportionately affecting women's experiences of the legal system.

A gender-sensitive approach promotes a more nuanced and comprehensive understanding of why women were disappeared and the range of crimes they experienced while disappeared. Consultations with family members of the disappeared will maximize the positive impact of exhumations, reburials, and material and symbolic reparations. The degree to which transitional justice mechanisms are effective in addressing enforced disappearances depends on their inclusiveness of women and their gendered experiences.

Notes

1. UN Working Group on Enforced or Involuntary Disappearances, *General Comment on Women*, February 14, 2013, 2. https://documents-dds-ny.un.org/doc/UNDOC/GEN/G13/112/57/PDF/G1311257.pdf?OpenElement

2. Beth Goldblatt, *Evaluating the Gender Content of Reparations: Lessons from South Africa*, 2006, 54. https://giwps.georgetown.edu/resource/evaluating-the-gender-content-of-reparations-lessons-from-south-africa/

3. Case file number 1583. See *"Argentina Comisión Nacional sobre la Desaparición de Personas," Nunca Más*, Part I ("The Repression: Health Conditions"), March 2015. https://www.ictj.org/sites/default/files/ICTJ-Global-Gender-Disappearances-2015.pdf

4. Julie Guillerot, International Center for Transitional Justice (ICTJ), *Morocco: Gender and the Transitional Justice Process*, September 2011, 11–12. https://

www.ictj.org/sites/default/files/ICTJ-Morocco-Gender-Transitional%20Justice-2011-English.pdf

5. See for example, *"Argentina Comisión Nacional sobre la Desaparición de Personas," Nunca Más*, Part II ("The Victims: The Disappeared According to Sex"), March 2015.

6. Elena Alvites and Lucía Alvites Sosa, *"Mujer y Violencia Política," Feminismos* 9 (n.d.): 121–37. https://rua.ua.es/dspace/bitstream/10045/3645/1/Feminismos_09_09.pdf

7. Amantha Perera, "War Widows Struggle in a 'Man's World,'" *Inter Press Service News Agency*, April 17, 2022. https://www.ipsnews.net/2012/12/war-widows-struggle-in-a-mans-world/

8. Christalla Yakinthou, "Living with the Shadows of the Past: The Impact of Disappearance on Wives of the Missing in Lebanon," ICTJ, April 20, 2015, 14. https://www.ictj.org/sites/default/files/ICTJ-Lebanon-Gender-Disappearance-2015.pdf; Yolima Bedoya González, *"El Impacto de la Población," Vulnerable*, April 21, 2009.

9. Dyan Mazurana, et al., "Making Gender-Just Remedy and Reparation Possible: Upholding the Rights of Women and Girls in the Greater North of Uganda," Feinstein International Center and ISIS Women's International Cross Cultural Exchange, 2013, 53. https://fic.tufts.edu/wp-content/uploads/Gender-Just-Remedy-and-Reparation-3-27-13-final.pdf

10. Yakinthou, "Living with the Shadows," 14.

11. Carlos Martín Beristain, *"Manual sobre perspectiva psicosocial en la investigación de derechos humanos," Hegoa* 46 (2010): 71–75. https://www.corteidh.or.cr/tablas/27117.pdf

12. Yakinthou, "Living with the Shadows," 11.

13. Carlos Martin Beristain, "The Value of Memory," *Forced Migration Review* (n.d.): 24–26. https://www.fmreview.org/camps/beristain

14. *Comisión para el Esclarecimiento Histórico, Guatemala Memoria del Silencio*, 1999. Volume III, 51, para. 2462.

15. Association of Parents of Disappeared Persons, *Half Widow, Half Wife?: Responding to Gendered Violence in Kashmir*, July 2011, 1. https://kafilabackup.files.wordpress.com/2011/07/half-widow-half-wife-apdp-report.pdf

16. Simon Robins, "Ambiguous Loss in a Non-Western Context: Families of the Disappeared in Post-Conflict Nepal," *Family Relations* 59, no. 3 (2010): 256. https://www.jstor.org/stable/40864538

17. Yakinthou, "Living with the Shadows," 21.

18. International Committee of the Red Cross (ICRC). *Accompanying the Families of Missing Persons in Relation to Armed Conflict or Other Situations of Violence*, 34. https://www.icrc.org/en/publication/accompanying-families-missing-persons-relation-armed-conflict-or-other-situations

19. Simon Robins, *An Assessment of the Needs of Families of the Missing in Timor-Leste*, Post-War Reconstruction and Development Unit, University of York, n.d., 49–50. https://www.academia.edu/3273798/An_Assessment_of_the_Needs_of_the_Families_of_the_Missing_in_Timor_Leste

20. ICRC, *Accompanying the Families of Missing Persons*, 34.

21. See, for example, Amrita Kapur and Polly Dewhirst, The Families of Vic-

tims of Involuntary Disappearance et al., "And They Shall Cry No More," International Center for Transitional Justice, 110; Simon Robins, "Towards Victim-Centred Transitional Justice: Understanding the Needs of Post-Conflict Nepal," *International Journal of Transitional Justice* 5, issue 1 (March 5, 2011): 75–98. https://academic.oup.com/ijtj/article-abstract/5/1/75/2356984?redirectedFrom=fulltext

22. Ambiguous loss is a "situation of unclear loss resulting from not knowing whether a loved one is dead or alive, absent or present." See Pauline Boss, *Ambiguous Loss: A Major Stressor* (Thousand Oaks, CA: Sage Publications, 2017), 3, 6.

23. This was the case in Argentina: Maitan Arnoso, et al. "*Mujeres jujeñas y sobrevivntes: narrativas del pasado represivo (1976–1983) argentino, consecuencias psicosociales y creencias acerca de la reparación.*" *Revista Mexicana de Ciencias Políticas y Sociales*, 57 (214): 141–61. *Universidad Nacional Automona de México, Facultad de Ciencias Políticas y Sociales.* https://www.researchgate.net/publication/262621174_Mujeres_jujenas_y_sobrevivientes_narrativas_del_pasado_represivo_1976-1983_argentino_consecuencias_psicosociales_y_creencias_acerca_de_la_reparacion; see also Margriet Blaauw and Virpi Lähteenmäki, "'Denial and Silence' or 'Acknowledgement and Disclosure'," *International Review of the Red Cross* 84, no. 848 (December 2002): 768. https://www.icrc.org/en/doc/assets/files/other/irrc_848_blaauw_virpi.pdf

24. Alvites and Alvites Sosa, "*Mujer y Violencia Política.*"

25. Ana Peluffo, "The Boundaries of Sisterhood: Gender and Class in the Mothers and Grandmothers of the Plaza de Mayo," *Contra Coriente* 4, no. 2 (Winter 2007): 79. https://projects.ncsu.edu/project/acontracorriente/winter_07/Peluffo.pdf; Diana Taylor, "Making a Spectacle: The Mothers of the Plaza de Mayo," *Journal for the Association for Research on Mothering* 3, no. 2 (2001): 102. https://jarm.journals.yorku.ca/index.php/jarm/article/view/2774

26. See Memorialize Turkey, *Saturday Mothers*, https://memorializeturkey.com/en/memorial/saturday-mothers/; Judith Warschawski, *Women in Black, Jerusalem*, http://www.gilasvirsky.com/id108.html; Human Rights in China (HRIC), *Tiananmen Mothers*, February 27, 2013. https://www.hrichina.org/en/content/6578. "A History of the Mothers of Kharavan," *Iran Tribunal*, n.d. https://irantribunal.com/mothers-of-khavaran/the-history-of-mothers-of-khavaran/

27. For more discussion, see Vasuki Nesiah et al., "Truth Commissions and Gender: Principles, Policies, and Procedures," ICTJ, July 1, 2006. https://www.ictj.org/sites/default/files/ICTJ-Global-Commissions-Gender-2006-English_0.pdf

28. *Argentina Comisión, Nunca Más*, Part I.

29. Philip E. Berryman, *Report of the Chilean National Commission on Truth and Reconciliation*, National Commission for Truth and Reconciliation (Notre Dame: University of Notre Dame, 1993), 648.

30. Beth Goldblatt, "Evaluating the Gender Content of Reparations,"; Ruth Rubio-Marín, ed. *What Happened to the Women? Gender and Reparations for Human Rights Violations* (New York: Social Science Research Council, 2006), 54–55.

31. Goldblatt, *What Happened to the Women?*

32. Simon Robins, "Challenging the Therapeutic Ethic: A Victim-Centred Evaluation of Transitional Justice Process in Timor-Leste," *International Journal of Transitional Justice* 6, issue 1 (March 2012): 21. https://academic.oup.com/ijtj/article-abstract/6/1/83/2357043?redirectedFrom=fulltext&login=false

33. South African Truth and Reconciliation Commission, *Report of the Human*

Rights Violations Committee, Volume 5, 539. https://www.justice.gov.za/trc/report/finalreport/Volume5.pdf

34. *Comisión de la Verdad y Reconciliación, Informe Final* VI (2003), 105. https://www.corteidh.or.cr/tablas/r08047-26.pdf

35. See Susana Navarro García, et al., "Exhumation Processes in Fourteen Countries in Latin America," *Journal for Social Action in Counseling and Psychology* 2, no. 2 (Fall 2010) 82–83. https://cupdf.com/document/navarro-garcia-s-perez-sales-p-fernandez-liria-a-2010-exhumation-in.html?page=1

36. Blaauw and Lähteenmäki, "Denial and Silence," 779; Navarro García, "Exhumation Processes," 50.

37. Navarro García, "Exhumation Processes," 49–50.

38. Navarro García, "Exhumation Processes," 50–52

39. Brandon Hamber, "Repairing the Irreparable: Dealing with the Double-Binds of Making Reparations for Crimes of the Past," *Ethnicity and Health* 5 no. 34 (August 2000): 215–26 https://www.researchgate.net/publication/12223317_Repairing_the_Irreparable_Dealing_with_the_double-binds_of_making_reparations_for_crimes_of_the_past

40. Peluffo, "The Boundaries of Sisterhood," 91.

41. Robins, "Victim-Centred Transitional Justice," 15.

42. Guillerot, *Morocco*, 27 (emphasis added).

43. ICTJ, *Beyond Relief*, 12.

44. Marcelo M. Suárez-Orozco, "The Heritage of Enduring a 'Dirty War': Psychosocial Aspects of Terror in Argentina, 1976–1988," *Journal of Psychohistory* 18, no. 4 (1991): 496. https://www.proquest.com/docview/1305586835?pq-origsite=gscholar&fromopenview=true

45. Nesiah, et al., "Truth Commissions and Gender," 37.

46. Goldblatt, *What Happened to the Women?* 68.

47. Christian Correa, *Reparation Programs for Mass Violations of Human Rights*, The Center for Civil and Human Rights, University of Notre Dame. 2014, 422. https://klau.nd.edu/assets/331778/correareparations2.pdf

48. Guillerot, *Morocco*, 155–56.

49. Law No 19.123 of Chile, that *Creates the National Corporation for Reparations and Reconciliation and Awards Benefits to those Persons Here Specified*, art. 29.

50. Ruth Rubio-Marín, et al., *Repairing Family Members: Gross Human Rights Violations and Communities of Harm*, (Cambridge: Cambridge University Press, 2009), 280. https://www.cambridge.org/core/books/abs/gender-of-reparations/repairing-family-members-gross-human-rights-violations-and-communities-of-harm/BDF4A0D551B3F236962B83B03157646C

51. Rubio-Marín, et al., *Repairing Family Members*, 281.

52. Law No 19.980 of Chile on *Reparations to Extend Benefits for Persons Here Specified*.

53. Truth and Reconciliation Commission of Peru, *Final Report*, Tomo IV, 190–92. https://www.usip.org/publications/2001/07/truth-commission-peru-01

54. Guillerot, *Morocco*.

55. In South Africa, "secondary victims" (family members) could only receive reparations if the "primary victim" was deceased.

56. ICTJ, *Beyond Relief*, 14.

57. Muslim Sharia laws, as the word is understood in the West, refers to the rules regulating relations among people. The laws are derived from the Qur'an and the Hadith. Sharia law may vary from one school to another on certain issues. For example, according to the Shi'a Jaafari school, the law of inheritance gives the daughters of the deceased parents the right to inherit all non-reserved parts of the estate in the absence of male siblings, while the Sunni schools do not.

58. ICTJ, *Beyond Relief*, 26, FN 128.

59. Correa, *Reparation Programs*, 425.

60. Goldblatt, *What Happened to the Women?* 73.

61. ICTJ, *Beyond Relief*, 14.

62. Goldblatt, *What Happened to the Women?* 73.

63. Correa, *Reparation Programs*, 7, 23–24.

64. Law No. 24.321 of Argentina on the *Law of Absence by Forced*, art. 1.

65. Maria José Guembe, "Economic Reparations for Grave Human Rights Violations," United Nations, *Rule of Law Tools for Post-Conflict States*, 36. https:// academic.oup.com/book/26106/chapter-abstract/194097072?redirectedFrom=full text

66. Christián Correa, *Reparations in Peru: From Recommendations to Implementation*, International Center for Transitional Justice, 21. https://www.ictj.org/sites/ default/files/ICTJ_Report_Peru_Reparations_2013.pdf

67. Law No. 20.377 of Chile on the *Disappearance of People*.

68. Brandon Hamber and Ingrid Palmary, "Gender, Memorialization, and Symbolic Reparations," Ruth Rubio-Marin, ed., *The Gender of Reparations: Unsettling Sexual Hierarchies while Redressing Human Rights*. (Cambridge: Cambridge University Press, 2009), 329. https://www.cambridge.org/core/books/abs/gender-of-reparations/gender-memorialization-and-symbolic-reparations/6B97CB54A6952 5657032ADF7174281B8

69. Simon Robins, "Constructing Meaning from Disappearance: Local Memorialization of the Missing in Nepal," *International Journal of Conflict and Violence* 8, no. 1 (2014): 11–12. https://www.ijcv.org/index.php/ijcv/article/view/3048

70. Hamber and Palmary, "Gender, Memorialization, and Symbolic Reparations," 358–69.

71. Hamber and Palmary, "Gender, Memorialization, and Symbolic Reparations," 339.

72. *Remembering the Filipino Desaparecidos*, Asian Federation Against Involuntary Disappearances (AFAD), July 13, 2010. https://afadsecretariat.wordpress. com/2010/07/13/remembering-the-filipino-desaparecidos/; Marielle Medina, "Families remember missing loved ones," *Philippine Daily Inquirer*, November 1, 2012. https://newsinfo.inquirer.net/299438/families-remember-missing-loved-ones

73. Remember Our Sisters Everywhere, *Mujeres en la memoria, Chile*.

74. American Convention on Human Rights, *Pact of San José, Costa Rica*, art. 8(1).

75. See, for example, "*Neira Alegría et al. v. Peru*," series C, no. 20, *Inter-American Court of Human Rights*, Judgment (Merits), para. 86, Jan. 19, 1995; "Caballero Delgado and Santana v. Colombia," series C, no. 22, *Inter-American Court of Human Rights*, Judgment (Merits), para. 64, December 8, 1995.

76. "Accusing party" in Latin America refers to the role of private prosecutors

that victims generally have in criminal trials. See "Genie-Lacayo v. Nicaragua," series C, no. 30, *Inter-American Court of Human Rights*, Judgment (Merits, Reparations and Costs), para. 75, January 29, 1997.

77. "Blake v. Guatemala," series C. no. 36, *Inter-American Court of Human Rights*, Judgment (Merits), paras. 96–97, January 24, 1998; "'White Van' (Paniagua-Morales et al.) v. Guatemala," series C, no. 37, *Inter-American Court of Human Rights*, Judgment (Merits), para. 156, March 8, 1998; "'Street Children' (Villagran-Morales et al.) v. Guatemala," series C, no. 63, *Inter-American Court of Human Rights*, Judgment (Merits), para. 227, November 19, 1999; "Durand and Ugarte v. Peru," series C, no. 68, *Inter-American Court of Human Rights*, Judgment (Merits), para. 130, August 16, 2000; "Bámaca-Velásquez v. Guatemala," series C, no. 70, *Inter-American Court of Human Rights*, Judgment (Merits), para. 182, November 25, 2000.

78. See, for example, "Bámaca-Velásquez v. Guatemala," series C, no. 70, *Inter-American Court of Human Rights*, Judgment (Merits), para. 201, November 25, 2000; "Castillo-Páez v. Peru," series C, no. 43, *Inter-American Court of Human Rights*, Judgment (Reparations and Costs), paras. 105–6, November 27, 1998; "Barrios Altos v. Peru," series C, no. 75, *Inter-American Court of Human Rights*, Judgment (Merits), para. 48, March 14, 2001; "Trujillo-Oroza v. Bolivia," series C, no. 92, *Inter-American Court of Human Rights*, Judgment (Reparations and Costs), paras. 100, 112–16, February 27, 2002.

Between Two Rivers

Sama Alshaibi

"Razor Wire"

"To Eat Bread"

Between Two Rivers re-empowers the image of Iraqi women, who were sub-jugated to the "selling of the war." The notion that women in Iraq, who once enjoyed the greatest freedoms of the Arab world, would be liberated by war under the guise of democracy is countered in this series of—so far—fifteen images, created in 2008–2009 and 2016 (see https://www.samaalshaibi.com/artwork/between-two-rivers).

Tribal tattoos, scarification, and historical Iraqi identity markers are subverted to speak about the once proud cradle of civilization; the photographs mirror the language of violence by physically altering the artist's own body through theater cosmetics. The protagonist's gaze reveals her resistance, paradoxically performing the dysfunctional Iraqi reality within the image of resolve.

—Sama Alshaibi

Editors' Note: Between 2003 and 2007, nearly 3,500 Iraqi women were missing, many likely trafficked into prostitution. This figure is surely underestimated. No one knows the exact numbers and they are almost impossible to find. Sadly, there are no recent records about Iraqi women's enforced disappearance. (Please see https://www.hrw.org/report/2011/02/21/crossroads/human-rights-iraq-eight-years-after-us-led-invasion)

The Organization of Women's Freedom in Iraq (OWFI) estimates that in the first four years since the 2003 United States invasion, 4,000 Iraqi women and girls went missing. It's difficult to determine how many are victims of sex trafficking. (See https://www.owfi.info/EN/) We thank Dirk Adriaensens for this information. Please see chapter 3, Dirk Adriaensens, "Iraq: Disappearance as a Tool of War."

THREE

Iraq

Enforced Disappearance as a Tool of War

Dirk Adriaensens

Iraq has been a member of the Convention for the Protection of All Persons from Enforced Disappearance since November 23, 2010 and was the twentieth country to implement its ratification. The treaty was finally implemented on December 23, 2010. The United States has not signed or ratified this convention. It claims its refusal to sign is because the text "did not meet our expectations," and offers no further explanation. Once again, the United States has placed itself outside the provisions of International Humanitarian law.

According to the Rome Statute of the International Criminal Court, which came into force on July 1, 2002, when committed as part of a widespread or systematic attack directed at any civilian population, a "forced disappearance" qualifies as a crime against humanity, and thus is not subject to a statute of limitations.[1] According to the United Nations Human Rights Council, "secret detention amounts to an enforced disappearance."

The practice of enforced disappearance reveals the fundamental nature of what is known as the Dirty War, first named in Latin America as *la guerra sucia* and which took place from 1974 to 1983. It was repeated with the worst excesses of the Vietnam War, from 1955 to 1975. The purpose of a dirty war[2] is to erase the identities of and then detain or kill actual resistance fighters. The target of dirty war is the civilian population. It is a strategy of State terrorism and collective punishment against an entire population with the objective of terrorizing it into submission. The same tactics used by the United States in Central America and Colombia were exported to Iraq. Even the architects of the dirty wars in El Salvador (Ambassador John Negroponte and Colonel James Steele) and in Colombia (Steven Casteel)[3] were transferred to Iraq to do the same dirty work. They recruited, trained, and deployed the notorious "Special Police Commandos," into which later, in 2006, death squads like the Badr Brigades and other militias were incorporated. The U.S. forces set up a high-tech operations center for the Special Police Commandos at an "undisclosed location" in Iraq. American technicians installed satellite telephones and computers with uplinks to the internet and U.S. forces networks. The command center had direct connections to the Iraqi Interior Ministry and to every U.S. forward-operating base in the country.

In January 2005, more than a year after the first reports about the Pentagon's planning for assassinations and paramilitary operations emerged, the "Salvador Option" hit the pages of *Newsweek* and other major news outlets. The report of the Human Rights Office of the United Nations Assistance Mission for Iraq (UNAMI), issued on September 8, 2005, written by John Pace, was very explicit, linking the campaign of detentions, torture, and extrajudicial executions directly to the Interior Ministry and indirectly to the U.S.-led Multi-National Forces.[4] The outsourcing of State terrorism to local proxy forces was regarded as a key component of a policy that had succeeded in preventing the total defeat of the U.S.-backed government in El Salvador. Pentagon-hired mercenaries, like DynCorp, helped form the sectarian militias that were used to terrorize and kill Iraqis and to provoke Iraq into civil war.

Forced disappearance is a systematic tool of mass repression generally diffused in States where government forces are unstable and opposition movements emerge. The logic behind this practice lies in the deterrent effect that follows its implementation, as well as in the need for protecting the State from allegations of having committed such atrocities. The practice of wiping out real or suspected political opponents, members of the resistance movements, supporters of these groups, civilians, and many others is diffused in many countries around the world, and its origins date back to Hitler's "Night and Fog" Decree of 1941.[5]

Since the invasion of Iraq in March 2003, the situation of missing persons and enforced disappearances in Iraq can be considered by all standards as dramatic, even apocalyptic. And since, upon a request for clarification by UNAMI,[6] the Multi-National Forces Iraq confirmed that the U.S. government continued to consider the conflict in Iraq an "international armed conflict," with procedures currently in force consistent with provisions of the Fourth Geneva Convention.[7] Iraq's missing persons and forced disappeared after the invasion in 2003 are the responsibility of the United States and the United Kingdom, which started this war, with coalition forces from other countries and, by extension, their installed Iraqi government. Therefore, they bear full accountability for the enforced disappearances that happened under their watch. Their militias and death squads have disappeared, tortured, brutally assassinated, secretly buried, and thrown thousands of bodies into the streets and rivers, many unidentifiable.

Paul-Henri Arni of the International Committee of the Red Cross (ICRC), noted that, after three conflicts—a war with Iran in the 1980s, the first Gulf War in 1991, and the U.S.-led operation in 2003, as well as comprehensive United Nations sanctions (1990–2003)—Iraq faced the highest number of missing people in the world.[8] The Geneva-based non-governmental organization (NGO), Alkarama, states that Iraq has had one of the highest numbers of enforced disappearances in the world with almost one million disappearances since the period of Saddam Hussein (r. 1979-2003). Three quarters of these disappearances happened following the U.S. invasion, making it a systematic phenomenon in the country.[9] The International Commission on Missing Persons (ICMP),[10] estimates Iraq's missing persons to be between 250,000 and more than 1 million. Iraq's Missing Campaign, the UN and the ICRC all claim one million people are missing, while other sources suggest as many as four million remain unaccounted for across the past four decades. Forty percent of the Iraqi population have a missing relative or know someone who has.[11]

The United Nations, the U.S. State Department, Amnesty International (AI), and Human Right Watch (HRW) estimate that during the twenty-four-year long reign of Saddam Hussein, thousands of innocent people were disappeared and killed. In May 2003, Human Rights Watch estimated that "as many as 290,000 Iraqis have been 'disappeared' by the Iraqi government over the past two decades. Many of these 'disappeared' are those whose remains are now being unearthed in mass graves all over Iraq."[12]

The Illegal Invasion of Iraq

The U.S.-led invasion of Iraq on March 19, 2003 was not just immoral, it was properly illegal. There was no "smoking gun," no *casus belli*. This was an illegal war of aggression, with no approval by the Security Council. The invasion could not be justified by chapter seven of the Charter of the

UN and qualified as self-defense, because Iraq had not attacked the United States and was no imminent threat, no justification for this so-called "preemptive war." Leading international personalities, officials, and lawyers made this clear. Kofi Annan—then UN Secretary-General[13]—and Hans Blix—then head of the weapons inspection committee for the UN[14]—openly declared that the Iraq invasion was illegal under international law. The report by the Dutch Commission Davids concluded that there was "no adequate international legal mandate for the invasion of Iraq."[15]

Benjamin Ferencz, a chief prosecutor of the 1945 to 1949 Nuremberg Trials addressed the issue, as well

A prima facie case can be made that the United States is guilty of the supreme crime against humanity, that being an illegal war of aggression against a sovereign nation. . . . The United Nations charter has a provision which was agreed to by the United States, formulated by the United States, in fact, after World War II. It says that from now on, no nation can use armed force without the permission of the UN Security Council. They can use force in connection with self-defense, but a country can't use force in anticipation of self-defense. Regarding Iraq, the last Security Council resolution essentially said, "Look, send the weapons inspectors out to Iraq, have them come back and tell us what they've found—then we'll figure out what we're going to do. The U.S. was impatient and decided to invade Iraq—which was all pre-arranged of course. So, the United States went to war, in violation of the charter."[16]

Iraq's Missing Persons during the U.S. Occupation: Disparate Tallies

Enforced disappearance has been a widespread challenge in Iraq since 2003, although the government insists it is a problem of the past and avoids admitting the ongoing, widespread, and systematic practice conducted by the U.S.-led coalition forces, terrorist groups, government forces, and government affiliated militias. The post-2003 period remains largely unexplored. The number of missing persons since is willfully downplayed, while investigations by the Iraqi government and the United States mainly focus on pre-2003 events. No proper framework has been established to deal with the numerous cases of enforced disappearance since 2003 and all cases in the past decade were related to the period beforehand.[17]

The policy of ambiguity followed by the U.S. occupation forces and the growing phenomenon of secret U.S. prisons in Iraq—which even international organizations have failed to locate—added to Iraq's own secret prisons (estimated by one Iraqi parliament member to exceed 420), have led to a large number of reported and unreported cases of forced disappearances, as described in 2012 by various NGOs to the Office of the United Nations High Commissioner for Human Rights (OHCHR) in the course of the Universal Periodic Review of the United States.[18]

Most victims of enforced disappearances in Iraq were abducted while going about their daily routine—on their way to work, school, or shopping centers. Some were picked up by police or security forces, others by uniformed militias.[19] Government forces or militias are known to shoot into the air to prevent witnesses from approaching the scene. Relatives receive no information about the charges, location of the detention, or the conditions of their loved ones. Many of those arrested were found killed, discarded in public areas, their bodies displaying signs of torture. The fates of the abducted remain unknown; they simply vanished. Iraq's Minister of Human Rights, Wijdan Mikhail, said that her ministry received more than nine-thousand complaints in 2005 and 2006 from relatives of the disappeared.

Human rights groups put the total number much higher. A report by AI, "New Order, Same Abuse," mentions that "several detainees have died in Iraqi custody due to torture or abuse by Iraqi interrogators and prison guards. AI reports that tens of thousands are held without charges and that guards won't confirm missing persons' whereabout to their relatives, which, for Iraqi families who had lost loved ones, was one of the most devastating aspects of the US occupation."[20]

Political Pressure to Lower the Death Toll and Ban on Releasing Morgue Data

The issue of civilian casualties has been politically charged since the start of the 2003 Iraq war, when U.S. and Iraqi officials forbade Baghdad's medical officials to release morgue counts. Thus, Iraq's health, interior, and defense ministries have consistently provided lower figures than those released by the morgue.[21]

There is no shortage of estimates, but they vary enormously. The Iraqi Ministry of Health initially tried to keep a count based on morgue records, but then stopped releasing figures under pressure from the U.S.-

supported government in the Green Zone.[22] The director of the Baghdad morgue, already under stress because of the mounting horror of his work, was threatened with death on the grounds that by publishing statistics he was causing embarrassment. The families of the bereaved wanted him to tell the truth, but like other professionals he came to the view that he had to flee Iraq. Dr Salih Mahdi Motlab al-Hasanawi, the health minister appointed after the Ministry's ban on releasing official morgue figures, said the survey was prompted by controversy over civilian casualties.[23]

An international official in Baghdad said Health Ministry officials cited the higher toll before lowering it in response to what he called political pressure. But in September 2006, the ministry confirmed that it planned to construct two new branch morgues in Baghdad and add doctors and refrigerator units to raise capacity to as many as 250 corpses a day.[24] The morgue expansion plans illustrate the dramatic surge in Baghdad violence. In 2002, before U.S.-led forces entered Iraq, the morgue averaged fifteen shooting victims a month, morgue officials said, but between 2006 and 2007, some 20,000 bodies were deposited at Baghdad's Medico-Legal Institute (MLI),[25] less than half of whom have been identified, the ICRC said. Unclaimed bodies are buried in cemeteries around the city.[26]

Iraq has no central database for linking unidentified bodies buried anonymously. In 2015, the government declared, "There is no system in Iraq to centralized information on the number of people who are supposed to be subjected to enforced disappearance."[27] Neither are there records of victims of sectarian violence who have been buried informally in unmarked plots.

Most of the disappeared are believed to be dead. But even those whose bodies have been found are not always identified quickly. Dr. Munjid Salah al-Deen, manager of Baghdad's central morgue, told the *New York Times* that during 2006 to 2009, his staff worked to identify twenty-eight-thousand bodies.[28] In April 2009, since the 2006 surge in sectarian violence, al-Deen said at least thirty-thousand unidentified bodies were delivered to the morgue. There was an average of three-thousand bodies a month in 2006, "a year of horror," he said.[29] "Ninety percent of the bodies received in 2006 were unidentified, compared with 50 percent in 2007 and 15 percent in 2008," said Dr. Munjid Salahuddin, the director of the Institute for Forensic Medicine, on October 25, 2009.[30]

In 2008, the Iraqi Red Crescent (IRCS) registered about seventy-thousand cases of missing persons since the American invasion began. Even the IRCS was not immune from the anarchy that plagued Iraq: in December 2006, thirty of its staff were kidnapped; thirteen were still missing a year later.[31]

Brian Conley and Isam Rashid of the Inter Press Service New Agency (IPS) were refused access to the central Baghdad morgue, and told journalists are forbidden to report on the conditions inside. "The last manager for this morgue, Faik Bakr, received death threats because he said there were more than seven-thousand Iraqis killed by death squads in recent months," an employee told them. "Most of the dead arrived with their hands tied behind their backs."[32]

"We are not authorized to issue any numbers," a doctor at the Baghdad morgue told IPS. "But I can tell you that we are still receiving human bodies every day; the men have no identity on them."[33] At the height of the killing, between fifty and 180 bodies were dumped on Baghdad's streets each day. Many more signs of torture, such as drill holes in their arms, legs, and skulls, or cigarette burns.[34]

Bodies Not Claimed for Fear of Reprisals

Looking for a missing relative was extremely complicated, very dangerous, and sometimes impossible because of the security situation. In several cases, families were contacted by anonymous individuals claiming to know the whereabouts of their missing relatives and demanding money in return for the information. But even if the family paid, the information might not be reliable.[35]

Iraqi human rights organizations have raised concerns that the mechanisms to address enforced disappearances are ineffective. Relatives were systematically mocked and insulted, if not told to go to another office. In some cases, inquiring relatives were abducted as an act of retaliation.

The bi-monthly UN Human Rights Report of November–December 2006 described the situation as

> notably graves in Baghdad where unidentified bodies killed execution-style are found in large numbers daily. Victims' families are all too often reluctant to claim the bodies from the six Medico-Legal Institutes (MLIs) around the country for fear of reprisals. The deceased's families are required to obtain permission from the police station which brought the body to the MLI, but many are too afraid and believe that police officers could be responsible for the disappearances and killings [. . .] The Baghdad Medico-Legal Institute is reported transporting some two hundred unidentified bodies every week to cemeteries in Najaf and Karbala which relatives do

not claim out of fear of reprisals. In addition, there are reports of bodies that end up buried in mass graves and are not recorded at the morgues.[36]

A *New York Times* headline blared, "Relentless Sectarian Violence in Baghdad Stalks Its Victims Even at the Morgue."[37] They had become a source of danger, at least for Sunni Arabs.[38] Shi'a militias were staking out Baghdad's central morgue in particular, and the authorities were receiving dozens of reports of kidnappings and killings of Sunni Arabs.[39]

The U.S. State Department Human Rights Report for 2007 stated that

> kidnappings and disappearances remained a severe problem . . . frequent accusations were directed at rogue police. The majority of the reported cases appeared to be sectarian-related. Police believed the great majority were unreported. Many Baghdad residents complained that rogue neighborhood police officers often arrested family members without an arrest warrant and then would later call for a ransom. Numerous reports indicated that rogue police were involved in sectarian-motivated, as well as criminal, kidnappings. . . . Incidents of political kidnappings occurred during the year, with frequent accusations directed at the police.[40]

Considering the ineffectiveness and risks of reporting disappearances to national authorities, numerous families raised their relatives' cases with human rights organizations in order to file complaints with the UN Committee on Enforced Disappearances (CED). Nevertheless, the Iraqi authorities have not clarified the victims' fates and whereabouts, showing little willingness to investigate disappearances.[41]

In 2017, a bill on enforced disappearances was drafted. In 2019, the Iraqi Council of Deputies reviewed the bill. The adoption of the legislative proposal has been repeatedly postponed and is still pending. If the draft legislation were adopted in its current wording, it would not meet a number of international standards. Among other things, the bill lacks a reference to enforced disappearance as a potential crime against humanity when committed in a widespread and systematic manner, as required by article 5 of the International Convention for the Protection of All Persons from Enforced Disappearance (ICPPED). In addition, law no. 10 of the Iraqi Supreme Court limits the possibility to qualify widespread and systematically committed enforced disappearances as crimes against humanity to those carried out between 1968 and 2003. Criminal liability of superiors, and article 40 of the Iraqi Criminal Code allows officials or officials who committed the crime to invoke the order of a superior as justification—in violation of article 6 of the ICPPED.[42]

On November 27, 2020, the CED issued its findings on Iraq, calling to incorporate the offense of enforced disappearances into domestic criminal legislation, and to ensure no person is held in secret detention. CED said it deeply regretted that a pattern of enforced disappearance persists over much of the territory of Iraq. The Committee said it is concerned by the delays in adopting the legislation, which have contributed to the continuing lack of criminalization of the offense of enforced disappearance in the country.[43]

"Time and again, the Iraqi government has announced investigations into recent alleged disappearances, but with little success," said Ceasefire Centre for Civilian Rights Executive Director Mark Lattimer. He went on to state

> The government now has an opportunity to put rhetoric into action by supporting the new bill to end enforced disappearance. . . . As there is currently no system to deal with disappearances, relatives of the missing are forced to move from prison to prison in search of information about their loved ones. This treatment is inhumane and causes even more suffering for families.[44]

2003–2011: How Many Iraqis Are Missing?

Asma Al-Haidari, an Amman, Jordan-based Iraqi human rights analyst and advocate, says the phenomenon of enforced disappearances in Iraq touches the whole population, irrespective of age, gender, ethnicity, or religious belief. "There is no safe place in Iraq. People can be disappeared and sent to secret, illegal detention centers anywhere in the country, without the knowledge of the family or the person's lawyer," she told the IRIN News Agency in 2011. "Many are assassinated and buried in secret. Many others are charged with trumped-up terrorism charges."[45]

UNHCR published findings in 2009 showing that many communities reported missing family members—30 percent of Internally Displaced Persons (IDP), 30 percent of IDP returnees, 27 percent of refugee returnees—indicating that they were missing because of kidnappings, abductions, and detentions and that they do not know what happened to their missing family members.

A rough estimate would therefore bring the number of missing persons among the refugee population and the internally displaced after "Shock and Awe"[46] to 260,000, most of them enforced disappearances.

Dahr Jamail, one of few unembedded U.S. journalists,[47] reported for the IPS in 2009 that in the al-Adhamiya area of Baghdad, what used to be a park was now a cemetery with more than five-thousand graves. The first body was buried there on May 21, 2006.

"Most of the bodies buried here are never reported in the media," Abu Ayad Nasir Walid, the cemetery's manager, told Jamail.

"Most of the dead were never logged by anyone, because we didn't check death certificates," Ali, a gravedigger, added. "We just tried to get the bodies into the ground as quickly as possible. I log their names in my book, but we've never had anyone come from the government to ask how many people are here. Nobody in the media nor the Ministry of Health seems to be interested."[48]

Such graveyards—and there are many—raise questions about the "official" number of enforced disappeared and missing persons in Iraq since 2003.

A video produced in 2011 by the Bureau of Investigative Journalism describes the scale of horror during the U.S. occupation

> The Missing Room at Baghdad's hospital morgue provides a slide-show of thousands of unidentified bodies. Many were mutilated before being dumped in the streets. Each picture is identified by a number and the word *majhoul*—unknown. Number 9,065 is a woman looking up at the sky with an expression of sublime calm, [oddly] because at that moment she had obviously been murdered. Number 12,568 is a man with half a face, whose remaining eye peers accusingly straight into the camera. Number 13,004 is a child with the look of shocked surprise, his hair standing on end as if from a blast. [A] man seems to be looking off camera in angry defiance. Most of the photographs were taken in haste. Few show any signs of respect. Some are naked or partly clothed. In one there is a 7-Up can next to the body.[49]

Unidentified Victims of Enforced Disappearance outside Baghdad

Many casualties outside Baghdad probably never appear in the official count, said Anthony Cordesman, a military analyst for the Center for Strategic and International Studies.[50] That explains why fatalities in Baghdad appear to account for such a large percentage of the total number, he told the *New York Times*.[51]

Since the U.S.-led invasion in 2003,[52] as many as forty thousand unidentified corpses were buried in Wadi al-Salam cemetery in the city of Najaf.[53] All corpses are numbered and photographed, and the location of burial is noted. Figures are recorded in a register so that families might eventually identify the bodies. Thousands more may have been hastily buried in the deserts surrounding Najaf.[54] Before the U.S. invasion, volunteers buried up to forty people every month. During the occupation's worst months (2005–2007), that figure increased fifty-fold.

In 2007, the head of the hospital's forensics department in Kut (southeast of Baghdad) described how unremitting the flow of bodies had become. "Up to now, we have received about five hundred bodies. Most of them have been shot or tortured. They are in an advanced state of decomposition, so you can't stand to be close to them for long." It took the bodies at least three days to float downstream from where they'd been dumped in the river. Most remain unidentified and were buried in mass graves.[55]

In 2008, Voices of Iraq reported that the number of unidentified bodies buried in the city of Karbala reached 2,043.[56]

Nima Jima'a, a morgue official in Baquba, told the IPS, "The morgue receives an average of four or five bodies every day. Many more are dropped in rivers and farms—or it is sometimes the case they are buried by their killers. The number we record here is only a fraction of those killed."[57]

More than 280 persons from the city of Fallujah were reported missing in 2005.[58] They are officially registered with names and photo by the city's authorities, yet it is estimated that the total number of the missing exceeds five hundred.

Large numbers of unidentified bodies were found in Diyala, Nineveh, Anbar, and Diwaniyah. They bore signs of torture and some were blindfolded, while others were decapitated.

Many other towns and villages where fighting and ethnic cleansing occurred during the U.S. occupation have no available reports. But each has a similar story.

According to *Forced Migration Review*, between 2003 and 2007, nearly 3,500 Iraqi women were missing, with a portion likely trafficked into prostitution.[59]

The number of people who were disappeared after being arrested at checkpoints in the capital increased significantly since 2007. The Iraqi Ministry of Human Rights said it has investigated many cases of Iraqis missing after being stopped at checkpoints, but claimed, "police officers have shown sufficient proof that they have not had anything to do with their disappearances."[60] Patrick Cockburn reported in the *Independent*

> A friend in Baghdad once told me, "No Iraqi can be proved to be paranoid because in our country there is always something to be frightened of." Habits of wariness and suspicion are slow to disappear. I was in the countryside near Taji, formerly a Sunni insurgent stronghold north of Baghdad this week. I met a farmer who said, "I know people from here who have not been to Baghdad for ten years because they are frightened of being picked up at government checkpoints."[61]

When Arsonists Become Firefighters

In April 2011, the Iraqi government set up a committee to trace thousands of Iraqis missing since the invasion. The committee included representatives from the ministries of Defense, Interior, National Security, and Human Rights, all from the Islamic Dawa Party, as well as representatives of the Health and Justice ministries from the Al Sadr Bloc and the Islamic Virtue Party, all of them Shi'a parties. Also included on the committee were members of the intelligence services and the anti-terrorism forces.[62] Many of these ministries and political parties have close links with the very militias that carried out most of the ferocious crimes of enforced disappearance, assassination, sectarian violence, and torture, in collaboration with the occupying forces. How could this committee investigate the very crimes for which their militias are responsible?

Over the years, the Geneva International Centre for Justice (GICJ) has reported extensively on cases of enforced disappearance in the al-Anbar, Diyala, and Salah ad-Din Provinces. It reported these cases to the CED, the High Commissioner, UNAMI, and the Working Group on Enforced or Involuntary Disappearances. On September 9, 2020, GICJ gave presentations at the 19th Session of the CED and submitted thousands of files of missing persons, highlighting the persistent situation of enforced disappearances in Iraq. The report further mentioned that

> Throughout the anti-government demonstrations raging in Iraq since the beginning of October 2019, there have been a growing number of demonstrators, human rights defenders and journalists

forcibly disappeared. It is almost certain that the killings and abductions are being carried out under Iraqi government orders, whether carried out by government security personnel or affiliated militias.

Enforced disappearances, especially of civil activists and members of the press, have become widespread. GICJ sources confirm that the total number of abducted at present exceeds 700 people and the whereabouts of many of them remains unknown, which caused and continues to cause much distress to family members. Most of the cases occurred while these activists were returning to their homes from demonstrations.[63]

The findings set out in the UNAMI report of August 20, 2020, indicate a pattern of disappearances of Sunni Arab males by pro-government forces during military operations conducted in Anbar in 2015 and 2016. Based on conservative estimates, the actions carried out by pro-government forces during those operations are likely to have resulted in more than one thousand men and boys being subjected to enforced disappearance and other frequently related human rights violations, including extrajudicial execution; torture; cruel, inhuman, or degrading treatment; and/or punishment and arbitrary detention.[64]

Incidents of kidnapping and enforced disappearance are often attributed to "the PMF," "PMF militias" or simply "militias" in official complaints, formal UN statements, human rights reports, and media accounts. The Popular Mobilization Forces (PMF) stem from a 2014 *fatwa* (a ruling or Islamic decree handed down by a religious authority) in which Grand Ayatollah Ali al-Sistani, Iraq's most influential Shi'a cleric, called on volunteers to join the national armed forces to defend the country's territory against Islamic State (ISIS) fighters. Former Prime Minister Nouri al-Maliki (r. 2006-2014) brought them together under an umbrella organization called *al-Hashd al-Sha'abi* (the PMF) and managed by a body referred to as *Hayat al-Hashd al-Sha'abi* (the PMF Committee). Of the approximately fifty paramilitary groups and entities that make up the PMF, only five have been publicly identified by name as perpetrators of kidnapping and enforced disappearance. These are: the PMF Security Directorate, the *Badr* Organization, *Kata'ib Hezbollah*, *Asai'b Ahl al-Haq*, and *Ansar Allah al-Awfiyah*. Victims and survivors consistently describe how masked men in civilian clothes forced them into unmarked vehicles, often without a license plate, as has been repeatedly shown on CCTV footage. This last point of anonymity becomes more important when one considers that, in those few cases where the specific PMF element has been identified, it was almost always the survivor, his or her lawyer, or a witness who made the identification—not the law enforcement officers.[65]

On August 30, 2021, the International Day of the Victims of Enforced Disappearances, thirty-three organizations jointly highlighted the systematic practice of enforced disappearance in the Middle East and North Africa (MENA) region and to call on states and multilateral and international institutions to take action to address impunity for this crime. About Iraq they wrote

> Although the country has a history of enforced disappearances, the crime is still committed today, with the number of cases peaking in recent years, including after the peaceful protests of 2019 in the country. Actors across the board, from security officials affiliated with the Iraqi State to non-State actors such as al-Qaeda, ISIS, and other armed groups, have been accused of being responsible for practices amounting to enforced disappearances in recent years. The UN Committee on Enforced Disappearances has received allegations of 420 places of secret detention, which often serve as sites for enforced disappearances. Although Iraqi authorities have indicated their willingness to investigate disappearance cases, no effective State-led investigations have been conducted.[66]

Case Study: Hakim Al-Zamili

Ali Al-Shimari, Health Minister of Iraq from 2006 to 2007, was aligned to the Shi'a cleric Moqtada al-Sadr's political movement, while his military arm, the Mahdi Army, was acting inside hospitals with impunity. Sick and wounded patients were abducted from public hospitals and later killed.[67] Increasingly, Iraqis were avoiding hospitals, which had become killing fields. Al-Shimari fled the country as soon as charges of sectarian acts were brought against officials at the ministry and was granted political asylum in the United States.[68] After a February 2006 bomb hit Samarra's *Askariya* Shrine, known as the Golden Mosque, one of the world's most important Shi'a sanctuaries,[69] Al-Shimari and his deputy, Hakim al-Zamili, a Mahdi Army commander, transformed the Ministry of Health into a torture and killing center. In September 2006, when the streets of Baghdad were swamped with thousands of brutally assassinated bodies, Prime Minister al-Maliki ordered the ministry not to release further figures about casualties to the United Nations.[70]

In 2007, occupation forces raided the ministry and arrested al-Zamili, accusing him of funneling money to the militias and using private ambulances and hospitals to carry out the killings. He was the key suspect in the kidnapping and (suspected) murder of his colleague, a deputy minister.[71] After a two-day trial, marred by accusations of witness intimidation, the charges were dropped and al-Zamili was freed after spending more than a year in U.S. custody.[72] According to Iraqi sources, he killed 160 persons, among them the general director of the health department in the city of Diyala.

According to an anonymous testimony, "The first thing al-Zamili did after being released was to kill Hassan Aziz, who tried to convict him. Now this criminal is a member of the Iraqi parliament!"

He was also one of the strongest advocates for the death sentence of former Deputy Prime Minister Tariq Aziz (r.1979-2003).[73] As well as being appointed head of the Iraqi parliament's security and defense committee, al-Zamili is also a top commander of the *Saraya al-Salam* brigades (peace brigades), a militia formed by Moqtada al-Sadr.[74]

Case Study: The Ministry of Higher Education Kidnapping

One incident sheds light on the reaction of the occupying forces to the wave of enforced disappearances that hit Iraq. In November 2006, between 140 and 150 members of the Ministry of Higher Education were abducted in full daylight. It was the largest kidnapping operation in Iraqi history. The raid took place in broad daylight, 1 kilometer from the Green Zone—the main base for coalition and Iraqi government officials—in an area that contained several high-security compounds, with a heavy presence of Iraqi troops and several checkpoints. The paramilitary force, estimated at between at least fifty and one hundred, wearing Iraqi National Police uniforms, arrived in a fleet of twenty to thirty camouflage pickup trucks of the kind employed by the Interior Ministry and rapidly cordoned off the area. The paramilitaries made their arrests according to lists, confirming the identities of those present by their ID cards, then handcuffed and blindfolded them, putting them into their vehicles and making their exit through heavy traffic without opposition, despite the reported presences of a regular police car. The majority of the detainees were murdered.

The fates of more than sixty are still unknown. No attempt was made to free them, although there were indications that the government and U.S. forces knew where they were held. A few months later, the same group kidnapped and killed three American soldiers. Within hours of the incident, U.S. planes located the hideout of the terrorist leader and bombed it, killing him and his aides.[75]

In October 2012, *Shafaq*, an Iraqi news agency, reported

> An official security source revealed . . . that a mass grave was found . . . on the outskirts of Sadr City, with bodies belonging to the staff of the Department of Missions of the Ministry of Higher Education and Scientific Research who disappeared in 2006. . . . Sixteen bodies were found. . . . Available intelligence reports that the bodies belong to employees of the Department of Missions. . . . Competent authorities are conducting DNA tests to make sure of the bodies' identities and inform their families.[76]

In the Future

Nineteen years after the U.S.-led invasion, Iraq remains mired in human rights abuses. The authorities have engaged in widespread detentions, torture, unfair trials, and executions. Iraq's security forces continue to evade accountability for enforced disappearances and other serious violations of human rights, much as the U.S. and British military forces have enjoyed impunity for the wrongs they committed while they occupied Iraq following the 2003 invasion.

To undo the legacy of enforced disappearance in Iraq takes more than criminalizing the crime. There are many factors that have made this practice possible, such as the widespread use of secret detention centers, the involvement of various armed groups in carrying out authorized arrests and detentions, and the lack of a unified reporting mechanism or search procedure for missing persons.

Therefore, a special rapporteur for Iraq should be appointed to

- Establish the responsibility of the United States and other occupying powers in the enforced disappearances that happened under their guard.
- Instruct all members of the police and security forces that it is

a crime to subject any individual to enforced disappearance and that any police, security, or other officials who order, perpetrate, acquiesce, or tolerate such crimes will be held fully accountable and will be liable to prosecution and possible imprisonment as well as dismissal from office.

- Establish mechanisms to ensure that all allegations of enforced disappearance are investigated promptly, thoroughly, transparently, and independently.
- Ensure that all detainees are taken only to officially recognized places of detention.
- Ensure that all persons who have been subjected to enforced disappearance and their families are promptly afforded all appropriate reparation by the State, including restitution, fair and adequate financial compensation, and any necessary medical care and rehabilitation.

Iraq's laws should be amended to bring them into full compliance with the UN Convention on Enforced Disappearance and other relevant international human rights law and standards and be implemented in practice.

Notes

1. https://www.un.org/en/observances/victims-enforced-disappearance

2. The term Dirty War was originally coined by the Argentine military junta or civic-military dictatorship of the period of State terrorism from 1974 to 1983 as a part of Operation Condor, a United States-backed campaign of political repression and State terror involving intelligence operations and assassination of opponents. For more, see, for example, Giles Tremlett, "Operation Condor: The Cold War Conspiracy that Terrorize South America," *Guardian*, September 3, 2020.

3. Steven Casteel worked in Colombia with paramilitaries called *Los Pepes* that have been responsible for most of the violence against civilians. Casteel founded the Special Police Commandos in his capacity as senior advisor to the Iraqi Interior Ministry. See https://nicolasdavies.blogspot.com/2006/03/what-is-us-role-in-iraqs-dirty-war.html

4. UN Assistance Mission for Iraq (UNAMI), *Human Rights Report*, July 1–31 August 31, 2005. https://www.ohchr.org/Documents/Countries/Jul-Aug05_en.pdf

5. Andrea Valeria Ciavatta, "Enforced Disappearance Under International Law: The Specific Case of 'Operation Condor,'" 2017/2018. https://tesi.luiss.it/19834/1/076272_CIAVATTA_ANDREA%20VALERIA.pdf

6. The United Nations Assistance Mission for Iraq was formed by United Nations Security Council Resolution 1500 on August 14, 2003, and supports national development efforts on political, electoral, and humanitarian levels

throughout Iraq. https://en.wikipedia.org/wiki/United_Nations_Assistance_Missi
on_for_Iraq

7. UN Assistance Mission for Iraq (UNAMI), *Human Rights Report*, January
1–June 30, 2008, 24. See also David Weissbrodt and Amy Bergquist, "Methods
of the 'War on Terror,'" *Minnesota Journal of International Law* 16, no. 371 (2007).
http://scholarship.law.umn.edu/faculty_articles/249; for more information, see
https://scholarship.law.umn.edu/cgi/viewcontent.cgi?article=1253&context=facul
ty_articles

8. James Kilner, "Accounting for Missing People is Vital for Stability in a Post-
War Scenario," International Committee of the Red Cross (ICRC), November 13,
2009. http://www.reliefweb.int/rw/rwb.nsf/db900SID/MUMA-7XS4PY?OpenD
ocument

9. Alkarama is a Geneva-based non-governmental human rights organization
established in 2004 to assist all those in the Arab world subjected to or at risk of
extrajudicial execution, enforced disappearance, torture, and arbitrary detention.
https://www.alkarama.org/sites/default/files/2019-04/UPR%20Iraq_EN_0.pdf

10. The International Commission on Missing Persons (ICMP) is an intergovernmental organization that addresses the issue of persons missing as a result of
armed conflicts, violations of human rights, and natural disasters. It is headquartered in The Hague, the Netherlands. It assists governments in the exhumation of
mass graves and DNA identification of missing persons, provides support to family
associations of missing persons, and assists in creating strategies and institutions to
search for missing persons. https://www.icmp.int/

11. The Bureau of Investigative Journalism, *Iraq's Missing People*, Vimeo. https://
www.thebureauinvestigates.com/stories/2011-07-03/in-video-iraqs-missing

12. Human Rights Watch Report, *The Mass Graves of al-Malawi: The Truth
Uncovered*, May 28, 2003. https://www.hrw.org/report/2003/05/28/mass-graves-al
-mahawil/truth-uncovered

13. *BBC News*, "Iraq War Illegal, Says Annan." http://news.bbc.co.uk/2/hi/mid
dle_east/3661134.stm

14. *BBC News*, "Iraq Inquiry: Former UN Inspector Blix Says War Illegal'" July
27, 2010. https://www.bbc.com/news/uk-politics-10770239

15. *Dutch Davids Commission Releases Report on Dutch Government Support for Iraq
Invasion*, Jan 12, 2010. The "Davids Commission," an independent Dutch commission chaired by Willibrord Davids, former head of the Dutch Supreme Court,
released its 551-page report on the Dutch government's decisions surrounding
the invasion of Iraq. The report, months in the making, provides the results of
an investigation into the political support given by the Netherlands to the Bush
administration's decision to invade Iraq. The Davids Commission charges that "the
Dutch government let politics override law when it supported the 2003 United
States invasion of Iraq and ignored intelligence that downplayed the threat of Saddam Hussein's weapons program." http://themoderatevoice.com/dutch-davids-co
mmission-releases-report-on-dutch-government-support-for-iraq-invasion/

16. Jan Frel, "Could Bush Be Prosecuted for War Crimes?" *AlterNet*, July 9,
2006. https://www.alternet.org/2006/07/could_bush_be_prosecuted_for_war_cri
mes/

17. "Iraq: Enforced Disappearance, A Widespread Challenge," *Shadow Report*

Submitted by *Geneva International Centre for Justice to the UN Committee on Enforced Disappearances*, the 9th session, September 7–18, 2015, Human Rights Council Geneva. http://www.gicj.org/articlespictures/CED_9thSESSION/GICJ_Report _for_CED_9_session_Iraq.pdf

18. UN General Assembly, *Human Rights Council Nineteenth Session*, joint written statement, February 28, 2012. http://ap.ohchr.org/documents/dpage_e.aspx?si =A/HRC/19/NGO/146

19. "Enforced Disappearance, A Widespread Challenge," *Shadow Report Submitted by the Geneva International Centre for Justice (GICJ) to the UN Committee on Enforced Disappearances*, 9th session, September 7–18, 2015. GICJ is an independent, non-profit, non-governmental organization dedicated to the promotion and reinforcement of commitments to the principles and norms of human rights. GICJ is headquartered in Geneva, Switzerland. Basing its work on the rules and principles of International Law, International Humanitarian Law, and International Human Rights Law, (GICJ) observes and documents human rights violations and seeks justice for their victims through all legal means available. https://tbintern et.ohchr.org/Treaties/CED/Shared%20Documents/IRQ/INT_CED_CSS_IRQ _21467_E.pdf

20. Shashank Bengali, "Amnesty International Slams Iraq Over Prison Torture," *McClatchy Newspapers*, September 14, 2010. https://www.mcclatchydc.com /news/nation-world/world/article24593161.html

21. Alister Bull, "Morgue Body Count Highlights Iraq Bloodshed," *New Zealand Herald*, August 10, 2006. http://www.nzherald.co.nz/world/news/article.cfm ?c_id=2&objectid=10395546

22. The Green Zone is the most common name for the International Zone of Baghdad. It was a heavily fortified 10-square-kilometer (3.9 sq mi) area in the Karkh district of central Baghdad, the governmental center of the Coalition Provisional Authority during the occupation of Iraq after the U.S.-led 2003 invasion and remains the center of the international presence in the city. Its official name beginning under the Iraqi Interim Government was the International Zone, though Green Zone remains the most used term. The contrasting Red Zone refers to parts of Baghdad immediately outside the perimeter but was also loosely applied to all unsecured areas outside the *off-site* military posts. Both terms originated as military designations.

23. Jonathan Steele and Suzanne Goldenberg, "What Is the Real Death Toll in Iraq?," *Guardian*, March 19, 2008. http://www.guardian.co.uk/world/2008/mar/19 /iraq

24. Ellen Knickmeyer, "Body Count in Baghdad Nearly Triples," *Washington Post*, September 8, 2006. http://www.washingtonpost.com/wp-dyn/content/article /2006/09/07/AR2006090700768_2.html

25. The Medico-Legal Institute in Baghdad oversees the work of provincial morgues throughout the country. By and large, these institutions confine their work to autopsies on bodies brought to them by the police and thus have little, if any, experience in crime scene investigation. The Baghdad Medico-Legal Institute has not received new equipment since the late 1980s. Since the end of the war, the institute has had to deal with an upsurge of firearm-related deaths. In the six months before the war, the institute documented approximately ninety-six such

deaths. By August 2004, the number had risen to 518 per month; *Human Rights Watch Discussion with Dr. Fa'eq Amin Bakr, Director, Medico-Legal Institute, Baghdad,* February 23, 2004. https://www.hrw.org/reports/2004/iraq1104/4.htm

26. Amy Serafin, "The Missing: A Hidden Tragedy," *Magazine of the International Red Cross and Red Crescent,* 2007. http://www.redcross.int/en/mag/magazine2008_1/4-9.html

27. *Iraqi High Commission for Human Rights Report about Implementation of the International Convention on Protection of All Persons from Enforced Disappearance,* presented to the UN Human Rights Council, August 2015. https://tbinternet.ohchr.org/Treaties/CED/Shared%20Documents/IRQ/INT_CED_NHS_IRQ_21392_E.pdf

28. Timothy Williams and Suadad Al-Salhy, "Fate of Missing Iraqis Haunts Those Left Behind," *New York Times,* May 24, 2009. http://www.nytimes.com/2009/05/25/world/middleeast/25missing.html

29. Mohammed Abbas, "Horror of War at Iraqi Morgue even as Attacks Fall', Reuters, April 16, 2009. http://www.reliefweb.int/rw/rwb.nsf/db900sid/MWAI-7R74BB?OpenDocument&query=disappeared iraq&cc=irq

30. Associated Press, "Iraqi Searches for Brothers in Ancient Cemetery," October 25, 2009. https://www.foxnews.com/story/iraqi-searches-for-brothers-in-ancient-cemetery

31. UNHCR Report, *Iraq Bleeds, Millions Displaced By Conflict, Persecution And Violence,* 2007. http://www.unhcr.org/4614f73f2.pdf

32. Brian Conley and Isam Rashid, "Baghdad Morgue Tells Story Statistics Can't," Inter Press Service News Agency (IPS), June 7 2006. https://original.antiwar.com/brian-conley/2006/06/08/baghdad-morgue-tells-story-statistics-cant/

33. Dahr Jamail, Ali Al-Fadhily, "Iraq Lies in Tatters Beneath a 'Surge' of False Claims," IPS News, February 19, 2008 http://www.alternet.org/world/77602/

34. Mohammed Abbas, "Horror of War at Iraqi Morgue even as Attacks Fall," Reuters, April 16, 2009. http://www.reliefweb.int/rw/rwb.nsf/db900sid/MWAI-7R74BB?OpenDocument&query=disappeared iraq&cc=irq

35. Report from International Committee of the Red Cross, *The Missing in Iraq: A Harsh reality, an Unsolved Tragedy,* August 29, 2007. https://reliefweb.int/report/iraq/missing-iraq-harsh-reality-unsolved-tragedy

36. UNAMI, *Human Rights Report,* November 1—December 31, 2006, published January 16, 2007. http://www2.ohchr.org/SPdocs/Countries/bimonthly_16012007.doc

37. Kirk Semple, "Relentless Sectarian Violence in Baghdad Stalks Its Victims Even at the Morgues," *New York Times,* July 30, 2006. http://query.nytimes.com/gst/fullpage.html?res=9507E4DB133FF933A05754C0A9609C8B63&pagewanted=all

38. Iraq is a multiethnic, multi-religious society. Arabs make up 80 percent of the Iraqi population, and 95 percent of those are Muslims. Since the independence of Iraq from British rule in 1920 until 2003, Iraq never had any major sectarian conflict, unlike Lebanon or other countries.

"Although the Shi'as had been underrepresented in government posts in the period of the monarchy, they made substantial progress in the educational, business, and legal fields. Their advancement in other areas, such as the opposition parties, was such that . . . from 1952 to 1963, before the Baath Party came to power, Shi'a held the majority of party leadership posts. Observers believed that in the late 1980s Shi'a were represented at all levels of the party roughly in proportion to government estimates of their numbers in the population." http://countrystudies .us/iraq/38.htm

Muhasasa is the system—laid in the early 1990s by Iraqi opposition groups— for distributing public offices, political positions and state resources along ethnic-sectarian lines between parties that are part of the ruling elite of the country. But muhasasa has driven sectarian tensions and torn the social fabric by putting ethnic-sectarian identities in the foreground. Iraq commentator Reidar Visser refers to the "selective de-Ba'athification" process given that historically, he notes, the Shi'a and Sunnis alike co-operated with the old regime in their millions.

"It is a historical fact that Shiites and Sunnis alike cooperated with the old regime in their millions . . . for example, Shiite tribes . . . cracked down on the 'Shi-ite' rebellion . . . in 1991. Nonetheless, the exiles who returned to Iraq after 2003 have tried to impose an artificial narrative in which the legacy of pragmatic coop-eration with the Baathist regime is not dealt with in a systematic and neutral fash-ion as such; instead, one singles out political opponents (often Sunnis) as 'Baathists' and silently co-opts political friends (especially if they happen to be Shi'a) with-out mentioning their Baathist ties at all. The result is a hypocritical and sectarian approach to the whole question of de-Ba'athification that will create a new Iraq on shaky foundations." http://gulfanalysis.wordpress.com/2010/01/08/why-ad-hoc -de-baathification-will-derail-the-process-of-democratisation-in-iraq/

The occupying authority practiced something new in Iraq: Ethnic cleansing, a divide-and-rule strategy, supporting Shi'a against Sunnis, and Sunnis against Shi'a. See Iraqi blogger Riverbend: http://www.riverbendblog.blogspot.com/2006_12 _01_riverbendblog_archive.html

Of interest, see also Saad Naji Jawad, professor of political science, College of Political Sciences, Baghdad University. Member of Iraq's Professors Association. Vice president of the Arab Association for Political Sciences, senior visiting fellow in Political Science, London School of Economics and Political Science. "Elections Won't Heal Iraqi's Scarred Democracy, Whatever the Results." *The Conversation*, May 13, 2014. http://tinyurl.com/564lsfsl

39. Report from International Committee of the Red Cross, *The Missing in Iraq: A Harsh Reality, an Unsolved Tragedy*, August 29, 2007. http://www.reliefweb.int/rw /RWB.NSF/db900SID/EVOD-76JGPZ?OpenDocument

40. UK Border Agency, *Country of Origin Information Report-IRAQ*, May 15, 2008, p. 65. http://www.refworld.org/pdfid/488efda42.pdf

41. Alkarama, *Iraq: Two Years After its Review by a UN Committee, Iraq is yet to Address the Issue of Enforced Disappearance*, July 26, 2017. Alkarama submitted to the UN experts its follow-up report, which highlights that the priority issues have not been addressed in the past two years. http://www.pressreleasepoint.com/iraq-two -years-after-its-review-un-committee-iraq-yet-address-issue-enforced-disappear ance

42. Linda Bergauer, "Protection for Victims of Enforced Disappearance in Iraq?," August 30, 2021. https://timep.org/commentary/analysis/protection-for-vi ctims-of-enforced-disappearance-in-iraq/

43. "Iraq: UN Committee Urges End to Impunity for Enforced Disappearances." https://www.ohchr.org/EN/HRBodies/HRC/Pages/NewsDetail.aspx?NewsID=26550&LangID=E

44. Ceasefire Centre for Civilian Rights, *The Forever Crime: Ending Enforced Disappearance in Iraq*, January 19, 2021. https://www.ceasefire.org/after-decades-of-disappearances-iraq-preparing-to-turn-the-page-new-report/

45. IRIN news service, "Enforced Disappearances—'A Long-Term Challenge,'" January 13, 2011. https://www.thenewhumanitarian.org/news/2011/01/13/enforced-disappearances-long-term-challenge. After nineteen years of humanitarian news and analysis, IRIN, originally the "Integrated Regional Information Networks," left the United Nations in January 2015 to relaunch as an independent, non-profit media venture. They have been providing ground reporting on humanitarian crises.

46. "The United States and its allies launched a massive aerial assault against Iraq on Friday. At 12:15 p.m. EST, anti-aircraft fire could be seen rising in the skies above Baghdad. Within an hour, tremendous explosions began rocking the Iraqi capital, as the Pentagon announced 'A-Day' was underway. The campaign was intended to instill 'shock and awe' among Iraq's leaders, and it was directed at hundreds of targets in Iraq, officials said. Plumes of fire could be seen rising above targets in Baghdad at 1:05 p.m. EST." CNN Correspondent Wolf Blitzer reported that in his thirty years of experience, he had never seen anything on the scale of Friday's attack on the Iraqi capital.

47. Embedded journalism refers to news reporters being attached to military units involved in armed conflicts. While the term could be applied to many historical interactions between journalists and military personnel, it first came to be used in the media coverage of the 2003 invasion of Iraq. This makes it impossible or, at least, extremely difficult, to get at the truth in order to analyze what is happening across the whole arena of conflict. Perhaps the most damaging effect of "embedding" is to soften the brutality of any military occupation and underplay hostile local response to it.

48. Dahr Jamail, "IRAQ: No Unemployment Among Gravediggers," IPS Inter Press Service News Agency, February 5, 2009. http://www.ipsnews.net/2009/02/iraq-no-unemployment-among-gravediggers/

49. Bureau of Investigative Journalism, "Iraq's Missing, in Video," July 2011. https://www.thebureauinvestigates.com/stories/2011-07-03/in-video-iraqs-missing The Bureau of Investigative Journalism is a non-profit organization based at London's City University.

50. The Center for Strategic and International Studies is a think tank based in Washington, DC.

51. Edward Wong and Damien Cave, "Iraqi Death Toll Rose Above 3,400 in July," *New York Times*, August 15, 2006. http://www.nytimes.com/2006/08/15/world/middleeast/15cnd-iraq.html

52. Middle East Online, "40,000 Unidentified Corpses Buried in Najaf since the Beginning of the US-Led Invasion," September 9, 2007. http://www.uruknet.info/?p=m36110&hd=&size=1&l=e

53. *Wadi Al-Salam*, meaning Valley of Peace in Arabic, is an ancient Islamic cemetery located near the holy city of Najaf, Iraq. The cemetery is located near the

shrine of Imam Ali ibn Abi Talib, the fourth Sunni Caliph and the first Shi'a Imam. Thus, many Shi'a in Iraq request that they be buried in this cemetery. This record-breaking cemetery contains approximately 5 million bodies, making it the largest graveyard on Earth. Ancient prophets, imams, kings, scientists, and civilians have been buried at this cemetery for nearly 1,500 years and it is estimated that 500,000 bodies continue to be placed at the site each year.

54. Michael Ware, "More Anonymous Dead Buried in Iraq Than Under Saddam," September 15, 2007. http://www.youtube.com/watch?v=P0JRzdCWR3g

55. One hundred and seventy-seven bodies were buried in mass graves in Kut from December 2006 to February 2007. Mona Mahmoud and Sebastian Usher, "Iraqi River Carries Grotesque Cargo," *BBC News*, July 17, 2007. http://news.bbc .co.uk/2/hi/middle_east/6902024.stm

56. This figure reflects June 2006–February 2008. Voices of Iraq, "64 More Unidentified Bodies Buried in Karbala," February 8, 2008. http://www.democratic underground.org/discuss/duboard.php?az=view_all&address=389x159667

57. Ahmed Ali, "IRAQ: Mass Graves Dug to Deal with Death Toll," IPS, July 17, 2007. http://www.ipsnews.net/2007/07/iraq-mass-graves-dug-to-deal-with-de ath-toll/

58. *First Periodical Report of Monitoring Net of Human Rights in Iraq*, November 11, 2005. The Monitoring Network for Human Rights (MHRI), which consists of more than twenty Iraqi organizations for Human Rights, made this report about the crimes and continuous violations of human rights in Iraq. http://brussellstribu nal.org/survey111105.htm

59. The UN Working Group on Enforced Disappearances submitted its report to the UN Human Rights Council in Geneva. The working group reported more than 43,000 cases from 88 countries still remained to be clarified. *UN: Enforced Disappearances Continue Unabated Globally*, September 15, 2014. https://www.voanews .com/a/enforced-disappearances-continue-unabated-around-globe/2450133.html

60. Report from IRIN, *Iraq: Hundreds Go Missing or Get Killed at Checkpoints*, June 6, 2007. https://reliefweb.int/report/iraq/iraq-hundreds-go-missing-or-get -killed-checkpoints

61. Patrick Cockburn, "Iraq Isn't as Dangerous as It Was—But Many Still Live in Fear," *Independent*, June 29, 2018. https://www.independent.co.uk/voices/iraq -danger-recovery-isis-war-us-syria-jihadis-a8422571.html

62. Joint written statement, "Violation of Women's Rights in Iraq," *Human Rights Council Nineteenth Session*, February 28, 2012. http://ap.ohchr.org/documents/dpa ge_e.aspx?si=A/HRC/19/NGO/145

63. "GICJ Updates the UN on the Situation of Enforced Disappearances in Iraq," *Summary of GICJ's Participation at the 19th Session of the UN Committee of Enforced Disappearances*, September 9, 2020. https://www.gicj.org/topics/enforced -disappearances/1868-update_ced_2020

64. *Enforced Disappearances from Anbar Governorate 2015–2016: Accountability for Victims and the Right to Truth, Report of the United Nations Assistance Mission for Iraq Office of the United Nations High Commissioner for Human Rights*, August 2020, Baghdad, Iraq. https://www.ohchr.org/Documents/Countries/IQ/UNAMI-OHC HR-report-enforced-disappearances.pdf

65. MENA Prison Forum (MPF), "'Rules of Engagement' Inside the Popular

Mobilization Forces' Iraq," October 17, 2021. https://www.menaprisonforum.org/observer_detail/9/

66. Freedom House, Joint statement, "A Call For Action on International Day of the Victims of Enforced Disappearances," August 30, 2021. https://freedomhouse.org/article/call-action-international-day-victims-enforced-disappearances

67. Amit R. Paley, "Iraqi Hospitals Are War's New 'Killing Fields,'" *Washington Post*, August 30, 2006. http://www.washingtonpost.com/wp-dyn/content/article/2006/08/29/AR2006082901680.html

68. Nermeen Al-Mufti, "Sadr's Men on Trial," Al-Ahram Weekly Online, February 21, 2008. http://weekly.ahram.org.eg/archive/2008/885/re82.htm

69. Ellen Knickmeyer and K.I. Ibrahim, "Bombing Shatters Mosque in Iraq," *Washington Post*, February 23, 2006. http://www.washingtonpost.com/wp-dyn/content/article/2006/02/22/AR2006022200454.html

70. Iraqanalysis, "Other Mortality Estimates," 2007. http://www.iraqanalysis.org/mortality/438

71. Ammar al-Saffar, "Senior Health Official Detained by US-Iraqi Forces," *Washington Times*, February 8, 2007. http://www.washingtontimes.com/news/2007/feb/8/20070208-115125-4889r/

72. Marc Santora and Michael R. Gordon. "Murky Candidacy Stokes Iraq's Sectarian Fears," *New York Times*, March 3, 2010, 8. http://www.nytimes.com/2010/03/04/world/middleeast/04baghdad.html?_r=1&ref=world

73. Milad Rizooqi and Dirk Adriaensens, "Sadrists Behind the Murder Of The Ministry Of Higher Education Officials In Iraq," Countercurrents.org, November 1, 2012. https://www.countercurrents.org/rizooqi011112.htm

74. http://www.gettyimages.co.uk/detail/news-photo/iraqi-mp-head-of-the-defence-and-security-committee-in-news-photo/503603436#iraqi-mp-head-of-the-defence-and-security-committee-in-parliament-picture-id503603436

75. Dr. Saad Naji Jawad, "Beyond Educide: Sanctions, Occupation and the Struggle for Higher Education in Iraq," *Recommendations of the International Seminar on the Situation of Iraqi Academics*, March 9–11, 2011, Ghent University, 26. https://www.amazon.com/Beyond-Educide-Sanctions-Occupation-Education/dp/9038218869

76. Dirk Adriaensens, "Crimes against Humanity: Iraq's Mass Graves," Global Research, October 23, 2012. https://www.globalresearch.ca/crimes-against-humanity-iraqs-mass-gravesvoting-the-stolen-election-of-2004-2/5309313; Iraq Turkmen Front News Portal, "A Mass Grave Found in Sadr City," October 22, 2012. http://www.kerkuk.net/eng/?p=7722

FOUR

Extraordinary Rendition

A Human Rights Analysis

David Weissbrodt

On September 13, 1995, local police in Croatia seized Egyptian national Talaat Fouad Qassem, and then handed him to agents of the United States Central Intelligence Agency (CIA). Qassem had fled Egypt after the Egyptian government accused him of involvement in the assassination of Anwar Sadat, the former President of Egypt. The Egyptian government subsequently sentenced Qassem to death in absentia. The CIA agents took him on board a ship in the Adriatic Sea and interrogated him. Then, they delivered Qassem to Egypt, where he disappeared. A human rights reporter in Egypt believed he had been executed.

During the summer of 2003, Kurdish soldiers in Iraq captured Iraqi national Hiwa Abdul Rahman Rashul somewhere in Iraq.[1] The Kurdish military handed Rashul over to operatives of the CIA who flew him to Afghanistan for interrogation. When a legal advisor for the CIA opposed the transfer, the CIA returned Rashul to Iraq. At the request of CIA Director George J. Tenet, United States Secretary of Defense Donald Rumsfeld endeavored to hide the location and identity of Rashul from the International Committee of the Red Cross. According to the *Washington Post*, the status of Rashul is unknown.

In December 2003, Khaled El Masri, who had German nationality and who was originally born in Iraq, boarded a bus in his home of Ulm, Germany, to travel to Skopje, Macedonia.[2] When he arrived at the Macedonian border on December 31, Macedonian police removed him from a bus, confiscated his passport, and detained him for three weeks. On January 23, 2004, a jet with tail number N313P, registered to Premier Executive Transport Services, a CIA front company, arrived in Macedonia from the island of Majorca. The CIA drove El Masri to the Skopje airport in Macedonia, where he was transferred to CIA officials. Men wearing black masks and black gloves, beat him, cut off his clothes, and then injected him with drugs. He was then placed on an airplane and flown, first, to Baghdad, and then to Kabul. When El Masri arrived in Afghanistan, U.S. officials interrogated him and held him in solitary confinement for nearly five months. On the order of U.S. Secretary of State Condoleezza Rice during May 2004, U.S. officials loaded El Masri on a plane, brought him back to Central Europe, and released him near a checkpoint on the Albanian border. His detention was apparently a case of mistaken identity. When El Masri returned home to Germany, he learned that his wife and children had gone to stay with her family in Lebanon; his wife thought he had abandoned the family.

The cases of Qassem, Rashul, and El Masri were part of the CIA practice of capturing suspected terrorists and sending them to countries, such as Afghanistan and Egypt, where the use of tortuous interrogation is commonplace. This strategy—commonly known as "extraordinary rendition"—was developed and refined by U.S. administrations during the past three decades, and has received assistance in its execution from dozens of countries, including Germany, Portugal, Austria, Sweden, and Finland. In total, more than fifty-four countries have participated in extraordinary rendition activities.

Due to the lack of relevant information and the use of secretive measures, the total number of cases involving extraordinary renditions is unknown.[3] Accordingly, it is widely speculated that the use of extraordinary renditions has dramatically increased since the September 11, 2001, terrorist attacks.[4] The increased use of extraordinary rendition is in part due to President George W. Bush's approval of expedited procedures giving the CIA more flexibility.[5] The more lenient use of extraordinary rendition has evolved in response to the United States' initiative to strengthen the "War on Terror."[6]

Extraordinary rendition generally involves the officials of a particular nation who abduct a person not formally charged with a criminal offense but is transported to a third country for detention and interrogation. World War II served as a basis for the twentieth-century movement to establish international human rights standards.[7] From these developments, extraordinary rendition has also emerged as an encouragement for human rights violations.[8] Extraordinary rendition is often utilized by governments expecting to avoid legal and moral constraints by denying their involvement with the abuses of detainees.[9] As more countries are now resorting to the use of extraordinary rendition as an alternative means of detaining and interrogating suspected enemies of the State, it is necessary to analyze how extraordinary rendition conflicts with the various international human rights instruments.

The Universal Declaration of Human Rights is the authoritative interpretation of the human rights obligations contained in the United Nations Charter.[10] The provisions of the Universal Declaration have been widely accepted as customary international law[11]—affirming the right to life; freedom from torture; freedom of thought, conscience, and religion; as well as the right to a fair trial[12]— and have inspired constitutional and legislative authority in many nations, including the United States, Greece, Chile, Afghanistan, Sweden, Guatemala, Ethiopia, New Zealand, and the Netherlands.[13]

Accordingly, the articles of the Universal Declaration provide broad human rights coverage: article 3 guarantees the "right to life, liberty, and security of person";[14] article 5 prohibits torture and cruel, inhuman or degrading treatment or punishment;[15] article 6 guarantees everyone a "right to recognition everywhere as a person before the law";[16] article 9 prohibits "arbitrary arrest, detention or exile";[17] articles 10 and 11 assure the right to a fair and public hearing on criminal charges along with a presumption of innocence until proven guilty by law.[18]

The use of extraordinary rendition clearly implicates violations of the Universal Declaration. The situations of Qassem, Rashul, and El Masri provide tangible examples of how extraordinary rendition subjects its victims to many of the most significant human rights violations, for example, abduction deprived these prisoners of their article 3 right to liberty and security. Further, article 5 violations were evident in each of these cases as the United States knowingly transferred these men to Afghanistan and Egypt—countries commonly criticized for systematic use of torture[19]—thus failing to protect against ill-treatment. During this process, U.S. agents and foreign police forces denied the prisoners proper access to counsel—violating the terms of article 6.[20] In all three situations the U.S. government performed arbitrary arrests by failing to file official criminal charges against the detainees—violating article 9. Accordingly, the lack of judicial process through fair and public hearings and a presumption of innocence, illustrates a clear breach of articles 10 and 11.[21] In sum, the use of extraordinary rendition as to Qassem, Rashul, and El Masri illustrates that many of the provisions of the Universal Declaration are directly violated, which is indicative of its malicious purpose in relation to recognized human rights instruments.

It is critical to know the status of the United States in regard to its acceptance of the respective human rights treaties. Currently, the United States has signed, but not ratified, the International Covenant on Economic, Social, and Cultural Rights. When a State, such as the United States, signs but does not ratify a treaty, it is not officially consenting to be bound by the treaty source but is rather simply agreeing to accept ratification upon further review or approval. The United States has both signed and ratified the International Covenant on Civil and Political Rights; the Geneva Conventions; and the Convention against Torture and Other Cruel, Inhuman or Degrading Treatment or Punishment. The United States has not signed or ratified the Convention for the Protection of All Persons against Enforced Disappearance, offering a legal explanation for its consistent use of extraordinary rendition.

While the Universal Declaration established a "common standard of achievement,"[22] the International Covenant on Civil and Political Rights (a.k.a., Covenant on Political Rights) codified many of its provisions.[23] The Covenant has a broad territorial reach. The Human Rights Committee has determined that a person does not need to be within a State Party's territory in order for that State to be subject to the terms of the Covenant—the person must merely be "within the power or effective control" of a State Party.[24] Therefore, no matter where a State Party detains a person, the State Party is required to afford all persons the protections enumerated in the Covenant on Political Rights.[25] The Covenant is especially important in relation to the use of extraordinary rendition by U.S. officials on Qassem, Rashul, and El Masri, because the detainees were never within U.S. territory.

The Covenant on Political Rights provides a broad range of human rights protections for detained persons: article 7 prohibits torture and other forms of cruel and inhuman punishments[26] and article 10 requires all State Parties to treat detained persons with humanity and respect.[27] Furthermore, the Human Rights Committee has broadly interpreted articles 2 and 7 to apply even when a State Party merely transfers a detainee to "another State where there are substantial grounds for believing he would be in danger of being tortured."[28] The guidance of the Human Rights Committee indicates that the protections of article 7 extend to cases of transfer.[29]

Again, the use of extraordinary rendition on Qassem, Rashul, and El

Masri reveals that multiple provisions of the Covenant on Political Rights were violated. In regard to article 7, the United States transferred all three detainees to locations where there were substantial grounds to believe that torture would ensue, violating its protections against reckless transfers of detainees to locations utilizing torture. Article 2 also requires that persons claiming a violation of the Covenant on Political Rights has "a right to remedy," however, the cases of Qassem, Rashul, and El Masri demonstrate that detainees rarely have a means of challenging their Covenant on Political Rights protections or transfers more generally.[30]

In 1966, the UN adopted the International Covenant on Economic, Social, and Cultural Rights as an addition to the Covenant on Political Rights.[31] Unlike the provisions of the Covenant on Political Rights, the protections enumerated in the International Covenant on Economic, Social, and Cultural Rights are not immediately enforceable, but rather should be implemented by State Parties "to the maximum of their available resources, with a view to achieving progressively the full realization of the rights."[32] Another divergence from the Covenant on Political Rights is that the International Covenant on Economic, Social, and Cultural Rights contains no jurisdictional limits.[33]

The International Covenant on Economic, Social, and Cultural Rights is violated when a government abducts and transports a person to a country where torture and other forms of inhuman or degrading treatment may ensue. Extraordinary rendition violates multiple provisions of the International Covenant on Economic, Social, and Cultural Rights. Articles 11 and 12 are violated when detainees are denied their right to adequate standard of living for themselves and their families,[34] and are further violated during transfer and interrogation if detainees are denied their right to be free from hunger,[35] and their right to mental and physical health.[36] An article 10 violation (protecting against separation of families) was demonstrated in El Masri's extraordinary rendition because, as previously noted, his family left Germany with the thought that El Masri had abandoned them during his detention.[37]

The Convention against Torture and Other Cruel, Inhuman, or Degrading Treatment, or Punishment (a.k.a., Convention against Torture) defines torture as "any act by which severe pain or suffering, whether physical or mental, is intentionally inflicted on a person."[38] The Convention against Torture requires minimal State action to implicate its provisions—the pain or suffering must be "inflicted by or at the instigation of or with the consent or acquiescence of a public official or other person acting in an official capacity."[39] The Convention against Torture is further broadened in scope by article 16, which requires that every State Party "undertake to prevent in any territory under its jurisdiction other acts of cruel, inhuman, or degrading treatment or punishment which do not amount to torture."[40]

The protections enumerated in article 3 of the Convention against Torture are particularly important in relation to extraordinary rendition because it prohibits "refoulement" to a State where there are substantial grounds to believe that a person would be in danger of being tortured.[41] To determine whether such substantial grounds exist, the article requires that authorities "take into account all relevant considerations."[42] Furthermore, article 2 explicitly forbids State Parties from attempting to justify the use of torture,[43] while articles 4, 5, and 7 require State Parties to criminalize all acts and attempts to torture through prosecution or extradition processes.[44]

The history of the drafting of the Convention against Torture helps to put its provisions in context with extraordinary rendition.[45] First, the drafters concluded that a State Party cannot use extraordinary rendition to circumvent the traditional methods of extradition,[46] and that a country engaging in extraordinary rendition cannot rely on extradition treaty reservations to avoid implicating article 3 protections.[47] As applied to the stories of Qassem, Rashul, and El Masri there is no evidence that traditional extradition procedures were used when transferring Qassem to Egypt or Rashul and El Masri to Afghanistan. Only Qassem was wanted on criminal charges.

Additionally, the history of the drafting of the Convention against Torture reveals that article 3 has a broadened extraterritorial scope.[48] The term "return" (in French, *refouler*) was added to article 3 during the drafting process with the intent that the article would cover all situations in which a person is transferred to another country. In fact, the CIA's transfer of Qassem, Rashul, and El Masri to third countries is prohibited by article 3.

The Committee against Torture has published two critical findings in regard to extraordinary rendition. First, in Khan v. Canada,[49] the Committee determined that transferring a person to a country that is not part of the Convention against Torture constitutes a violation of article 3 because the transfer exposes the person to danger, and the person would not be able to seek protection under the convention.[50] The Committee affirmed this ruling in Agiza v. Sweden, where it determined that the transfer of detainee Ahmed Agiza to Egypt constituted a violation of article 3 because Sweden's officials "[knew] or should have known" that Egypt resorted to consistent use of torture.[51]

Second, extraordinary rendition may also constitute a conspiracy to commit torture, which also qualifies as a violation of the Convention against Torture. Countries that merely facilitate the practice by providing intelligence or material assistance may violate article 1's prohibition on State "consent or acquiescence."[52] The U.S. officials involved in extraordinary rendition have admitted that they were aware that the transfers were likely to result in torture.[53]

The Geneva Conventions of 1949 enacted protections tailored toward persons involved in armed conflict.[54] First, the Geneva Convention Relative to the Treatment of Prisoners of War (a.k.a., the POW Convention) protects prisoners of war (POWs) that are detained as a result of armed conflict.[55] The POW Convention covers a broad range of persons, including members of the armed forces held in enemy hands,[56] members of militias or voluntary forces, and members of organized resistance movements[57] (members in this category are subject to additional requirements to be eligible for protection).[58] Extraordinary rendition implicates grave breaches in the POW Convention's protections against willful killing, serious bodily harm, and torture.[59] Extraordinary rendition also violates the POW Convention's protections against the separation of families, and "moral suffering" through sadistic punishment methods,[60] and further protects POWs who are "willfully" transferred to a country that utilizes ill-treatment and torture.[61]

Article 4 of the Civilian Convention protects all civilians from ill-treatment and torture so long as they are not in the hands of their own government.[62] Extraordinary rendition violates article 49 of the Civilian Convention, which protects all civilians against transfer or deportation out of an occupied territory, except if it is due to military evacuation.[63] Article 49 is intended to prohibit all forms of forcible transfer of persons protected under the Civilian Convention, regardless of their legal status in the occupied territory. Therefore, the United States' extraordinary rendition of protected civilians, such as Rashul, violates article 49 of the Civilian Convention.

More recently in 2006, the United Nations Human Rights Council adopted the International Convention for the Protection of All Persons from Enforced Disappearance (a.k.a., Enforced Disappearance Convention).[64] The Enforced Disappearance Convention was specifically created to prevent enforced disappearance, noting that the use of enforced disappearance qualifies as a crime against humanity.

Article 2 of the Enforced Disappearance Convention defines enforced disappearance as "the arrest, detention, abduction, or any other form of deprivation of liberty by agents of the State or by persons or groups of persons acting with the authorization, support, or acquiescence of the

State, followed by a refusal to acknowledge the deprivation of liberty or by concealment of the fate or whereabouts of the disappeared person, which places such a person outside the protection of the law."[65] Article 1 prohibits the use of enforced disappearance without the possibility of justification from State Parties.[66] The Enforced Disappearance Convention proactively prevents enforced disappearance by requiring State Parties to investigate all suspected activities pertaining to article 2,[67] and mandating that State Parties hold anyone involved with the practice of enforced disappearance criminally liable.[68]

Article 17 pertains closely to extraordinary rendition by requiring all State Parties to maintain official registers of all persons who are deprived of liberty.[69] The registers must promptly be made available to any competent authority at their request. The register must include information documenting the date and time of release or transfer to another place of detention, along with the authority that will be responsible for the transfer. Article 18 allows all relatives of persons who are victims of enforced disappearance to have access to the date and time of abduction and transfer, the location of detention, and all information regarding the health of the detainee.[70]

Extraordinary rendition implicates multiple violations of the Enforced Disappearance Convention and other human rights treaties. Qassem, Rashul, and El Masri were each abducted and placed outside of the control of the law while CIA officials failed to admit responsibility for the deprivation of liberty, breaching article 2. Furthermore, the U.S. government failed to uphold the protections of articles 6 and 7 by failing to maintain a record of Qassem's, Rashul's, and El Masri's exact location and health status. As a result of these failures to maintain appropriate records, the location and health of Qassem and Rashul are still unconfirmed. In order to avoid the reoccurrence of extraordinary rendition, it is crucial that government officials, particularly within foreign intelligence agencies, keep accurate and extensive records of all abductions, while simultaneously ensuring that abducted foreign citizens are not placed in the hands of nations known to use torture Furthermore, the United Nations must encourage strict guidelines for all States that resort to the use of extraordinary rendition.

Notes

The author wishes to thank his Research Assistant, Peter Economou, University of Minnesota Law School, Class of 2019, for his outstanding assistance in preparing this paper.

1. Jane Meyer, "Outsourcing Torture: The Secret History of America's Extraordinary Rendition Program," *New Yorker*, February 24, 2005, 106, 109; Dana Priest, "Memo Lets CIA Take Detainees Out of Iraq: Practice Is Called Serious Breach of Geneva Conventions," *Washington Post*, October 24, 2004, A1.

2. Details of Khalid El Masri's abduction are reported in numerous sources. See Bruce Zagaris, "U.S. Extraordinary Renditions Subject to Foreign and US Investigations and Oversight," *International Enforcement Law Reporter* 21 (2005): 188; Michael Hirsh et al., "Aboard Air CIA," *Newsweek*, February 28, 2005, 32; Scott Shane et al., "CIA Expanding Terror Battle Under Guise of Charter Flights," *New York Times*, May 31, 2005, A1; Craig Whitlock, "Europeans Investigate CIA Role in Abductions," *Washington Post*, March 13, 2005, A1; "CBS News: CIA Flying Suspects to Torture?" (CBS, March 6, 2005).

3. See Meyer, supra note 1, 107 (noting that Representative Markey complained that after repeated requests of CIA officials to provide an accurate count of the number of people transferred, "[t]hey refuse to answer. All they will say is that they're in compliance with the law").

4. See Shannon McCaffrey, "Canadian Sent to Syrian Prison Disputes U.S. Claims Against Torture," *Knight Ridder/Trib. News Service*, July 29, 2004.

5. See Douglas Jehl, "Pentagon Seeks to Shift Inmates from Cuba Base," *New York Times*, March 11, 2005, A1; Douglas Jehl and David Johnston, "Rule Change Lets CIA Freely Send Suspects Abroad to Jails," *New York Times*, March 6, 2005, 1.

6. See generally "War on Terror Is 'Inaccurate' Label for War on Insurgency," *Inside the Navy* 18 (June 20, 2005). But see Richard W. Stevenson, "President Makes It Clear: Phrase is 'War on Terror,'" *New York Times*, August 4, 2005, A12.

7. See Johannes Morsink, *The Universal Declaration of Human Rights: Origins, Drafting, and Intent* (Philadelphia: University of Pennsylvania Press, 1999), 36–91 (explaining the role of World War II as a catalyst for the human rights protections in the Universal Declaration of Human Rights).

8. The U.S. Department of Justice has used this term since the late 1980s.

9. See Dana Priest, "CIA's Assurances on Transferred Suspects Doubted," *Washington Post*, March 17, 2005, A1 (quoting an unnamed U.S. official as saying, "They say they are not abusing them, and that satisfies the legal requirement, but we all know they do").

10. See Hurst Hannum, "The Status of the Universal Declaration of Human Rights in National and International Law," 25 *Georgia Journal of International and Compartative Law* 25 (1996): 287, 352–53 ("The most important multilateral treaty in the field of human rights is perhaps the UN Charter. . . . Legally and politically, it is the Universal Declaration of Human Rights which defines the Charter's human rights provisions.").

11. Hannum, "The Status of the Universal Declaration of Human Rights," 289.

12. See U.N. Economic and Social Council [ECOSOC], "Commentary on Human Rights," *Preliminary Report by the Special Representative of the Commission, Mr. Andres Aguilar, Appointed Pursuant to Resolution 1984/54, on the Human Rights Situation in the Islamic Republic of Iran*, para. 14–15, UN Doc. E/CN.4/1985/20, February 1, 1985.

13. See Hannum, "The Status of the Universal Declaration of Human Rights," supra note 11, 312–17.

14. *Universal Declaration of Human Rights* art. 3, G.A. Res. 217A, 71, UN GAOR, 3d Sess., lst plen. mtg., UN Doc A/810, December 12, 1948.

15. *Universal Declaration of Human Rights*, art. 5.

16. *Universal Declaration of Human Rights*, art. 6.

17. *Universal Declaration of Human Rights*, art. 9.

18. *Universal Declaration of Human Rights*, arts. 10 and 11.

19. See U.S. Department of State, *Country Reports on Human Rights Practices for 2004*, 2004. http://www.state.gov/g/drl/rls/hrrpt/2004 (noting that receiving countries' use of torture is "systematic" [Egypt, Morocco, Saudi Arabia, and Uzbekistan], or "a common occurrence" [Syria]).

20. See, e.g., McCaffrey, "Canadian Sent to Syrian Prison," supra note 4 (reporting that "most of the detainees are never heard from again").

21. See *Universal Declaration of Human Rights*, supra note 14, art. 10 ("Everyone is entitled in full equality to a fair and public hearing by an independent and impartial tribunal, in the determination of his rights and obligations and of any criminal charge against him."); *Universal Declaration of Human Rights*, art. 11(i) ("Everyone charged with a penal offence has the right to be presumed innocent until proved guilty according to law in a public trial at which he has had all the guarantees necessary for his defense.").

22. See *Universal Declaration of Human Rights*, pmbl.

23. *International Covenant on Civil and Political Rights*, entered into force Mar. 23, 1976, S. Exec. Doc. E, 95-2, 999 UNT.S. 171.

24. See United Nations, "Human Rights Committee," *General Comment 31, Nature of the General Legal Obligation on States Parties to the Covenant*, UN Doc. CCPR/C/21/Rev.1/Add.13, 2004, para. 10:
State Parties are required by Article 2, Paragraph 1, to respect and to ensure the Covenant rights to all persons who may be within their territory and to all persons subject to their jurisdiction. This means that a State Party must respect and ensure the rights laid down in the Covenant to anyone within the power or effective control of that State Party, even if not situated within the territory of the State Party. . . . This principle [that enjoyment of the Covenant is not limited by nationality] also applies to those within the power or effective control of the forces of a State Party acting outside its territory, regardless of the circumstances in which such power or effective control was obtained.

25. The Special Rapporteur on torture stated the obligation under Article 2(l) in broad terms: "[I]t is the essential responsibility of States . . . to prevent such acts [of torture and other forms of ill-treatment] by not bringing persons under the control of other States if there are substantial grounds for believing that they would be in danger of being subjected to torture." See *Report of the Special Rapporteur on Torture and Other Cruel, Inhuman or Degrading Treatment or Punishment*, para. 27, delivered to the General Assembly, UN Doc. A/59/324, September 1, 2004.

26. See *International Covenant on Civil and Political Rights*, supra note 24, art. 7.

27. See *International Covenant on Civil and Political Rights*, art. 10(1).

28. United Nations, *Human Rights Committee*, 60th Sess., Comm. No. 692/1996, UN Doc. CCPR/C/60/D/692/1996, para. 3.3, July 28, 1997.

29. Cf. "Soering v. United Kingdom," 161 Eur. Ct. H.R. (ser. A) para. 91, 1989

(holding that article 3 of the European Convention for the Protection of Human Rights and Fundamental Freedoms, which provides that no one shall be subjected to torture or to inhuman or degrading treatment or punishment, is implicated when there is a real risk that a person will be subjected to such treatment or punishment upon return). The Human Rights Committee has cited favorably to Soering in interpreting article 7 obligations. See "Kindler v. Canada," Comm. No. 470/1991, UN Doc. CCPR/C/48/D/470/1991, para. 15.3, July 30, 1993.

30. See, e.g., McCaffrey, supra note 4 (reporting that "most of the detainees are never heard from again").

31. See David Weissbrodt et al., *International Human Rights: Law, Policy, and Process* 9, 3d. ed. (2001).

32. *International Covenant on Economic, Social and Cultural Rights*, entered into force January 3, 1976, 993 UNT.S. 3.

33. Compare, e.g., *International Covenant on Economic, Social and Cultural Rights*, supra note 33, art. 2(1) ("Each State Party to the present Covenant undertakes to take steps, with a view to achieving progressively the full realization of the rights recognized in the present Covenant by all appropriate means, including particularly the adoption of legislative measures."), with *Convention against Torture and Other Cruel, Inhuman or Degrading Treatment or Punishment*, opened for signature February 4, 1985, S. TREATY Doc. No. 100–20, 1465 UNT.S. 85 ("Each State Party shall take effective legislative. Administrative, judicial or other measures to prevent acts of torture in any territory under its jurisdiction.").

34. See *International Covenant on Economic, Social and Cultural Rights*, supra note 33, art. 11(1).

35. *International Covenant on Economic, Social and Cultural Rights*, art. 11(2).

36. *International Covenant on Economic, Social and Cultural Rights*, art. 12(1).

37. *International Covenant on Economic, Social and Cultural Rights*, art. 10.

38. *Convention against Torture*, supra note 33, art. 2(1).

39. *Convention against Torture*, art 1(1).

40. *Convention against Torture*, art. 16.

41. *Convention against Torture*, art. 3(1).

42. *Convention against Torture*, art. 3(2).

43. *Convention against Torture*, art. 2(2) ("No exceptional circumstances whatsoever, whether a state of war or a threat of war, internal political instability or any other public emergency, may be invoked as a justification of torture.").

44. *Convention against Torture*, arts. 4(1), 5, 7.

45. See generally J. Herman Burgers and Hans Danelius, "The United Nations Convention against Torture: A Handbook on the Convention against Torture and OTHER Cruel, Inhuman or Degrading Treatment or Punishment" 3, 1988 (tracing the actions and deliberations of the United Nations General Assembly and United Nations Commission on Human Rights between 1977 and 1984 that led up to the entry into force of the Convention against Torture).

46. See Michael Scheuer, "Talk of the Nation: Policy of Extraordinary Rendition" (National Public Radio, April 7, 2005).

47. See Burgers and Danelius, "The United Nations Convention against Torture," supra note 45, at 126–27.

48. Burgers and Danelius, "The United Nations Convention against Torture," 125. In the Refugee Convention, protection is given to refugees, i.e., to persons who are persecuted in their country of origin for a special reason, whereas article 3 of the present Convention applies to any person who, for whatever reason, is in danger of being subjected to torture if handed over to another country.

49. See Comm. No. 15/1994, *Report of the Committee against Torture*, UN GAOR, 50th Sess., Supp. No. 44, 45, UN Doc. A/50/44, Annex V, 1994.

50. See *Report of the Committee against Torture*, para. 12.5, 55. It is important to note that simply because a receiving country is a party to the Convention against Torture does not ensure that transfer to that country comports with the protections of Article 3. See "Alan v. Switzerland," Comm. No. 21/1995, *Report of the Committee against Torture*, UN GAOR, 51st Sess., Supp. No. 44, para. 11.5, at 75, UN Doc. A/51/44, Annex V, 1995.

51. Comm. No. 233/2003, *Report of the Committee Against Torture*, UN GAOR, 60th Sess., Supp. No. 44, para. 13.4, 34, UN Doc. A/60/44, Annex VIII, 2003.

52. *Convention against Torture*, supra note 33, art. 1(1).

53. See Jehl and Johnston, "Rule Change," supra note 5 ("[I]n interviews, a half-dozen current and former government officials said they believed that, in practice, the administration's approach may have involved turning a blind eye to torture.").

54. All of the countries mentioned above as participants in extraordinary rendition, including Afghanistan and Iraq, where the most recent armed conflicts have occurred, are High Contracting Parties to all four Geneva Conventions. See U.S. Department of State, *Treaties in Force 3*, 2004. http://www.state.gov/documents/organization/38569.pdf

55. See *Geneva Convention Relative to the Treatment of Prisoners of War*, adopted August 12, 1949, 6 U.S.T. 3316, 75 UNT.S. 135.

56. "Geneva Convention," art. 4(a)(1).

57. "Geneva Convention," 4(a)(1)(2).

58. The four requirements are, "(a) That of being commanded by a person responsible for his subordinates; (b) That of having a fixed distinctive sign recognizable at a distance; (c) That of carrying arms openly; (d) That of conducting their operations in accordance with the laws and customs of war." Id. art. 4(a)(2). The authoritative commentary of Jean S. Pictet confirms that these requirements are only imposed on members of resistance movements, and not on members of the armed forces of a Party to the conflict. See 4 Int'l Comm. of the Red Cross, "Commentary," IV *Geneva Convention Relative to the Protection of Civilian Persons in the Time of War* 50 (Jean S. Pictet ed., 1958).

59. "Geneva Convention," supra note 55, art. 130.

60. III Int'l Comm. of the Red Cross, "Commentary," *Geneva Convention Relative to the Treatment of Prisoners of War* 627 (Jean S. Pictet ed., 1958).

61. "Geneva Convention," supra note 55, art. 12, para. 3.

62. *Geneva Convention Relative to the Protection of Civilian Persons in Time of War*, August 12, 1949, 6 U.S.T. 3516, 75 UNT.S. 287.

63. *Geneva Convention*, art. 147.

64. *Rep. of the Human Rights Council on Its Sixty-First Session*, UN Doc. A/61/448, at 7–8, December 8, 2006.

65. *Rep. of the Human Rights Council*, art. 2.
66. *Rep. of the Human Rights Council*, art. 1.
67. *Rep. of the Human Rights Council*, art. 6.
68. *Rep. of the Human Rights Council*, art. 7.
69. *Rep. of the Human Rights Council*, art. 17(3)(a)-(h).
70. *Rep. of the Human Rights Council*, art. 18(1)(a)-(g).

Abu Ghraib

Nancy Maron

The perpetrator, the falsely accused, the tortured, the torturers, Christ like-figure, the scapegoat. Why does he/she have those wires attached to his/her body?

—Nancy Maron

Editors' note: During the United States-led invasion of Iraq, members of the U.S. Army and Central Intelligence Agency (CIA) indulged in an orgy of torture, physical and sexual abuse, sodomy, rape, and murder at Abu Ghraib Prison, then took pictures of their crimes. These documents of profound violations of the United Nations Universal Declaration of Human Rights—the Geneva Conventions—were discovered, prompting an investigation. The George W. Bush administration claimed the abuses were isolated events. But human rights organizations note that the cruelties at Abu Ghraib were part of a pattern at other U.S. detention centers in Iraq, as well as Afghanistan, Guantanamo Bay, and elsewhere. Bush apologized, promising that perpetrators of the maltreatment would be brought to justice, then falsely pledging that he would prevent future abuse. Lower-ranking officials were blamed. Seventeen soldiers and officers were removed from duty. Thirteen soldiers were variously convicted, and a brigadier general demoted to the rank of colonel. (For a timeline of events, please see https://www.cnn.com/2013/10/30/world/meast/iraq-prison-abuse-scandal-fast-facts/index.html)

In the run up to the invasion, the U.S. Justice Department prepared "Torture Memos," authorizing "enhanced interrogation" and arguing that the Geneva Conventions did not apply to American interrogators abroad. Several Supreme Court decisions following Abu Ghraib overturned the Bush policy, ruling that the Geneva Conventions do apply. But in 2022, the court upheld the government's privilege to invoke "state secrets." (See https://www.vox.com/2022/3/3/22959954/supreme-court-torture-poland-zubaydah-state-secrets-stephen-breyer-neil-gorsuch)

For a more thorough discussion of the prohibition of torture as stated in the Universal Declaration of Human Rights, please see chapter 4, David Weissbrodt, "Extraordinary Rendition: A Human Rights Analysis."

FIVE

Lives in Limbo

Afghanistan's Epidemic of Disappearances

Dallas Mazoori and Stefan Schmitt

Throughout Afghanistan's four decades of armed conflict, tens of thousands of Afghans have been subjected to enforced disappearance by State agents or non-State actors—arrested, detained, their whereabouts or fates concealed, placing them outside the protection of the law. Most are believed to have been tortured and summarily executed, their bodies disposed of in mass graves, some of which have been uncovered. Thousands more went missing during military operations, displacement or through irregular channels of migration. Many families of the disappeared and missing will never know the fates of their loved one or the circumstances in which they disappeared. They are condemned to a life of eternal limbo, a suffering that, in the case of an enforced disappearance, has itself been recognized as a human rights violation. Such is the scale of enforced disappearances in Afghanistan since the Saur Revolution of April 1978 that there is seldom an Afghan family that hasn't experienced the disappearance of a loved one. Despite the scale of Afghanistan's enforced disappearance epidemic, there has been little acknowledgement or any real effort to find the disappeared or hold the perpetrators to account.

Patterns of Enforced Disappearances in Afghanistan

On April 27, 1978, a coup d'état in the capital Kabul brought to power the *khalq* faction of the *hezb-e demokratik-e khalq-e Afghanistan*, or People's Democratic Party of Afghanistan (PDPA), in what became known as the Saur Revolution.[1] Under the leadership of Nur Mohammad Taraki and Hafizullah Amin, the PDPA set out to radically transform Afghanistan from a culturally and religiously conservative tribal society into a modern communist state. Between April and November 1978, the new order was promulgated in eight decrees. Reforms relating to land redistribution, compulsory education, and abolishment of the bride price were opposed by much of the population, the forced abolition of such practices on the local level even more so. Resistance to the PDPA's agenda was met with brutal repression, including widespread arbitrary arrests, disappearances, and summary executions of those perceived to be in opposition. Those targeted included intellectuals, religious leaders, landowners, former government officials, members of the royal family, teachers, ethnic minorities, and even those from within the PDPA's own *parcham* (banner or flag) faction. Typically, uniformed PDPA officers or plain-clothed agents of the regime's intelligence service, *da Afghanistan gato satonki idara* (AGSA)[2] or Department for Protecting the Interests of Afghanistan, would arrest victims at home, transfer them to prison or another place of detention and subsequently execute them. At the epicenter of this brutal architecture was the notorious Pul-e Charkhi prison on the eastern outskirts of Kabul.

The following account of one woman's efforts to find her husband is indicative of the experiences of the families of the disappeared

> My husband promised me that we would be going downtown, and I was waiting for him, but he didn't come home. I passed the night waiting for him. The next day my husband's uncle went to his office and asked his colleagues where he was, and his colleagues told him that a few people had come and had put him in the car and had taken him away. . . . I went several times to AGSA and asked after the health of my husband. But they didn't show him to me, instead they said he was not there. I went to Pul-e Charkhi prison several times and took his clothes for him. But the officials of Pul-e Charkhi said that he was not there. . . . From that time on I couldn't find my husband. Even when the lists of those killed were published, I couldn't find my husband's name on them.[3]

This pattern of conduct was repeated across the country on a massive scale, with thousands of people being disappeared in the twenty months prior to the Soviet invasion of December 1979. As one man who was detained in Kandahar during this period recalled, "every night, they blindfolded people and tied their hands. During what they called investigations, they pulled people out and beat them and then those people disappeared."[4]

Another detainee, from a northern province, stated that, "every night, at around 9 or 10 pm, officers and soldiers would come with a list which they would read, and take those who responded out of the prison. I was in the prison for four and a half months. Over a period of approximately ten nights, sixty to seventy prisoners were removed from the prison and never seen again."[5]

Following the Soviet invasion in December 1979, Babrak Karmal from the PDPA's parcham faction was installed with Soviet support as the new president. An initial amnesty saw the release of more than two thousand prisoners from the infamous Pul-e Charkhi prison and, in February 1980, the Ministry of Planning was authorized to register missing persons based on information received from their families and friends. The registration effort was reportedly abandoned just three weeks later, after twenty-five thousand persons had been reported missing, a larger figure than previously estimated.[6] Human rights violations continued, with a shift toward targeting those who supported or were perceived to support the *mujahidin*, armed opposition groups that emerged to fight the regime.

One of the first actions of the new administration was the creation of the *khidamat-e ettila'at-e dawlati* (KhAD) or State Information Services, a successor to previous intelligence agencies modelled on the Soviet *Komitet Gosudarstvennoy Bezopasnosti* (KGB) or Committee for State Security, and the East German *Staatssicherheitsdienst* (Stasi) or State Security Service. Disappearances were almost always accompanied by torture in prisons such as Pul-e Charkhi, Sedarat, and Shash Darak in Kabul, and in places of detention throughout the country. Thousands of detainees were executed on the orders of a Special Revolutionary Court that afforded no due process and no prospect of appeal to those who came before it. In its efforts to wipe out the mujahidin, the Soviets subjected the countryside to aerial bombardment and scorched-earth tactics, decimating entire districts. As millions of Afghans fled the country, families frequently became separated, not knowing whether their missing family member had been arrested, conscripted, or killed, or had managed to seek refuge in another district, across the Afghan border, or in a third country. These missing people were not disappeared within the legal definition of enforced disappearance;[7] however, this fact does not lessen the pain and suffering experienced by their families and communities.

As the mujahidin took control of rural and urban areas, they too engaged in abuses perpetrated against the civilian population. The historical narrative widely disseminated outside of Afghanistan during the latter stages of the Cold War was one characterized by romantic notions of the mujahidin as freedom fighters, liberating their people from the scourge of communism and Soviet occupation. In reality, many Afghans recall the mujahidin as little more than thieves and murderers. A woman from Kandahar related her daughter's kidnapping at the hands of the mujahidin in the early years of Babrak Karmal's rule as follows

> All the streets became full of mujahidin taking all the houses under their rule and doing wrong to people. They killed some people in their houses. They disgraced some women and burned the houses. In our house they shot my husband and took my young girl away with them. They left all the people shocked and saddened with the grief of their loved ones. My dear girl is still disappeared, and we don't know if she is alive or dead. My husband became ill with tuberculosis because of what happened to his daughter and the stigma of it and passed away after two years. I am still alive with my three remaining girls, but the pain of my missing daughter is still tearing at my heart.[8]

Following the fall of Kabul to the mujahidin in April 1992, new patterns of enforced disappearance emerged at the hands of the various armed groups that now sought to control the capital. All mujahidin groups, including the government of the Islamic State of Afghanistan, committed violations with impunity. Arbitrary arrest, detention, torture, rape, disappearances, and summary executions were characteristically perpetrated upon ethnic lines. One man who was detained in Kabul in February 1993 stated that "of the forty other people who were imprisoned with me, we never heard of them again, or found them. We have talked to their families: none of them was ever returned, and no one ever saw them again."[9]

The Cooperation Centre for Afghanistan (CCA) documented 671 disappearances in West Kabul from 1992 to 1995 with the objectives of compiling and disseminating accurate information on the missing, assisting the families of the missing and facilitating the release of the detainees, where possible.[10] Although CCA researchers were able to secure the release of a small number of detainees after confronting commanders, such instances were rare. Commanders, regardless of affiliation, would systematically deny that their forces were keeping detainees and almost all the 671 disappeared individuals documented were never seen again.[11]

The Taliban emerged from the lawlessness and abuses that were replicated by the mujahidin in Kandahar.[12] Like its predecessors, the Taliban engaged in arbitrary arrest, detention, torture, disappearances, and summary executions, targeting ethnic and religious minorities in particular for such treatment. When the Taliban captured the northern city of Mazar-e Sharif on August 8, 1998, they massacred at least two thousand and as many as six-to-eight thousand predominantly Shi'a Hazara civilians.[13] Mullah Abdul Manan Niazi, the Taliban-appointed Governor of Balkh Province, delivered speeches at mosques throughout the city inciting the destruction of Shi'a Hazaras. Such speeches typically denounced Hazaras as Shi'a and infidels, announced that Hazaras would be killed wherever they went, and that anyone who was hiding Hazaras would suffer the same fate. Male Hazaras who were not killed immediately on the streets or in their houses were rounded up by Taliban forces and taken away. On the morning of August 9, 1998, trucks were parked in front of Shi'a mosques and all those who came out were placed in them and taken to prison. Once the prison in Mazar-e Sharif was full, prisoners were transferred to prisons elsewhere in Afghanistan, particularly in Shiberghan, Herat, and Kandahar. At least ten to twelve large metal container trucks, each containing an estimated 110 to 130 Hazara prisoners, were taken to Shiberghan during the first six days after August 8. In at least two instances, almost all the prisoners inside died of asphyxiation, although many other trucks transported the majority of their human cargo without this result.[14] The UN Special Rapporteur found that "many, possibly several thousand persons, were brought to Hairatan and Shiberghan for investigation, and most are believed to have been killed. . . . Some containers were filled with children (boys and girls), who were taken to an unknown destination after their parents had been killed."[15] The fate of many of those detained during the massacre in Mazar-e Sharif remains unknown.

The Taliban ruthlessly enforced edicts banning women from education, work, leaving the home without a male relative, and appearing in public without the *chaadari*, also known as a *burka*. Women whose husbands or other male family members had been killed or disappeared were forced to take extraordinary risks in the hope of being able to feed themselves and their children, as exiting the home with no male guardian made them liable to public beatings, arrest, and detention by the Taliban.

Many of the violations suffered under previous regimes and phases of the armed conflict did not end with the United States military intervention in late 2001 and the subsequent fall of the first Taliban government. A resurgent Taliban and other armed groups, including the Islamic State Khorasan Province (ISKP), continue to massacre civilians throughout the period of the current Islamic Republic of Afghanistan. The government of Afghanistan and its allies have been accused of holding detainees incommunicado, as well as torture, cruel treatment, and outrages upon personal dignity. The Afghan National Police (ANP) in Kandahar have been accused of numerous enforced disappearances throughout the latter stages of this period.[16] One of the better documented cases of disappearances, torture, and arbitrary killings by international forces, the so-called "A-Team Killings," appeared in *Rolling Stone* magazine. It is alleged that United States Special Forces operating in Nerkh district of Wardak Province in 2012 disappeared ten civilians, killing a further eight.[17] It wasn't until family members in search of their missing loved ones began digging up human remains around the former U.S. Special Forces base in Nerkh district in 2013 that the case became public and led to investigations by both the Afghan and U.S. governments. Neither investigation resulted in anything but the arrest of one of the Afghan translators who had been working with the U.S. Special Forces team.

With the fall of Kabul on August 15, 2021, the Taliban returned to power, following their seizure of most of the country in a lightning offensive during the United States' withdrawal. As the world watched with horror, fleeing Afghans fell to their deaths from airplanes, the so-called "Taliban 2.0" went about government departments methodically searching and seizing personnel files, CCTV footage, and data. Their public offer of amnesty to all of those affiliated with the previous government of the Islamic Republic of Afghanistan stood in stark contrast to the situation on the ground, with reports of summary executions and disappearances emerging almost immediately.

For many Afghans, the reality is that while the actors and levels of impunity might have changed, they continue to be victims of the impunity of those that govern their lives, some of whom are well-known power brokers in Afghanistan's modern history.

The Right to the Truth of Families of the Disappeared

For the families of the disappeared, knowing the truth about the circumstances of their loved one's fate may provide some closure, allowing them to move on with their lives. Similarly, a society that has experienced egregious human rights violations may find that acknowledging the truth about what happened allows people to move beyond their own localized narrative of suffering and see that "everyone suffered," thereby contributing to reconciliation. The right to the truth about gross human rights violations is recognized in international human rights law as inalienable and autonomous, linked to the duty and obligation of the State to protect and guarantee human rights, to conduct effective investigations, and provide effective remedy and reparations.[18] It has been endorsed by the United Nations General Assembly,[19] is expressly provided for in treaty,[20] and has been upheld by the regional human rights courts.[21] The right to the truth is most often invoked in relation to enforced disappearances, one of the elements of which is a refusal to acknowledge the deprivation of liberty or concealment of the fate or whereabouts of the disappeared person, placing that person outside the protection of the law. The suffering experienced by the families of the disappeared by a refusal to provide them with information about the whereabouts or fate of a disappeared person has been recognized as a human rights violation by regional human rights courts.[22] The International Court of Justice and International Criminal Tribunal for Former Yugoslavia have held that within the context of a genocide, the suffering of families of the disappeared may constitute serious mental harm as an act of genocide.[23]

Transitional "Justice" in Afghanistan

Afghanistan's transition following the fall of the first Taliban government in 2001 was marred from the outset by the failure of the international community to address the country's decades of armed conflict and egregious human rights violations at the 2001 Bonn Conference. The lack of a long-term vision for the country rooted in accountability and justice as the foundation for a sustainable peace allowed many individuals widely accused of bearing responsibility for war crimes and crimes against humanity to occupy positions of power with the knowledge—and support—of the international community, without fear of being vetted, prosecuted, or ever held to account for their crimes. This resulted in an endemic culture of impunity which fed protracted armed conflict, corruption, refugee flows and the ongoing commission of serious human rights violations and war crimes by State and non-State actors, many of which find their origins back in the late 1970s.

The first significant attempt to address transitional justice came in January 2005 with the publication of the Afghanistan Independent Human Rights Commission (AIHRC) report, *A Call for Justice*. AIHRC was established by Presidential Decree in 2002 and is mandated by article 58 of the Constitution to promote, protect, and monitor human rights. *A Call for Justice* details the results of a national consultation on the issue of past human rights violations and their legacy. The report found that 69 percent of 4,051 respondents identified themselves or their immediate families as victims of human rights violations during the 1978–2001 conflict era.[24] Ninety-five percent of respondents were of the view that it was important to establish the truth about violations,[25] with 76.4 percent of respondents of the view that bringing war criminals to justice would increase stability and bring security.[26] While there was strong support for criminal justice, in a country where fair trial procedures are effectively nonexistent, it bears mentioning that the term "justice" in Afghanistan doesn't necessarily relate to what would be conceived as internationally accepted criminal trials.

The release of the AIHRC report was supposed to be accompanied by the release of a mapping report of open-source accounts of human rights violations that occurred during the 1978–2001 period produced by the United Nations Office of the High Commissioner for Human Rights (OHCHR). UN officials reportedly pressed the High Commissioner, Louise Arbour, not to make the report public, fearing that public release would endanger UN staff, complicate demobilization negotiations with powerful militias, and raise expectations of accountability—something neither the UN nor the government of Afghanistan could provide.[27] The refusal of OHCHR to release a mapping report consolidating what was information already in the public domain is yet another indicator of the reluctance of the international community to promote any form of formal and institutional truth seeking, accountability, or justice for Afghanistan's decades of war crimes and human rights violations.

In 2005, the government of Afghanistan commissioned the drafting of a national transitional justice action plan. The Action Plan on Peace, Reconciliation, and Justice contained five key actions: (1) acknowledging the suffering of the Afghan people; (2) ensuring credible and accountable State institutions; (3) truth-seeking and documentation; (4) promoting reconciliation and the improvement of national unity; and (5) establishing effective and reasonable accountability mechanisms. Although the Action Plan provided a useful advocacy tool for Afghanistan's nascent civil society, there was little if any political will to implement it, and it remained almost entirely unimplemented at its expiration. Despite Key Actions 4 and 5 providing that there should be no amnesty for war crimes, crimes against humanity, and other gross violations of human rights, in 2008, a controversial amnesty law, the National Reconciliation, General Amnesty, and National Stability Law, came into effect. The law purports to provide a blanket amnesty to all of those involved in Afghanistan's decades of conflict, including those currently involved in hostilities, provided that they join the peace process and accept the Constitution.[28] In July 2010, the Afghanistan Peace and Reintegration Program (APRP) was launched with the stated aim of facilitating the reintegration of fighters in armed opposition groups. The High Peace Council, established to oversee its implementation, has been criticized for its composition, lack of transparency, and the perception that reintegration only benefits criminals, as well as the assumption that the Taliban and other armed opposition groups are interested in peace—an assumption at odds with the daily reality of mass murder of Afghan civilians perpetrated by such groups.

In 2012, in a rare case of Afghan "justice" following twenty years of pretrial detention at the hands of different armed groups and seven years of judicial proceedings in which he was initially sentenced to death, Assadullah Sarwari, the former head of AGSA, was convicted by the Military Appeals Court of crimes including misuse of power and neglect of duty, illegal detention, murder, and treason and sentenced to a twenty-year prison term. He was released from prison in 2016.

In November 2017, the Prosecutor of the International Criminal Court (ICC) requested authorization from the Court's Pre-Trial Chamber to open an investigation into alleged war crimes and crimes against humanity committed on the territory of Afghanistan in the period since May 1, 2003, the date that Afghanistan's accession to the Rome Statute entered into force, as well as other alleged crimes that have a nexus to the armed conflict in Afghanistan and were committed on the territory of other State Parties since July 1, 2002.[29] In April 2019, the Pre-Trial Chamber rejected the prosecutor's request, finding that the commencement of an investigation would not be "in the interests of justice," essentially putting it in the too-hard basket. The prosecutor appealed this decision and on March 5, 2020, the Court's Appeals Chamber overturned the Pre-Trial Chamber's decision, unanimously authorizing the prosecutor to commence an investigation.[30] The prosecutor's request does not contemplate investigating the crime against humanity of enforced disappearance. However, it does contemplate investigating conduct frequently associated with enforced disappearance, such as the crime against humanity of imprisonment or other severe deprivation of physical liberty and the war crimes of cruel treatment, torture, and outrages upon personal dignity. Despite the fact that enforced disappearance is widely regarded as a continuing crime, the Court only has jurisdiction over enforced disappearances if they occurred in the context of a widespread or systematic attack directed against a civilian population, with the requisite knowledge, after the entry into force of the Rome Statute.[31] This places the overwhelming majority of Afghanistan's enforced disappearances outside the Court's temporal jurisdiction.

In September 2020, purported peace talks between the Taliban and the government of Afghanistan commenced in Doha, Qatar. The Taliban negotiating team included alleged perpetrators of war crimes, most notably commander and former Army Chief of Staff Mullah Fazl Mazlum, one of the "Guantanamo Five" released in a prisoner swap deal in exchange for the American soldier Bowe Bergdahl after more than a decade in Guantanamo Bay. Many Afghans were rightly skeptical about the process, and within a year the Taliban were back in power.

Efforts to Acknowledge and Address Afghanistan's Legacy of Enforced Disappearances

In the absence of a meaningful transitional justice process at the State-level, there have been numerous efforts by Afghan civil society, media organizations, and others to acknowledge and document Afghanistan's enforced disappearances.

The AIHRC was mandated by Key Action 3 of the Action Plan to "increase and accelerate efforts to document past human rights abuses in Afghanistan, including on gender-based violence, to complement and enrich the existing work." The AIHRC implemented this key action in the form of a conflict mapping project, which aimed to reconstruct the chain of events of the conflict in Afghanistan between April 27, 1978 (Saur Revolution) and December 5, 2001 (Bonn Conference); ascertain which war crimes and crimes against humanity may have been committed; determine who bears greatest responsibility for the commission of these crimes; and make recommendations for accountability. The program was based upon a similar exercise undertaken in Sierra Leone by the international non-government organization (NGO) No Peace Without Justice (NPWJ). The broader aims and objectives of AIHRC conflict mapping were to contribute to a historical record through on-the-ground information gathering, validate the experiences of victims and assist in the identification of victims and the circumstances of their deaths. Over a number of years, AIHRC researchers conducted 7,890 interviews with witnesses and key people in every province of Afghanistan, 929 of which focused on enforced disappearances. Wherever they went across the country, AIHRC researchers were presented with lists of the disappeared compiled by local communities. It was hoped that by demonstrating that "everyone has suffered," the final conflict mapping report might serve as a foundation for a national reconciliation process. In terms of accountability, it was hoped that the report could be used to vet alleged perpetrators from government posts and might serve as a pre-trial document or foundation upon which criminal investigations—domestic or international—could be built in the future. After several years of work on the conflict mapping report, it became increasingly clear that it too would fall victim to Afghanistan's climate of "acceptable impunity." The report was ultimately deemed too sensitive for public release and as a result has never been published.

Human rights reports, such as those published by the Afghanistan Justice Project and Human Rights Watch, have documented individual incidents and patterns of enforced disappearances. UN Women published an oral history project that focused specifically on women's experiences of violations from 1978–2008, including the impact upon women of the killing or disappearance of male family members.[32] There have been consultations on the legacy of violence, such as those undertaken by the Afghanistan Research and Evaluation Unit and Afghan Civil Society Forum, which have included accounts of family members of the disappeared. The Afghanistan Human Rights and Democracy Organization (AHRDO) has worked extensively with victims and affected communities through arts-based documentation projects including participatory theater and memory boxes. In 2019, AHRDO opened the Afghanistan Centre for Memory and Dialogue, which serves as both a museum and memorial to Afghanistan's war victims. It is important to note that all these projects were funded by international donors hoping to give civil society a chance to participate in Afghanistan's political process. The result, however, was that both the donors and the few Afghan civil society organizations involved weren't given any mandate, formal recognition, or access to participate in any justice process.

One of the most enduring examples of the public consciousness surrounding enforced disappearances in Afghanistan is found in the form of a radio program titled "In Search of the Missing." Born out of producer/correspondent Zarif Nazar's search for his own missing relatives, the program has been broadcast biweekly, since February 2004, on Radio Azadi, one of the country's most popular radio stations. Family members and people "in search of the missing" record a message regarding their missing loved one via telephone message, Facebook, or email. A typical message contains information about the missing or disappeared person, where they are from, where they were last seen and provides contact details should anyone have any information about the person. The messages are then compiled and played during each program, which has been credited with a number of family reunions.

In 2006, the International Forensic Program at the U.S. NGO, Physicians for Human Rights (PHR), was asked by the United Nations Assistance Mission in Afghanistan (UNAMA) to assess the issue of mass graves in Afghanistan, in particular one of the country's more prominent reported mass graves at Pul-e Charkhi. PHR subsequently worked for the next decade to build local capacity in crime-scene documentation and mass-grave exhumation techniques. A paraprofessional mass grave team trained by PHR in 2010 mobilized to form the Afghanistan Forensic Science Organization (AFSO), an NGO that advocates for the protection of mass graves from unlawful destruction and the use of forensic documentation tools to work toward determining the identity of the victims. In 2016, the team conducted the first professional mass grave exhumation in Afghanistan in Bamyan province. The remains of at least seven males ranging in age between seventeen and seventy years were exhumed, some of which displayed gunshot wounds. As no potential family members came forward to claim the remains, which might have allowed for DNA reference samples to be taken for the purposes of identification, the remains were reburied with dignity in accordance with traditional Islamic burial rites. Unfortunately, there has never been any political will, domestically or internationally, for an integrated human identification effort that could identify the disappeared buried in Afghanistan's many mass graves.

On September 18, 2013, the greatest acknowledgement to date of Afghanistan's epidemic of enforced disappearances came with the publication by the Netherlands National Prosecutor's Office and National Police of a list of 4,782 names of those executed by the PDPA regime in 1978–1979.[33] The list was simultaneously published in Afghanistan by the daily newspaper *8 sobh*. Dutch investigators obtained the list during their examination into Amanullah Osman, the former chief of AGSA's Interrogation Department, who was suspected of having committed war crimes, including torture, and who had unsuccessfully sought asylum in the Netherlands. The list was made public following the death of the suspect and subsequent end of the investigation. The Netherlands had previously prosecuted the former head of the *KhAD-e nezami* or Military Intelligence Service, Hesamuddin Hesam, and a former head of its Interrogation Department, Habibullah Jalalzoy, for torture offenses and sentenced them to twelve and nine years in prison respectively. Across Afghanistan and the world, families who found their relatives' names on the list held funerals for them, decades after their disappearance. One individual, now living in Australia, described the impact of his father's disappearance and finding his name on the list

> The impact of my father's disappearance has been huge on every member of my family. Personally, I lost part of my childhood. I suddenly became the eldest male member of the family at the age of seven. I had to attend most of the important social gatherings to fill in for my father. We had to live with the unknown. We lived with hope that he might come back. We have hardly accepted that he is dead. Maybe our minds know that he is "gone," but our hearts are still not convinced. The release of the list has brought some form of closure for some of us. We became able to mourn and say and hear things that we did not dare to say and hear before. But I don't think complete closure will ever be possible.
>
> Justice for the death of my father would be to know more about how everything had happened. For me justice is not to see a lengthy criminal trial but to be able to know how my father's last days were. Justice for me is to know as much as possible.[34]

The absence of a meaningful transitional justice process in Afghanistan has denied many families their right to know the truth about what happened to their disappeared relatives. Documentation projects that might have provided some answers have fallen victim to the very impunity that they sought to address. Evidence of the fate of the disappeared lies in the human remains found in the country's many mass graves, but there is no international and hence no national political will for exhumations. Identification of the victims and repatriation of their remains to their families remains as elusive as peace for the country. The publication of the list of 4,782 Afghans executed by the PDPA regime in 1978–1979 confirmed the fears of many Afghans that their disappeared relatives were dead, however, for many families, the tyranny of not knowing what happened to their loved ones continues.

Notes

1. The PDPA had been established in January 1965 in Kabul, with many of its founding members belonging to Marxist study circles at Kabul University. The party was split into two factions, *Khalq* (people), which was in power from April 1978 until December 1979 under the leadership of Presidents Nur Mohammad Taraki and Hafizullah Amin; and *Parcham* (banner or flag), which came to power with the Soviet invasion in December 1979, led by Presidents Babrak Karmal and Najibullah. The *khalq* faction drew much of its support from newly educated rural Pashtuns whereas the more moderate parcham faction was more ethnically diverse and urban. Internal purges, including the enforced disappearance of parchamis by khalqis and vice versa, were common.

2. Later AGSA was renamed *kargari istikhbarati muassisa* (KAM) or Workers' Intelligence Department.

3. Interview conducted by Afghanistan Independent Human Rights Commission (AIHRC), January 2010.

4. Interview conducted by AIHRC, April 2007.

5. Interview conducted by AIHRC, April 2009.

6. UN Commission on Human Rights, *Report on the Situation of Human Rights in Afghanistan Prepared by the Special Rapporteur, Mr. Felix Ermacora, in Accordance with Commission on Human Rights Resolution 1985/38*, UN Doc E/CN.4/1986/24, February 17, 1986, 11.

7. Article 2 of the *International Convention for the Protection of All Persons from Enforced Disappearance* defines enforced disappearance as the arrest, detention, abduction or any other form of deprivation of liberty by agents of the State or by persons or groups of persons acting with the authorization, support, or acquiescence of the State, followed by a refusal to acknowledge the deprivation of liberty or by concealment of the fate or whereabouts of the disappeared person, which places such a person outside the protection of the law. Article 3 of the Convention obliges State Parties to take appropriate measures to investigate and prosecute acts of enforced disappearance carried out by persons or groups acting without the authorization, support or acquiescence of the State. Article 7(2)(i) of the Rome Statute of the International Criminal Court defines the crime against humanity of enforced disappearance as the arrest, detention, or abduction of persons by, or with the authorization, support, or acquiescence of, a State or a political organization, followed by a refusal to acknowledge that deprivation of freedom or to give information on the fate or whereabouts of those persons, with the intention of removing them from the protection of the law for a prolonged period of time (when committed as part of a widespread or systematic attack directed against any civilian population, with knowledge of the attack). The differences in definition may be attributed to the different purposes of international human rights law (State responsibility) and international criminal law (individual criminal responsibility). Afghanistan is a State Party to the Rome Statute but not the Convention.

8. UN Women, *Like a Bird with Broken Wings: Afghan Women Oral History 1978–2008* (Kabul: UN Women, 2013), 34.

9. Human Rights Watch, *Blood-Stained Hands: Past Atrocities in Kabul and Afghanistan's Legacy of Impunity* (New York: Human Rights Watch, 2005), 89–90. https://www.hrw.org/reports/2005/afghanistan0605/afghanistan0605.pdf

10. Cooperation Center for Afghanistan, *The Prisoners and the Missing, Kabul, Afghanistan 1992–1995* (Peshawar: Cooperation Centre for Afghanistan, 1996), ii.

11. Human Rights Watch, *Blood-Stained Hands*, 51.

12. The Taliban ("students," a plural of the Arabic) are a fundamentalist Sunni Islamic movement which emerged from the anarchy of the mujahidin period in Kandahar in 1994, under the leadership of Mullah Mohammad Omar. Since 2016, the Taliban's leader has been Mawlawi Hibatullah Akhundzada.

13. Shi'a Islam or Shi'ism is one of the two main branches of Islam. Shi'a believe that the Islamic prophet Mohammad designated his cousin and son-in-law Ali ibn Abi Talib as his successor. This view contrasts with that of Sunni Islam, whose adherents believe that Mohammad did not appoint a successor before his death and consider the prophet's companion, Abu Bakr to be the rightful caliph. Hazaras are one of Afghanistan's largest, and most persecuted, ethnic minorities. Their distinctive Asian appearance and majority adherence to Shi'a Islam have seen them endure persecution since before the establishment of the modern Afghan State.

14. Human Rights Watch, *Afghanistan: The Massacre in Mazar-I Sharif* (1998), 11.

15. *Interim Report on the Situation of Human Rights in Afghanistan Submitted by the Special Rapporteur of the Commission on Human Rights in Accordance with General Assembly Resolution 52/145 and Economic and Social Council Decision 1998/267*, UN Doc A/53/539, October 26, 1998, Annex, 5–6.

16. *Treatment of Conflict-Related Detainees: Implementation of Afghanistan's National Plan on the Elimination of Torture*, UNAMA, April 2017, 33–34. https://unama.unmissions.org/sites/default/files/treatment_of_conflict-related_detainees_24_april_2017.pdf

17. Matthieu Aikins, "The A-Team Killings," *Rolling Stone*, November 6, 2013, https://www.rollingstone.com/interactive/feature-a-team-killings-afghanistan-special-forces/

18. OHCHR, *Promotion and Protection of Human Rights: Study on the Right to the Truth*, UN Doc E/CN.4/2006/91, February 8, 2006. thttps://digitallibrary.un.org/record/567521

19. *Declaration of the Basic Principles of Justice for Victims of Crime and Abuse of Power*, UN Doc A/RES/40/34, November 29, 1985; *Basic Principles and Guidelines on the Right to a Remedy and Reparations for Victims of Gross Violations of International Human Rights Law and Serious Violations of International Humanitarian Law*, UN Doc A/RES/60/147, December 16, 2005, arts. 22(b), 24; *Proclamation of 24 March as the International Day for the Right to the Truth Concerning Gross Human Rights Violations and for the Dignity of Victims*, UN Doc A/RES/65/196, December 21, 2010.

20. *International Convention for the Protection of All Persons from Enforced Disappearance*, UN Doc A/61/488 (2006) entered into force December 23, 2010, 2716 UNTS 3, arts. 18, 24(2); *Protocol Additional to the Geneva Conventions of 12 August 1949 and Relating to the Protection of Victims of International Armed Conflicts* (1977) entered into force December 7, 1978, 1125 UNTS 3, art. 32.

21. "Velásquez Rodríguez v. Honduras," *Inter-American Court of Human Rights*, Ser. C, No. 4, July 29, 1988, 181.

22. See, for example, "Kurt v. Turkey," no 24276/94, *European Court of Human Rights*, May 25, 1998, 134; "Bazorkina v. Russia," no 69481/01, *European Court of Human Rights*, July 27, 2006, 146.

23. "Application of the Convention on the Prevention and Punishment of the Crime of Genocide (Croatia v Serbia)," *International Court of Justice*, February 3, 2015,356, 160; "Prosecutor v. Karadžić," *ICTY Trial Chamber Judgment*, March 24, 2016, IT-95–5/18-T, 5664–65; "Prosecutor v. Blagojević and Jokić," *ICTY Trial Chamber Judgment*, January 17, 2005, IT-02–60-T, 653; "Prosecutor v. Popović," *ICTY Trial Chamber Judgment*, June 10, 2010, IT-05–88-T, 846.

24. *A Call for Justice* (Kabul: Afghanistan Independent Human Rights Commission, 2005), 8.

25. *A Call for Justice*, 29.

26. *A Call for Justice*, 17.

27. Patricia Gossman and Sari Kouvo, *Tell Us How This Ends: Transitional Justice and Prospects for Peace in Afghanistan* (Kabul: Afghanistan Analysts Network, 2013), 22.

28. "National Reconciliation, General Amnesty and National Stability Law," Gazette No. 965, *Qaus* 9, 1387 (equivalent to November 29, 2008), art. 3(2).

29. Public redacted version of *Request for Authorization of an Investigation Pursuant to Article 15*, ICC-02/17–7, November 20, 2017.

30. *Judgment on the Appeal against the Decision on the Authorization of an Investigation into the Situation in the Islamic Republic of Afghanistan*, ICC-02/17–138, March 5, 2020.

31. *Elements of Crimes* (The Hague: International Criminal Court, 2011), 11.

32. UN Women, *Like a Bird With Broken Wings*.

33. Searchable versions of the list in English and Dari are available at https://www.om.nl/onderwerpen/internationale-misdrijven/documenten/publicaties/internationale-misdrijven/brochures/map/afghaanse-dodenlijsten/

34. Personal communication with author, October 31, 2017.

SIX

Vanishing Nation

Enforced Disappearance in Syria

Sareta Ashraph and Nicolette Waldman

In March 2011, protests erupted on the streets of the Syrian Arab Republic. By mid-February 2012, the spreading unrest had metastasized into a brutal civil war, the brunt of which has been borne by civilians. Ten years after the violence first ignited, an estimated half a million men, women, and children have been killed.[1] Today, the war grinds on. As the sound and fury of the battlefield begin to subside, a quieter, more insidious violence continues to be perpetrated.

Between March 2011 and August 30, 2020, nearly one hundred thousand Syrians have been forcibly disappeared.[2] Most are adult men who have been arrested or abducted from their homes, workplaces, universities, and at checkpoints. Others vanished while seeking or providing treatment at hospitals and clinics. The majority—84,371 people, an estimated 85 percent[3]—have been seized by agents of the Syrian government.[4] The government's use of enforced disappearance to target actual and perceived opponents, and to crush restive sections of Syrian society, long predates both the current conflict and the tenure of President Bashar al-Assad,[5] but accelerated sharply during Syria's most recent descent into violence.

Those abducted by anti-government armed groups are often taken as hostages, their detention publicized so as to trade them for ransom or to facilitate a prisoner exchange. The Islamic State of Iraq and Al-Sham

(ISIS), which emerged in Syria in 2013 and lost the last of its territory in March 2019, made greater use of enforced disappearance. As of August 2020, the armed group had been found to be responsible for more than 8 percent of all confirmed disappearances in Syria.[6]

Syria's Criminal Code does not criminalize enforced disappearances as an autonomous crime. Any act of enforced disappearance, however, violates fundamental rights enshrined in the 2012 Syrian Constitution,[7] the Arab Charter on Human Rights, and the International Covenant on Civil and Political Rights, to which Syria is party.[8] When committed as part of a widespread or systematic attack directed against a civilian population, enforced disappearance is a crime against humanity.

Civil Unrest (March 2011–February 2012)

From the earliest days of Syria's unrest, the government employed the tactic of enforced disappearance to silence and punish its opponents, and to terrorize current and nascent dissenters. Victims were arrested or abducted by intelligence and security officers as well as by the army, sometimes in conjunction with pro-government militias.

Between March and July 2011, the government attacked demonstrators, killing hundreds.[9] As protests were violently dispersed, government forces undertook mass arrests.[10] In restive areas, such as Homs city, the army and security agencies conducted house and hospital searches, arresting and abducting known and suspected demonstrators, activists, and media workers. Hundreds vanished in the first six months of the unrest.[11] Many of those who disappeared in 2011 have not yet reappeared.

As defections mounted, the government turned its attention on its own troops. Those who refused orders or were suspected of harboring anti-government sentiment disappeared following their arrest at military bases.[12] Medical staff who treated protesters also began to vanish.[13]

When the target of a particular arrest could not be found, government forces sometimes arrested or abducted their family members. Defectors and protesters later provided accounts of relatives disappeared in their place.[14]

Civil War (February 2012–Present Day)

By mid-2012, the unrest had spiraled into civil war, drawing in an increasing number of Syrian and international actors. The latter included Hezbollah, Iraqi Shi'a militias, Iranian military advisers, and the political and ultimately military support of Russia, bolstering the Assad Government; the more inconsistent support of the United States, Turkey, Jordan, and the Gulf States to the anti-government armed groups; and foreign fighters who flooded to ISIS from all around the world, particularly after the group's June 2014 declaration of their "caliphate."[15] As armed groups multiplied and the government's response became increasingly ferocious, more civilians became victims of crimes, including enforced disappearance.

The government, faced by a rising armed opposition and in possession of a complex network of holding sites, remained the main perpetrator of enforced disappearance. As defections increased and armed groups seized territory throughout 2012 and into the summer of 2013, it was apparent that the government's attacks, including its use of enforced disappearance, had failed to silence those calling for the fall of Assad's regime.

Yet, the number of people disappeared by the government continued to climb, suggesting that the punitive element of disappearance had moved to the fore. The government's strategy as it sought to reclaim territory was to make life unbearable for civilian populations living in areas controlled by armed groups.[16] This was accomplished by a multi-pronged strategy including intense bombardments of restive localities;[17] the prolonged use of siege warfare;[18] the targeted destruction of medical infrastructure, food and water sources, and schools;[19] and the continued use of enforced disappearance, a gateway to torture and killing. Many believed the enforced disappearance of thousands of men and women was also designed to irreversibly rend the social fabric of communities opposing the government.[20]

Suspected fighters and supporters of anti-government armed groups and their families were targeted. In March 2014, the army searched the Bab Amr neighborhood of Homs city, taking dozens of young men with them as they left. A similar scene unfolded two months later in Hama city, where sons of those killed or disappeared in the Government's 1982 crackdown, also vanished. Any injured civilian seeking medical attention at a national hospital risked being disappeared.[21]

Thousands disappeared traversing the official and makeshift[22] checkpoints mushrooming across Syria. As bombardments and sieges intensified in areas held by armed groups, civilians who fled to find relative safety in government-held areas had no choice but to move through checkpoints. Where cities such as Homs and Aleppo were besieged, some women made the heart-wrenching decision to flee with their young sons and leave their husbands behind, as the sons were growing to an age where they were in danger of being abducted at the encircling checkpoints.

The Syrian government's eventual dominance of the battlefield owed less to their own forces than to external intervention and support. This included Hezbollah's integral role in the recapture of Al-Qusayr in June 2013; the on-the-ground support of Iraqi Shi'a militias; and the logistical, technical, and financial support provided by Iran and Russia. Most significant, however, was the Russian military intervention which officially began in September 2015 and was indispensable to the December 2016 re-taking of Aleppo, the last major city in which anti-government armed groups held territory. As 2020 came to a close, the Syrian Government controlled most of the country, with the northern Syrian province of Idlib being the last remaining stronghold controlled by forces opposed to President Bashar al-Assad.

As the government retook territory, men who were evacuated from rebel-held areas into government-held territory were arrested and disappeared. As families fled the final onslaught on eastern Aleppo in late 2016, they crossed into the west of the city which was controlled by the Government. Government forces, aided by pro-government militias, separated the men from their relatives. Some were forcibly conscripted; hundreds of others reportedly disappeared.[23] None have since been reported as having reappeared.[24]

Opportunists have leveraged the government's widespread use of disappearance for their own benefit, reporting colleagues and acquaintances to Syrian intelligence agencies and pro-government militias for payment or simply to settle personal grievances.[25]

Throughout the conflict, armed groups repeatedly formed, merged, and dissolved. Some were organized, structured units; others were small groups of local men, bearing whatever weapons they could muster. Attempts to bring the armed groups under a central command were ultimately unsuccessful for reasons beyond the scope of this chapter. It is unwise, therefore, to speak of armed groups as a monolith, but it holds true that their use of enforced disappearance—in contrast to various armed groups' involvement in hostage-taking, torture, and/or summary executions—was very limited.[26]

ISIS, however, made greater use of enforced disappearance, as compared to all other armed groups (though not as compared to the government). The Syrian Network for Human Rights (SNHR) estimated that ISIS is responsible for 8,648 individuals being disappeared, constituting approximately 8 percent of all documented disappearances between March 2011 and August 2020. This figure displayed a sharp increase from the height of the group's territorial control between 2014 and 2015;

as of August 2016, the SNHR found that ISIS was responsible for only 1,479 disappearances, representing only 1.98 percent of all documented disappearances.[27] The spike after August 2016 is a direct consequence of the crumbling of ISIS's self-described "caliphate," with the group's last toehold in Syria—Baghuz village in the eastern governorate of Dayr Az-Zawr—lost in March 2019. Civilians who had been previously unreachable could now report the violations they and their families had suffered, including disappearances.[28] As ISIS was driven out of Syria, families who had been living in ISIS-controlled areas came forward to report thousands more disappearances in the hope of receiving any information on the fate of their relatives.[29]

The number of men, women, and children who have reportedly been forcibly disappeared by the government continues to mount. With many Syrian families too terrified to make public inquiries lest they further endanger their disappeared relatives or put their remaining family at risk,[30] the actual number of the disappeared is likely to be much higher that the statistics quoted here suggest. The scale of disappearances during the unrest and subsequent conflict in Syria may not be fully grasped for many years to come.

The Fate of the Disappeared

A minority of those who were disappeared by the government have been released, bringing with them an invaluable and terrifying insight into what those who have vanished suffer. Almost all describe being held in government detention centers where they lived unrecognized existences, cut off from friends, family members, and the outside world for weeks, or, more commonly, months or years.[31]

In August 2020, the Syrian Network for Human Rights established that the vast majority of detainees held by the Syrian Government were subsequently classified as forcibly disappeared persons, at a ratio of approximately 65 percent.[32] The largest proportion of these disappeared between 2011 and 2013. Most were disappeared immediately or shortly after their arrests.[33] Others disappeared later in their detentions, often during transfer from one detention center to another. Former detainees, as well as former guards and officials, have consistently described individuals held by the government after 2011 being subjected to a horrific catalogue of human rights abuses; serious violations of international humanitarian law; and crimes against humanity including not only enforced disappearance, but also torture, rape, murder, and extermination.[34]

Most detainees in Syria are tortured or mistreated from the moment of their arrest, usually in the form of beating. Upon their arrival at a detention facility, many are subjected to more severe and prolonged beatings, commonly referred to by former detainees and guards as "welcome parties."[35] Officials from security and intelligence agencies and prison authorities torture detainees during their interrogations in an effort to extract false "confessions" used as the basis of detainees' convictions in trials that are either flagrantly unfair or, in the case of the Military Field Court, so shambolic they cannot even be considered judicial proceedings.[36] Torture sessions during interrogations usually last several hours and occur periodically over the course of weeks or months. When a detainee is transferred to a new detention center, he or she will usually be subjected to a new round of interrogation and torture.

Some of the most common methods of torture include severe beatings, often with objects such as batons or steel bars; electric shocks; sexual violence including rape; the pulling out of finger- and toenails; and holding detainees in painful stress positions for prolonged periods of time.[37] These methods are often used in combination. Disappeared detainees, the vast majority of whom are men but who also include hundreds of children and thousands of women,[38] are held in appalling conditions. They are systematically denied access to food, water, medicine, medical care, and sanitation, and they are held in filthy cells so overcrowded that detainees are often forced to take turns sleeping. As a result, detainees routinely suffer from scabies, lice, infections, and diseases.[39] Many also develop serious mental illnesses such as psychosis and anxiety disorders.[40]

Since 2011, tens of thousands of disappeared detainees have been killed as a result of torture and inhuman conditions. Many of these deaths are preventable and result from untreated health conditions such as gastrointestinal illnesses and infections. The Human Rights Data Analysis Group, an independent nonprofit organization that analyses human rights violations around the world, found that at least 17,723 people are likely to have died in the custody of the Syrian Security Forces between March 2011 and December 2015 due to torture and inhuman conditions.[41] In 2016, the Commission of Inquiry on Syria found that the government had a "calculated awareness" that the conditions it inflicted in its detention centers would cause the mass deaths of detainees and occurred in the pursuance of a State policy to attack a civilian population. Consequently, it determined that the government's conduct amounted to extermination, as a crime against humanity.[42]

Thousands more disappeared detainees have been killed in secret extra-judicial executions. In a 2017 report, Amnesty International detailed how the victims of executions at Saydnaya Prison are condemned to death in "trials" lasting between one and three minutes at the Military Field Court in the Al-Qaboun neighborhood of Damascus.[43]

Some have been released from government detention—having survived torture and inhuman conditions and avoided extrajudicial execution. The physical and psychological scars of their experiences will likely endure for the rest of their lives. As one former detainee told Amnesty International: "Being with my family again was very strange. It was as if I had a cancer, and then someone told me I was healed. Just because they tell me this doesn't make it true . . . I will never overcome [my detention]."[44]

To date, monitors have been largely unable to identify people who were released after being disappeared by ISIS, adding weight to the belief that many of these people have been executed.

Impact on Relatives of the Disappeared

Across Syria, and throughout the Syrian refugee community, tens of thousands of men, women, and children suffer as they await news of their disappeared relatives. The anguish of Syrian families is multilayered and includes deteriorating physical and psychological health of adults and children, economic hardship, legal difficulties, and, for most, a marked fear of their own government.

Lacking information on the fate or whereabouts of their relatives, families can neither mourn nor adjust to their loss. One woman, whose son disappeared in 2011, explained to Amnesty International, "If someone dies, you can grieve for them. . . . But with my son missing I am always wondering: Is he sleeping enough? Did he get enough to eat today? Is he hurt? But then again maybe none of this worry matters. Maybe he is dead."[45] Another woman, whose mother disappeared in 2013, said, "Every morning, I forget. I will think to myself, 'I didn't call my mother,' and then I remember she is gone. . . . It's like each day she disappears again."[46] The anguish of the families is so great and often so prolonged that it is likely to rise to the level of torture or inhuman treatment and constitutes a crime in itself.[47]

With no official explanation of the fate of the disappeared, relatives are forced into a legal limbo. Without death certificates, property cannot be inherited or sold. Syrian law compounds the difficulties for wives of disappeared men. Under the Personal Status Law,[48] the father assumes guardianship of their own or others' children, which includes consenting to provision of medical treatment, education, marriage and all other matters involved in the care of a legal minor. Women whose husbands are disappeared cannot assume guardianship over their own children, creating numerous legal problems. Syrian law also gives no automatic right of divorce to women, and so, in the absence of a death certificate, women are unable to divorce or to remarry, even years after the disappearance of their husbands.

An untold number of Syrian children, already traumatized by war and displacement, have lost one or more of their parents or guardians to disappearance. Some were present when their fathers and mothers were taken away, not to be seen again. One woman, speaking to the Commission of Inquiry on Syria, described her young daughter as crying "when she sees a military uniform" after her father was abducted by Military Intelligence officers in Hama in December 2011.[49] As most of the disappeared are men, there is a generation of Syrian children who are growing up without male role models in their immediate, and sometimes also extended, families. Many Syrian boys leave school to fill the role of breadwinner for their families, the disappearance of older men having created financial hardship. Syrian girls, left without a male guardian and in a situation where security is absent or fragile, risk being pushed into early and forced marriages.

Documentation and Accountability

Enforced disappearance—a violation characterized by the absence of information—is particularly difficult to document. As a result, only a fraction of the disappearances carried out by the government since 2011 have been properly recorded.[50]

The primary challenge for documentation remains the government's refusal to provide any information on the tens of thousands of detainees in its custody, a flagrant violation of its obligations under international law. Additionally, families have refused to report disappearances due to well-justified fears of reprisals, which have been documented as including travel bans, arrests, or being forcibly disappeared themselves.[51]

Due to the risks involved in speaking publicly, many families opt to deal directly with an intermediary, commonly referred to as a "middleman" or "broker," to secure the release of their disappeared relatives. The bribes families are forced to pay—which range anywhere from hundreds to thousands of U.S. dollars—are often a source of shame and lead families to treat disappearance as a private matter.[52] In some cases, families have paid for inaccurate or false information.

There has been a noticeable gap in the systematic documentation of disappearances in Syria by international and national organizations. While several local organizations have compiled extensive lists of disappeared individuals, they have been reluctant to share this information, whether due to not obtaining informed consent to share, a lack of trust between groups or because they have been forced to compete for limited donor funds. International efforts have been similarly ineffective. Due, perhaps, to the enormity of the task, no international organization or non-governmental organization has stepped forward thus far to spearhead and harmonize international and national efforts to record disappearances. The impact of these problems has been exacerbated by access constraints due to ongoing hostilities and the fact that Syrians have fled to so many countries around the world. The combined outcome is that documentation by monitoring groups to date has been piecemeal and uncoordinated.

Public advocacy has been only slightly more successful. Aside from a small number of research reports and campaigns by international and non-governmental organizations, advocacy efforts have largely been led by Syrian civil society organizations. Several such organizations have come together to establish groups to provide support for survivors of disappearance and detention, as well as for the family members of the disappeared.[53]

The UN Working Group on Enforced and Involuntary Disappearances and the Commission of Inquiry on Syria both found that the Syrian Government's campaign of enforced disappearance constitutes a crime against humanity.[54] Nevertheless, justice remains out of reach. Syria is not a party to the Rome Statute, and it is unlikely the UN Security Council will refer the situation to the International Criminal Court due to the exercise of veto powers by Russia, Assad's ally. Hopes lie with cases being brought in national courts,[55] potentially supported UN General Assembly's December 2016 establishment of International Impartial and Independent Mechanism for Syria.[56] While a small number of cases—mainly taking place in courts of Germany and Sweden have sought to hold individuals responsible for crimes committed in Syria,[57] no one from any of the warring parties has yet been charged with the crime of enforced disappearance.

The fate and whereabouts of tens of thousands of Syrians remain unknown. Their families wait in agony. As the war is fought to its bitter end, Syrians warn that the deep wounds of the conflict may never heal without information being provided about what has happened to the legions of the missing and disappeared, and without accountability for what they and their families have suffered.[58] It is the responsibility of the international community to ensure that the victims of enforced disappearance are placed at the heart of peace negotiations and the pursuit of justice.[59]

Notes

1. Syrian Observatory for Human Rights, *About 500,000 Persons Were Killed in Syria during 81 Months after the Syrian Revolution Started*, December 10, 2017.

2. Syrian Network for Human Rights, *Ninth Annual Report on Enforced Disappearance in Syria on the International Day of the Victims of Enforced Disappearances*, August 30, 2020, 2. https://sn4hr.org/wp-

3. The Syrian Network for Human Rights (SNHR) estimated that approximately 84,371 people were disappeared by the government, an estimated 85 percent of all documented disappearances between March 2011 and 30 August 2020; *SNHR—Ninth Annual Report*, 8.

4. This includes the four branches of the Security Forces—the Military Intelligence, Air Force Intelligence, Political Security and General Intelligence (sometimes referred to as State Security), as well as the Armed Forces, and pro-government militias. This is widely recognized: Syrian Network for Human Rights, *Where Are They?*, August 30, 2016, 4. . Available at https://sn4hr.org/wp-. See also Amnesty International, *Between Prison and the Grave: Enforced Disappearances in Syria*, November 2015; available at https://www.amnesty.org.uk/files/embargoed_-_between_prison_and_the_grave_final.pdf and Independent International Commission of Inquiry on the Syrian Arab Republic, "Without A Trace: Enforced Disappearances in the Syrian Arab Republic," December 19, 2013, *Commission of Inquiry on Syria—Without a Trace*, paras. 2–4, htttp://www.ohchr.org/Documents/HRBodies/HRCouncil/CoISyria/ThematicPaperEDInSyria.pdf

5. From 1971 to 2000, during the presidency of Hafez al-Assad, enforced disappearances were a major human rights concern. In the 1980s, more than 17,000 people are said to have disappeared, notably from Hama following the uprising there in 1982; see Syrian Network for Human Rights, *The Prolonged Pain*, August 30, 2016, 1, http://sn4hr.org/wp-content/pdf/english/The_Extended_pain_en.pdf

6. SNHR, *Ninth Annual Report*, 8.

7. The Syrian Constitution, while not explicitly prohibiting enforced disappearance, prohibits holding any detainee incommunicado. Article 33 states: "Every detained individual shall be informed within 24 hours of the cause(s) of his detention and cannot be interrogated without the presence of an attorney, where requested. A detainee cannot be kept for more than 48 hours before the administrative authority, unless so ordered by the judicial authority."

8. These rights include the right to liberty and security of persons, the right not to be arbitrarily detained, the right not to be subjected to torture or to cruel, inhuman or degrading treatment or punishment, the right to a fair trial and the right of all persons deprived of their liberty to be treated with humanity and with

the inherent dignity of the human person. Enforced disappearances also violate and imperil the right to life.

9. Independent International Commission of Inquiry on the Syrian Arab Republic, *Commission of Inquiry on Syria. —A/HRC/S-17/2/Add.1*, A/HRC/S-17/2/Add.1, November 23, 2011, paras. 41–46.

10. Independent International Commission of Inquiry on the Syrian Arab Republic, A/HRC/19/69, February 22, 2012, paras. 58–59.

11. Commission of Inquiry on Syria, *Without a Trace*, paras. 12–15; *Commission of Inquiry on Syria—A/HRC/S-17/2/Add.1*, paras 59–60; Commission of Inquiry on Syria, A/HRC/19/69, paras 58–61.

12. Commission of Inquiry on Syria, *Without a Trace*, para. 19.

13. In attacking doctors, nurses, and other medical staff, who were often well known in their communities, the government sent an unambiguous message that no one was above the consequences of aiding the opposition. See Amnesty International, *Health Crisis: Syrian Government Targets the Wounded and Health Workers*, October 2011, https://www.amnesty.org/en/documents/MDE24/059/2011/en/; Independent International Commission of Inquiry on Syria, *Assault on Medical Care in Syria*, A/HRC/24/CRP, September 2, 2013, http://www.ohchr.org/EN/HRBod ies/HRC/IICISyria/Pages/Documentation.aspx; Commission of Inquiry on Syria, *Without a Trace*, para. 21.

14. Commission of Inquiry on Syria, *Without a Trace*, para. 20

15. BBC News, "Isis rebels declare 'Islamic State in Iraq and Syria," June 30, 2014, https://www.bbc.com/news/av/world-middle-east-28091637

16. While the government focused its firepower on anti-government armed groups from the outset of the conflict, it did not direct the full force of its military weight against ISIS until 2016, a fact which aided the terrorist group's entrenchment in Syria.

17. Amnesty International, *Left to Die Under Siege: War Crimes and Human Rights Abuses in Eastern Ghouta, Syria*, https://www.amnesty.org/en/documents/mde24/2079/2015/en/

18. Amnesty International, "Squeezing the Life Out of Yarmouk: War Crimes Against Besieged Civilians," press release, March 10, 2014, https://www.amnesty .org/en/press-releases/2014/03/syria-yarmouk-under-siege-horror-story-war-cri mes-starvation-and-death/

19. Physicians for Human Rights, *Aleppo Abandoned: A Case Study on Healthcare in Syria*, November 2015, https://phr.org/wp-content/uploads/2015/11/alep po-abandoned-executive-summary.pdf; Amnesty International, "Syrian and Russian Forces Targeting Hospitals as a Strategy of War," press release, March 2016, https://www.amnesty.org/en/latest/press-release/2016/03/syrian-and-russian-forc es-targeting-hospitals-as-a-strategy-of-war/

20. Interview with Fadel Abdul Ghany, Director of the Syrian Network for Human Rights, July 11, 2017; interview with Bassam Al-Ahmed, Director of Syrians for Truth and Justice, July 13, 2017.

21. Commission of Inquiry on Syria, *Assaults on Medical Care*; Commission of Inquiry on Syria, *Without a Trace*, para. 25.

22. Makeshift checkpoints were also set up by pro-government militias which abducted people, quickly handing them over to government detention centers.

23. Independent International Commission of Inquiry on the Syrian Arab Republic, A/HRC/34/64, 2, February 2017, https://www.ohchr.org/en/hr-bodies/hrc/iici-syria/documentation; See also BBC News, "Aleppo Battle: UN Says Hundreds of Men Missing," December 9, 2016, http://www.bbc.com/news/world-middle-east-38260388

24. Interview with Bassam Al-Ahmed, director of Syrians for Truth and Justice, July 13, 2017.

25. Amnesty International, *Between Prison and the Grave*, 51. Amnesty International's research suggested those who exploit the system of enforced disappearance are driven by two primary motivations: first, the pursuit of financial profit, and second, the settling of personal grievances.

26. Commission of Inquiry on Syria, *Without a Trace*, para. 28–30.

27. See SNHR, *Prolonged Pain*, 4.

28. Email correspondence with Fadel Abdul Ghany, director of the Syrian Network for Human Rights, September 7, 2017.

29. *Guardian*, "The Missing of Raqqa: Families Search for Loved Ones Disappeared by ISIS," January 6, 2018.

30. Where the State maintains a climate in which family members are too intimidated to inquire about detentions by security services, this is tantamount to a refusal or a denial of the person's fate.

31. The Syrian Network for Human Rights found that, of the 65,116 disappearance cases they documented between March 2011 and August 2015, 16 percent of victims were forcibly disappeared for one month, 12 percent for two months, 10 percent for six months, 9 percent for one year, 11 percent for two years, 23 per cent for three years, and 19 percent for four years. Email correspondence with SNHR director, cited in Amnesty International, "Between Prison and the Grave," 15.

32. SNHR—Ninth Annual Report, 12. See also, Independent International Commission of Inquiry on Syria, *Out of Sight, Out of Mind: Deaths in Detention in the Syrian Arab Republic*, February 2016, 4, https://www.ohchr.org/sites/default/files/Documents/HRBodies/HRCouncil/CoISyria/A-HRC-31-CRP1_en.pdf; see also Amnesty International, *It Breaks the Human: Torture, Disease, and Death in Syria's Prisons*, August 16, 2016, https://www.amnesty.org/en/documents/mde24/4508/2016/en/; Human Rights Watch, *If the Dead Could Speak Mass Deaths and Torture in Syria's Detention Facilities*, December 16, 2016 https://www.hrw.org/report/2015/12/16/if-dead-could-speak/mass-deaths-and-torture-syrias-detention-facilities

33. Amnesty, *Between Prison and the Grave*, 15.

34. The Syrian Network for Human Rights documented that anti-government armed groups were responsible for 3,262 disappearances (2.4 percent of the total number of disappearances between March 2011 and August 2020); Kurdish armed forces as being responsible for 2,056 disappearances (2.06 percent of all disappearances between March 2011 and August 2020); and Hay'at Tahrir Al Sham as being responsible for 2,007 disappearances (or 2.02 percent of all disappearances between March 2011 and August 2020); SNHR, *Ninth Annual Report*, 8.

35. One man recounted his "welcome party" at Saydnaya Prison to Amnesty International: "You are thrown to the ground, and they use different instruments for the beatings: electric cables with exposed copper wire ends—they have little hooks, so they take a part of your skin—normal electric cables, plastic water pipes

of different sizes and metal bars. . . . All you see is blood: your own blood, the blood of others. After one hit, you lose your sense of what is happening. You're in shock. But then the pain comes." Amnesty International, *Human Slaughterhouse: Mass Hangings and Extermination in Saydnaya Prison, Syria*, February 2017 https://www.amnesty.org/en/documents/mde24/5415/2017/en/, 32

36. Amnesty, *Human Slaughterhouse*, 15.

37. Typical stress positions include the "flying carpet," where the victim is strapped face-up on a foldable wooden or metal board, and one end is brought near the other, effectively folding the victim in on themselves; and *shabeh*, which involves the victim being suspended by his wrists for several hours. Human Rights Watch, *Torture Archipelago: Arbitrary Arrests, Torture and Enforced Disappearances in Syria's Underground Prisons since March 2011*, July 2012, https://www.hrw.org/report/2012/07/03/torture-archipelago/arbitrary-arrests-torture-and-enforced-disappearances-syrias

38. The Syrian Network for Human Rights has confirmed the forcible disappearance of 1,738 children and 4,982 women by the Syrian government between March 2011 and 30 August 2020. SNHR, *Ninth Annual Report*, 8.

39. Commission of Inquiry on Syria, *Out of Sight, Out of Mind*, paras. 26–33.

40. For more details on the psychological implications of detention, see Amnesty International, *It Breaks the Human*, 41. Human Rights Watch listed "mental anguish" as a principal cause of death for detainees, noting that several former detainees "described a state of mind they called *fasl*, or losing one's mind and cutting off interaction with others, which would lead afflicted detainees to get disoriented, hallucinate, become unaware of their surroundings, and stop eating and drinking. According to many of the detainees who witnessed such cases in their cells, after about a week in this condition, an afflicted detainee could die." Human Rights Watch, *Torture Archipelago*, 65.

41. Human Rights Data Analysis Group, *Technical Memo for Amnesty International Report on Deaths in Detention*, August 2016, https://www.zora.uzh.ch/id/eprint/129519/

42. Commission of Inquiry on Syria, *Out of Sight, Out of Mind*, 17.

43. On the day of the executions, detainees are told they will be transferred to a civilian prison. They are instead brought to a basement room of another building on the grounds of the prison, where they are hanged. These hangings take place in the middle of the night and in the utmost secrecy. The victims are told that they have been sentenced to death only minutes before the executions are carried out, and they do not know how they will die until the nooses are placed around their necks. Amnesty International, *Human Slaughterhouse*, 15.

44. Amnesty, *It Breaks the Human*, 63.

45. Amnesty, *Between Prison and the Grave*, 21.

46. Amnesty, *Between Prison and the Grave*, 21.

47. The "flying carpet" and shabeh stress position methods are often used in combination. See endnote 37. Commission of Inquiry on Syria, *Without a Trace*, paras. 44–50; and Human Rights Watch, *Torture Archipelago*.

48. The Personal Status Law of 1953 (amended by Law 34 of 1975 and Law 18 of 2003) regulates the family affairs of the overwhelming majority of the population in Syria, namely Sunni, Shi'a and Alawite Muslims. For more details, see Amnesty

International. *Submission to the Committee on the Elimination of Discrimination against Women (CEDAW)*, in advance of its 58th pre-sessional meeting, September 16, 2013, http://www.refworld.org/topic,50ffbce51b1,50ffbce51c6,525bdcce4,0,AMN ESTY,COMMENTARY,SYR.html

49. Commission of Inquiry on Syria, *Without a Trace*, para. 45.

50. The UN Working Group for Enforced and Involuntary Disappearances has received 236 reports of enforced or involuntary disappearance in Syria between 1980 and 2015. This is a stark contrast to the Syrian Network of Human Rights' estimate that more than 74,000 Syrians were forcibly disappeared between March 2011 and August 2015. See Human Rights Council, *Report of the Working Group on Enforced or Involuntary Disappearances*, 2016, 32, http://www.ohchr.org/EN/Issues/ Disappearances/Pages/Annual.aspx; see also SNHR, *Prolonged Pain*, 5.

51. See Commission of Inquiry on Syria, *Without a Trace*; Amnesty, *Between Prison and the Grave*.

52. Amnesty, *Between Prison and the Grave*, 17.

53. For example, The Day After, a Syrian organization, formed an association of survivors of Saydnaya Prison, and the group Families for Freedom. They have brought together Syrian families whose relatives have been disappeared or abducted by any of the warring parties.

54. Commission of Inquiry on Syria, *Without a Trace*; Office of the UN High Commissioner for Human Rights, *Syria: Group of Experts Call for Action into Enforced Disappearances as Crime Against Humanity*, March 20, 2014, http://www.ohchr.org/ EN/NewsEvents/Pages/DisplayNews.aspx?NewsID=14410&LangID=E

55. Many of the cases brought before national courts will likely be based on universal jurisdiction, that is to say, a national court may prosecute individuals for any serious crime against international law—such as crimes against humanity, war crimes, and genocide—based on the principle that such crimes harm the international community or international order itself, which an individual State may act to protect. Generally, universal jurisdiction is invoked when other, traditional bases of criminal jurisdiction do not exist, for example: the defendant is not a national of the State, the defendant did not commit a crime in that State's territory or against its nationals, or the State's own national interests are not adversely affected. The definition and exercise of universal jurisdiction varies around the world. A national or international court's authority to prosecute individuals for international crimes committed in other territories depends on the relevant sources of law and jurisdiction, such as national legislation or an international agreement, which may, for example, require that only individuals within the country's national territory be subject to prosecution.

56. On December 22, 2016, the United Nations General Assembly adopted resolution 71/248 establishing the *International, Impartial and Independent Mechanism to Assist in the Investigation and Prosecution of Persons Responsible for the Most Serious Crimes under International Law Committed in the Syrian Arab Republic since March 2011* (the "Independent Mechanism for Syria"). See A/RES/71/248, para. 4.

57. TRIAL International, *Universal Jurisdiction Database*, https://trialinternational.org/resources/universal-jurisdiction-database/?keywords=&country=1457& topic=&resource_type=Trial+Watch&body=&orderBy=date&submitted=1

58. *Wall Street Journal*, "Syria's Festering War Wound: Legions of the Missing," January 5, 2018, https://www.wsj.com/articles/syrias-festering-war-wound-legions -of-the-missing-1515148201

59. On August 2, 2017, 169 Syrian civil society organizations wrote to the then UN Special Envoy for Syria, Staffan de Mistura, in a letter stating that the Syrian people feel "increasingly disillusioned with a process that continues to fail them," and called on the UN Special Envoy to "ensure progress on the detainee file including by securing (i) a comprehensive plan for the release of detainees beyond small-scale prisoner exchanges; (ii) information about the fates of all Syrians forcibly disappeared; (iii) access by international monitors to all detention facilities; and (iv) a halt to execution orders, particularly in regime security and military facilities, as well as in those run by armed groups." The text of the letter is available at https://www.syriauk.org/2017/08/

Do Not Forget Us, La Tanssana

Helen Zughaib

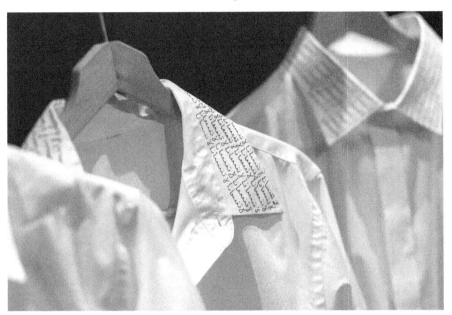

Locked away, in an underground Syrian prison, are thousands of
  people that have just "disappeared."
In cells packed so tightly, they take turns lying down to sleep.
In one of these cells, a prisoner was finally released, and in the
  darkness of the cell, the other prisoners hugged him and
  whispered, "Don't forget us."
He did not. The names of the other eighty-two prisoners were written
  in blood and rust with a chicken bone on torn pieces of cloth and
  sewn into the collar and cuffs of his shirt.
When he was at last free, he resolved to try to find the families of the
  other prisoners, to let them know where their loved ones were.
Of the eighty-two families, he could only locate eleven. Of those
  families, four of the prisoners had died in custody, the other seven
  were either freed or taken to other secret prisons.

—Helen Zughaib

Editors' note: *Do Not Forget Us, La Tanssana* was first exhibited in 2020 at Creative Alliance in Baltimore, Maryland. It is constructed of shirts belonging to the artist's Syrian father. The installation is based on the experience of journalist and activist Mansour Omari, who worked for the Syrian Center for Media and Freedom of Expression, documenting the names of the disappeared, when he was arrested by military police. He spent nearly a year in prison and, with his release in 2013, was charged by his fellow prisoners to smuggle out their messages. In 2017, the five fragile, original pieces of fabric were displayed at the United States Holocaust Museum in Washington, D.C., in an exhibit titled *Syria: Please Don't Forget Us* (See https://www.ushmm.org/information/exhibitions/museum-exhibitions/syria-please-dont-forget-us). Omari was eventually given asylum in Sweden. His efforts are featured in a documentary, *Syria's Disappeared*, directed by Sara Afshar (see https://syriasdisappeared.com).

SEVEN

Politics of Silence and Denial

1988 Enforced Disappearances and Executions in Iran

Ashraf Zahedi

> Savagery is a defining condition of the animal kingdom, but only
> humans, blessed with reason, can invent death camps, inquisitions,
> the subtle instrumentation of torture, and mass executions. We con-
> tinually amaze ourselves with viciousness, the cause of which is less
> often bloodlust or brutality than it is mere expediency.
>
> —Robert Coover, *Kissing the Sword: A Prison Memoir*

This statement resonates with the brutality of the Islamic Republic of Iran
and the mass executions of its opponents in the summer of 1988. Thousands
of political prisoners affiliated with the banned political organizations—the
Mojahedin, Fadaian, Peykar, and Komala, among others—became targets
of this brutality.

Eye-witness accounts depict a gruesome picture of this massacre in the
capital, Tehran. Mehdi Aslani, a member of the Fadaian Organization,
imprisoned in Gohardasht Prison from 1985 to 1989, explained

> One late night in early August, . . . we saw a number of masked
> people loading and unloading a refrigerated truck of meat. We rec-
> ognized masked prison guards from their green Revolutionary out-
> fits . . . sanitizing the area. Later we learned that when they hanged
> people, the smell of feces and urine at the execution site took over

the whole area. Apparently, because of the extreme heat of August, to fight the stench, they felt sanitizing was necessary.[1]

Ebrahim Mohammad Rahimi, a member of the Mojahedin Organization, imprisoned from 1979 to 1981, had a similar account of the executions in Evin Prison:

> The windows were barred, but we twisted one of the bars so there was a small space through which we could take turns watching what was happening outside. We could see the guards dragging corpses and putting them into large black trash bags or body bags. The guards were throwing the bodies inside these bags, into the back of a nearby truck.[2]

Reza Ghaffari, imprisoned from 1981 to 1991, on suspicion of being a member of a socialist group, described how the executed bodies were removed from Gohardasht Prison

> One day, a lorry stopped within clear view. It was loaded with large parcels. Each parcel was wrapped in plastic sheeting, tied with twine at either end. From the unsteady way in which the guards found their footing as they jumped from the truck onto the parcels, it was obvious what was in the packages—bodies.
>   There had been a constant movement of these meat-wagons to an unknown graveyard for at least two months.[3]

These prisoners did not know who the executed prisoners were, but they recognized their prison-issued plastic slippers. Monireh Baradaran of the Revolutionary Workers Organization, who was imprisoned from 1981 to 1990 and whose brother was executed, explained in her memoir, *A Simple Truth*, that some prisoners had seen a prison staff member " pushing a hand wagon full of slippers."[4] The slippers gave the political prisoners a clue about what was awaiting them, and each felt his or her life hanging by a thread.

What explains the Islamic Republic's executions of thousands of Iranians in 1988? The answers lie in the making of the revolution and in post-revolutionary political developments.

Power Struggles and the Revival of Repression

The Iranian revolution was the culmination of decades of mobilization by political forces, secular and religious. These forces shared a common goal: to overthrow Shah Mohammad Reza Pahlavi. They regarded the Shah's regime as illegitimate. After World War II, Iran was experiencing democracy: freedom of expression, freedom of the press, freedom of assembly, and the right to membership in political parties of various persuasions. In 1951, the democratically elected prime minister, Mohammad Mossadegh, a Swiss-educated lawyer, led a campaign to nationalize Iranian oil, which was under control of the British Anglo-Persian Oil Company. Mossadegh's political party, the National Front of Iran (Jebh-ye Melli Iran) formed in 1949, was the largest secular pro-democracy organization. The Front, along with the leftist Tudeh Party of Iran (*Hezb-e Tudeh Iran*), created in 1941, as well as a number of smaller political groups succeeded in their oil nationalization campaign, and, drawing on that support, Mossadegh nationalized the Anglo-Persian Oil Company 1951.

In the context of the Cold War, Iran's political stance threatened to undermine British economic and geopolitical interests and thus raised the ire of the British and United States governments. In 1953, the United States Central Intelligence Agency (CIA), via "Operation Ajax," and the British Secret Intelligence Service (MI6), with "Operation Boot," removed Mossadegh and reinstated the Shah.[5]

Sixty years later, in 2013, the CIA acknowledged its role in the 1953 coup.[6] By forcibly overthrowing Mossadegh and installing the Shah, the United States and Britain secured the flow of Iranian oil to the Western market, controlling its price, and curbing the influence of the Soviet Union, their Cold War rival.[7]

The Shah's opponents resisted his oppressive rule, but his repression notwithstanding, Iran benefited from his many modernizing policies, such as the enfranchisement of women, free and compulsory education, and the formation of a literacy corps. But ultimately, his uneven socioeconomic developments along with arrests, imprisonments, and executions led to his downfall. He had underestimated the strength of his opponents, particularly the religious factions.

By 1978, two underground revolutionary organizations were gaining popular support inside Iran. The Organization of Iranian People's Fadaian, *Sazman-e Fadaian-e Khalq-e Iran*, founded in 1963, adhered to Marxism-Leninism. The People's Mojahedin Organization of Iran, *Sazman-e Mojahedin Khalq-e Iran*, formed in 1965, adhered to an ideology drawn from

Shi'a Islam and egalitarian aspects of Marxism. The two organizations had strong support among the Iranian intelligentsia and youth.

Meanwhile, Ayatollah Ruhollah Khomeini, an Iranian Shi'a religious leader living in exile in Paris,[8] tried appealing to large segments of the Iranian population, speaking of a *qiyam-e mardomi*, or popular uprising, rather than an Islamic uprising, which would be more likely to attract Iranians who feared religious rule.[9] He drew on vast networks of mosques throughout Iran exploiting Islamic ideologies to mobilize a revolution.

Secular forces inside Iran, mostly in disarray, failed to present an alternative to Khomeini and, fearing the loss of public support, they shied away from directly criticizing him. Though they did not accept Khomeini's leadership, they accepted his anti-imperialist and anti-Shah stands.

Khomeini, whose use of Islamic language resonated with traditional segments of population, emerged as the leader of the upcoming revolution. In late 1978, Iranians—mobilized by old as well as newly formed political organizations[10]—took to the streets demanding the Shah's departure, leading to the 1979 Revolution.[11]

Khomeini adamantly refused to include the word "democracy" in the title of the Revolution or the Iranian Constitution. Once the Revolution was secured, Khomeini and the ruling clerics embarked on the Islamization of Iran and set forth to suppress any opposition. Political groups received the brunt and were disbanded.

In overpowering its adversaries, the regime benefited greatly from the attack by Iraq's Saddam Hussein on Iran on September 22, 1980, which led to the eight-year Iran-Iraq war and gave the regime the opportunity to heighten Iranian nationalism. It labeled its opponents as unpatriotic and, worse, agents of Saddam Hussein or the United States.

To exert political control, the clerics broached no dissent, even among their own rank and file. When the first president of the Islamic Republic, Abolhasan Banisadr (elected in 1980) disagreed with the regime over domestic and international matters, he was impeached in 1981. This brought thousands of protestors to the streets, who were met with violence, arrest, and imprisonment.

In response to ongoing repression and the rulers' refusal to share power with political groups, the Mojahedin Organization began a campaign of terror. In June 1981, they assassinated several Iranian officials and detonated bombs in the head office of Islamic Republic Party, killing seventy-three high-ranking Iranian officials, hoping to weaken the regime and empower the disillusioned population to overthrow it. Yet this campaign served only to intensify the regime's determination to eliminate its adversaries. According to historian Ervand Abrahamian, "In 1981–85, the regime executed 4,995 Mojahedin and 547 Marxists. These figures do not include those killed in armed struggle with the regime."[12]

With "Revolutionary Rage and Rancor": *Fatwa* and Executions

By 1988, thousands of Iranians—men, women, old, and young, from various social classes, ethnic, and religious backgrounds—were imprisoned. Members of the Baha'i faith and the Kurdish ethnic minority suffered the impact of the regime's oppression. Some prisoners belonged to banned Iranian organizations, some were merely sympathizers, others were wrongfully arrested simply on suspicion of being opposed to the regime.

Physical and mental torture forced prisoners to confess to alleged oppositional activities and profess allegiance to the regime. The most common forms of torture, Abrahamian recorded, "were whipping—sometimes on the back but most often on the feet with the body tied to an iron bed—sleep deprivation, suspension—by the arms—from ceilings and high walls, twisting of forearms until they broke, crushing of hands and fingers in metal presses, insertion of sharp instruments under fingernails, cigarette burns, submersion under water, standing in one place for hours on end, and mock execution."[13]

It is believed the torture also included sexual abuse and rape.[14] These unbearable torments drove many male and female prisoners to suicide[15] with broken glass to slit their wrists or intestines, by drinking disinfectant, or hanging.

By 1988, the Iran-Iraq war had reached an impasse, and in July, Khomeini reluctantly accepted the United Nations Security Resolution 598, calling for a cease-fire.

Five days later, Mojahedin leadership, now exiled in Iraq and enjoying the support of Saddam Hussein, waged a military attack on Western Iran, hoping their incursion, *Forough-e Javidan* (Eternal Lights), would lead to a general uprising. The regime succeeded in driving them back to Iraq within days.

The Mojahedin attack only heightened people's nationalistic sentiments, giving the regime a greater opportunity to wage war against its opponents, some of whom were already in prison. Their supporters, in general, accepted their version of the sequence of events. Former political prisoners, however, concur with scholars and human rights organizations that these executions were planned before the Mojahedin's attack, and were coldly premeditated, authorized at the highest levels of government.[16]

Even before the Mojahedin's incursion, the regime had categorized its opponents into believers and non-believers in Islam and the Islamic Republic. Special commissions with instructions to execute "Mojaheds as *mohareb* (those who war against God) and leftists as *mortad* (apostates from Islam)" were set up.[17] The Mojahedin Organization was labeled *monafeqin* (hypocrites).

On July 19, 1988, with no prior notice, prisons holding political prisoners were closed.[18] Prisoners were ordered to stay in their cells. Scheduled visits from families were cancelled. What was awaiting them? The answer came in a *fatwa* (a decree issued by an Islamic religious authority) from Khomeini regarding members and sympathizers of the Mojahedin Organization.

In an undated letter distributed to prison authorities throughout Iran, Ayatollah Khomeini declared, "It is decreed that those who are in prisons throughout the country, who remain steadfast in their support for the monafeqin are considered to be mohareb and are condemned to execution. . . . It is naïve to show mercy to mohareb. The decisiveness of Islam before the enemies of God is among the unquestionable tenets of the Islamic regime. I hope that you satisfy almighty God with your revolutionary rage and rancor against the enemies of Islam."[19]

Ayatollah Hussein-Ali Montazeri, Khomeini's designated heir, objected to the fatwa. In a July 31, 1988 letter, he referred to the executions as unlawful and against the principles of Islam and warned that they could be perceived as acts of vengeance and vendetta.[20]

Nevertheless, the task of implementing the fatwa in Tehran was entrusted to a judicial panel comprising Hossein Ali Nayyeri, a religious judge, Morteza Eshraqi, a Tehran prosecutor, Ebrahim Raisi, Eshraqi's deputy prosecutor, and Mostafa Pour Mohammadi, representative of the Intelligence Ministry. Prisoners in Tehran referred to them as the "Death Committee." The panels differed depending on their provinces.

On July 29, 1988, the "Death Committee" convened to begin the first wave of executions.[21] It quickly determined each prisoner's fate. None had legal representation. The panel started with Mojahedin members and sympathizers some of whom had already completed their prison sentences but were not released. If they admitted they had been members of the Mojahedin, the questioning ended, and the panel concluded the prisoner was still loyal to the organization. But if the prisoner referred to the Mojahedin as hypocrites—as the regime labeled them—the interrogation continued with questions such as

- Are you willing to go on camera and denounce your organization?
- Will you name the members and sympathizers of the Mojahedin?
- Are you willing to go to the war front and walk on Iraqi minefields?

On August 26, 1988, the panel began the second wave of executions.[22] This time, the targets were prisoners belonging to or sympathizing with dissolved leftist organizations, such as Fadaian. The leftist prisoners, however, had neither supported the Mojahedin Organization nor its military incursion against the regime.[23] The prisoners were asked

- Are you a Muslim?
- Do you believe in Allah?
- Do you pray?
- Will you go on camera and denounce your leftist beliefs?

As with the Mojahedin, the leftist prisoners who were steadfast in their beliefs and loyalties were sent to the execution halls. When the first series of prisoners answered the questions truthfully and ended up dead, the remaining prisoners decided to provide tactical answers (*pasokh-ha-ye taktiki*), twisting the truth to save their lives.[24]

In Tehran, executions took place in Ghohardasht and Evin prisons. Gallows were erected in lecture halls or amphitheaters. Blindfolded prisoners in groups of six were stood on chairs, nooses around their necks. Their bodies were dumped in a meat truck and carried away. Throughout Iran, bodies were buried in unmarked graves and vacant lots. With thousands killed, managing the dead and secretly disposing of bodies became the regime's immediate concern.

Unmarked and Mass Graves

In Tehran, executed Mojahedins were taken to Behesht-e Zahra, the main Muslim cemetery. Some were interred in unmarked or old existing graves. To avoid public attention to the magnitude of these burials, the regime inscribed false names and dates of burial on the tombstones. Some were buried in mass graves in canals, which were then covered with cement, rendering them undetectable.

Authorities believed that the leftists, as apostates, should not be buried among Muslims. Therefore, in 1981, a vacant land in southeast Tehran, later called Khavaran, was allocated for them.[25] Khavaran is a vast burial site in southeast Tehran,[26] divided into sections, each allotted to non-Muslim religious minorities such as Christian Armenians and Baha'i.

In Khavaran, the bodies of executed leftists were dumped into a secret mass grave adjacent to the Baha'i cemetery. It was discovered by Afghans living and working in the area, who alerted the families of political prisoners about the comings and goings of meat trucks and bodies buried in shallow graves at night. Heavy rains washed away the soil exposing the bodies. Stray dogs, detecting the smell of flesh, "dragged these hastily buried bodies out," Shahla Talebi wrote in *Ghosts of Revolution*.[27] Families "came face-to-face with shocking proof of their [loved ones'] deaths in their traumatic encounter with the uncovered arms, legs, or faces of the young dead men, who had been buried with their clothes on,"[28] as opposed to wrapped in customary white shrouds.[29]

Families informed other families, who rushed to Khavaran and dug with their bare hands, uncovering bones, body parts, and articles of clothing. In shock and tears, they took photos to document the mass grave. They placed flowers on random sites referred to by the regime as *Lana-tabad*, or "Place of the Damned," and renamed it *Golzar-e Khavaran*, or "Flower Garden of Khavaran."

Despite continuous disruptions of their gatherings at the site by the authorities, the families made Khavaran a cemetery of their own. Gradually, more mass graves were discovered in Khavaran and throughout Iran.

Impact on the Families

In October–November 1988, the families of political prisoners were finally allowed into the prisons to visit. A limited number of them got to see their loved ones. Others, however, were informed that their loved ones were no longer there or were handed two plastic bags, one containing belongings, the other a last testament. Families were told the prisoners died of natural causes, or "that the prisoner had been killed during a prison riot or had been executed for taking part in a riot."[30] Many families never got answers nor did the authorities release the bodies. Their loved ones simply disappeared.[31]

Families were instructed by the authorities not to talk about the executions. They were not to hold funeral services at home, in mosques, or in cemeteries. They were not allowed the customary seventh and fortieth memorial days. Families who did not receive the bodies of their executed loved ones remain in an ambiguous state of perpetual loss and deprived of closure.

For cultures such as Iran's, proper burial is an essential observation and sanctification of death. A grave enshrines the deceased's identity and is significant for coming to terms with loss and reaching closure. Shahla Talebi, who lost her husband, Hamid, to the executions remarked, "[M]y Hamid and other loved ones were denied not only their lives but also their deaths."[32] Even without graves, she felt the urge to talk to her loved ones and have them hear her through the soil that covered them.[33]

Nina Toobaei expressed her need for a grave for her executed brother, Siamak. She lamented, "I wish I could visit his grave and talk to his bones."[34] Maryam Nuri, whose husband was executed, stated, "I needed Rahmat to have a grave. I needed to see what we had heard was his grave, even though it was a common grave."[35]

There are no definitive figures on the number of executions. The Mojahedin Organization estimates thirty thousand.[36] Based on information provided by families, political parties, and organizations, the names of about five thousand executed political prisoners have been compiled.[37] This does not include those whose families, fearing retaliation, have not shared the names. Moreover, between 1981 and 1988, around twenty-thousand dissidents disappeared, either dying under torture or executed by firing squad or hanging.[38]

This wave of executions came to an end before the tenth anniversary of the Islamic Republic in February 1989. To mark the anniversary, Khomeini gave amnesty to repenting political prisoners.[39] Why did the Islamic Republic take such draconian measures against its opponents in the first place? Khomeini, then dying of cancer and sensing political divisions that could undermine the regime, accelerated the process of eliminating the opposition. His order "was intent upon preserving his creation: an Islamic Republic without opposition."[40]

Khomeini did not leave Ayatollah Montazeri's objection to the fatwa unpunished and admonished him for lacking qualifications to serve as heir designate.[41] Khomeini died in June 1989. Gradually all political prisoners were released. Thanks to the silence inside Iran, as well as the tacit silence of the international community, the Islamic Republic managed to cover up the 1988 executions.

The Significance of Silence

Political silence can be both the outcome of political repression and a contributing factor to its continuation. Some post-revolutionary regimes draw on revolutionary rage in dealing with their opponents, therefore setting the stage for muzzling any objections.

Sadly, the Islamic Republic has capitalized on rage from its earliest days by establishing the Revolutionary Tribunal to determine the fates of the Shah's officials and thus their executions. Many prominent figures, such as Ayatollah Mohammad Kazem Shariatmadari, Abdol Karim Lahigi—an important human rights lawyer—and the regime's Prime Minister, Mehdi Bazargan, (April–November 1979) a well-respected politician, objected to the executions. Yet the tribunal carried on. In total, 497 individuals were executed,[42] including the Shah's prime minister, Amir Abbas Hoveyda (1965–1977).

Many Iranian political organizations were complicit. The Mojahedin Organization, the Fadaian Organization, and the Tudeh Party, each with a significant base of support among the public, did not object to the executions.[43] They, too, believed in *Ghahr-e Enghelabi*, or revolutionary violence. Had they objected to the executions, they could have sensitized the public to the rights of the accused and in turn elevated human rights in Iran. By not objecting to the use of revolutionary violence, they effectively normalized it and themselves became the subjects of revolutionary rage captured in Khomeini's fatwas.

The scope and secrecy of the 1988 executions depict one of the darkest periods in Iranian history. Yet most Iranians claim they did not know about these executions. The Islamic Republic had indeed succeeded in keeping them secret, while generating fear, which in turn produced silence even among those who were aware of the executions.

Arts and literature of resistance have been deeply rooted in Iranian culture and Iranian intellectuals, through their work, have opposed repression. Faraj Sarkohi, an Iranian literary critic,[44] decried the unprecedented silence of Iranian intellectuals in Iran.[45] "We Iranian intellectuals inside Iran had remained silent. . . . I do not forgive myself for this silence."[46]

The silence of the international community was noteworthy considering that Amnesty International, in a comprehensive 1988 report, brought the massacre to the world's attention.[47] Iranians in diaspora, including political organizations abroad, as well as families of the executed and disappeared, continued to expose the Islamic Republic's atrocities by holding rallies in which photos of the victims were displayed. They lobbied the United Nations to investigate. The international community, particularly European countries, pleased with the success of the Iran-Iraq 1988 cease-fire, focused on postwar reconstruction. When issues of human rights violations were raised, they were told by the Islamic Republic that those executed had been involved in armed conspiracy and acted against the regime's sovereignty. European countries accepted this narrative and secured access to the Iranian market.[48] More disturbing was the silence of the Soviet Union and China. Their silence disillusioned Iranian intellectuals, Marxists, Leninists, or Maoists, who looked up to them as revolutionary models and sources of inspiration. But these countries maintained their vested interests in the Islamic Republic, which they considered to be anti-imperialist and anti-American, meanwhile benefiting from Iran's resources and growing consumer market. The United States, self-appointed champion of human rights, also stayed silent about the 1988 massacres.

All this can be attributed to the politics of the Cold War and the ways in which the West in general, and the United States in particular, used religion as a powerful weapon against communism and its various ideologies.[49] Despite open enmity between the United States and Iran, they shared an anti-communist agenda. Thus, there were extensive contacts between the Jimmy Carter administration (1977–1981) and Ayatollah Khomeini while he was still in Paris before the 1979 Iranian Revolution.[50] Despite publicly upholding an embargo against selling arms to Iran, President Ronald Reagan (1981–1989) secretly approved weapons sales to Iran in what became known in 1986 as the Iran-Contra Affair.

Mobilizing Islam as a buffer against communism was part of the United States' Cold War strategy.[51] The Islamic Republic's executions of communists, Maoists, and Islamists influenced by Marxist ideology effectively corresponded with the U.S. anti-communist Cold War agenda. Moreover, Iran's 1988 executions took place at the time when the United States was heavily involved in combating the spread of the Soviet Union's influence in Afghanistan, Iran's neighbor to the east.[52]

Thus, U.S. silence was in line with its global Cold War strategy. The U.S. Congress continues to claim supporting human rights in Iran but has not, as of this writing, passed a resolution condemning the executions.[53]

The UN reaction to the events of 1988 was mild, considering its magnitude. The UN Special Rapporteur on the situation of human rights in the Islamic Republic of Iran, Reynaldo Galindo Pohl (1986–1995), brought the violations to the United Nations' attention in his 1989 report on the Situation of Human Rights in the Islamic Republic of Iran, where he expressed grave concern and pointed out that "there was a renewed wave of executions in the period July–September whereby [during which] a large number of persons died because of their political convictions."[54]

Galindo Pohl's written complaint about the "wave of executions" received the Islamic Republic's usual responses that these killings occurred during the encounter with the Mojahedin. Yet despite his awareness of the Islamic Republic's concealment of the truth, Galindo Pohl failed[55] to further investigate, despite what he had seen.

The United Nations special procedure which continues to this day pursuing the 1988 crimes is the Working Group on Enforced or Involuntary Disappearances (WGEID). Yet the WGEID's continual requests to visit Iran are declined. By not complying with the UN, the Islamic Republic benefits from the geopolitical power dynamics between Russia, China, and a host of other undemocratic regimes which favor it.

Revealing the Truth: Mothers of Khavaran

In the face of the Islamic Republic's atrocities, the Mothers of Khavaran have shown unwavering determination to bring the executions and the enforced disappearances into light.[56] The group is a loose network of mothers, their families, and friends seeking justice for their loved ones. They number in the thousands and are divided by social class and ideology, secular and religious, yet they are united in presenting the true narrative of what happened to thousands of Iranian political prisoners.

The Mothers have continued to demand accountability, redress, and access to truth. They met with high-ranking Iranian officials including Ayatollah Montazeri who opposed the executions. They wrote to then-United Nations Secretary General Javier Perez de Cueller (1982–1991). Inspired by the Mothers of the Plaza de Mayo in Argentina, the Mothers of Khavaran are the sole advocacy group for those who perished in Iran.

The Islamic Republic's response has ranged from blocking the entrance to Khavaran to, in 2009, bulldozing parts of the cemetery,[57] and arresting and imprisoning protestors. Nevertheless, the Mothers continue to make their presence felt and demand justice for their loved ones. Their quest for truth, accountability, and prosecution of those involved in the 1981 to 1988 executions have brought them international recognition. In 2014, the Mothers of Khavaran were awarded the prestigious South Korean Gwangju Prize for Human Rights.[58]

They have also been instrumental in revealing the truth and its details to Iranians in diaspora, international human rights organizations, as well as the UN. Sadly, they are aging, many have passed away, while their quest for justice has remained unfulfilled.

Mobilization for Justice in Diaspora

After the executions in 1988, the regime gradually released political prisoners. Some left Iran taking residence primarily in Europe, Canada, or the United States. A number wrote their prison memoirs in Persian or English, which have offered a more complete picture than would ever be possible inside Iran of what happened in the prisons and provided detailed accounts of the 1988 executions. Ex-prisoners' memoirs have greatly contributed to the preservation of this grim history.[59]

These historical memories have received significant attention from Iranians in exile. Iranian human rights organizations[60] are actively contributing to the documentation of the 1988 executions and to seeking justice. The Iranian Tribunal—a grassroots organization established in 2007 by the families of the victims and human rights activists—has sought to hold the Islamic Republic accountable for its crimes.[61] In 2012, they organized an international tribunal modeled after Bertrand Russell's People's Tribunal.[62] At a three-day hearing held at the Peace Palace in The Hague, seventy-five survivors and families of those executed provided testimonies on camera and revealed the range of atrocities committed by the Islamic Republic. Based on these testimonies, the judges, international legal experts, Johann Kriegler (South Africa), Makau Mutua (Kenya), Margaret Ratner Kunstler (United States), Michael Mansfield (United Kingdom), among others, concluded that the Islamic Republic has indeed committed crimes against humanity.[63]

From Denial to Destruction of Evidence

For years, the Islamic Republic has denied the 1988 mass executions. But new evidence has challenged this denial. A forty-minute audio file of the late Ayatollah Montazeri, who had objected to Khomeini's fatwa, was released online by his son Ahmad in 2016.[64] In this file, Montazeri speaks vehemently to members of the "Death Committee" (Hossein Ali Nayyeri, Morteza Eshraqi, Ebrahim Raisi, and Mostafa Pour Mohammadi), criticizing them for their complicity in the slaughters: "In my view, the biggest crime of the Islamic Republic for which history will condemn us, has been committed at your hands. They will write your names as criminals in history."[65]

Montazeri's audio file verified the executions and triggered strong reaction from the regime. The authorities set out to destroy any evidence that could prove and incriminate its atrocities. According to a joint report by Justice for Iran, an Iranian human rights organization based in London, and Amnesty International, Iran has been actively destroying mass graves in cities across the country.[66] Based on satellite imagery from Google Earth,[67] video footage, and photographs,[68] the report illustrates that "There may be more one hundred and twenty [mass grave] locations across Iran that contain the remains of these victims."[69] The Islamic Republic has accelerated the pace of destroying mass graves by "bulldozing, hiding the mass graves beneath new burial plots, constructing concrete slabs, building roads over the graves, and turning them into rubbish dumps."[70]

The destruction of mass graves and the evidence of the 1988 mass executions has been expedited now that Ebrahim Raisi is in power as the president of Iran (term: 2021– 2025). Raisi, a member of "Death Committee," played a key role in the extrajudicial executions of thousands of political prisoners in 1988.[71]

In June 2022, Iranian authorities began erecting high concrete walls and installing security cameras around the perimeter of Khavaran to restrict family access. The walled cemetery will allow the Islamic Republic to further destroy any evidence of the executions: the bones. Raisi's rise to the presidency is a further blow to human rights protection in Iran and the quest for accountability and justice.

A Path Forward

The United Nations could play a central role in holding the Islamic Republic accountable for the 1988 executions and enforced disappearances. After decades of inaction, in 2020, seven UN human rights experts, including Luciano Hazen, Chair-Rapporteur of the Working Group on Enforced or Involuntary Disappearances, and Javaid Rehman, Special Rapporteur on the Situation of Human Rights in the Islamic Republic of Iran, sent a letter to the government of Islamic Republic demanding accountability.[72] They called for investigation of the 1988 executions and enforced disappearances by a UN–authorized team and expressed concern, "that the situation may amount to crimes against humanity."[73]

Should the Islamic Republic refuse to comply with its legal obligations under international human rights laws, the UN experts are prepared to call for establishment of an international investigation of the events of 1988.[74] The unequivocal UN letter was a positive development but, as of this writing, the Islamic Republic has not responded to this letter. Nevertheless, the United Nations should continue to exert pressure on Iran.

Human rights organizations concur that the Islamic Republic has committed grave crimes against humanity.[75] Unfortunately, Iran is not signatory to more recent United Nations instruments such as the 2007 International Convention for the Protection of All Persons from Enforced Disappearance. But Iran is a signatory to the Universal Declaration of Human Rights of 1948 and the International Covenant on Civil and Political Rights of 1966, which states in article 7 that "no one shall be subjected to torture, inhumane or degrading treatment or punishment." The Islamic Republic has not only breached international human rights treaties but its own Constitution as well.[76]

Addressing the gruesome events of 1988 requires comprehensive measures and partnership by the UN and the Islamic Republic of Iran, which must allow the United Nations Special Rapporteur on Human Rights in the Islamic Republic of Iran and the United Nations Working Group on Enforced or Involuntary Disappearances to visit Iran to investigate.

With that investigation, the Islamic Republic would be obliged to provide the names of the executed political prisoners and reveal the locations of their graves. With the consent of the families, graves might then be exhumed by independent professional forensic experts and the remains of bodies properly preserved. The bodies should be accurately identified and buried according to the families' religious and cultural traditions. Families would necessarily be consulted and engaged throughout the process.

The tragedy of Iran's 1988 executions and disappearances, as in so many places worldwide, must be seen, spoken aloud, admitted, victims' names reinstated, and restitution take place to restore victims and survivors in history.

Notes

I would like to thank former Iranian political prisoners and the families of the executed and disappeared for sharing their painful memories with me. My gratitude to Payam Akhavan for reviewing this chapter and providing insightful comments. Likewise, I am grateful to Jafar Yaghoobi for his enthusiastic support and in-depth review of the chapter. My many thanks to Jennifer Heath for her fine editing of this chapter.

1. Mehdi Aslani, in *The Massacre of Political Prisoners in Iran 1988. Witness Testimonies and Official Statements: An Addendum.* (Washington, DC.: Abdurrahman Boroumand Foundation, 2013), 51–60, 57.

2. Ebrahim Mohammad Rahimi in *The Massacre of Political Prisoners in Iran 1988*. (Washington, D.C.: Abdurrahman Boroumand Foundation, 2013), 209–12, 212.

3. Reza Ghaffari, *A State of Fear: My 10 Years Inside Iran's Torture Jails* (London: John Blake Publishing, 2012), 28.

4. Monireh Baradaran, *Haghighate Sadeh* (*A Simple Truth*) (Essen, Germany: Nima Verlog, 2000), 402.

5. Mohammad Mossadegh was arrested and tried in a military court and sentenced to three years imprisonment. Upon his release from prison, he was kept under house arrest until his death on March 5, 1967. The Shah's regime denied him a public funeral.

6. The National Security Archive, "CIA Confirms Role in 1953 Iran Coup," *National Security Archive Briefing*, Book No. 4, 435, August 19, 2013. This declassified document was posted on George Washington University website, https://nsarchive2.gwu.edu/NSAEBB/NSAEBB435/

7. Soviet Union influence in Iran was mainly exercised through the pro-Soviet Tudeh Party and through support for the Iranian separatist movements of Iranian Azerbaijan (1945) and Iranian Kurdistan (1946).

8. Khomeini lived in exile in Iraq from October 1965 until October 6, 1978, when he was expelled by Saddam Hussein. Khomeini then settled in Paris.

9. Amir Taheri, *The Persian Night: Iran Under the Khomeinist Revolution* (New York: Encounter Books, 2009), 78.

10. For a list of political organizations please refer to *The Massacre of Political Prisoner in Iran 1988*, 385–94.

11. While Iranians in general refer to the revolution as *Enqelab-e Iran*, or Iranian Revolution, Khomeini and his supporters declared the revolution as *Enqelab-e Islami*, or Islamic revolution.

12. Ervand Abrahamian, *Tortured Confessions: Prisons and Public Recantations in Modern Iran* (Berkeley: University of California Press 1999), 131.

13. Abrahamian, *Tortured Confessions*, 139.

14. Shadi Sadr and Shadi Amin, *Crime and Impunity* (London: Justice for Iran, 2012), 171–89.

15. Abrahamian, *Tortured Confessions*, 215; Baradaran, *Haghighate Sadeh*, 228 and 295.

16. Abrahamian, *Tortured Confessions*, 218; Reza Afshari, *Human Rights in Iran: The Abuse of Cultural Relativism* (Philadelphia: University of Pennsylvania Press, 2011), 38; Kaveh Shahrooz, "With Revolutionary Rage and Rancor: A Preliminary Report on the 1988 Massacre of Iranian Political Prisoners," *Harvard Human Rights Journal* 20, 2007, 227–61, 251; Amnesty International, *Iran: Violations of Human Rights 1987–1990*, (AI Index 13/21/90)13; Human Rights Watch, *Ministers of Murder* (2005), 2; https://www.hrw.org/legacy/backgrounder/mena/iran1205/; Iran Human Rights Documentation Center, *Deadly Fatwa: Iran's 1988 Prison Massacre* (New Haven: Iran Human Rights Documentation Center,2009), 1. https://iranhrdc.org/deadly-fatwa-irans-1988-prison-massacre/

17. Abrahamian, *Tortured Confessions*, 210.

18. Abrahamian, *Tortured Confessions*, 209.

19. *The Massacre of Political Prisoners in Iran 1988*, 28.

20. Iran Human Rights Documentation Center, *Deadly Fatwa*, 94.

21. *The Massacre of Political Prisoners in Iran 1988*, 373.

22. *The Massacre of Political Prisoners in Iran 1988*, 374.

23. Sharooz, "With Revolutionary Rage and Rancor," 251.

24. Abrahamian, *Tortured Confessions*, 213.

25. Nasser Mohajer, *Jonbesh-e Madaran-e Khavaran* (*Mothers of Khavaran Movement*) (2009), 231. https://www.bidaran.net/spip.php?article

26. Khavaran Cemetery is in southeast Tehran on Khavaran Road, off Lapeh Zanak Street. It is ten miles from Tehran on Imam Reza Highway (Tehran-Mashhad Highway).

27. Shahla Talebi, *Ghosts of Revolution: Rekindled Memories of Imprisonment in Iran* (Redwood City, CA: Stanford University Press, 2011), 33.

28. Talebi, *Ghosts of Revolution*, 34.

29. Ritually washing the body and wrapping it in a white shroud, with some variations, apply to Muslims, Jews, and Christian Armenians who were also among the executed.

30. Jafar Yaghoobi, *Let Us Water the Flowers: The Memoir of a Political Prisoner in Iran* (New York: Prometheus Books, 2011), 320.

31. Amnesty International has recognized prisoners' disappearances in Iran as enforced. Amnesty International and Justice for Iran, *Criminal Cover up: Iran Destroying Mass Graves of Victims of 1988 Killings* (2018), 5.

32. Talebi, *Ghosts of Revolution*, 36.

33. Talebi, *Ghosts of Revolution*, 31.

34. Author's interview with Nina Toobaei, December 12, 2015.

35. Maryam Nuri in *The Massacre of Political Prisoners in Iran* (1988), 239–250, 249.

36. National Council of Resistance of Iran, *1988 Massacre of Political Prisoners in Iran*, https://www.ncr-iran.org/en/1988-massacre-of-political-prisoners-in-iran

37. Babak Emad, "How History Will Judge Us," *Iran Tribunal*, 2009. https://irantribunal.com/how-history-will-judge-us/

38. Emad, "How History Will Judge Us." The names and profiles of the executed and disappeared political prisoners are posted on a number of Iranian websites in diaspora, *Iran Tribunal*, https://irantribunal.com/mass-executions/list-of-executions; *Bidaran*, "Khavaran-e Majazi," http://www.bidaran.net/spip.php?rubrique19; and Iraj Mesdagi's website, http://irajmesdaghi.com/

39. Shahrooz, "With Revolutionary Rage and Rancor," 241.

40. Iran Human Rights Documentation Center, *Deadly Fatwa*, 63.

41. Iran Data Portal, *Letters Dismissing Ayatollah Montazeri*, March 26, 1989. http://irandataportal.syr.edu/letter-dismissing-montazeri. On March 29, 1989, Montazeri resigned as the heir designate.

42. Abrahamian, *Tortured Confessions*, 125.

43. Michael Axworthy, *Revolutionary Iran: A History of Islamic Republic* (Oxford: Oxford University Press, 2013), 148; Shadi Sadr and Shadi Amin, *Crime and Impunity*, 49.

44. Faraj Sarkohi was cofounder and editor in chief of Iranian magazine, *Adineh* (1988–1996). It was a significant magazine of art and culture in 1980s and 1990s Iran. https://en.wikipedia.org/wiki./Faraj_Sarkohi

45. Sarkohi, *Vakonesh-e roshanfekran-e dakhel-e keshvar dar barabar-e koshtar-e 67* (*The Reaction of Intellectuals inside Iran Toward the 1988 Executions*), October 13, 2006. http://asre-nou.net/1385/mehr/21/m-1367.html

46. Sarkohi, *Vakonesh-e.*

47. Amnesty International, *Urgent Action: Iran Political Executions*, AI Index MDE 13/14/88, September 22, 1988, 2.

48. Germany, France, Former Yugoslavia, and Romania, to name a few, benefited from a growing consumer market in Iran.

49. Dianne Kirby, ed. *Religion and the Cold War.* (New York: Palgrave, 2003).

50. Saeed Kamali Dehghan and David Smith, "U.S. Had Extensive Contact with Ayatollah Khomeini Before the Iran Revolution," *Guardian*, June 10, 2016. https://www.theguardian.com/world/2016/jun/10/ayatollah-khomeini-jimmy-carter-administration-iran-revolution; Kambiz Fattahi, "Two Weeks in January: America's Secret Engagement with Khomeini," *BBC News*, June 3, 2016. https://www.bbc.com/news/world-us-canada-36431160

51. Robert Morrison, "Faith Fights Communism: The United States and Islam in Saudi Arabia During the Cold War" (master's thesis, University of North Carolina, 2009).

52. From 1979 to 1989, the CIA, in what was dubbed "Operation Cyclone," spent billions of dollars arming and financing Islamist fighters, Afghan and non-Afghan, to fight Communism and drive the Soviet army out of Afghanistan.

53. Nevertheless, much later, Resolution 159 (September 2016) and Resolution 188 (May 2017) were introduced to the U.S. House of Representatives, but no further action was taken. Author's email exchange with the Law Librarian of Congress, March 6, 2019.

54. Reynaldo Pohl, *Report on the Situation on Human Rights in the Islamic Republic of Iran*, resolutions adopted by the General Assembly, 43rd Session, January 1, 1989, 211. http://repository.un.org/bitstreams/handle/11176/164166/A_RES-43-137-EN.pdf?sequence=3&isAllowed=y

55. Afshari, *Human Rights in Iran*, 38; Shahrooz, "With Revolutionary Rage and Rancor," 242.

56. For more information on Mothers of Khavaran, please check the following sources in Persian: *Dastan-e Na Tamam-e Madaran va Khanevadeha-ye Khavaran* (*The Unfinished Tale: The Mothers and Families of Khavaran: Three Decades of Pursuit of Truth and Justice*) (London: Justice for Iran 2015); Nasser Mohajer, *Jonbesh-e Madaran-e Khavaran* (*Mothers of Khavaran Movement*) 2009, article 231. http://www.bidaran.net/spip.php?

57. Amnesty International, Iran, *Preserve the Khavaran Grave Site for Investigation into Mass Killings*, AI Index: MDE 13/006/2009, January 20, 2009.

58. The award is given in recognition of individuals and groups contributing to human rights and democracy. This award was shared between the Mothers of Khavaran and Adilur Rahman Khan, a human rights defender from Bangladesh.

59. Political Prisoners: The Art of Resistance in the Middle East, a website sponsored by University of Toronto, provides the list of these memoirs. https://womenpoliticalprisoners.com

60. Abdurrahman Boroumand Foundation (Washington, D.C.), the Iranian Tribunal (Sweden and England), the Center for Human Rights in Iran (New York),

Iran Human Rights Documentation Center (Connecticut), and Justice for Iran (London) are just some of these organizations.

61. For more information on this tribunal refer to Payam Akhavan, "Is Grass-roots Justice a Viable Alternative to Impunity? The Case of the Iranian's People's Tribunal," *Human Rights Quarterly* 39 (2017): 73–103.

62. Bertrand Russell and Jean-Paul Sartre Tribunal, known as International War Crimes Tribunal, was a campaign against the American atrocities in the Vietnam War (1965–1967).

63. *Findings of the Truth Commission of International People's Tribunal* (Iran Tribunal: Sweden 2013), 7.

64. Ahmad was forced by the Iranian authorities to remove the audio file, but it had already been posted on other websites.

65. The audio file, with English captions, was posted on YouTube on September 16, 2016. https://www.youtube.com/watch?v=48lhBXm-dNo&t=362s

66. Justice for Iran and Amnesty International, *Criminal Cover-Up: Iran Destroying Mass Graves of Victims of 1988 Killings*, April 2018. AI Index: MDE 13/8259/2018

67. Justice for Iran and Amnesty International, *Criminal Cover-Up*, 6.23.

68. Justice for Iran and Amnesty International, *Criminal Cover-Up*, 5.

69. Justice for Iran and Amnesty International, *Criminal Cover-Up*, 4.

70. Justice for Iran and Amnesty International, *Criminal Cover-Up*.

71. In addition to his role on the "Death Committee," Raisi, as deputy to the Chief Justice (2004–2014), played a visible role in the crackdown on protestors contesting the reelection of then-President Mahmoud Ahmadinejad in 2009. The United States has imposed sanctions on Raisi for his human rights violations.

72. Office of the United Nations High Commissioner for Human Rights, AL.IRN 20/2020, September 3, 2020. https://spcommreports.ohchr.org/TMResultBase/DownLoadPublicCommuniactionFile?gld=25503

73. Office of the United Nations High Commissioner for Human Rights, 8.

74. Office of the United Nations High Commissioner for Human Rights.

75. Human Rights Watch, *Ministers of Murder: Iran's New Security Cabinet*, 2005, 3; Amnesty International, *Blood-Soaked Secrets: Why Iran's 1988 Prison Massacres are ongoing Crimes Against Humanity*, 2017, Index: MDE 13/9421/2018, 18; Center for Human Rights in Iran, *Stop Destruction of Mass Graves at Khavaran: Evidence of Crime Against Humanity Being Deliberately Wiped*, February 5, 2009. https://www.iranhumanriths.org/209/02/khavaran/

76. Iranian Constitution of 1979, chapter 3 in general and articles 34–39, prove the Islamic Republic has violated political prisoners' rights, https://www.iranchamber.com/government/laws/constitution_ch03.php

The Eyes

Yassi Golshani

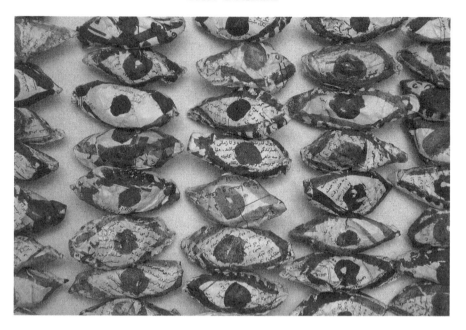

The Eyes represents the social pressures that result from self-censorship. These social pressures include the traditional values that control every person in society through the eyes of the family, neighbors, and the public.

Persian newspapers in exile carry much meaning in my work. When I arrived in Paris in 1996, I was excited to see they existed without censorship and therefore signaled freedom.

Morad Qashqa'i was the son of family friends. Everyone more or less knew what was going on in the prisons and had friends, relatives, or acquaintances executed. Another friend had been killed a few years before and was buried en masse in Khavaran Cemetery. Morad was imprisoned without charge at the age of nineteen and sentenced to seven years. He was to be released in 1988. When the authorities called on his parents to go to Evin Prison, they looked forward to their reunion. When they arrived, they were informed of the execution and given his belongings. He was twenty-five. (See https://www.iranrights.org/memorial/story/-5340/morad-qashqai)

—Yassi Golshani

Editors' note: For more about the crimes against humanity perpetrated by Iran's Islamic Republic, as well as a history of Kharavan Cemetery, please refer to chapter 7, Ashraf Zahedi, "Politics of Silence and Denial: 1988 Enforced Disappearances and Executions in Iran."

EIGHT

The Legacy of Wartime Rape in Bosnia and Herzegovina

Edina Bećirević and Majda Halilović

The website of the Vilina Vlas Hotel in the mountainous eastern Bosnian town of Višegrad appeals to tourists seeking wellness and retreat:

> The Višegrad spa is a balneo-climatology treatment center in which the direct and indirect effects of the water and air provide excellent conditions for all forms of rehabilitation and recreation. Medical programs are based on the use of natural medicinal thermo-mineral waters in modern applications of physical medicine and rehabilitation.[1]

What the website fails to mention is that the hotel served as a detention center in 1992 and 1993, where Bosniak (Muslim) women, adolescents, and even young girls were the victims of rape and other daily sexual violence. Around two hundred women and girls were tortured, raped, and killed in the hotel during this time.[2]

Jasmina Ahmetspahić, twenty-four-years-old, after being raped in June 1992 jumped from the hotel's third floor and took her own life.[3] Jasmina and other victims at Vilina Vlas suffered what one survivor later called "unspeakable" abuse, which went well beyond the brutality of sexual violence alone, to include the vile degradation of women's bodies. One of the survivors from Vilina Vlas described being burned with cigarettes, cut with knives, and having flesh "ripped" from her mouth, as well as being locked in a room with her hands bound at all times; recounting that "[e]veryday they threw us bread which we had to catch with our teeth . . . The only time they untied us is when they raped us."[4]

In 2008, when Australian artist Kym Vercoe stayed in the hotel during a tour of the Balkans, she knew nothing of its dark past but was haunted nonetheless by feelings of discomfort. Upon her return to Australia, she researched Vilina Vlas and learned that it had been used as what the United Nations has called a "rape camp."[5] The experience inspired her to write the play, *For Those Who Can Tell No Tales*—adapted later by filmmaker Jasmila Žbanić to the screen—which exposed the culture of denial that has left many women survivors of wartime rape in the shadows of Bosnian society.

Vilina Vlas was not the only place in Bosnia and Herzegovina (BiH) where women were systematically raped during the 1992–1995 war. In fact, well over twenty thousand women were victims of wartime sexual violence, many of whom were kept in captivity and tortured, and some of whom were subjected to forced pregnancy.[6] Several thousand men are also believed to have been victims of wartime rape in BiH.[7] According to the UN, men were not only subjected to wartime sexual assault, but were also "forced to rape women and to perform sex acts on guards or each other," and were sometimes sexually mutilated.[8] Male victims, however, have remained almost entirely invisible, as prevailing gender norms allow no room for recognition of their trauma. Moreover, while men undoubtedly suffered a range of human rights violations during the war, rape was most often targeted at women; and in BiH, the methodical rape of women was part of a wider genocidal plan by Serb forces.

Rape as a Mechanism of Genocide by Serb Forces during the 1992–1995 War in BiH

The war in BiH extended from the process of dissolution that transformed Former Yugoslavia and is considered one of the "Yugoslav wars of the 1990's," among which a common feature was the instigating role of Serbia. But Serbia's aggression in BiH was the bloodiest of these conflicts. It claimed some hundred thousand Bosnian lives, led to the largest displacement of people in Europe since World War II, and engulfed the country in a humanitarian crisis of an almost inconceivable scale.[9]

In March 1992, under the influence of Serbian media, controlled by Serbian strongman Slobodan Milošević, Bosnian Serbs largely boycotted a democratic referendum in which their fellow Bosnian citizens overwhelmingly voted for independence. The position of Serb nationalist leaders like Milošević was that BiH should remain part of a rump Yugoslav State, but that if it sought independence, "Serb territories" within BiH belonged to Serbia. This echoed a century-old call for the creation of a "Greater Serbia," the realization of which was impossible without forcibly changing demographic realities on the ground.[10]

By the time the new State of Bosnia and Herzegovina received international recognition shortly after declaring independence, the Serb aggression—planned well in advance—had already begun; and would continue for the next three and a half years. During this time, between twenty thousand and fifty thousand women were victims of a systematic rape campaign, a figure that remains difficult to ascertain, as many survivors have chosen to keep silent about their wartime experiences.[11] This reticence is not uncommon in victims of sexual violence in any context, but there is a unique stigma for women survivors of wartime rape in BiH, as the crimes committed against them were employed as a weapon of war. In other words, Serb soldiers wielded this weapon, in systematic fashion, against non-Serb women—especially Bosniak (Muslim), but also Bosnian Croat, women—not only as a crime of domination but also with the intention to impregnate them, in order to "make *četnik* [Serb] babies."[12] Indeed, one of the most horrifying features of the conflict was the Serb practice of detaining women in rape camps into the late stages of pregnancy, and then releasing them to cross back into territory held by the Bosnian Army as proof of the lengths Serbs were willing to go to meet their genocidal objectives.

The genocidal campaign waged by Serbs in BiH relied on certain standard tactics across the country. Bosniak and Croat populations were terrorized and "cleansed" in concentration camps, or were forcibly displaced by the incessant bombing of occupied cities where citizens were intentionally starved. Within this larger campaign of genocide, the systematic way in which rape was used by Serb forces against non-Serb women had all the elements of a planned military strategy, and it reasonable to claim—as many scholars have—that, "when utilized in ethnic conflicts, as in the Bosnian case, sexual violence is employed as a weapon of demoralization against entire societies."[13]

Rape by Non-Serb Forces during the War in BiH

Most wartime rapes perpetrated in BiH were committed by Bosnian Serb forces. The majority of victims were Bosniak women, but Bosnian Croat and Bosnian Serb women were also raped during the war. Notably, the UN found that "few reports of rape and sexual assault [were] between members of the same ethnic group."[14] Yet, in the aftermath of the conflict, Bosniak and Croat victims were the only ones to speak about their experiences of sexual violence, as Serb victims kept wholly silent. Because rape had been part of the genocidal campaign unleashed by Serb forces, an organized post-war effort among Serb leaders to conceal the part played by those forces in weaponizing rape against non-Serb women contributed to an active denial of wartime sexual violence in the public and media discourse of the predominantly Serb part of BiH. This made it especially difficult for Bosnian Serb women to say publicly, or report to authorities, that they were also victims of wartime rape.

This silence among Bosnian Serb women is one of the reasons that literature acknowledging the "well established fact" that Serb women "were also victims of . . . sexual violence during the war"[15] nonetheless tends to cite interviews and testimonies from almost exclusively Bosniak women. This is also why collective activism is most prominent among Bosniak victims. For the most part, Serb victims of wartime violence have only recently been willing to identify themselves as such; and political hostility has kept them from reaching beyond their own ethnic spheres to explore the possibility of building common identities or drawing strength in joint activism based on gender rather than ethnicity. Yet, some Bosniak women who have given voice to their experiences say they have escaped feelings of shame and guilt because they feel part of a wider collective.[16] Hence, while it is important to acknowledge the genocidal nature of the sexual violence committed by Serb soldiers against non-Serb women, there may be significant value for survivors in shifting the focus to the *gendered* nature of wartime rape, and away from the ethnic filter through which so many Bosnian social issues are viewed.

Confronting Wartime Rape in the Post-War Era

Immediately following the war in BiH, women of all ethnicities were reluctant to speak publicly about the rape they had suffered, fearing condemnation, shame, and the stigma that is so often attributed to women victims of sexual violence. Still, over time, some survivors became more vocal; and their brave voices have stood in opposition to this social stigma, forcing a number of their rapists to face justice in both international and domestic courts. In the interest of justice, women have provided painful, detailed testimony to these courts, illustrating the extreme brutality and horrifying inhumanity that was weaponized against them. Some of these women have spoken in public forums as well, helping normalize discourse on wartime sexual violence.[17]

Before the war was even over, both the international community and the broader public had come to realize that systemized mass rape was occurring in BiH, and the need to address this planned pattern of sexual violence became unavoidable. In judgements issued in cases in The Hague (at the International Criminal Tribunal for the Former Yugoslavia, or ICTY), wartime rape was recognized for the first time as a war crime and a crime against humanity. This acknowledgement by the Tribunal of the suffering caused by the weaponization of sexual violence was important. Numerous studies and interviews conducted after the war with women survivors of rape indicate that their rape marked a traumatic turning point in their lives. The experience will resonate forever, in their relationships with their partners and children, their attitudes toward their own bodies, and their sense of place in their communities.[18] As one survivor explained, "that time changed my life completely. . . . When I see Vilina Vlas it all comes back. This is something that cannot be erased . . . no matter how strong I am, I can't overcome it." She told an interviewer that the "only consolation . . . would be to see [her perpetrator] admit his crimes . . . accept the gravity of his actions and admit his guilt."[19]

The sad truth for most victims, however, is that their rapists will never face justice. The sheer numbers of both perpetrators and victims of wartime rape in BiH make it impossible to prosecute more than a small percentage of cases, and any satisfaction that convictions bring to victims is tempered by that fact that other known wartime rapists live unpunished in their communities. Nonetheless, the prosecution of any perpetrator does offer some sense of justice to most victims; and the willingness of women to speak out has helped expand the reach of international criminal law and establish judicial precedents for the prosecution of rape as a war crime, a crime against humanity, and a crime of genocide.[20]

Bosnian women who have spoken openly about their experiences of wartime rape, along with media coverage of trials and the persistence of some local and international NGOs, have contributed to changing the social climate in BiH, so that twenty-five years after the war, the topic of wartime sexual violence is discussed in public as never before. High-profile media attention on specific cases of wartime rape in BiH has also inspired films such as *In the Land of Blood and Honey* (2011), directed by Angelina Jolie, which piqued global interest in the topic. For Jolie, the film became a platform for activism that resulted in a worldwide campaign to end impunity for war-related sex crimes, resulting in a "Declaration of Commitment to End Sexual Violence in Conflict," signed by 144 countries so far, including Serbia.[21]

Importantly, Jolie's film portrays the cruelty of Serb soldiers but also humanizes them, revealing their brutality not as an inherent "wickedness of Serbs as people" but as the result of a "systematic, institutionalized policy of persecution and killing" and as part of "an organized genocide."[22] Indeed, the scale of the mass rape perpetrated against Bosniak women was unprecedented, and fit a clear pattern; there is no question that it necessitated top-down organization, and victims have testified at the International Criminal Court in The Hague that their rapist(s) acknowledged they had been ordered to commit sexual violence or impregnate them. But among the strongest evidence that mass rape in BiH was in fact organized by Serb authorities has been their willingness to protect high-level perpetrators, such as Dragan Zelenović, the wartime deputy commander of the military police in the eastern Bosnian town of Foča. In 2007, Zelenović—who was arrested in Moscow—pleaded guilty to aiding and abetting rape as well as committing rape himself, and also for torturing, beating, and starving women in rape camps. At the ICTY, his lawyer told the court during a hearing that Zelenović "was told to leave Foča" and go to Belgrade, and that when he arrived, "he went to the police station . . . where documents were issued to him, a passport with a visa of the Russian Federation, and a personal identity card in the name of Branislav Petrović."[23] His case illustrates that the post-war mechanism to protect Serb war criminals stretches from Banja Luka and Belgrade all the way to Moscow.

Cases such as that of Zelenović have helped raise public awareness of wartime rape and give rise to more serious civic debate in BiH on the subject of rape more generally, from its "causes" to possible approaches to preventing it. This has been a factor in overcoming antiquated myths within Bosnian society, such as that rape is a product of the uncontrollable biological urges of men. Feminist voices have driven this dialogue toward a critical examination of misogyny–already widespread in Bosnian society before finding its most brutal expression in the war. To some degree, this has been possible because women have entered politics and the law in greater numbers, occupying prominent positions that enable them to offer alternative perspectives on rape and give rape victims a voice. But the hope of some activists that a collective examination of the views and attitudes directed at women would occur immediately after the war in BiH, or that their experience of rape on such a large scale would inspire the better treatment of women and decrease their exposure to violence, has not been realized. Indeed, women in BiH are exposed to insupportable rates of violence to this day. The latest Organization for Security and Co-operation in Europe (OSCE) survey on violence against women (2019) found that 48 percent of women in BiH have experienced some form of violence, including intimate partner violence, stalking, and sexual harassment, from the age of fifteen; and that nearly four in ten women (38 percent) have experienced psychological, physical, or sexual violence in their adult lives.[24]

Many years before the war in BiH, Susan Brownmiller wrote that men are groomed by patriarchal culture to loathe women and are then enabled by wartime circumstances to express that loathing.[25] It is clear that misogyny fuels the abuse of women even in peacetime, but that it especially inspires the commission of atrocities such as those perpetrated against women during the Bosnian war, meaning that women become even less safe when social order collapses.[26] Nena Močnik emphasizes that BiH is really no different than anywhere else when it comes to how sex is stigmatized, mystified, and controlled in local culture vis-à-vis a patriarchal ideology that shapes intimate relationships. Across the world, societies replicate a heteronormative discourse on sexuality, and disturbing evidence of mass rape campaigns in conflicts that have taken place in more recent years—in Darfur, Syria, Northern Iraq, and Liberia, for example—highlight the importance of raising international awareness about wartime gendered violence and generating the political will to prevent and end it. The 2017 testimony of a Yazidi rape survivor that she "was raped every day for six months"[27] too closely echoes the experiences of Bosnian women from twenty-five years ago.

Unpacking the Legacy of Wartime Sexual Violence in BiH

While misogyny and patriarchy certainly inform our understanding of the sexual violence committed against women during the conflict in BiH, these factors do not account entirely for the organized and mass nature of these crimes. For many Bosnian women, the question that lingers is *how* it was possible in a country where they were at least declaratively and legally equal to men that so many women were raped and so many men participated. To answer this, it is necessary to recognize that the dynamics of Bosnian society at the time of the war cannot be explained through the lens of misogyny and patriarchy alone, for this overlooks the nuances of social relations in BiH and how they were instrumentalized in the years *before* the war.

The war itself, and the mass atrocities committed once it began, were in fact manifestations of an existing misogynistic and patriarchal culture, but the narratives that created a climate for war and fueled the grievances that drove people to violence were linked to a more complex set of factors, intertwined with both history and myth. In this sense, it is significant that the victims of wartime rape in BiH were predominantly Bosniak women and the perpetrators were predominantly Serb soldiers, not because it assigns blame or is meant to deny that rape was committed by forces on all sides of the conflict, but because it speaks to the way sexual violence was weaponized as a tool of war against an "enemy" population. What occurred in BiH was a systematic and planned pattern of rape, deliberately targeting one group. This "enemy" group had been designated long before the war began with rhetoric that simultaneously dehumanized Bosniaks and implied that they posed an existential threat to Serbs. In other words, the answer to how mass rape could have occurred in a society that at least declaratively viewed women and men as equals is that it was not merely gender but *ethnicity and gender* that made someone a target, inspired by an ideology of Serb ethno-nationalist extremism.

Though rape is among the most traumatic crimes that any woman (or man) can experience, the fact that rape was used as a weapon of war in BiH, and therefore that victims (mostly Bosniak women) were targeted for their ethnic belonging and not primarily because of their gender, is significant in terms of how survivors have dealt with related trauma. According to Inger Skjelsbæk, these women feel a sense of solidarity in belonging to a group that was targeted by sexual violence, which makes it easier for them to reach out to each other, knowing their experience is likely to be understood. This solidarity can sometimes transcend the traditional patriarchal divisions within families, crossing gender lines; as corroborated by the stories of women survivors whose husbands have felt that they, too, suffered and survived these crimes.[28]

However, the reality for most victims of wartime rape in BiH and elsewhere is not one of spousal solidarity and understanding, which is more often the exception than the rule. Instead, many of these women have turned to women's organizations and associations for support, quite a few of which emerged in the early post-war period and actively worked to empower survivors. These organizations have been vital to helping communities learn to cope with the level of violence that occurred during the war. According to Sophie Yohani, societies in shock often lack means to cope with this kind of violence, especially if they adhere to socio-cultural taboos relating to sexuality. If a community does not know how to confront the societal trauma of mass rape and chooses a policy of denial, victims feel isolated and are further traumatized.[29]

Despite social taboos, Bosnian society has managed to engage in a collective discourse, talking increasingly openly about wartime rape. And this has been relatively unique; for the gender-specific nature of this crime typically correlates to public silence. Indeed, feminist scholars have emphasized that misogyny motivates not only the use of rape during war, but the practice of silence that obscures this crime after a war is over.[30] Still, creating space in BiH for public dialogue regarding wartime sexual violence has not relieved victims of facing prejudice, stigma, and denial, which continue to prevent many wartime rape victims from obtaining adequate assistance from the State. Whereas the families of fallen soldiers and civilian victims were recognized immediately after the war, and their entitlements awarded with relative ease, it took many years of persistent advocacy and engagement by women's organizations to secure benefits for victims of wartime rape; and in some parts of BiH, this struggle is still ongoing, meaning that entitlements for these victims are inconsistent across the country. For example, in one entity, the Federation of BiH (FBiH), a special status is awarded to survivors of wartime rape as civilian victims of war, but this status does not exist in the law of the other entity, the Republika Srpska (RS).

Under the provisions of RS law, benefits are awarded to individuals who sustained injuries from wartime violence, including rape, resulting in a minimum 60 percent disability. This formulation discourages many victims from reporting their experience and pursuing assistance because it is difficult (and can be retraumatizing) to prove that a disability relates to the specific trauma associated with rape. In the FBiH, the qualification of survivors of wartime sexual violence as a unique category of civilian victim means that monetary benefits and other entitlements are awarded to them without having to prove a degree of disability. This includes health insurance, psychological and professional rehabilitation services, professional re-training, and continuing education. In some cantons in the FBiH, women victims of wartime rape are also given priority in employment, housing, and legal aid.

BiH must develop a comprehensive and consistent approach to supporting wartime victims of sexual violence in all parts of the country, and from every ethnic group. This will improve the status and position of all women victims of war and will help expand existing measures and benefits and ensure equal access.[31] Moreover, a special status for victims of wartime rape reflects that this crime is viewed as different from other forms of rape in some important ways. Beyond the fact that the circumstances of war place victims in an inherently coercive environment where they are extremely vulnerable to any number of physical threats, Yohani and Kristine Hagen underscore that the weaponization of rape in wartime is also characterized by public humiliation (as perpetrators are emboldened to act in full view), sexual slavery, and forced reproduction.[32]

Research by Trial International in 2017 found that some defendants accused of wartime rape have nonetheless been acquitted in Bosnian courts because, among other things, a victim did not resist.[33] This speaks to the power of courts and prosecutors to shape the social narrative around this crime. Judicial proceedings and court decisions can reinforce lasting myths and prejudices, or they can lead to a new recognition of the seriousness of the crime of rape and a social rejection of the idea that it can ever be justified. But as Trial International documented, in BiH, a number of (patriarchal) biases continue to manifest in the language of judgements in these cases, as well as in the questions asked of victims in the courtroom and the way protective measures are applied. For instance, while questions about a victim's sex life are not permitted in court, defense lawyers often refer to a victim's sexual experiences prior to being raped, hoping to influence judges who may hold an implicit or explicit bias toward the idea that "promiscuous" victims of sexual violence are somehow responsible for the crime committed against them, even in wartime.[34] In fact, the practices of some defense lawyers in these cases undoubtedly disincentivize many survivors of rape—whether the crime occurred during wartime or peacetime—from seeking justice.

The language used in trial proceedings also has the power to implicitly minimize the seriousness of wartime rape, as well as the crime of rape more broadly. Sometimes, prosecutors refer to mere "sexual intercourse," noting, for instance, that an alleged perpetrator "took the injured party away and had sexual intercourse with her," or describing that a defendant "engaged in sexual intercourse with her on the bed and then he told her to take a shower. . . . After the shower, he had sexual intercourse with her again." Some legal professionals have used language that goes even further to infer mutuality, claiming for instance that "the defendants sexually pleasured each other."[35] This twists the crime of rape completely, particularly in the context of war, implying that it is driven by a shared sexual desire between the victim and perpetrator, rather than by the expression of misogynistic loathing described by Brownmiller or as part of the genocidal campaign that we know motivated wartime sexual violence in BiH.

It is clear that much work must still be done to fight the gender-based prejudice and myths that persist in Bosnian society, yet it is important to emphasize that progress *is* being made. According to the OSCE Mission to BiH, both male and female judges and prosecutors have demonstrated growing awareness in their handling of rape cases, significantly advancing the capacity of the judicial system to prosecute the crime of wartime rape over the past two decades. The total number of indictments issued in BiH for wartime of sexual violence remains low compared to the substantial number of crimes known to have been committed, even if one accepts the functional reality that only a small portion of perpetrators can ever face justice in a courtroom.

But justice can take other forms as well, and in BiH, these forms must begin to address the country's legacy of wartime sexual violence by recognizing that the trauma rooted in that violence extends beyond its women victims, and beyond ethnicity. While many women who are victimized individually by systemic campaigns of rape feel burdened by how their personal story contributes to a wider social trauma, this is not the burden of women to carry alone, and it is crucial that post-war societies create mechanisms which enable the larger collective to face and share this burden. If, as Sideris has observed, "when one woman [is] raped, the whole community [is] raped,"[36] then it is the whole community that must confront the trauma of that violence. And in BiH, it is especially important that "the specific socio-cultural issues and the systemic forces of oppression that gave rise to rape as a tool of war"[37] are understood, both to avert another conflict and to unwind the ways in which misogyny poses a threat to both women and to men, in peacetime and in war.

Notes

1. See (in local language): https://vilnalas.com/

2. United Nations Security Council, *Final Report of the Commission of Experts Established Pursuant to Security Council Resolution 780 (1992)*, S/1994/674, May 27, 1994. Also see: Amnesty International, *"We Need Support, Not Pity": Last Chance for Justice for Bosnia's Wartime Rape Survivors*, September 2017.

3. "*Sjetimo se lijepe Jasmine, djevojke koja je bježeći od zločinaca skočila u smrt,*" (Let's Remember the Beautiful Jasmine, the Girl who Jumped to her Death while Fleeing from Criminals) *Oslobodenje*, June 14, 2020. https://www.oslobodje nje.ba/vijesti/bih/sjetimo-se-lijepe-jasmine-djevojke-koja-je-bjezeci-od-zlocinaca -skocila-u-smrt-564740

4. Nidzara Ahmetasevic, Nerma Jelacic, and Selma Boracic. "Visegrad Rape Victims Say Their Cries Go Unheard," *Balkan Insight*, December 10, 2007.

5. United Nations Security Council, *Final Report of the Commission.*

6. United Nations Security Council, *Final Report of the Commission.*

7. *Rape Myths in Wartime Sexual Violence Trials: Transferring the Burden from*

Survivor to Perpetrator (Sarajevo, Bosnia/Herzegovina: Trial International, 2017), 19.

8. United Nations Security Council, *Final Report of the Commission*, 56.

9. Ewa Tabeau and Jakub Bijak. "War-Related Deaths in the 1992–1995-Armed Conflicts in Bosnia and Herzegovina: A Critique of Previous Estimates and Recent Results," *European Journal of Population* 21 (2005): 187–215.

10. For more on history, propaganda, and sociological analysis of genocide in Bosnia and Herzegovina, see Edina Bećirević, *Genocide on the Drina River* (New Haven: Yale University Press, 2014).

11. Alexandra Stiglmayer, "The Rapes in Bosnia-Herzegovina," in *Mass Rape: The War against Women in Bosnia-Herzegovina* (Lincoln: University of Nebraska Press, 1994); Amnesty International, *"We Need Support, Not Pity."*

12. United Nations Security Council, *Final Report of the Commission*, Annex IX, 24.

13. Earl Coneth-Morgan, *Collective Political Violence: An Introduction to the Theories and Cases of Violent Conflicts* (Oxfordshire: Routledge, 2019), 22.

14. Coneth-Morgan, *Collective Political Violence*, 60.

15. Inger Skjelsbæk, "Victim and Survivor: Narrated Social Identities of Women Who Experienced Rape During the War in Bosnia-Herzegovina," *Feminism & Psychology* 16, no. 4 (2006): 373–403, 378.

16. Interview by author with four victims of wartime rape, October and November 2014.

17. Majda Halilović, "Wartime Sexual Violence and Post-War Gender-Based Violence," *What is the Gender of Security? 20 Years of the Security Council Resolution 1325 "Women, Peace and Security" and Its Implementation in Bosnia and Herzegovina* (Sarajevo, Bosnia/Herzegovina: Sarajevo Open Centre, 2020), 235–56.

18. C. Snyder, W. Gabbard, D. May, and N. Zulčić, "On the Battleground of Women's Bodies: Mass Rape in Bosnia-Herzegovina," *Journal of Women and Social Work* 21, no. 2 (2006): 184–95.

19. BIRN BiH, "A Month in the Hands of Milan Lukić," *Justice Report*, November 6, 2009. https://www.justice-report.com/en/articles/for-the-record-a-month-in-the-hands-of-milan-lukic

20. Women from Rwanda, who were subjected to genocidal rape in 1994, have also testified in trials that have changed international discourse on this subject. It is estimated that up to half a million women were raped during the Rwandan genocide, and the Judgement in the trial of Jean-Paul Akayesu specifically cited rape as a form of genocide. See: Judgement, "Prosecutor v. Jean-Paul Akayesu," No. ICTR-96-4, September 2, 1998.

21. See the Declaration here: https://www.peacewomen.org/content/declaration-commitment-end-sexual-violence-conflict-0

22. Marko Hoare, "Angelina Jolie," *Spirit of Bosnia/Duh Bosne* 7, no. 3 (2012).

23. Court Proceedings, "Prosecutor v. Zelenović," No. IT_96–23/2, February 23, 2007, 529.

24. OSCE, *Well-Being and Safety of Women: OSCE-led Survey on Violence Against Women* (Sarajevo: OSCE, 2019).

25. Susan Brownmiller, *Against Our Will: Men, Women and Rape* (New York: Simon and Schuster, 1975).

26. Cindy S. Snyder, Wesley J. Gabbard, J. Dean May, and Nihada Zulčić, "On the Battleground of Women's Bodies: Mass Rape in Bosnia-Herzegovina," Consortium on Gender, Security, and Human Rights (Boston: University of Masssachusetts, 2006).

27. *BBC News*, "Surrviving ISIS," July 24, 2017. Available on YouTube at: https://www.youtube.com/watch?v=XDniN3k5aQ8&pbjreload=101

28. Inger Skjelsbæk, "Victim and Survivor: Narrated Social Identities of Women Who Experienced Rape During the War in Bosnia-Herzegovina," *Feminism and Psychology* 16, no. 4: 373–403.

29. Kristine T. Hagen and Sophie C. Yohani, "The Nature and Psychosocial Consequences of War Rape for Individuals and Communities," *International Journal of Psychological Studies* 2, no. 2 (2010): 14–25.

30. For example, see: Brownmiller, *Against Our Will*.

31. Esther Garcia Fransioli, *Annual Report on the State of Women's Rights in Bosnia and Herzegovina in 2013* (Sarajevo, Bosnia/Herzegovina: Sarajevo Open Centre, 2013).

32. Kristen Hagen and Sophie Yohani, "The Nature and Psychosocial Consequences of War Rape for Individuals and Communities," *International Journal of Psychological Studies, Canadian Centre of Science and Education* 2, no. 2 (December 2010).

33. Kyle Delbyck, *Rape Myths in Wartime Sexual Violence Trials: Transferring the Burden from Survivor to Perpetrator* (Sarajevo, Bosnia/Herzegovina: Trial International, 2017), 36.

34. Delbyck, *Rape Myths in Wartime Sexual Violence Trials*, 25–29.

35. Delbyck, *Rape Myths in Wartime Sexual Violence Trials*, 43.

36. Tina Sideris, "Rape in War and Peace: Social Context, Gender, Power, and Identity," in Anu Pillay Sheila Meintjes and Meredith Turshen, eds., *The Aftermath: Women in Post-Conflict Transformation* (New York: Zed Books, 2001), 147.

37. Hagen and Yohani, "The Nature and Psychosocial Consequences of War Rape," 20.

NINE

Genocide of the Rohingya

Elena Sarver and Akila Radhakrishnan

Myanmar is a country composed of a majority (two-thirds) Burman (Bamar), largely Buddhist population and a minority comprising more than one hundred different ethnicities, with several major groups including Shan, Karen, Kachin, Rakhine, Chin, Mon, Rohingya, and Kayah.[1] Many of these groups have "distinct cultures, languages, traditions, and sometimes religions" and "live mainly in the peripheral areas, near the borders with Bangladesh, China, India, and Thailand."[2] Among these populations more than one hundred languages are spoken.[3] With respect to religion, some minorities are Buddhist along with the Burman majority and there are also groups of Christians, Hindus, and Muslims.[4]

Against this diverse background, Myanmar's military has a long history of violence, systematic discrimination, and policies of exclusion and marginalization. Out of unliteral power over the past decade, Myanmar's military staged a coup in February 2021, jailing political opponents and asserting control over the country. As of this writing, the military faces immense opposition from Myanmar's populace, who largely support the National Unity Government (NUG).

Ongoing since the 1960s, conflict in Myanmar's ethnic states continues unabated despite the country's quasi-democratic transition and the signing of various ceasefire agreements—conflicts which have been exacerbated in the wake of the coup, with armed ethnic groups forming a key component of the resistance to military rule. Mass violence in Rakhine State and targeting of the Rohingya, a Muslim ethnic minority, must be considered and understood alongside the continued conflict between Myanmar's military and various armed ethnic groups, including violence in Shan and Kachin States. In Kachin and Shan States, as well as other ethnic states, there have been decades of complicated conflict motivated by a struggle for greater independence. According to the United Nations Independent International Fact-Finding Mission (FFM) on Myanmar, these conflicts have been driven "against what [these minority populations] perceive to be a central government that has favored Bamar-Buddhists politically and economically . . . fueled by the exploitation of natural resources; land use and major infrastructure projects; and narcotics trading . . . [and] in a context of severe discrimination on ethnic and religious grounds, often with persecutory intent."[5]

The Rohingya, like many of Myanmar's ethnic minorities, have suffered from widespread discrimination. As the FFM on Myanmar states, "[t]he Rohingya are in a situation of severe, systematic, and institutionalized oppression from birth to death. Their extreme vulnerability is a consequence of State policies and practices implemented over decades, steadily marginalizing the Rohingya and eroding their enjoyment of human rights."[6] The situation of the Rohingya in Myanmar has been aptly described as apartheid.[7] The military has recognized eight ethnic groups (Kachin, Kayah, Karen, Chin, Bamar, Mon, Rakhine, and Shan) as "those who 'belong' in Myanmar; all others, regardless of how many generations they have lived in Myanmar, are considered outsiders or immigrants. This includes the Rohingya."[8]

Effectively deprived of nationality under the 1982 Citizenship Law and denied recognition as an official ethnic group, the Rohingya are a predominantly Muslim ethnic minority living in Rakhine State in northern and western Myanmar. "The Rohingya trace their origins in the region to the fifteenth century, when thousands of Muslims" migrated to the historical Kingdom of Arakan, on the border of what is now Bangladesh.[9] "Many others arrived during the nineteenth and early twentieth centuries, when Rakhine was governed by colonial rule as part of British India."[10] Prior to the resurgence of conflict in 2016, approximately one million of the world's 3.5 million Rohingya lived in Rakhine State.[11] Many of the Rohingya population are spread worldwide in such countries as Bangladesh, Thailand, Malaysia, and Indonesia.[12] Since the late 1970s, when the military initiated a process to register citizens that "led to more than 200,000 Rohingya fleeing to Bangladesh"[13] (one of several periodic flights of the Rohingya out of Myanmar), the Rohingya population in Myanmar has been subject to increasing restrictions on their rights including their freedom of movement, marriage, access to education, and healthcare, and, in some cases, even their ability to have children, such as by controlling the number and spacing of children permitted or requiring contraception use with penalties for noncompliance.[14] Furthermore, Myanmar's former government, civilian and military alike refused to recognize the "Rohingya" (the term they use to self-identify) and instead most often called them "Bengali," which is viewed as a "derogatory term implying they are illegal immigrants from Bangladesh."[15] This refusal to recognize, coupled with their denials of citizenship, renders the Rohingya as one of the largest stateless populations in the world.[16] This stateless status renders them even more vulnerable, by denying the protections of the State and ability to access and exercise a wide range of rights, and exposing them to exploitation, detention, and abuse.[17]

Against this background, in October 2016, Burmese military (Tatmadaw), Border Guard, and police forces (collectively referred to here as Burmese Security Forces) initiated a wave of violence targeting the Rohingya. The crackdown came after an attack by an armed group now known as the Arakan Rohingya Salvation Army (ARSA) on three security posts in northern Rakhine State that resulted in the death of nine officers.[18]

Formed in 2012, following "violence between Buddhist and Muslim communities in Rakhine State,"[19] "ARSA is the first operational Rohingya armed force in Myanmar in decades" with the goal to restore Rohingya rights.[20] Reports from various non-governmental agencies (NGOs) indicate the group is not well organized, funded, or trained[21] and "operates from within Rohingya villages, using cells of villagers who have been given some basic training but most of whom do not have access to firearms, only bladed weapons and some improvised explosive devices (IEDs)."[22] According to Amnesty International, there is evidence showing the group is responsible for committing human rights abuses.[23]

Security Forces responded to this attack by carrying out disproportionate and brutal "clearance operations" on all Rohingya in northern Rakhine State, comprising unlawful killings, rape, enforced disappearances, arbitrary detentions, and other forms of torture.[24]

In August 2017, ARSA carried out a second wave of larger and more coordinated attacks.[25] Again, Burmese Security Forces responded with violence on a mass scale which was characterized by increased ferocity and horror.[26] Survivors report indiscriminate killings, rape, and sexual violence, arbitrary detention, torture, beatings, and forced displacement.[27]

The Burmese Security Forces' attacks since August 25, 2017 have impacted a massive number of victims. Estimates indicated nearly 6,700 Rohingya were killed in the first month of violence alone following the start of the attacks.[28] Burmese Security Forces attacked Rohingya civilians en masse and with machine-like consistency, destroying almost four hundred villages in Rakhine State and forcing more than 700,000 Rohingya to flee across the border to neighboring Bangladesh in the months following August 2017.[29] Smaller numbers of Rohingya fled to Malaysia, Indonesia, and India, often on treacherous boat journeys.[30]

The gender-based international crimes—which arise to crimes against humanity and genocide—committed during the 2016 and 2017 campaigns are the primary focus of this chapter. We will also highlight the role gender played in the design and commission of these crimes, and the importance of an inclusive gender analysis as justice processes take shape and advance forward. We will conclude with a discussion of the existing accountability efforts, structural barriers hindering these efforts, and an emphasis on why justice is critical for the Rohingya.

Gendered Nature of the Crimes Committed

Burmese Security Forces committed a range of heinous acts against the Rohingya population in Rakhine State. Killings often were carried out in differentiated ways against men and boys and against women and girls. After initial waves of indiscriminate attacks, Burmese Security Forces systematically swept through Rohingya villages, calling out families from their homes, singling out men and boys for instantaneous execution, and women and girls for physical and sexual assault before murder.[31] Entire villages were razed and burned. In the commission of these crimes, gender was integral to the actions of the Burmese Security Forces. Sexual and gender-based violence have long been the weapon of choice for Myanmar's Security Forces, documented for decades as carried out (primarily) against ethnic women and girls in conflict situations and occupied areas,[32] with the attacks against the Rohingya as no exception to this pattern.

Beginning in October 2016, Rohingya women and girls were targeted for particularly brutal manners of killing, rape, sexual violence, torture, and forced displacement.[33] Perpetrators showed no mercy, targeting pregnant and disabled women, as well as girls as young as five. Many women reported being gang raped, some by as many as eight perpetrators. Rapes were accompanied by physical violence, threats, humiliation, and cruelty. Women were beaten, punched, kicked, and subjected to invasive body searches. Their bodies were mutilated, their breasts and nipples cut off and vaginas slashed. According to one report, after a pregnant woman was raped, her stomach was slit open and her unborn baby killed with a knife.[34] These violations were often performed in public or in front of family members, traumatizing both the victims and the witnesses. They were also widespread: in one instance, 52 percent of women interviewed reported they had been raped or subject to sexual violence.[35] Men and boys were also victims of sexual violence, with one report identifying the three most common forms of sexual violence against men as forced witnessing, genital violence, and anal rape.[36] There was profound mental suffering caused by the perpetrators' violence, which was compounded by humiliation, terror, and trauma.[37]

The violence was not limited to sexual crimes. Women have been targeted and subject to a variety of crimes that are informed by their gender. Rohingya women and girls were often murdered by being burned alive or butchered by knives used for slaughtering animals—methods of killing that mirror the destruction of objects and property, demonstrating the Burmese Security Forces' misogyny.[38] Even upon fleeing these horrors and arriving in displacement camps, women confront particularly harsh consequences: cultural obstacles to receiving humanitarian aid and medical and psychosocial care, lasting consequences and discrimination from sexual violence crimes, including ostracization by their own community, and increased risk for sexual violence and exploitation. This increased risk can be due to a number of factors, including, but not limited to, the vulnerable conditions in the displacement camps such as insufficient access to basic health services, lack of privacy, heightened stress, and deficient employment or educational opportunities.[39] Further, long-embedded discriminatory legal systems within Myanmar limit Rohingya women's reproductive choices and family life, by, in some cases, restricting the number of children permitted, requiring the spacing of children, and contraception use.[40] These limiting systems reflect institutionalized and gendered persecution.

Genocide and Crimes against Humanity

There is strong evidence that these acts committed by Burmese Security Forces against the Rohingya during the 2016 and 2017 attacks constitute genocide and crimes against humanity, including by carrying out specifically designed gender crimes.

International crimes have historically been considered those that are of the "most serious . . . concern to the international community as a whole,"[41] including crimes against humanity and genocide. Crimes against humanity occur when certain acts are "committed as part of a widespread or systematic attack directed against any civilian population, with knowledge of the attack."[42] Individual acts amount to genocide when they are committed with intent to destroy a national, ethnic, racial, or religious group, in whole or in part.

Brazen and pervasive sexual and gender-based violence was used by Myanmar's Security Forces as "collective punishment" and as a "push factor" to destroy and coerce the Rohingya to flee Myanmar.[43] As such, the crimes against Rohingya women and girls form the basis of the crimes against humanity of murder, persecution, forcible transfer or deportation, rape and other sexual violence of comparable gravity, and torture; as well as the genocidal acts of killing, causing serious bodily or mental harm, inflicting conditions of life calculated to bring about physical destruction, and imposing measures intended to prevent births within the group. These classifications show how gender permeates the commission and effects of international crimes, a pattern seen time and time again across history, including, for example, in Darfur, Rwanda, and Guatemala, where "perpetrators intentionally commit[ed] rapes of women and girls publicly," thereby employing sexual violence as part of "a genocidal strategy, aim[ing] to destroy the victim as an incremental step to annihilating the group."[44]

The crimes against humanity committed against the Rohingya are the result both of the widespread and systematic nature of the campaigns of violence, as well as the network of laws and policies that deprive the Rohingya of fundamental rights and freedoms such as citizenship, marriage, reproductive choice, movement, and healthcare access.

The violence also showed clear patterns, demonstrating planning and intentionality. The multiple crimes detailed throughout this chapter indicate the mistreatment of the Rohingya population—a mild description for the killings, rape, and other crimes of sexual violence repeatedly perpetrated against the targeted group of civilians. Indeed, evidence indicates the violence was not isolated or random but rather committed in planned, systematic ways. For example, a Fortify Rights report details the Burmese Forces' deliberate preparations for the crimes carried out since October 2016, including

> disarm[ing] Rohingya civilians . . . systematically [tearing] down fencing and other structures around Rohingya homes . . . train[ing] and arm[ing] local non-Rohingya citizens in northern Rakhine

State . . . depriv[ing] Rohingya civilians of food and other aid . . . build[ing] up state security forces in northern Rakhine State . . . [and] commit[ing] human rights violations against Rohingya civilians, including imposing discriminatory curfews.[45]

There is also clear evidence that these acts amount to genocide. While most conceptions of genocide focus on the mass killing of members of a group, genocide can be committed in myriad ways that do not result in the physical "destruction" of the group but may occur through breaking the bonds holding the protected group together, including with rape and other forms of sexual violence, destroying the ability of the group to reproduce and the transfer of children from one group to another.

As genocide is a crime of "specific intent," it is often the intent attached to genocide that sets it apart from other international crimes (which may be comprised of the same underlying acts). However, there is strong evidence indicating that the acts committed by Myanmar's Security Forces were accompanied by the requisite intent. Factors supporting this conclusion include the unprecedented scale of atrocities—with estimated reports that the August 2017 operations alone resulted in more than ten-thousand casualties,[46] longstanding discrimination against the Rohingya, systematic patterns of attack, brutal and public sexual and gender-based violence crimes—and statements of Burmese government officials and Burmese Security Forces. The notion that such statements support inferences of requisite intent are bolstered by victim testimony—which include instances of ethnic and religious references during attacks, and specifically during acts of sexual violence—that make clear the connection between Security Forces' conduct and Rohingya ethnic and religious identity.[47] Specific examples of such statements include soldiers asserting Islam was not the "religion of Myanmar," calling the Rohingya "Bengalis," stating that Rohingyas would be "eliminated from Myanmar," that "all Muslims . . . would be 'vanish[ed],'" and indicating that attacks were collective punishment for alleged support for 'insurgents.'"[48]

Justice and Accountability Efforts

The international community has, at long last, begun to recognize the imperative to ensure justice and accountability for the crimes committed by Burmese Security Forces and the impossibility of justice in Myanmar's domestic system. As the evidence of genocide against the Rohingya becomes clearer, the call for justice is not just a moral imperative, but a legal one for the international community.

Under the Convention on the Prevention and Punishment of the Crime of Genocide, all States are obliged to prevent, suppress, and punish genocide, wherever it occurs.[49] In order to fulfill these obligations, the international community must recognize and punish all forms of genocidal violence, including gendered genocidal crimes. Myanmar is a party to the Convention on the Punishment and Prevention of the Crime of Genocide, and, as such, is compelled to take measures to comply with its obligations under the Convention. These include the prevention and cessation of any acts of genocide, as well punishment of responsible individuals.

Even before the February 2021 military coup, the opportunities for accountability in Myanmar were limited. As human rights advocates have long argued, until structural barriers to accountability in Myanmar are confronted, justice is not available to the Rohingya or any other ethnic minority in Myanmar's domestic courts or by any other domestic mechanism. This includes such mechanisms as the Independent Commission of Enquiry, which was deemed by the UN Independent International Fact-Finding Mission on Myanmar not to meet the standards of an "impartial, independent, effective, and thorough human rights investigation"[50] and whose report does not lay the groundwork for justice. In addition, Myanmar's previous civilian government was historically unable to hold perpetrators accountable due to structural barriers that preclude the possibility of justice. Myanmar lacks domestic legislation on international crimes, rendering its court system unable to prosecute any potential crimes against humanity or genocide. Furthermore, constitutionally imposed limits under the 2008 constitution on the power of the civilian government over the military, coupled with Myanmar's constitutional protections for the military from prosecution, have long ensured that it remains immune from accountability. More specifically, Myanmar's military is granted 25 percent of the seats in Parliament and because constitutional amendments require a more than 75 percent vote, the military has retained a veto over any amendments.[51] Even as some of the relevance of these constitutional provisions are called into question post-coup, they remain essential to the framework that allowed the Rohingya genocide to occur.

Without significant domestic legal and constitutional reforms and as the military retains control under the coup, Myanmar's national judicial system is neither available nor able to carry out proceedings for crimes committed by its Security Forces against any ethnic group, including the Rohingya. Historically Myanmar's authorities—civilian and military alike—also failed to demonstrate any willingness to investigate or hold perpetrators accountable. In fact, the previous civilian government variously denied any wrongdoing, ignored the problem, failed to conduct genuine investigations, or impose sanctions or accountability on perpetrators of these crimes.[52] Furthermore, the previous civilian government actively denied and dismissed the existence of sexual violence; for example, it stated in a February 2019 report to the Committee on the Elimination of Discrimination against Women that "[d]espite repeated accusations that Myanmar Security Forces committed a campaign of rape and violence against Muslim women and girls residing in Rakhine State, there is no evidence to support these wild claims."[53]

Against this backdrop of a long history of impunity and structural barriers, the February 2021 military coup has further exacerbated the accountability crisis in Myanmar.

Therefore, it is critical that the international community act expeditiously to jumpstart justice and accountability efforts for crimes committed against the Rohingya. Notably, on November 11, 2019, the Republic of The Gambia filed suit against the Republic of the Union of Myanmar in the International Court of Justice (ICJ) for violating the Genocide Convention. Two months later at the request of The Gambia, the ICJ ordered the government of Myanmar to take certain actions to protect the Rohingya via "provisional measures" while the case proceeds. In February 2022 the ICJ held public hearings on Myanmar's preliminary objections regarding the Court's jurisdiction to hear the case. This historic lawsuit brings a critical focus to Myanmar's responsibility as a State for the Rohingya genocide, and in the long term may bring about a measure of justice for them. However, since the court is a state-to-state court—a court that only hears disputes between States—individuals will not be held to account, and the possibility of direct redress for the Rohingya is remote.

Additionally, the International Criminal Court (ICC) has recognized the potential jurisdiction over a limited subset of crimes that have an element occurring in Bangladesh, including deportation (which, for example, involves the crossing of an international border), persecution, and other inhumane acts.[54] The limited scope is due to jurisdictional requirements, since Myanmar is not a State Party to the Rome Statute of the ICC, although Bangladesh is. The ICC has authorized an investigation "with broad parameters" on any crimes "committed, at least in part, on the territory of Bangladesh (or any other State Party or State formally accepting the jurisdiction of the ICC), insofar as the crimes are sufficiently linked to the situation, and irrespective of the nationality of the perpetrators."[55] In short, where a part of the crime occurred on the territory of Bangladesh. However, the Court's decision leaves open the possibility that, in any ICC case built on this jurisdictional theory, other crimes occurring solely within Myanmar will inevitably be left behind—including the crimes of rape and sexual violence—with such crimes serving as contextual elements, at best. Thus, this authorization is not an absolution of the international community's duties to act.

Another accountability avenue has been opened with a case in November 2019 by the Burmese Rohingya Organization UK, supported by Mothers of the Plaza de Mayo and the Fundación Servicio Paz y Justicia, in an Argentinian court under the principle of universal jurisdiction, urging the criminal prosecution of senior officials from Myanmar who are responsible for the Rohingya genocide. Further, the UN's Independent Investigative Mechanism for Myanmar (IIMM), established by the UN Human Rights Council in September 2018, is collecting evidence and preparing case files for the most serious international crimes and violations of international law occurring in Myanmar. The IIMM's case files are intended to contribute to prosecutions of individuals in national, regional, or international criminal proceedings (such as in Argentina), but could also support cases claiming State responsibility, including in The Gambia v. Myanmar case at the ICJ.

As these cases move forward, it is important to keep in mind that, although the stories of the gendered experiences of the violations against the Rohingya—in particular the mass gang rape of women and girls—are central to the rhetorical narrative about the violence, there is a long history of failing to pursue justice for these crimes. Justice for Rohingya women and girls will take individual and collective action from States and international organizations alike, require laser focus in each case to center gendered experiences and employ a strong gender perspective, and, most importantly, ensure that Rohingya women and girls are involved in the design and decision-making in all such processes. One positive turn in this context has been a pledge by Canada and the Netherlands to intervene in the ICJ Gambia v. Myanmar case with special attention paid to "crimes related to sexual and gender-based violence, including rape."[56]

Justice is not only necessary to assign responsibility and hold individuals to account but is also a necessary precursor for the safe, voluntary, and dignified return and reintegration of the Rohingya to Rakhine State. Such repatriation should include a number of factors, such as the consent of those returning, repatriation of any confiscated land, equal participation of women in all decision-making processes related to these efforts, and relevant legal reform such as amending the problematic Citizenship Law.

Unfortunately, the February 2021 military coup has exacerbated barriers to repatriation efforts, as there is no safety in return when those who committed genocide of the Rohingya remain in absolute power. Impunity for acts committed by the Burmese military has long been the norm in Myanmar and is in fact codified in the country's constitution. The Rohingya, like Myanmar's other ethnic minorities, must see justice and accountability for the crimes committed against them.

As a result of the scope and scale of the crimes, justice will likely need to be pursued in a myriad of venues, both international and domestic, and must set the stage to ensure effective remedy and reparations to victims, including restitution, compensation, rehabilitation, satisfaction, and guarantees of non-repetition. Women and girls must not be left behind in these efforts. As noted above, history has shown that while women's experiences and stories have long been used to illustrate the horrors of conflict, they are rarely carried forward into justice efforts. For example, while sexual violence in Rwanda has formed an integral part of the narrative of the Rwandan genocide, outside the seminal *Akayesu* case—the first to find rape and other acts of sexual violence as constitutive acts of genocide—it has only been reflected in the jurisprudence of the genocide in limited form.[57]

The quest for accountability has been made all the more pressing by the February 2021 military coup in Myanmar. While the motivations behind the coup are unclear as of this writing, there is no doubt that the structural and persistent impunity of the military for human rights abuses are an emboldening factor. The failure to hold the military accountable for any of its actions, including the genocide of the Rohingya, has given them a signal that they will not face meaningful consequences for their actions, no matter how harmful or extreme. The imperative for the international community to hold the military accountable has never been stronger or more important. In June 2020 the newly formed parallel civilian government, the National Unity Government, issued a policy statement recognizing the human rights violations committed against the Rohingya, yet stopped short of naming the crimes genocide.[58] While significant, recognition is not coextensive with comprehensive accountability, which still remains to be seen. Further, actions taken by the NUG as they relate to the Rohingya, as of this writing, do not satisfy the demands of the Rohingya community. As the international community pursues justice and accountability—whether through investigations in the United Nations system, International Criminal Court, or third-party States—it is essential that the gender dynamics underpinning the crimes committed against Rohingya women and girls are a central and omnipresent concern.

NOTE: This chapter was initially drafted in 2019 and the authors wish to note that its contents reflect events and understandings at the time of writing. While efforts have been made to update the content and address more recent developments in Myanmar in advance of publication, the situation is in constant flux and it is impossible to fully capture all events as they occur in real-time.

Notes

1. David Steinberg, "Myanmar's Perpetual Dilemma: Ethnicity in a 'Discipline-Flourishing Democracy.'" (Honolulu: East-West Center Working Papers—Politics, Governances and Security Series, No. 22, April 2011), 1; Human Rights Council, *Report of the Detailed Findings of the Independent International Fact-Finding Mission on Myanmar*, U.N. Doc. A/HRC/39/CRP.2, September 17, 2018, para. 84. https://www.ohchr.org/sites/default/files/Documents/HRBodies/HRCo uncil/FFM-Myanmar/A_HRC_39_CRP.2.pdf

2. Human Rights Council, *Report of the Detailed Findings.*

3. Minority Rights Group International, *Myanmar/Burma.* https://minorityrig hts.org/country/myanmarburma/

4. Minority Rights Group International, *Myanmar/Burma.*

5. Human Rights Council, *Report of the Detailed Findings*, paras. 109, 110, 112.

6. Human Rights Council, *Report of the Detailed Findings*, para. 458.

7. Emanuel Stoakes and Hannah Ellis-Petersen, "Myanmar: UN Threatens to Withdraw Aid Over 'Policy of Apartheid' against Rohingya," *Guardian*, June 16, 2019. https://www.theguardian.com/world/2019/jun/17/myanmar-un-threate ns-to-withdraw-aid-over-policy-of-apartheid-against-rohingya

8. Human Rights Council, *Report of the Detailed Findings*, para. 85.

9. Council on Foreign Relations, *The Rohingya Crisis*, January 23, 2020. https:// www.cfr.org/backgrounder/rohingya-crisis?gclid=EAIaIQobChMI9PTg_5-h4AI VDFqGCh2Rww7jEAAYAiAAEgJrSPD_BwE

10. Council on Foreign Relations, *The Rohingya Crisis.*

11. Council on Foreign Relations, *The Rohingya Crisis.*

12. Council on Foreign Relations, *The Rohingya Crisis.*

13. Human Rights Council, *Report of the Detailed Findings*, para. 475.

14. Refugees International, *Field Report, Reluctant Refugee*, 4; Amnesty International, *Caged Without a Roof*, 20, 36, citing Office of the High Commissioner for Human Rights (OHCHR), *Situation of Human Rights of Rohingya Muslims and Other Minorities in Myanmar*; *Report of the United Nations High Commissioner for Human Rights*, UN Doc: A/HRC/32/18, June 29, 2016, paras. 43, 44; Fortify Rights, *Policies of Persecution: Ending Abusive State Policies Against Rohingya Muslims in Myanmar*, February 2014, 24–30.

15. Antoni Slodkowski, "Safety and 'Identity' Key for Rohingya Returnees: U.N. Chief in Myanmar," *Reuters*, June 6, 2018. https://www.reuters.com/article /us-myanmar-rohingya-un-idUSKCN1J21G1

16. Amnesty International, *Caged Without a Roof*, 20.

17. Refugees International, *Field Report, Reluctant Refugee*, 4.

18. For a detailed description of ARSA and its activities, see International Crisis

Group, *Myanmar's Rohingya Crisis Enters a Dangerous New Phase*, Asia Report no. 292, December 7, 2017; Amnesty International, *Caged Without a Roof*, 9, 23; Refugees International, *Field Report, Reluctant Refugee*, 4.

19. Amnesty International, *Myanmar: New Evidence Reveals Rohingya Armed Group Massacred Scores in Rakhine State*, May 22, 2018.

20. U.S. Holocaust Museum & Fortify Rights, *"They Tried to Kill Us All": Atrocity Crimes Against Rohingya Muslims in Rakhine State, Myanmar*, November 2017, 6.

21. U.S. Holocaust Museum & Fortify Rights, *"They Tried to Kill Us All."*

22. International Crisis Group, *Myanmar's Rohingya.*

23. Amnesty International, "Myanmar."

24. OHCHR, *Report of OHCHR Mission to Bangladesh*, February 3, 2017, 42. https://www.ohchr.org/Documents/Countries/MM/FlashReport3Feb2017.pdf; United Nations, *Report of the Special Rapporteur on the Situation of Human Rights in Myanmar*, UN Doc. A/HRC/37/70, March 9, 2018, paras. 42–49.

25. Amnesty International, *Caged Without a Roof*, 24.

26. Amnesty International, *Caged Without a Roof*, 24.

27. OHCHR, *Report of OHCHR Mission to Bangladesh*, para. 42; United Nations, *Report of the Special Rapporteur.*

28. United Nations, *Report of the Special Rapporteur*, para. 46.

29. United Nations, *Report of the Independent International Fact-Finding Mission on Myanmar*, UN Doc. A/HRC/39/64, para. 42.

30. Council on Foreign Relations, *The Rohingya Crisis.*

31. United Nations, *Report of the Special Rapporteur.*

32. Women's League of Burma, *Same Impunity, Same Patterns*, January 2014. https://womenofburma.org/sites/default/files/2018-06/2014_Jan_SameImpunity SamePattern_English-final.pdf; Burma Campaign UK, *Burma Briefing: Rape and Sexual Violence by the Burmese Army*, July 2014, 6.

33. For a detailed legal analysis regarding the gender-based crimes committed against the Rohingya, see Global Justice Center, *Discrimination to Destruction: A Legal Analysis of Gender Crimes Against the Rohingya*, September 2018. https://www .globaljusticecenter.net/files/Discrimination_to_Destruction.pdf

34. OHCHR, *Mission Report of OHCHR Rapid Response Mission: 13–24 Sept. 2017*, 7. https://www.ohchr.org/sites/default/files/Documents/Countries/MM /CXBMissionSummaryFindingsOctober2017.pdf

35. OHCHR, *Mission to Bangladesh*, 10.

36. Women's Refugee Commission, *"It's Happening to Our Men as Well": Sexual Violence Against Rohingya Men and Boys*, November 2018, 18. https://www.womens refugeecommission.org/wp-content/uploads/2020/04/Rohingya-Report-Final.pdf

37. Global Justice Center, *Discrimination to Destruction*, 34–35.

38. OHCHR, *Mission to Bangladesh*, 16.

39. Global Justice Center, *Discrimination to Destruction*, 31–32.

40. OHCHR, "Situation of Human Rights of Rohingya Muslims and Other Minorities in Myanmar," *Report of the United Nations High Commissioner for Human Rights*, UN Doc: A/HRC/32/18, June 29, 2016, paras. 43, 44; Fortify Rights, *Policies of Persecution.*

41. Rome Statute of the International Criminal Court, art. 5(1). https://legal.un .org/icc/statute/english/rome_statute(e).pdf

42. Rome Statute, art. 7(1).

43. *Statement by the Special Representative of the Secretary-General on Sexual Violence in Conflict, Ms. Pramila Patten, UN Security Council Briefing on Myanmar,* December 12, 2017. https://www.un.org/sexualviolenceinconflict/statement/stat ement-by-the-special-representative-of-the-secretary-general-on-sexual-violence -in-conflict-ms-pramila-patten-security-council-briefing-on-myanmar-12-decem ber-2017/

44. Global Justice Center, *Beyond Killing: Gender, Genocide, and Obligation Under International Law,* December 2018, 19. https://www.globaljusticecenter.net/files /Gender-and-Genocide-Whitepaper-FINAL.pdf

45. Fortify Rights, *"They Gave Them Long Swords." Preparations for Genocide and Crimes Against Humanity Against Rohingya Muslims in Rakhine State, Myanmar,* July 2018, 41 https://www.fortifyrights.org/downloads/Fortify_Rights_Long_Swords _July_2018.pdf

46. Human Rights Council, *Report of the Detailed Findings,* para. 1395.

47. Global Justice Center, *Discrimination to Destruction,* 46–49.

48. Global Justice Center, *Discrimination to Destruction,* 46–49. Citing OHCHR, *Report of OHCHR mission to Bangladesh,* 21, 42; *Statement by the Special Representative of the Secretary-General on Sexual Violence in Conflict, UN Security Council Briefing on Myanmar,* December 12, 2017; Antoni Slodkowski, et al., "How a Two-Week Army Crackdown Reignited Myanmar's Rohingya Crisis," *Reuters,* April 25, 2017; Human Rights Watch, "Burma: Security Forces Raped Rohingya Women, Girls." https://www.hrw.org/news/2017/02/06/burma-security-forces-raped-rohingya -women-girls#; U.S. Holocaust Memorial Museum and Fortify Rights, *"They Tried to Kill Us All,"* 12.

49. *Convention on the Prevention and Punishment of the Crime of Genocide,* art. 1, 78 UNTS 277, December 9, 1948. https://www.un.org/en/genocideprevention/docu ments/atrocity-crimes/Doc.1_Convention%20on%20the%20Prevention%20and %20Punishment%20of%20the%20Crime%20of%20Genocide.pdf

50. Global Justice Center. *Myanmar's Independent Commission of Enquiry: Structural Issues and Flawed Findings* (Feb. 2020), https://globaljusticecenter.net/files/20 200203_ICOEfact_sheet.pdf (citing Human Rights Council, *Report of the Independent International Fact-Finding Mission on Myanmar,* UN Doc. A/HRC/39/64, September 12, 2018, para. 96).

51. Global Justice Center, *Structural Barriers to Accountability for Human Rights Abuses in Burma,* October 2018, https://globaljusticecenter.net/files/Structural-Ba rriers---Burma.pdf (citing Constitution of the Republic of the Union of Myanmar, 2008, at ch. IV, arts. 74, 109(b), 141(b) [for 25% military appointees] and ch.XII, art. 436(a) [for amendments to the Constitution]).

52. Human Rights Council, *Report of the Special Rapporteur,* para. 73; UN Human Rights Council, "Statement by Mr. Marzuki Darusman, Chairperson of the Independent International Fact-Finding Mission on Myanmar, at the 37th session of the Human Rights Council," Press Statement, March 12, 2018. https:// www.ohchr.org/en/statements/2018/03/statement-mr-marzuki-darusman-chairpe rson-independent-international-fact-finding

53. Akila Radhakrishnan. "Rohingya Symposium: From Rhetoric to Justice– Ensuring a Gender Perspective in Accountability Proceedings for the Rohingya

Genocide," Opinion Juris, August 26, 2020. http://opiniojuris.org/2020/08/26/ro hingya-symposium-from-rhetoric-to-justice-ensuring-a-gender-perspective-in-ac countability-proceedings-for-the-rohingya-genocide/; Committee on the Elimination of Discrimination Against Women, *Consideration of Reports Submitted by States Parties Under Article 18 of the Convention on the Elimination of All Forms of Discrimination against Women: Myanmar: Report on an Exceptional Basis*, UN Doc. CEDAW/C/MMR/4–5/Add.1, February 6, 2019, para. 11. https://www.un.org/wo menwatch/daw/cedaw/reports/18report.pdf

54. "Situation in the People's Republic of Bangladesh/Republic of the Union of Myanmar," Case No. ICC-01/19, *Decision Pursuant to Article 15 of the Rome Statute on the Authorization of an Investigation into the Situation in the People's Republic of Bangladesh/Republic of the Union of Myanmar*, November 14, 2019, para. 62, 110-11. https://www.icc-cpi.int/CourtRecords/CR2019_06955.PDF

55. Alison Smith and Francesca Basso, "No Peace Without Justice, Justice for the Rohingya: What Has Happened and What Comes Next?" Coalition for the International Criminal Court, February 13, 2020. https://www.coalitionfortheicc .org/news/20200213/justice-rohingya-what-has-happened-and-what-comes-next For more information on the progress of the court case at the ICC, see International Criminal Court, *Bangladesh/Myanmar*. https://www.icc-cpi.int/bangladesh -myanmar

56. *Joint Statement of Canada and the Kingdom of the Netherlands Regarding Intention to Intervene in The Gambia v. Myanmar Case at the International Court of Justice*, September 2, 2020. https://www.government.nl/documents/diplomatic-stateme nts/2020/09/02/joint-statement-of-canada-and-the-kingdom-of-the-netherlands -regarding-intention-to-intervene-in-the-gambia-v.-myanmar-case-at-the-intern ational-court-of-justice

57. Global Justice Center, *Beyond Killing*, 2.

58. Republic of the Union of Myanmar National Unity Government, "Policy Position on the Rohingya in Rakhine State," Press Release, June 3, 2021. https:// gov.nugmyanmar.org/2021/06/03/policy-position-on-the-rohingya-in-rakhine-st ate/

The Elephant and the Pond of Blood

Leang Seckon

The phrase "the elephant and the pond of blood" is known and remembered by the Cambodian people. It is a frightening phrase. People once associated it with a fortunate Buddhist saying that looks to the future. The killing fields of the mid-1970s gave it a much darker meaning. In the Buddhist verse, an elephant stands in blood that rises, eventually reaching its belly. The elephant is the biggest, strongest, and most powerful animal, but it is also soft. In ancient times, people used elephants to help build temples; they also rode elephants into battle. Nowadays, elephants are used for touring the temple complex at Angkor Wat.

Please look at this painting: the elephant is decorated with flowers to look like a royal elephant. The passengers are a tiger and a dog. They represent stupid people who kill millions of other people. Blood floods over the field where the elephant walks. A storm of blood blows incense smoke that comes from the center of people's hearts. The blood covers belief, peace, culture, and knowledge; and it destroys temples, Buddhist statues, and Buddhism.

Does *The Elephant and the Pond of Blood* come from Buddhist scripture? In the last life of his lives, the Buddha spends much of his energy suffering without eating to achieve enlightenment—and to bring peace to the world. Where does the phrase come from? And why does it sound so painful and frightening?

—Leang Seckon

TEN

The Khmer Rouge Bureaucrats

Counting the Missing

James A. Tyner

On December 27, 1976, a woman named Kaing Kîm Lien was arrested and detained at a secretive "prison" designated "S-21." Located in Phnom Penh, the security center was one of approximately two hundred detainment sites situated throughout Democratic Kampuchea—as Cambodia was renamed. During its formal existence, between October 1975 and January 1979, more than eighteen thousand men, women, and children were warehoused under inhumane conditions.[1] Many were tortured and forced to confess to various crimes; all but a handful were eventually executed, either within the greater S-21 compound or at the nearby "killing fields," known as *Cheooung Ek*. These deaths were but a subset of countless other people who were purged by members of the Khmer Rouge security apparatus. Indeed, tens of thousands—if not hundreds of thousands—of people simply disappeared during the Khmer Rouge regime, their lives and eventual deaths unrecorded, their corpses dumped in unmarked mass graves.

The death of Kaing Kîm Lien is but one of approximately two million people who died during the Cambodian genocide. Between April 1975 and January 1979, the Communist Party of Kampuchea (CPK; better known as the "Khmer Rouge") carried out a program of State-led mass violence that, in many respects, remains unfathomable.[2] In just under four years approximately one-quarter of the country's pre-1975 population died. Many of these deaths resulted from starvation, disease, and exhaustion; others were murdered outright.[3] And still more were tortured and executed, including those at the S-21 security-center, such as Kaing Kîm Lien.

The Cambodian genocide was born of geopolitical machinations. Throughout the 1950s and 1960s the ongoing armed conflict between the Democratic Republic of Vietnam (DRV, colloquially known as "North Vietnam"), the Republic of Vietnam ("South Vietnam"), and the United States bled into the neutral State of Cambodia. Despite the efforts of Norodom Sihanouk, Cambodia's prince and head of state, Cambodia became, in the words of William Shawcross, a bothersome sideshow.[4] As the United States intensified its military campaigns throughout both South Vietnam and North Vietnam, the military forces of the DRV and its southern allies, the National Liberation Front (NLF; derisively known as the "Viet Cong"), used Cambodian territory as sanctuary and as a means of transporting troops, weapons, and war material. In turn, the U.S. military redirected much of its arsenal toward Cambodia. For one fifteen-month period, for example, more than 3,800 B-52 sorties were flown over Cambodia, dropping more than 100,000 tons of bombs. The carnage was devastating, as hundreds of thousands of Cambodians were killed or displaced by the encroaching war. Out of the morass of the Vietnam War emerged the Khmer Rouge. Their ascent to power was hastened, in no small part, following the coup of Sihanouk in 1970 and the subsequent civil war (1970–1975) that carried war to the entirety of the country.

When Khmer Rouge forces entered Phnom Penh on April 17, 1975, their future was very much in doubt. The Khmer Rouge constituted neither a centralized, efficient political party nor military force. The Khmer Rouge "achieved" victory not because they were united in principle and ideology with the Khmer populace; indeed, the revolution enacted by the CPK was not the end result of a popular uprising but rather the result of a repressive cadre of individuals that brutally outmaneuvered both their political opponents and allies.[5] Subsequently, the fragility of CPK rule contributed, in part, to the development of a massive security apparatus designed to seek out and "smash" perceived external and internal enemies.

Very little is known of Kaing Kîm Lien. Records simply identify her as "wife of Chham Khân." No known documents have survived that might indicate why she was arrested—other than the fact that she was the wife of Chham Khân, was employed by the "railway," and was arrested from Kompong Som, a coastal city south of Phnom Penh.[6] As for Chham Khân, his name is currently not found among the various documents. For all intents and purposes, he simply disappeared.

On the day of Kaing Kîm Lien's arrest, two other people, both women, were also detained: Ing Vann and Uk Siep. They also were employed with the railway and arrested from Kompong Son. Ing Vann as identified as "wife of Por Sameth" and Uk Siep was recorded as "wife of Yîm Dam." We know that Por Sameth was thirty years old at the time of his arrest (date unknown) and that he was associated with the "railroad repairing section"; there is no record for Yîm Dam.

Kaing Kîm Lien, Ing Vann, and Uk Siep were executed on December 28, 1976, all within twenty-four hours of their being processed at S-21. No doubt they were part of a wider purge associated with suspected traitors employed in the railway sector located in Kompong Som.[7] Between December 2 and December 28, 1976, at least twenty-eight men and women employed in the railway sector were arrested and executed. Most were executed within one week of their arrest.[8]

In Democratic Kampuchea, to be accused was to be guilty; to be guilty was to be sentenced to death. Indeed, the Khmer Rouge phrase for those imprisoned was *neak tos*, meaning, literally, "those who are already convicted." Such Orwellian logic underscored the pervasive *bureaucratic* nature of CPK administrative practice and forms the context within which to gain insight into the day-to-day machinations of the Khmer Rouge regime.

The impetus and premise for this chapter, but also of my broader project of detailing the Khmer Rouge security apparatus, is tied to current events, namely the legal proceedings of the Extraordinary Chambers in the Courts of Cambodia (ECCC), better known as the "Khmer Rouge tribunal."[9] The ECCC's first trial, Case 001, convened four years after the establishment of the tribunal. On July 31, 2007, Kaing Guek Eav (alias "Duch"), commandant of the S-21 security-center, was formally indicted by the co-investigating judges of the ECCC with crimes against humanity and grave breaches of the Geneva Conventions of 12 August 1949.[10] The initial hearing of Duch was held in Phnom Penh on February 17, 2009, with the substantive part of the trial beginning on March 30, 2009. The actual trial lasted seventy-seven days, culminating on November 27, 2009. A final verdict was delivered on July 26, 2010, with Duch being found guilty of crimes against humanity, including extermination, enslavement, imprisonment, torture, rape, and other inhumane acts. He was also found guilty of grave breaches of the 1949 Geneva Conventions, including the willful causing of great suffering or serious injury to body or health, willfully depriving a prisoner of war or civilian of fair trial rights, and of unlawful confinement of civilians.[11] Following an appeals proceeding, Duch was in 2012 sentenced to life imprisonment in Cambodia for his crimes.[12]

On September 15, 2010, Nuon Chea (former Deputy Secretary of the

CPK), Khieu Samphan (former President of Democratic Kampuchea), Ieng Sary (former Minister of Foreign Affairs), and Ieng Thirith (former Minister of Social Affairs) were indicted on charges of crimes against humanity, genocide, and grave breaches of the Geneva Conventions of 1949. The following year the Trial Chamber decided to sever the charges in Case 002 into a series of smaller trials. The first, Case 002/01, commenced on November 21, 2011. For many observers, the advanced age of the defendants was of great concern. Both Nuon Chea and Ieng Sary were eighty-five years old, Khieu Samphan was eighty, and Ieng Thirith was seventy-nine. It was noted, also, that because of their advanced age, even if convicted, they were unlikely to serve a significant portion of any prison sentence handed down.[13] These fears only added to a more pervasive sense that the tribunal was, ultimately, too little, too late. Indeed, prior to the commencement of the trial, in August 2011, Ieng Thirith was diagnosed with dementia and subsequently declared incompetent to stand trial. She died on August 22, 2015, and never stood trial for her crimes. Ieng Sary died prior to the completion of the trial.

On August 7, 2014, a verdict was rendered in Case 002/01 against Nuon Chea and Khieu Samphan. Both were found guilty of crimes against humanity, and both were sentenced to life imprisonment. In reaching its verdict, the Trial Chamber determined that both men were guilty of participation in a "joint criminal enterprise," the purpose of which "was to implement rapid socialist revolution." The Trial Chamber concluded also that "certain policies formulated by the Khmer Rouge involved the commission of crimes as the means to bring the common plan to fruition" and that these included "a policy to forcibly remove people from urban to rural areas" and "a policy to target officials of the former Khmer Republic."[14] Case 002/02, in which Nuon Chea and Khieu Samphan were charged with a series of crimes, including genocide, commenced on October 17, 2014 and the presentation of evidence began on January 8, 2015.[15]

Notably, in September 2012, the Supreme Court Chamber of the ECCC ordered that 1,749 documents of the tribunal be made public. In addition, a total of 13,383 documents related *solely* to S-21 have been declassified; these include S-21 daily entry logs, monthly entry logs, yearly entry logs, periodical entry logs, sectional entry logs, prisoner biographies, interrogation lists, and execution lists.[16] Most of these documents have not widely been incorporated into the scholarly account of the Cambodian genocide. Indeed, it is not uncommon still for some scholars to lament the "lack of materials" available; or—incredulously—to conclude that documentation and administrative protocol were anathema to CPK officials. Many of these records were initially archived by the staff at the Documentation Center of Cambodia (DC-CAM).[17] DC-CAM is the principal archive of documentary materials related to the Cambodian genocide and includes two main types of documents: primary documents (i.e., those produced during the genocidal years) and secondary documents (i.e., those produced after 1979, including interviews with both Khmer Rouge members and survivors of the genocide). Overall, the archives at DC-CAM include approximately one million pages of documents from the Khmer Rouge period, including meeting minutes, telegrams, reports, party periodicals, and files from the Khmer Rouge secret police. In addition, the archives include documentation of over 20,000 mass grave sites, 196 prisons, 60,000 photos from the Khmer Rouge period, 260 documentary films shot during and directly after the Khmer Rouge regime, and approximately 50,000 interviews conducted by DC-CAM staff with perpetrators and survivors.

From Documenting Life to Living Documents

In her book, *Paper Cadavers*, Kirsten Weld details how documents, at different historical moments, may represent distinct archival logics. Writing in the context of Guatemala's violent past, Weld identifies two organizing principles surrounding the voluminous materials archived by Guatemala's secret police. The first logic, Weld explains, "was one of surveillance, social control, and ideological management," while the second, "emerging from the records" rescue, is one of "democratic opening, historical memory, and the pursuit of justice."[18] In Cambodia, before the many Khmer Rouge documents were archived at DC-CAM or the ECCC, they were stored by the Khmer Rouge in countless file cabinets, binders, or desks throughout Democratic Kampuchea. Lawyers and scholars have given these documents a second life.[19] Less attention has focused on the "first life" of these documents: their original production, circulation, and usage.[20] Thus, as Weld notes, I want to "document the process, not to process the documents."[21] My overriding purpose is to redirect attention toward the processes of documentation; to interpret the documents *as they were produced by the CPK* toward particular purposes. In other words, my intent is not to document so much what the Khmer Rouge did as it is to understand why the Khmer Rouge documented the way they did. It was the bureaucratic procedures instituted by the CPK that facilitated the disappearance, and ultimately death, of so many men, women, and children.

The politics of how archives are compiled, created, and opened are strongly tied to the politics and practices of government.[22] Consequently, a focus on the documentary processes of the CPK sheds insight into the broader coordinates of governance both as envisioned and practiced by the Khmer Rouge, for as Ann Stoler relates, "Filing systems and disciplined writing produce assemblages of control and specific methods of domination."[23] Such a journey, therefore, requires that we step into the mundane world of the bureaucrat—a passage that seems incongruous with more conventional understandings of the Cambodian genocide. To speak of the Khmer Rouge is to recall black-clad youth wielding AK-47s; bureaucrats, conversely, are mild-mannered administers toiling behind desks, all but forgotten in their tiny cubicles. And yet, as the voluminous materials compiled by both DC-CAM and the ECCC demonstrate, Democratic Kampuchea was flush with documents. These documents did not materialize in a vacuum but instead were the products of innumerable men and women, many of whom wielded weapons but, crucially, were armed also with pens, paper, and typewriters.

Documents are essential for bureaucratic rule. Indeed, recent scholarship has shown how bureaucratic documents are produced, used, and experienced through procedures, techniques, aesthetics, ideologies, cooperation, negotiation, and contestation.[24] Two functions are particularly notable. First, as Matthew Hull points out, "documents promote control within organizations and beyond not only through their links to the entities they document but through the coordination of perspectives and activities."[25] Second, bureaucratic documents entail a "generative capacity" in that they bring *things* into existence.[26] Marie-Andrée Jacobs, for example, details how documents—but especially consent forms—generate "form-made persons." Jacobs elaborates that while documents "answer the bureaucratic needs for efficiency and for comparability of documents" they also "make political subjects visible." In turn, these subjects may more readily be "archived, classified, measured, compared, and controlled on a mass scale."[27] In short, documents "are central to how bureaucratic objects are enacted in practice."[28]

A focus on bureaucratic documents calls to question the materiality of power as it is administered behind the scenes, for here we see how seemingly mundane technologies—files, charts, and records—become the means which enable a few to know about or to rule over many.[29] Indeed, as Kenneth Dauber describes, "record keeping makes it possible to characterize and administer large populations with a (relatively) small staff."[30] This observation holds considerable purchase when understanding, for example, the rule of the Khmer Rouge throughout Democratic Kampuchea. The

Communist Party of Kampuchea never enjoyed mass popular support; in fact, many of those cadre who fought and died in the civil war leading up to the CPK's revolutionary victory did so not for ideological reasons, but rather in support of their deposed prince, Sihanouk, or in response to the American bombing campaign. Consequently, it was incumbent upon the CPK to effectively wield power over an increasingly discontented population. Direct force was used; and this violence has been well documented by scholars of Democratic Kampuchea. But so too was control facilitated through mundane exercises of power.

Accounting In/For S-21

Prior to assuming power in April 1975, the CPK had established a security apparatus known as *santebal*. The term itself is a contraction of the Khmer words *santesokh* (security) and *nokorbal* (police). According to Chandler, the santebal functioned not unlike the East German Stasi and even the United States Federal Bureau of Investigation (FBI) and Britain's MI5, in that it was a national security police.[31] However, unlike these other security forces, the santebal had no central policy-making office and did little in the way of primary investigations. Rather, the primary function was simply to arrest, detain, and execute both external and internal "enemies of the State."

The overarching Khmer Rouge security apparatus was tasked with three functions: to re-educate, refashion, or purge men and women determined to be guilty of having committed, or were likely to commit, criminal activities. Within the broader administrative structure, S-21 was unique in that it was established not to reform or rehabilitate but to specifically document and punish perceived criminal offenses against the Party. In other words, S-21 was administratively a State-level security-center designed to eliminate principally those who committed treason or otherwise betrayed the Party, the Revolution, and Democratic Kampuchea. In this way, S-21 functioned not as a "concentration" camp or "extermination" camp, such as found throughout Nazi-occupied Europe but instead as an "investigative" apparatus.

S-21 was a complex bureaucracy that, over its lifespan, had a staff of approximately 2,300 men and women.[32] Collectively, staff members at S-21 kept meticulous records of their activities. Surviving documents include: arrest forms on individual prisoners; personal biographies of prisoners; day-by-day arrest schedules; mug-shot arrest photographs; daily charts on the prison population; handwritten or type-written confessions; typed summaries of confessions; daily schedules for interrogation; summaries of torture methods used; photographs of tortured prisoners; post-mortem photographs of prisoners who were executed or died during torture; reports on medicines administered to prisoners; signed execution orders; signed daily execution schedules; elaborate diagnostic flow charts of "conspiratorial networks"; and summaries of "plots" uncovered to overthrow the Party. Various other documents include photographs and personal biographies of S-21 staff, notebooks indicating procedures for conducting interrogations, notebooks from political education sessions, work schedules for guards, and correspondence between S-21 and the Standing Committee.[33]

Perhaps no department epitomizes the bureaucratic nature of S-21 as does the Documentation Unit. Supervised by Suos Thy, this unit was responsible for transcribing tape-recorded confessions, typing handwritten notes, preparing summaries of confessions, and maintaining the prison's files.[34] The unit also was responsible for the compilation of both prisoner biographies and staff biographies. Within this unit was the photography sub-unit. Also under the supervision of Suos Thy, but on a day-to-day basis headed by Nim Kimsreang, the photography sub-unit was tasked primarily with photographing prisoners upon their arrival. Photographers were also required to take photographs of prisoners who died in captivity and of "important" prisoners after they were executed. The sub-unit also took identification photos that were included in the files of all staff members.[35]

Surviving documents—but also testimony at the ECCC by surviving S-21 staff members—reveal a concerted effort on behalf of the CPK bureaucrats to amass sufficient evidentiary records to justify (in their minds) the guilt of suspected persons. Annotated comments scrawled on copied confessions, telegrams sent between members of the Standing Committee and S-21 staff, and other written memos linking myriad other units expose an exceptionally engaged bureaucracy. Before any decision to arrest an individual was rendered there needed to be some form of "actionable-evidence." And regardless of how flimsy that may appear now, it does not belie the observation that from the CPK's point of view, information was essential. For example, considerable "evidence" was derived from the compilation of observations: a man may have been overheard complaining of inadequate food rations; a woman may have been seen stealing a coconut. Often, branch-level cadres would "evaluate" this evidence and make an initial decision regarding punishment. Rudimentary interrogative techniques may have been applied; and following some level of physical or psychological abuse, a list of suspected persons may have been forwarded to the upper echelon for additional interrogation. Furthermore, cadres at various levels would generate lists of associates through these confessions.

Confessions were a stalwart of S-21. However, S-21 was far from unique in this respect. Throughout the entirety of the Khmer Rouge security apparatus interrogators used torture to force confessions from persons adjudged guilty. In practice, confessions became working documents, in the sense that confessions were written and rewritten many times, depending on the prisoner in question. Initially, there was little standardization to the form of confessions; by 1976, and especially at S-21, confessions assumed a more standard form. Prisoners were required to recount their life stories, including names of family members, friends, and associates; prisoners were also forced to confess to their traitorous activities, including planned criminal acts that they might have carried out if not caught. No doubt the vast majority of confessions were false; under physical and psychological abuse, prisoners invariably admitted guilt to whatever charges their interrogators put forth.

For any person whose name appeared on a list, they immediately came under suspicion and subsequently were observed, questioned, and possibly arrested. For example, on October 30, 1977, Ren, a staff member of the Revolutionary Army of Kampuchea, informed S-21 that thirty-six "bad elements" were removed. Of these, ten people were named specifically. A female comrade named Yean was accused of committing moral offenses and encouraging other cadre to steal; a man named Saroeun was listed as a militiaman, but "worked in a liberal manner"; while another man, Hok, was considered a "malingerer" and considered "very liberal." Both Makara and Keu Ly were deemed "dishonest and slothful." Twenty-six other persons went unnamed but were to be sent to S-24; the letter stated: "We are tracing them. Their offenses have not yet been categorized." In signing off, Ren requested further comments to help determine how to proceed.[36] In short, the charge of "bad elements" is exceptionally vague and thus exceptionally wide-ranging. Any behavior, any statement, or any association could and often was misconstrued by party members as evidence of disloyalty or treason.

"Evidence" was also gathered through the evaluation of personal biographies. Personal biographies, especially at the branch level, were written on sheets of paper. If the person in question was illiterate, or could not write, a cadre would transcribe the relative information. Other institutions, such as the Ministry of Commerce or S-21, would provide prepared forms that would be filled out either by the man or woman or a staff member. For example, a brief biography of Khim Met was prepared when she was transferred to S-21 as a staff member. The document indicates that she was twenty-years-old; was born in Chonlus Village, Tuol Kreul Sub-district, Kampong Svay District, Kampong Thom Province. Prior to the revolution she worked as a farmer and was classified as a "middle-class peasant."[37] She joined the revolution on November 3, 1974, introduced by a person named Den. Her father, Khim Chin, was deceased and her mother, Pen Morn, worked at a cooperative. Khim Met was not married and had no children. She was transferred to S-21 for unknown reasons on October 12, 1977.[38]

The biography of Khim Met is telling, in that it demonstrates how the bureaucratic procedures initiated by the CPK facilitated the construction of social "networks" that were so vital to the purges. Precise information was requested not only of family members; but also of other individuals with whom one may have associated. Information was routinely gathered on previous units in which one served, thus establishing implicitly wider networks of suspicion. Khim Met, for example, previously served in Unit 450 and, prior to her transfer to S-21, was part of Unit 17. If either of these two units came under suspicion, so too would Khim Met.

Confessions of detainees at lower-level security-centers were also used to initiate investigations. On August 10, 1977, Sou Met, Secretary of Division 502, wrote to Duch requesting information on the confession of a man from Battalion 512, named Sem. Sem had previously been sent to S-21 for interrogation. Sou Met writes

> I sent this person, whose name had been extracted from the confession of A Sa Um to you for a long time. I would like to have his confession shortly, because in the confession of A Sa Um this person was alleged to have betrayed the party, with the instruction from a political assistant, Phal. Phal is working with me. I would like to know whether A Sa Um has provided thorough and precise answers, or if we need to take Sem's confession into further consideration.[39]

This letter highlights not only the crucial role of confessions and how these were used to construct elaborate theories of conspiratorial "strings of traitors," but also the iterative component of investigations throughout the administrative hierarchy.

Life Disappearing

The final administrative function was that of execution. Duch referred to the process as the activity line (not unlike kill-chains) for it was the activity of the S-21 Committee to follow orders and make sure the process was smooth, that the prison would not become overcrowded, and that prisoners were executed at the appropriate time.[40] For those prisoners considered unimportant and not worthy of interrogation, such as spouses or the children of the accused, the process was relatively quick, but no less brutal and no less deadly. These detainees were often held for a few days or weeks until such time they were taken to be executed. During mass purges, prisoners were not even processed and detained, but taken straightaway to be killed. Throughout December 1978, according to Duch, prisoners from the East Zone were never interrogated but taken away immediately to be "smashed."[41]

For those men and women who had been interrogated, it was important that their execution be confirmed by Duch and his superiors. Once established, it was up to the mid-level bureaucrats to carry out the executions. A prisoner list dated July 1, 1977, for example, indicates sixty-three women who were scheduled to be smashed that day. These were mostly women who were wives of male prisoners who had already been purged.[42] Another execution schedule, dated July 2, 1977, lists eighty-five sons and daughters of previously executed prisoners.[43] Lists would also be compiled of prisoners who had already been executed. A report dated June 11, 1977, indicates that 198 prisoners from Division 310 had been smashed the previous day.[44] One month later it was reported that 173 prisoners from the North Zone had been smashed on July 8. According to an annotation on this report, Sao Khun (alias Kim) had not yet been sent to be executed, as this individual was "kept for doing documentation work."[45] Also killed that day were eighteen female prisoners.[46] Later that month a report confirmed on July 23, 1977, that 178 persons—of whom 160 were unnamed children—were also smashed.[47] Apart from these daily recordings, summary reports of prisoners smashed would be compiled. One document for example indicates that 162 prisoners died between March 2 and 30, 1976. Of these deaths 153 had been smashed while nine died of sickness.[48] Collectively, these documentary materials provide evidence of an intricate bureaucratic apparatus that managed—literally—the life and death of Democratic Kampuchea's citizenry. Untold lives were reduced to lines on a list; a scribble here, an annotated comment there, could spell the difference, albeit fleetingly, the difference between immediate execution and an opportunity to live one day longer.

For many of those men, women, and children who perished at S-21 or at any of the other security centers located throughout Democratic Kampuchea, their lives and deaths were recorded in the cold, matter-of-fact manner typical of any bureaucracy. For countless others, nothing tangible remains—other than memories held by survivors. And herein lies the crux of the issue. During his trial, Helen Jarvis writes, Duch frequently tried to deny that certain persons were imprisoned, tortured, or executed at S-21. However, when confronted with documentary evidence, such as lists of prisoners or photographic mugshots, Duch conceded that the account must be true. For Jarvis, Duch's actions provide a clear lesson: "If such 'proof' was not provided he continued his denial. For Duch, the paper traces are the only true records."[49]

Life Reappearing

The decision to arrest and ultimately to send a person to S-21 was a multi-faceted process that included the efforts of CPK leaders and military commanders. But it was a process that also included the mundane workings of bureaucrats who typed reports, delivered messages, photographed prisoners, and transcribed confessions. In so doing, the simple act of compiling lists, or of recording an observation, translated into the disappearance of countless men, women, and children.

Today, the disappeared are slowly reappearing, if only as names inscribed on sheets of paper. Staff associated with the Tuol Sleng Genocide Museum, the Documentation Center of Cambodia, and the Extraordinary Chambers in the Courts of Cambodia are meticulously bringing to life those who died at the hands of the Khmer Rouge.[50] As Jarvis explains, "the written reports and photographs of the graves, as well as the remains and the names and photographs of the victims, are crucial evidence for the co-prosecutors and provide support for the testimony of the Civil Parties."[51] In the process, survivors and the descendants of those who perished have gained precious insight and understanding of *why* one-quarter of Cambodia's pre-1975 population died. To this end, it is necessary to account for the actions not solely of those senior leaders adjudged "most responsible," but also of those ordinary bureaucrats, without whom the CPK could not have wielded the power of life and death.

Michel Foucault postulates that knowledge is inseparable from power. He explains that power and knowledge directly imply one another, that there is no power relation without the correlative constitution of a field of knowledge, nor any knowledge that does not presuppose and constitute at the same time power relations.[52] This is a radically different understanding of power than is normally conceived in, say, genocide studies or studies of violence. Unlike more conventional approaches, whereby power is equated with force, following Foucault, power is *exercised* rather than *possessed*. Foucault elaborates: "Power must be analyzed as something which circulates, or rather as something which only functions in the form of a chain. It is never localized here or there, never in anybody's hands, never appropriated as a commodity or piece of wealth."[53]

Given the assertion that power circulates, we can postulate that power circulates through documents; that files and folders, invoices and inventories, are the material manifestation of authorial power. Here, authorial power assumes a dual function, implying both authorship and authoritarian behavior. In other words, knowledge is produced through the combined actions of writing and documentation. Democratic Kampuchea exemplifies the calculative power of bureaucratic rule. Significantly, the documents produced by the Khmer Rouge are currently being used to prosecute crimes against humanity. And it is through the "second life" of these documents that survivors and their descendants may hope to achieve some measure of justice.

Notes

1. *Annex F.1-Revised OCIJ S-21 Prisoner List*, archived by the Extraordinary Chambers in the Courts of Cambodia (ECCC) at http:eccc.gov.kh/en. For a broad overview of S-21, see David Chandler, *Voices from S-21: Terror and History in Pol Pot's Secret Prison* (Berkeley, CA: University of California Press, 1999).

2. Good introductions to the Cambodian genocide include David Chandler, *The Tragedy of Cambodian History: Politics, War, and Revolution since 1945* (New Haven: Yale University Press, 1999); Ben Kiernan, *The Pol Pot Regime: Policies, Race and Genocide in Cambodia under the Khmer Rouge* (New Haven: Yale University Press, 1996); Elizabeth Becker, *When the War was Over: Cambodia and the Khmer Rouge Revolution* (New York: Public Affairs, 1998); and Boraden Nhem, *The Khmer Rouge: Ideology, Militarism, and the Revolution that Consumed a Generation* (Santa Barbara, CA: Praeger, 2013).

3. For an insightful account into the killings, see Alexander L. Hinton, *Why Did They Kill? Cambodia in the Shadow of Genocide* (Berkeley: University of California Press, 2005); for discussions on famine-induced deaths, see James A. Tyner, *From Rice Fields to Killing Fields: Nature, Life, and Labor under the Khmer Rouge* (Syracuse: Syracuse University Press, 2017); James A. Tyner and Stian Rice, "To Live and Let Die: Food, Famine, and Administrative Violence in Democratic Kampuchea, 1975–1979," *Political Geography* 52 (2016): 47–56; James A. Tyner and Stian Rice, "Cambodia's Political Economy of Violence: Space, Time, and Genocide under the Khmer Rouge, 1975–79," *Genocide Studies International* 10, no. 1 (2016): 84–94; and Stian Rice and James A. Tyner, "The Rice Cities of the Khmer Rouge: An Urban Political Ecology of Rural Mass Violence," *Transactions of the Institute of British Geographers* (2017). https://doi.org/10.1111/tran.12187

4. William Shawcross, *Sideshow: Kissinger, Nixon and the Destruction of Cambodia*, rev. ed. (New York: Cooper Square, 2002).

5. See for example Ben Kiernan, "Origins of Khmer Communism," *Southeast Asian Affairs* (1981): 161–80; Ben Kiernan, *How Pol Pot Came to Power: A History of Communism in Kampuchea, 1930–1975* (London: Verso 1985); and Steve Heder, *Cambodian Communism and the Vietnamese Model: Imitation and Independence, 1930–1975* (Bangkok: White Lotus Press, 2004).

6. Both men and women were subject to arbitrary arrest, detainment, and possible execution. This does not indicate, however, that gendered forms of violence did not take place. Women for example were subject to sexual abuse and were often targeted for alleged immoral actions. See Nakagawa Kasumi, *Gender-Based Violence during the Khmer Rouge Regime: Stories of Survivors from the Democratic Kampuchea (1975–1979)* (Phnom Penh, Cambodia: n.pub. 2007); Rachel Killean, "An Incomplete Narrative: Prosecuting Sexual Violence Crimes at the Extraordinary Chambers in the Courts of Cambodia," *Journal of International Criminal Justice* 13 (2015): 331–52; and Maria Elander, "Prosecuting the Khmer Rouge Marriages," *Australian Feminist Law Journal* 42 (2016): 163–75.

7. Khmer Rouge cadres typically constructed networks or "strings of traitors" based on personal associations of those who came under suspicion. If a sector chief of a particular unit for example was accused of treasonous activities, it was not uncommon for most if not all known associates of that chief to come under suspicion and subject to arrest, detainment, and execution. Also, it was common practice for the Khmer to eliminate spouses, children, extended family members, and friends of those who came under suspicion.

8. For an overview of arrests and executions at S-21, see James A. Tyner, et al., "An Empirical Analysis of Arrests and Executions at S-21 Security-Center during the Cambodian Genocide," *Genocide Studies International* 10, no. 2 (2016): 268–86; and James A. Tyner, et al., "Emerging Data Sources and the Study of Genocide: A Preliminary Analysis of Prison Data from S-21 Security-Center, Cambodia," *GeoJournal* 81, no. 6 (2017): 907–18.

9. See for example James A. Tyner, *The Politics of Lists: Bureaucracy and Genocide under the Khmer Rouge* (Morgantown: West Virginia University Press, 2018).

10. Office of the Co-Investigating Judges (OCIJ), *Closing Order, Case File No.: 002/19-09-2007-ECCC-OCIJ* (Phnom Penh: Extraordinary Chambers in the Courts of Cambodia, 2010).

11. Franziska C. Eckelmans, "The *Duch* Case: The ECCC Supreme Court Chamber's Review of Case 001.," in Simon M. Meisenberg and Ignaz Stegmiller, eds. *The Extraordinary Chambers in the Courts of Cambodia* (Berlin: Springer, 2016), 159–79, at 161.

12. For overviews of the Khmer Rouge Tribunal, see Alexander L. Hinton, *Man or Monster? The Trial of a Khmer Rouge Torturer* (Durham: Duke University Press, 2016) and Peter Manning, *Transitional Justice and Memory in Cambodia: Beyond the Extraordinary Chambers* (New York: Routledge, 2017).

13. Donald W. Beachler, "The Quest for Justice in Cambodia: Power, Politics, and the Khmer Rouge Tribunal," *Genocide Studies and Prevention* 8, no. 2 (2014): 67–80, at 71.

14. Russell Hopkins, "The Case 002/01 Trial Judgement: A Steppingstone from

Nuremberg to the Present?" in *The Extraordinary Chambers in the Courts of Cambodia*, ed. by Simon M. Meisenberg and Ignaz Stegmiller (Berlin: Springer, 2016), 181–201, at 184.

15. See the website of the Extraordinary Chambers of the Courts of Cambodia at http://www.eccc.gov.kh/en

16. Document No. E393.1, *The OCIJ S-21 Prisoner List and Explanation of the Applied Methodology*, archived by the Extraordinary Chambers in the Courts of Cambodia (ECCC) at http:eccc.gov.kh/en

17. "Supreme Court Chamber Orders to Declassify Over 1,700 Confidential Documents," Press release, Supreme Court Chamber of the Extraordinary Chambers in the Courts of Cambodia, September 6, 2012.

18. Kirsten Weld, *Paper Cadavers: The Archives of Dictatorship in Guatemala* (Durham: Duke University Press, 2014), 6.

19. Ben Kiernan, "Bringing the Khmer Rouge to Justice," *Human Rights Review* 1, no. 3 (2000): 92–108; Michelle Caswell, "Khmer Rouge Archives: Accountability, Truth, and Memory in Cambodia," *Archival Science* 10, no. 1–2 (2010): 25–44; and Michelle Caswell, "Using Classification to Convict the Khmer Rouge," *Journal of Documentation* 68, no. 2 (2012): 162–84.

20. Though see Michelle Caswel, "Hannah Arendt's World: Bureaucracy, Documentation, and Banal Evil," *Archivaria* 70 (2010): 1–25; and Stewart Clegg, Miguel Pina e Cunha, and Arménio Rego, "The Theory and Practice of Utopia in a Total Institution: The Pineapple Panopticon," *Organization Studies* 33, 12 (2012): 1735–57.

21. Weld, *Paper Cadavers*, 23.

22. Weld, *Paper Cadavers*, 13.

23. Ann Laura Stoler, *Along the Archival Grain: Epistemic Anxieties and Colonial Common Sense* (Princeton: Princeton University Press, 2009), 33.

24. Matthew S. Hull, "Documents and Bureaucracy," *Annual Review of Anthropology* 41 (2012): 251–67, at 253.

25. Hull, "Documents and Bureaucracy," 257.

26. Hull, "Documents and Bureaucracy," 259.

27. Marie-Andrée Jacob, "Form-Made Persons: Consent Forms as Consent's Blind Spot," *PoLAR: Political and Legal Anthropology Review* 30, no. 2 (2007): 249–68, at 251.

28. Hull, "Documents and Bureaucracy," 259.

29. Kenneth Dauber, "Bureaucratizing the Ethnographer's Magic," *Current Anthropology* 36, no. 1 (1995): 75–95, at 75.

30. Dauber, "Bureaucratizing the Ethnographer's Magic," 76.

31. Chandler, *Voices from S-21*, 15.

32. Document No. D390 (00744663), *Co-Prosecutors" Rule 66 Final Submission (Public Redacted Version)*, archived by the Extraordinary Chambers in the Courts of Cambodia (ECCC) at http://www.eccc.gov.kh/en

33. David Hawk, "Tuol Sleng Extermination Centre," *Index on Censorship* 15, no. 1 (1986): 25–31, at 25; see also David Hawk, *Khmer Rouge Prison Documents from the S-21 (Tuol Sleng) Extermination Center in Phnom Penh* (Ithaca: Cornell University Press, 1984).

34. Chandler, *Voices from S-21*, 27.

35. Chandler, *Voices from S-21*, 27; Document No. D390 (00744663), *Co-Prosecutors" Rule 66 Final Submission (Public Redacted Version)*, archived by the Extraordinary Chambers in the Courts of Cambodia (ECCC) at http://www.eccc.gov.kh/en; staff members at S-21 were themselves subject to arrest and execution.

36. Document No. E3/1044 (00875624), *Request for the Removal of Bad Elements, Which Were Divided into Three Categories*, archived by the Extraordinary Chambers in the Courts of Cambodia (ECCC) at http://www.eccc.gov.kh/en

37. This accusation, of being a "middle-class peasant," suggests that Khim Met was viewed as having bourgeois or revisionist tendencies.

38. Document Number E2/80/4.2 (00347466), *Brief Biography*, archived by the Extraordinary Chambers in the Court of Cambodia (ECCC) at http://www.eccc.gov.kh/en

39. Document No. E3/1043 (00224319), "Dear Beloved Brother Duch," archived by the Extraordinary Chambers in the Courts of Cambodia (ECCC) at http://www.eccc.gov.kh/en

40. Document No. E1/34.1 (00342829), *Transcript of Trial Proceedings—Kaing Guek Eav "Duch" Public*, Case File No. 001/18-07-2007-ECCC/TC, June 17, 2009, Trial Day 30, archived by the Extraordinary Chambers in the Courts of Cambodia (ECCC) at http://www.eccc.gov.kh/en

41. Document No. E1/34.1 (00342829), *Transcript of Trial Proceedings—Kaing Guek Eav "Duch" Public*, Case File No. 001/18-07-2007-ECCC/TC, June 17, 2009, Trial Day 30, archived by the Extraordinary Chambers in the Courts of Cambodia (ECCC) at http://www.eccc.gov.kh/en

42. "Execution Schedule for July 1, 1977," compiled in David Hawk, *Khmer Rouge Prison Documents from the S-21 (Tuol Sleng) Extermination Center in Phnom Penh* (Ithaca, NY: Cornell University Press, 1984).

43. "Execution Schedule for July 2, 1977," compiled in David Hawk, *Khmer Rouge Prison Documents from the S-21 (Tuol Sleng) Extermination Center in Phnom Penh* (Ithaca, NY: Cornell University Press, 1984).

44. Document No. E3/2131 (00182876), *List of Prisoners from Military Division Smashed on 10-6-1977 Division 310*, archived by the Extraordinary Chambers in the Courts of Cambodia (ECCC) at http://www.eccc.gov.kh/en

45. E3/3861 (00657714), *List of Prisoners "Smashed" on 8-7-77, North Zone*, archived by the Extraordinary Chambers in the Courts of Cambodia (ECCC) at http://www.eccc.gov.kh/en

46. Document No. E3/3861 (00657725), *List of Prisoners "Smashed" in the Section of Brother Huy Sre*, archived by the Extraordinary Chambers in the Courts of Cambodia (ECCC) at http://www.eccc.gov.kh/en

47. Document No. E3/2133 (00242285), *Prisoners' Names Smashed by Brother Huy Sre*, archived by the Extraordinary Chambers in the Courts of Cambodia (ECCC) at http://www.eccc.gov.kh/en

48. Document No. E3/1540 (00182892), *Names of Prisoners Who Died at Office S-21 C*, archived by the Extraordinary Chambers in the Courts of Cambodia (ECCC) at http://www.eccc.gov.kh/en

49. Helen Jarvis, "Powerful Remains: The Continuing Presence of Victims of the Khmer Rouge Regime in Today's Cambodia," *Human Remains and Violence* 1, no. 2 (2015): 36–55, at 48.

50. The scale and scope of the atrocities meant that restitution would be impossible and compensation in the form of individual financial payments unfeasible; however, the ECCC has made (some would argue "minimal") attempts to provide "collective and moral reparations" for victims. Thus far, these have mostly taken the form of memorials erected to recognize the victims. See Renée Jeffery, "Beyond Repair?: Collective and Moral Reparations at the Khmer Rouge Tribunal," *Journal of Human Rights* 13 (2014): 103–19, at 104.

51. Jarvis, "Powerful Remains," 48.

52. Michel Foucault, *Discipline and Punish: The Birth of the Prison*, trans. by Alan Sheridan (New York: Vintage Books, 1979), 27.

53. Michel Foucault, "Two Lectures," in Colin Gordon, ed., *Power/Knowledge: Selected Interviews and Other Writings, 1972–1977* (New York: Pantheon Books, 1980), 78–108, at 98.

Lynch Fragments

Melvin Edwards

"Memory of Winter"

Melvin Edwards's *Lynch Fragments* highlight his exploration of intersectional identity, social justice, and political awareness. It spans three periods: the early 1960s, when Edwards responded to racial violence in the United States; the early 1970s, when his activism concerning the Vietnam War motivated him to return to the series; and from 1978 to the present, as he continues to investigate a variety of themes, including his personal connection to Africa, where he now lives in Dakar, Senegal.

—Alexander Gray Associates

Editors' note: Lynchings are public killings of individuals without due process. Law enforcement in the United States and elsewhere have consistently been complicit under the pretext of justice. Today's extrajudicial murders of Black men and women by men and women charged with upholding the law, can be considered

"Jom Time"

lynchings, though they don't necessarily involve hanging. Other desecrations, such as immolation, emasculation, beheading, strangling, or shooting, are also historically part of the lynching inventory. A practice still used variously to terrorize and subjugate African Americans, there were 4,743 hangings in the U.S. from 1882 to 1968 in the American south (see https://naacp.org). In 1964, Malcolm X (1925–1965) launched the Organization of Afro American Unity, whose goal was to submit "the case of the American Negro before the United Nations" in hope of global intervention under the banner of human rights (see Manning Marable, *Malcolm X: A Life of Reinvention* (New York: Viking, 2011), 337).

Lynchings of Mexican Americans in the West were also devastating, with, for example, reportedly 473 per 100,000 people slaughtered between 1848 and 1870 (see https://daily.jstor.org/the-untold-history-of-lynching-in-the-american-west). The 1871 massacre of Chinese immigrants in Los Angeles, California, is considered one of the worst—yet most often forgotten—lynchings in U.S. history, victimizing nineteen people (out of a mere 172 residing in the city). Ironically, they were residents of LA's so-called "Negro Alley" (see https://www.nationalgeographic.com/history/article/the-bloody-history-of-anti-asian-violence-in-the-west).

ELEVEN

Our Resilient Bodies

*The Role of Forensic Science and Medicine in Restoring the
Disappeared to History*

Soren Blau

[T] hese figures refer to real human beings with first and last
names, with families and friends still longing to know what has
happened to them.

> —Luis Fondebrider, "The Applications of Forensic Anthropology
> to the Investigation of cases of Political Violence:
> Perspectives from South America"

For generations, the systematic, large-scale illegal detention, torture, extra-judicial killing, and enforced disappearance of individuals have been means of domination and suppression, either hidden or resulting in humanitarian and human rights crises.[1] The actions of perpetrators of political, ethnic, and/or religious violence very often silence individuals (death), and in cases of ethnic cleansing, obliterate target groups. Following death, attempts may be made to hide or destroy evidence including the deceased's identity. These attempts have included concealment of remains in single or mass burials,[2] which may be located in a variety of locations such as fields of crops, forests, military compounds, factories, non-descript buildings, formal cemeteries,[3] wells,[4] or latrines.[5] In some contexts, bodies have been dumped in rivers, seas,[6] or volcanoes; or thrown from airplanes; or disposed of using fire, chemicals, or explosives.[7]

Attempts to "disappear" individuals from history through the disposal and concealment (including burial) of all types of evidence including the body itself will, no doubt, continue to be a modus operandi for perpetrators of crime involving murder. Primo Levi, a member of the Italian anti-fascist front during the Second World War, described perpetrators of crime involving mass murder as typically going to extreme lengths to dispose of individuals: "There will perhaps be suspicions, discussions, research by historians, but there will be no certainties, because we will destroy the evidence together with you."[8] Such notions are, however, contrary to the founding principle of forensic science espoused by Dr. Edmond Locard, a French scientist working in the early twentieth century. Locard's so-called "exchange principle" established that "it is impossible for a criminal to act, especially considering the intensity of a crime, without leaving traces of this presence."[9] While this exchange principle originally related to trace evidence (such as fibers, hair, soil, wood, gunshot residue, and pollen),[10] in cases of purposeful attempts to conceal evidence (including bodies), the principle also applies. Regardless of the scale of the crime or the passage of time between the atrocity and the investigation, typically there will be some kind of surviving evidence; it is only a question of finding it. While physical evidence may play a role in establishing the truth of what happened in the past,[11] it equally may contribute to identifying deceased individuals,[12] and thus restoring the so-called "disappeared" to history.

As outlined in the Geneva Conventions, there is a legal obligation under international humanitarian law (as applied to international and armed conflicts) to search for and identify the dead,[13] which, it has been argued, is focused on affording dignity to the dead and protecting the interests of the families of the deceased.[14] However, physical evidence to assist in identification is only useful if it can be accurately located and systematically recovered and analyzed.[15] Over the past forty years there has been increased awareness of the powerful nature of forensic science and medicine to professionally locate, recover, and analyze evidence to assist in human identification.[16]

Restoring the Disappeared: The Process of a Forensic Approach to Human Identification

The identification of a deceased person, that is, the attribution of a correct name to the body,[17] is a legal obligation and facilitates a number of important social and legal requirements. Identification not only restores dignity to the dead, but is required, usually, to initiate mourning and traditional death rituals to allow family and community closure. Although not absolutely necessary, identification also enables mortality statistics to be developed (tabulating cause and manner of death and demographics of the dead).[18] Legally, identification may be required to aid in effective prosecution, to facilitate settlement of estate and/or inheritance or the right of the remaining partner to remarry.

While identification is clearly important for a number of reasons, there is tremendous variation in the range of identification techniques used and the amount of effort employed in identifying the dead.[19] Identification of the deceased is normally overseen by organizations such as institutes of forensic medicine, medical examiners offices, and offices of prosecutors. Under controlled circumstances, a recently deceased person is typically visually identifiable by a family member or friend.[20] However, there are a number of circumstances where visual identification is not possible, for example, if a family member or friend cannot be located to view the deceased; if the family members feel that a visual identification is too stressful; or if the deceased is physically traumatized, significantly decomposed (which may be associated to the time between death and discovery), and/or burnt and physical features are no longer recognizable. In these circumstances alternative methods must be sought and typically include the comparison of ante- and post-mortem fingerprint records, dental records, DNA profiles, or medical records (e.g., where the deceased may have evidence of surgical intervention).[21] The method used to identify the deceased person will depend on a number of variables.

Locating the remains: It is axiomatic that identification cannot progress until human remains are located. In many contexts people are reported missing but the success of physically locating remains is influenced by many variables including political will to initiate and undertake a search,[22] time since the event (which in turn impacts on the ability to locate witnesses, the reliability of witness information, and the effectiveness of specific technical equipment),[23] the environment, and resources,[24] including experts[25] and technical equipment.[26]

Quality of the recovery of remains: Depending on the context of the death, forensic specialists may be required to recover human remains in varying states of preservation. The advantages of using forensic experts during the search and recovery of human remains are well established.[27] In cases where the body is badly decomposed or skeletonized (potentially due to the effects of one or more variables including the nature of the environment, time passed since the event, and/or mode of death), unprofessional recovery may result in incomplete remains. When the necessary experts are not involved in the recovery efforts, anatomical parts which are essential for analysis and comparison (e.g., teeth) may fail to be recognized and thus not collected.

Preservation—completeness and condition of the remains (post-mortem data): Assessment of the preservation is a critical first part of the examination of human remains. The completeness of the remains (i.e., intact skeleton versus fragmentary single skeletal element), as well as condition (e.g., where the soft tissue may be mummified or the skeletal elements weathered) will affect the methods which can be considered for identification.[28] Different techniques will be used depending on whether the individual is recently deceased (fresh body) or whether significant time has passed (partially or fully skeletonized). For example, it is obviously not possible to use fingerprints for identification when the hands/palms of the individual are fully skeletonized. Peri-mortem trauma and/or post-mortem actions may affect the condition of the remains: for example, in the case of a bomb blast with associated fire it is possible that the dentition and DNA may be affected.

Quality and quantity of ante-mortem data: The identification process relies on the ability to compare information provided by surviving family members and/or friends about the missing person when they were last seen alive (so called "ante-mortem" data) with information obtained by forensic medical and science experts through an examination of the deceased person (so called "post-mortem" data). There may be cases where only general information such as the age and sex of the missing person is available, which does not provide enough detail for individual comparison with the results of the examination of human remains. The absence of, or inability to locate, medical, dental and/or fingerprint records (so-called "primary identifiers") may also make it impossible to reach a positive (that is, scientific) identification.[29] In the case of initial attempts to identify the large number of deceased following the atrocities committed in Former Yugoslavia in the 1990s, such problems, together with the fact that only anecdotal information was supplied by family members, significantly inhibited preliminary attempts to identify the thousands of individuals recovered from mass graves.[30] Ultimately this issue in Former Yugoslavia was addressed by large scale DNA-led identification programs.[31]

In contexts where it is not possible to obtain primary identifiers, circumstantial information must be considered when developing the identification hypothesis.[32] However, depending on the context, even circumstantial information may be difficult to locate.[33]

Open or closed disasters: A closed disaster refers to a situation where the exact number and names of missing individuals is known. An example is a plane crash where details of the number and names of people on the plane would be available prior to flight departure. Following the disaster (whether accidental or human-induced), the exact number and names of the missing people are known, enabling ante-mortem data to be more readily searched and obtained. In contrast, an open disaster implies the exact number of individuals unaccounted for as a result of the disaster or atrocity is unknown because no manifest of missing persons exists. Terrorist bombings, tsunamis, bushfires, earthquakes, public transport and ferry disasters, and deaths resulting from mass migration[34] are all examples of open cases. Typically, in the early period after an open disaster, the number of persons reported to authorities as missing will exceed the actual number involved in the incident.[35]

The Contributions of Forensic Science and Medicine to Identification: Key Historical Events

In 1947, the United States Army established a Central Identification Laboratory in Hawaii which was charged with recovering and identifying war dead.[36] While such an act was pivotal to facilitating the development of many forensic techniques still used in identification today (particularly in the disciplines of forensic anthropology, archaeology, and DNA), the mandate was and continues to be the identification of U.S. war dead (rather than all deceased).[37] It was not until the mid-1980s that forensic science and medicine were systematically and sustainably applied to questions relating to identification.

Under the First Geneva Convention of 1949, exhumations were supported in order to locate the remains of deceased soldiers for the purpose of repatriation to their country of origin or to move the bodies to permanent military cemeteries. While aspects of forensic science were applied to investigations of mass graves resulting from the massacre in April/May 1940 of more than twenty-five thousand Polish officers, soldiers, and civilians in the Katyn Forest in Russia,[38] the questions which were addressed focused on accountability rather than identification.[39]

The importance of the recovery process in aiding the potential to identify a deceased individual is highlighted by the events following the return of civilian rule in Argentina in 1983. In an effort to investigate the tens of thousands of individuals (estimated at more than ten thousand)[40] who were abducted and murdered during the seven years (1976–1983) of military dictatorship under General Jorge Rafael Videla,[41] a National Commission on the Disappeared (CONADEP) was established by the newly elected president Raul Alfonsin. Part of the work undertaken by CONADEP involved exhumations. The initial attempt to exhume unmarked graves was, however, undertaken in an uncontrolled manner by cemetery gravediggers aided by heavy earth-moving equipment.[42] This haphazard approach resulted in a mass of unprovenanced bones lying heaped next to opened graves. The loss of forensic and identification evidence, as well as criticism from the families of the disappeared, highlighted the need for an improved approach to recovery.

While some have argued that it is difficult to assess the number of cases which have in some way failed because a forensic anthropologist (or archaeologist) was not included in the recovery process,[43] there are case studies which highlight where the failure to include forensic practitioners (specifically forensic archaeologists and anthropologists in the search/recovery phase) has significantly hindered the case. Typically, errors made at the time of search or recovery stages include not understanding soil stratigraphy and therefore not digging deep enough,[44] time wasted on fruitless digging,[45] or implementing a process which does not involve a rigorous methodology. Such mistakes have serious implications for the subsequent attempted identification. Similar to the events in Argentina in the mid-1980s, in Colombia in 1990, an investigation into the whereabouts of forty-three peasants who were disappeared by a paramilitary group involved an exhumation undertaken by police officers (untrained in professional recovery) using heavy machinery. While six of the deceased were visually identified, many other individual remains were badly destroyed due to inexperience using heavy machinery. All the individuals were subsequently buried as "No Names" in a cemetery. These actions resulted in government-led inquiries, and the case was brought before the Inter-American Court of Human Rights. The Colombian government was found to be negligent in its recovery of remains and subsequent handling of the bodies.[46]

Similar issues have also been observed in Rwanda. While there were two brief forensic investigations undertaken in Rwanda following the 1994 genocide,[47] a program of exhumation of individuals from single and mass burials was also undertaken by government organizations. The lack of forensic expertise within these groups resulted in the separation and piling of thousands of bones. While it has been argued that the goal of these actions was to "produce an experience of memory,"[48] nonetheless, the process resulted in the deceased individuals being rendered anonymous.[49]

Based on the premise that one grave excavated using archaeological techniques will yield more evidence than several hundred demolished by bulldozers,[50] in 1984, local Argentine anthropologists and archaeologists were trained by experts from the United States. Most notably, Dr. Clyde Snow (1928–2014), a pioneer in the application of forensic anthropology and archaeology in international human rights forensic work,[51] provided training to individuals who became experts in the location and recovery of human remains and associated evidence. This training ultimately resulted in the formation of the Argentine Forensic Anthropology Team (*Equipo Argentino de Antropologia Forense*, EAAF).[52] The forensic excavations provided evidence both for the trials of the junta and assisted in the process of identifying individuals. As the new democratically elected president of Argentina began enacting legislation which brought an end to the trials of those responsible for the disappearances, the focus of EAAF's work shifted to concentrating solely on questions of identification.[53] Over the past forty years, EAAF has played a significant role in the application of forensic science and medicine (mainly forensic anthropology, forensic archaeology, and genetics) to the investigations of human rights violations worldwide.[54] Following the establishment of the EAAF, other forensic anthropology teams with similar approaches were created in Chile (1989), which also had cases in Guatemala (1992), Peru (1999) and Colombia (2004)[55] where misidentifications led to the realization that forensic medicine was essential to the identification process.[56]

Following the breakup of Former Yugoslavia and the ensuing violence between 1991 and 1992, hundreds of thousands of individuals went missing or were killed.[57] In 1996 extensive investigations commenced in the Balkans under the auspices of the International Criminal Tribunal for the Former Yugoslavia (ICTY). At the time, the excavations were the largest on-going forensic investigations in the world, and highlighted the value of forensic science to international investigations.[58] However, identification of the dead was not seen as the main purpose of the excavations with the cause and manner of death the main focus of the ICTY.[59] While evidence of personal identification was collected, it was not deemed necessary to know the name of a person in order to pursue convictions for murder and genocide.[60] For prosecutions relating to genocide charges, establishing group identity was seen as sufficient; individual identification was not necessary.[61]

While there was demonstrated value in the application of forensic science and medicine (specifically archaeology and anthropology) to the collection of evidence for prosecution in international courts,[62] the humanitarian (and some may argue justice) needs of the families to know the identity of their relatives were not being met. To address this gap, the International Commission of Missing Persons (ICMP) was established in 1996.[63] ICMP employed excavation teams and forensic anthropologists for the recovery and analysis of unidentified human remains[64] with the majority of identifications being achieved through a DNA-led approach.[65]

In 2003, the International Committee of the Red Cross (ICRC) highlighted the importance of the humanitarian, rather than just the legal aspects of the investigation of the missing.[66] Following a series of workshops conducted in 2002—with government and non-government organizations involved in the investigation of missing persons from armed conflicts and other types of violence—a series of recommendations and best practices were developed and adopted by the ICRC and Red Crescent.[67] The ICRC emphasizes the right of families to know the fate of the missing as specified in international humanitarian and human rights law.[68] In 2003, the ICRC developed a forensic unit which advocates a multidisciplinary approach to the dignified recovery, management, and identification of the dead in armed conflicts and other challenging contexts,[69] including active violence (e.g., Libya), urban violence (e.g., Brazil), and migration (e.g., México, Europe). The ICRC runs exclusively humanitarian missions which place the victims and their families, rather than the judicial investigations, at the center of the forensic investigations.[70]

Identification in the Context of Political, Ethnic, and/or Religious Violence

The approach to identification in cases of political, ethnic, and/or religious violence is complicated by a number of factors.[71] In some contexts people are disappeared over a relatively long period of time and often at various locations. In addition, the number of individuals missing (presumed deceased) often extends into the tens of thousands.[72] The scale of missing persons may be so large that it is often difficult to establish a reliable list of names from which to seek ante-mortem information (see above). Further, until some degree of political stability has resumed, it is not possible to undertake the search for the missing. Consequently, investigations often take place many years after the atrocity/ies in which people went missing occurred. For example, in 1981, the Salvadoran Armed Forces carried out "scorched earth" massacres in El Mozote and surrounding towns. At least 978 people were killed, the majority children under twelve years of age.[73]

Forensic investigations did not begin until 1992, and, due to the passing of an Amnesty Law in 1993, work was halted with new exhumations not beginning again until 1999.[74] It was not until 2017 that charges were brought against eighteen former military officers and work could commence on identifying the deceased.[75]

The delay in time between the atrocity being committed and an investigation being initiated potentially has significant impacts on both post- and ante-mortem data. With the passage of time, decomposition progresses (human remains may become skeletonized—see above for identification implications), and the preservation of associated evidence diminishes. Further, as time passes surviving relatives and/or witnesses grow older and therefore, potentially less able to recall information about where individuals went missing (resulting in difficulties in locating bodies) or specific details about their loved ones (e.g., clothing and personal belongings, health status, etc.). In some situations, surviving relatives move away from the place where the violence occurred. If ante-mortem information, including a family-reference DNA sample, is never provided by surviving family members, identification may be impossible. Further, in many human rights violation cases, the affected populations are often relatively poor and live in rural areas where concepts of health may vary. Typically, such populations also do not have access to health services (doctor and/or dentist). Consequently, there are no available ante-mortem records and where they do exist there are no laws for protection of records.[76]

Finally, the attempted forensic identification of victims of political, ethnic, and/or religious violence is often led by non-governmental organizations (NGOs) rather than, as outlined above, official State institutions. This is predominantly because in many countries the relatives of the missing do not trust State agencies which may include military, police, covert paramilitary groups, and lawyers, as well forensic pathologists, and doctors. The State often does not inquire or investigate sufficiently and, in some capacity, may have been involved in perpetrating the atrocities.[77] (See C. Moon, C. C. Snow, and B. E. Anderson for examples.[78]) Consequently, families become dissatisfied and often are no longer able to cope, hence the request to NGOs for assistance.

The Politics of Identifying the Dead

It is well established that the provision of justice is often protracted (one example of many being the conviction of only three people after twelve years for crimes against humanity committed by the Khmer Rouge between 1975 and 1979),[79] and that it comes with a cost, as demonstrated by the significant budgets allocated to organizations such as the International Criminal Court and the Internal Criminal Court for the Former Yugoslavia.[80] Similarly, as outlined above, the identification of a deceased person is a process that often takes time and typically requires significant resources. However, there is often disparity in the allocation of resources and the time and effort invested in a death investigation and personal identification depending on the context of the death and who goes missing. Compare, for example, the resources devoted by the United States government to identifying U.S. unrecovered war dead (regardless of the time passed or preservation of the remains),[81] or the expenditure of more than $80 million on the investigation of the 2001 New York terrorist attacks (including a promise to identify all 21,800 human remains fragments)[82] versus the limited financial investment in identifying individuals killed during the Santa Cruz massacre in Timor-Leste (East Timor),[83] or those who die during attempts to migrate.[84] There are often also inequalities in the time and resources allocated to identifying vulnerable individuals living below the poverty line,[85] or socially isolated elderly people living alone.[86] Such disparity has been described as "inequality in death and identification."[87] It has also been argued that a forensic system that privileges specific kinds of evidence such as DNA, fingerprints, and dental records favors the rich, and therefore, also creates inequity.[88] While identification is a legal obligation, there are many contexts where identifications are not immediately (if at all) pursued.[89] This may be either for political reasons, for example, where the conflict is still active and/or the scale of the incident results in the local infrastructure being overwhelmed (such as currently in Libya or Syria). While cultural complexities may impact on the identification process (see J. Levinson and S. Blau, for example[90]), ultimately actions taken to restore the disappeared to history remain political decisions. It is perhaps a sad truism that the many, many thousands of individuals who die anonymously every year will remain unidentified.

Conclusion

The ability to identify a deceased person has psychological, emotional, and legal consequences for surviving relatives. While it has been recognized that there is the possibility "of absolute annihilation without a trace,"[91] forensic science and medicine continue to strive to minimize this potential,[92] to ensure the disappeared are not like ghosts, neither alive nor dead,[93] and that we move past seeing mortal remains as "only bones." Following the wave of democratization across Latin America that commenced in the 1980s and the following pursuit of transitional justice and truth and reconciliation commissions across the world, the importance of identification in all these processes has been highlighted.[94] While it is a sad reality that the social context in which the dead are located can obscure the possibilities of identification, forensic science, and medicine have, and continue to significantly contribute to, restoring the names of those missing as a result of past conflict (e.g., Argentina, Peru, Timor-Leste (East Timor), the Balkans, Republic of Georgia, Spain, and Cyprus),[95] active conflict (e.g., Syria), urban violence (e.g., Brazil) and migration (e.g., worldwide).[96]

Notes

I am grateful for the comments provided by Stephen Cordner on a draft of this chapter.

1. Donald G. Dutton, E. O. Boyanowsky, M. H. Bond, "Extreme Mass Homicide: From Military Massacre to Genocide," *Aggression and Violent Behavior* 10 (2005): 437–73; Stefan Schmitt, "Mass Graves and the Collection of Forensic Evidence: Genocide, War Crimes and Crimes Against Humanity," in William D. Haglund, Marcella H. Sorg, eds., *Advances in Forensic Taphonomy: Method, Theory and Archaeological Perspectives* (Boca Raton, FL: CRC Press, 2002), 277–92.

2. Haglund. "Mass Graves and the Collection of Forensic Evidence," 244–61.

3. Jean M. Morgan, *Proving Genocide: Forensic Anthropologist's Role in Developing Evidence to Convict those Responsible for Genocide* (Tallahassee: Florida State University Libraries, 2011).

4. Mario Šlaus, David Strinović, Vedrana Petrovečki, Vlasta Vyroubal, "Contribution of Forensic Anthropology to Identification Process in Croatia: Examples of Victims Recovered in Wells," *Croatian Medical Journal* 48, no. 4 (2007): 503–12.

5. Alison Des Forges, "Leave None to Tell the Story: Genocide in Rwanda," *Human Rights Watch* (New York: International Federation of Human Rights, 1999).

6. Amanda M. Quinn, *Identifying Desaparecidos: The Development of Forensic Anthropology in Chile* (Syracuse: Syracuse University, 2014).

7. Luis Fondebrider, "The Applications of Forensic Anthropology to the Investigation of Cases of Political Violence: Perspectives from South America," in Soren Blau, Douglas H. Ubelaker, eds., *Handbook of Forensic Anthropology and Archaeology* 2nd. ed. (New York: Routledge, 2016), 65–74; Mario Ranalletti, "When Death Is Not the End: Towards a Typology of the Treatment of Corpses of 'Disappeared Detainees' in Argentina from 1975 to 1983," in Elizabeth Anstatt, Jean-Marc Dreyfus, eds., *Destruction and Human Remains* (Manchester, England: Manchester University Press, 2016), 146–79; Laura C. Fulginiti, Kristen M. Hartnett-McCann, Detective Frank Di Modica, "Sealed for your Protection: A Triple Homicide Involving the Use of a Corrosive Agent to Obscure Identity," in

Heather M. Garvin, Natalie R. Langley, eds., *Case Studies in Forensic Anthropology: Bonified Skeletons* (Boca Raton, FL: CRC Press; 2020), 99–107.

8. Primo Levi, *The Drowned and the Saved* (New York: Vintage International, 1989).

9. Robert C. Shaler, *Crime Scene Forensics: A Scientific Method Approach* (Boca Raton, FL: CRC Press; 2012).

10. John Horswell, "Crime Scene Investigation," in John Horswell, ed., *The Practice of Crime Scene Investigation* (Boca Raton, FL: CRC Press; 2004), 1–44.

11. Chip Colwell-Chanthaphonh, "History, Justice and Reconciliation," Barbara J. Little, Paul A Shackel, eds., *Archaeology as a Tool of Civic Engagement* (Lanham, MD: AltaMira Press, 2007), 23–46; Soren Blau, Jon Sterenberg, "The Use of Forensic Archaeology and Anthropology in the Search and Recovery of Buried Evidence," in Jason. Payne-James, Roger. Byard, eds., *Encyclopaedia of Forensic and Legal Medicine*, 2nd ed. (London: Elsevier, 2015), 236–45.

12. Luis Fondebrider, "Reflections on the Scientific Documentation of Human Rights Violations," *International Review of the Red Cross* 84 (2002): 848; Patricia Bernardi, Luis Fondebrider, "Forensic Archaeology and the Scientific Documentation of Human Rights Violations: An Argentinean Example from the Early 1980s," in Roxana Ferllini, ed., *Forensic Archaeology and the Investigation of Human Rights Abuses* (Springfield, IL: Charles C. Thomas, 2007), 205–32.

13. Anna Petrig, "The War Dead and Their Gravesites," *International Review of the Red Cross*, 91, issue 874 (2009): 341–69; Claire Moon, "Extraordinary Deathwork," in Roberto C. Parra, Sara C. Zapico, Douglas H. Ubelaker, eds., *Forensic Science and Humanitarian Action.* (London: Wiley, 2020), 37–48.

14. Éadaoin O'Brien, *The Exhumation of Mass Graves by International Criminal Tribunals: Nuremberg, the former Yugoslavia and Rwanda* (Galway: National University of Ireland Galway, 2011).

15. Bernardi and Fondebrider, *Forensic Archelogy*, 205–32; Dennis C. Dirkmaat, Luis. L. Cabo, Stephen D. Ousley, Steven A. Symes, "New Perspectives in Forensic Anthropology," *American Journal of Physical Anthropology* 137 (2008): 33–52.

16. For example, Parra et al., *Forensic Science and Humanitarian Action: Interacting with the Dead and the Living*.

17. Laura Major, "Unearthing, Untangling and Re-Articulating Genocide Corpses in Rwanda," *Critical African Studies* 7 no. 2 (2015):164–81.

18. Eric J. Bartelink, "Identifying Difference: Forensic Methods and the Uneven Playing Field of Repatriation," in Krista E. Latham, Alison J. O'Daniel, eds., *Sociopolitics of Migrant Death and Repatriation, Bioarchaeology and Social Theory* (London: Springer; 2018), 129–41.

19. Bartelink, "Identifying Difference," 129–24; Soren Blau, Jeremy Graham, Lyndall Smythe, Samantha Rowbotham, "Human Identification: A Review of Methods Employed within an Australian Coronial Death Investigation System," *Internaitonal Journal of Legal Medicine* 135, no. 1 (2021):375–85.

20. Soren Blau, "It's All about the Context: Reflections on the Changing Role of Forensic Anthropology in Medico-Legal Death Investigations," *Australian Journal of Forensic Sciences* 8 no. 4 (2018): 1–11.

21. Soren Blau, David Ranson, Chris O'Donnell, *An Atlas of Skeletal Trauma in Medico-Legal Contexts* (London: Elsevier, 2018).

22. Zoe Crossland, "Buried Lives: Forensic Archaeology and the Disappeared in Argentina," *Archaeological Dialogues* 7 no. 2 (200): 146–59; Roxana Ferllini, "The Development of Human Rights Investigations Since 1945," *Science and Justice* 43 no. 4 (2003): 219–24; Layla Renshaw, *Exhuming Loss: Memory, Materiality and Mass Graves of the Spanish Civil War* (Walnut Creek, CA: Left Coast Press, 2011).

23. Dominic Sarsalora, Pasquale Poppa, Alberto Amadasi, Deborah Mazzarelli, Daniele Gibelli, Emma Zanotti "The Utility of Ground-Penetrating Radar and Its Time-Dependence in the Discovery of Clandestine Burials," *Forensic Science International* 253 (2015): 119–24.

24. Naomi Kinsella, Soren Blau, "Searching for Conflict Related Missing Persons in Timor-Leste: Technical, Political and Cultural Considerations," *Stability: International Journal of Security and Development* 2, no. 1 (2013): 1–14.

25. For example, Aandrea M. Szkil. "'It's Like Every Other Job': A Consideration of Forensic Specialists' Professional Identities in Bosnia and Herzegovina," *Human Remains and Violence* 2, no. 1 (2016): 75–94; Anne Marie Mires, "The Use of Forensic Archaeology in Missing Person Cases," in K. S. Moran, C. Gold, eds., *Forensic Archaeology* (New York: Springer, 2019), 111–41.

26. Abate Dante, C. Sturdy Colls, Noly Moyssi et al., "Optimizing Search Strategies in Mass Grave Location through the Combination of Digital Technologies," *Forensic Science International: Synergy*, 1 (2019): 95–107; Soren Blau, Jon Sterenberg, Patrick Weeden, Fernando Urzedo, Richard Wright, Chris Watson, "Exploring Non-invasive Approaches to Assist in the Detection of Clandestine Human Burials: Developing a Way Forward," *Forensic Sciences Research* 3, no. 4 (2018): 304–26.

27. Tosha L. Dupras, John J. Schultz, Sandra M. Wheeler, Lana J. Williams, *Forensic Recovery of Human Remains: Archaeological Approaches*, 2nd ed. (Boca Raton, FL: CRC Press; 2011).

28. Soren Blau, "Missing Persons Investigations and Identification: Issues of Scale, Infrastructure, and Political Will," in Stephen J. Morewitz, C. Sturdy Colls, eds., *Handbook of Missing Persons* (Switzerland: Springer Nature, 2016), 227–35; Soren Blau, Samantha Rowbotham, "Not So Simple: Understanding the Complexities of Establishing Identity for Cases of Unidentified Human Remains in an Australian Medico-Legal System," *Forensic Science International* (2022): 330. https://doi.org/10.1016/j.forsciint.2021.111107

29. Soren Blau, "Forensic Human Identification: An Australian Perspective," in Roberto C. Parra, Sara C. Zapico, Douglas H. Ubelaker, eds., *Humanitarian Forensic Science: Interacting with the Dead and the Living* (London: Wiley and Sons, 2020), 593–602.

30. Caroline Alyce Tyers, *Hidden Atrocities: The Forensic Investigation and Prosecution of Genocide* (Knoxville: University of Tennessee Press, 2009).

31. Edwin Huffine, J. Crews, B. Kennedy, K. Bomberger, A. Zinbo, "Mass Identification of Persons Missing from the Break-up of the Former Yugoslavia: Structure, Function, and Role of the International Commission on Missing Persons," *Croatian Medical Journal* 42, no. 3 (2001): 271–5; Dragan Primorac, "The Role of DNA Technology in Identification of Skeletal Remains Discovered in Mass Graves," *Forensic Science International* 146 (2004): S63–4; Thomas J. Parsons, Rene M. L. Huel, Zlatan Bajunović, Adnan Rizvić, "Large Scale Identification of the Missing," in: Heny Erlich, Eric Stover, Thomas J. White, eds., *Silent Witness:*

Forensic DNA Analysis in Criminal Investigations and Humanitarian Disasters (Oxford: Oxford University Press; 2020), 193–207.

32. Soren Blau et al., *Human Identification*, 2021; Jose-Pablo Baraybar, "When DNA is Not Available, Can We Still Identify People? Recommendations for Best Practice," *Journal of Forensic Sciences*, 53, no. 3 (2008): 533–40.

33. The father of Brendan Hughes (a leading Irish Republican and Commanding Officer of the Belfast Brigade of the Provisional Irish Republican Army) purposely destroyed every family photograph attempting to deter the British from identifying Hughes. Patrick Radden Keefe, *Say Nothing: A True Story of Murder and Memory in Northern Ireland* (London: William Collins, 2018), 29.

34. Thomas P. Gocha, Martha Katherine Spradley, Ryan Strand, "Bodies in Limbo: Issues in Identification and Repatriation of Migrant Remains in South Texas," in Krista E. Latham, Alyson J. O'Daniel, eds., *Sociopolitics of Migrant Death and Repatriation, Bioarchaeology and Social Theory* (London: Springer, 2018), 143–55.

35. Soren Blau, T. Hill, "Disaster Victim Identification: A Review," *Minerva Medicolegale* 129 (2009): 35–46; Stephen M. Cordner, Noel Woodford, Richard Bassed, "Forensic Aspects of the 2009 Victorian Bushfires Disaster," *Forensic Science International* 205, no. 1–3 (2011): 2–7.

36. Thomas Holland, John Byrd, Vincent Sava, "Joint POW/MIA Accounting Command's Central Identification Laboratory," in Michael W. Warren, Heather A. Walsh-Haney, Laurel Freas, eds., *The Forensic Anthropology Laboratory* (Boca Raton: CRC Press, 2008), 47–63.

37. Clyde Collins Snow, "Forensic Anthropology," *Annual Review of Anthropology* 11 1982): 97–131.

38. Telford Taylor, *The Anatomy of the Nuremberg Trials, A Personal Memoir* (New York: Knopf Doubleday, 1992).

39. Roxana Ferllini, *Science and Justice*, 219–24; D. Debons, A. Fleury, J. F. Pitteloud, eds., *Katyn and Switzerland: Forensic Investigators and Investigations in Humanitarian Crises 1920–2007* (Geneva: Georg editeru, 2009).

40. R. H. Kirschner, "The Application of the Forensic Sciences to Human Rights Investigations," *Medical Law Review* 13 (1994): 451–60.

41. Chistopher Joyce, Eric Stover, *Witnesses from the Grave: The Stories Bones Tell* (Boston: Little, Brown, 1991).

42. Eric Stover, M. Ryan, "Breaking Bread with the Dead," *Historical Archaeology* 35, no. 1 (2001): 7–25.

43. Martin Paul Evison, Rafaela A. Francisco, Marco A. Guimarães, "Utility in Forensic Anthropology: Findings Contributing to Case Conversion," *Forensic Science Policy and Management: An International Journal* 3, no. 3 (2012): 113–25.

44. Meagan Dillon, "Murder Accused Killed Wife Colleen Adams with Metal Bar at Family Home, SA Court hears," *ABC News*, August 10, 2020.

45. Richard Wright, "Shallow and Grave," Letter to the Editor, *The Australian*, September 2, 2003.

46. R. H. Kirschner, *Medical Law*, 451–60; A. M. López, A. P. Umaña, "Who is Missing? Problems in the Application of Forensic Archaeology and Anthropogy in Colombia's Conflict," Roxana Ferllini, ed., *Forensic Archaeology and Human Rights Violations* (Springfield, IL: Charles C. Thomas, 2007), 170–204.

47. The aims of the forensic examinations undertaken in Rwanda were to estab-

lish patterns of injury and cause of death, and to collect and preserve evidence, as opposed to identifying the individuals; Physicians for Human Rights, *Forensic Investigations of Human Remains at Kibuye Roman Catholic Church and Home St. Jean Complex Expert Report Submitted on Behalf of the Prosecution in the trial of Prosecutor v. Kayishema and Ruzindana*, ICTR-95-1-T, 3; Éadaoin O'Brien, *The Exhumation of Mass Graves*.

48. Sara Guyer, "Rwanda's Bones," *Boundary 2* 36 no. 2 (2009): 155–75.

49. Major, *Critical African Studies*, 164–81.

50. Joyce, *Witnesses from the Grave*.

51. O'Brien, *The Exhumation of Mass Graves*; McFadden, "Clyde Snow, Sleuth Who Read Bones from King Tut's to Kennedy's, Dies at 86," *New York Times*, May 17, 2014.

52. Stover, *Historical Archeology*, 113–25; Mercedes Doretti, Clyde Collins Snow, "Forensic Anthropology and Human Rights: The Argentine Experience," in Dawn W. Steadman, ed., *Hard Evidence: Case Studies in Forensic Anthropology* (Upper Saddle River, NJ: Prentice Hall, 200), 3, 290–310.

53. Zoe Crossland, "Violent Spaces: Conflict Over the Reappearance of Argentina's Disappeared," in John Scholfield, William G. Johnson, Colleen M. Beck, eds., *Material Culture: The Archaeology of the Twentieth-Century Conflict* (London: Routledge, 2002), 115–31.

54. Merceds Doretti, Luis Fondebrider, "Science and Human Rights—Truth, Justice, Reparation and Reconciliation: A Long Way in Third World Countries," in Victor Buchli, Gavin Lucas, eds., *Archaeologies of the Contemporary Past* (London: Routledge, 2001), 138–44; Mercedes Salado Puerto, Laura Catelli, Carola Romanini, Magdalena Romero, Carlos Maria Vullo, "The Argentine Experience in Forensic Identification of Human Remains," in Roberto C. Parra, Sara C. Zapico, Douglas Ubelaker, eds., *Forensic Science and Humanitarian Action*, (London: Wiley and Sons, 2020), 549–58.

55. Mercedes Doretti, J. Burrell, "Gray Spaces and Endless Negotiations: Forensic Anthropology and Human Rights," in Richard Fox, Les Field, eds., *Anthropology Put to Work* (Oxford, England: Berg, 2007), 45–64.

56. Krista E. Latham, Ryan Strand, "Digging, Dollars, and Drama: The Economics of Forensic Archeology and Migrant Exhumation," in Krista E. Latham, Alyson J. O'Daniel, eds., *Sociopolitics of Migrant Death and Repatriation, Bioarchaeology and Social Theory* (London: Springer, 2018), 99–113.

57. Jon Sterenberg, "Dealing with the Remains of Conflict: An International Response to Crimes Against Humanity, Forensic Recovery, Identification and Repatriation in the Former Yugoslavia," in Soren Blau, Douglas H. Ubelaker, eds., *Handbook of Forensic Anthropology and Archaeology*, 1st ed. (Walnut Creek, CA: Left Coast Press, 2009), 416–25; M. Djuric, "Dealing with Human Remains from Recent Conflicts; Mass Grave Excavation and Human Identification in a Sensitive Political Context," in Soren Blau, Douglas H. Ubelaker, eds., *Handbook of Forensic Anthropology and Archaeology*, 2nd ed. (London: Routledge, 2016), 532–44.

58. Djuric, "Dealing with Human Remains from Recent Conflicts."

59. O'Brien, *The Exhumation of Mass Graves*; Tyers, *Hidden Atrocities*.

60. Stephen M. Cordner, Morris Tidball-Bin, "Humanitarian Forensic Action—Its Origins and Future," *Forensic Science International* 279 (2017): 65–71; G. T. Ble-

witt, "The Role of Forensic Investigations in Genocide Prosecutions Before an International Criminal Tribunal," *Medicine, Science and the Law* 37 no. 4 (1997): 284–8; Stephen M. Cordner, Helen McKelvie, "Developing Standards in International Forensic Work to Identify Missing Persons," *International Review of the Red Cross* 84, issue 848 (2002): 867–84.

61. Debra Komar, "Is Victim Identity in Genocide a Question of Science or Law? The Scientific Perspective, with Special Reference to Darfur," *Science and Justice* 48, no. 3 (2008): 146–52.

62. Melanie Klinker, "Forensic Science Expertise for International Criminal Proceedings: An Old Problem, A New Context and a Pragmatic Resolution," *The International Journal of Evidence and Proof* 13 (2009): 102–29.

63. Sarah E. Wagner, *To Know Where He Lies: DNA Technology and the Search for Srebrenica's Missing* (Berkeley: University of California Press, 2008).

64. Sterenberg, *Handbook of Forensic Anthropology*, 416–25.

65. Huffine et al., *Croatian Medical Journal*, 271; Andreas Kleiser, Thomas J. Parsons, "Large Scale Identification of the Missing," in Henry Erlich, Eric Stover, Thomas J. White, eds., *Silent Witness: Forensic DNA Analysis in Criminal Investigations and Humanitarian Disasters* (Oxford: Oxford University Press, 2020), 193–207.

66. Shula M. Drawdy, Cheryl Katzmarzyk, "The Missing Files: The Experience of the International Committee of the Red Cross," in Derek Congram, ed. *Missing Persons: Multidisciplinary Perspectives on the Disappeared* (Toronto: Canadian Scholars Press, 2016), 60–73.

67. Anon, *The Missing and Their Families, Action to Resolve the Problem of People Unaccounted For as a Result of Armed Conflict or Internal Violence and to Assist Their Families* (Geneva, Switzerland: International Committee of the Red Cross, 2003).

68. Cordner et al., *International Review of the Red Cross*, 867–84.

69. Cordner et al., *International Review of the Red Cross*, 867–84.

70. Drawdy et al., *Missing Persons: Multidiscciplinary Perspectives*, 60–73.

71. Blau, *Handbook of Missing Persons*, 227–35.

72. Fondebrider, *Handbook of Forensic Anthropology*, 65–74; Cordner et al. *Forensic Science International*, 65–71; Kirsten Juhl, *The Contribution by (Forensic) Archaeologists to Human Rights Investigations of Mass Graves* (Stavanger, Norway: Museum of Archaeology, 2005).

73. Leigh Binford, *The El Mozote Massacre: Human Rights and Global Implications* (Tucson: University of Arizona Press, 2016).

74. Doretti et al., *Hard Evidence*, 290–310.

75. Anon, *The Massacre of El Mozote: 36 Years of Struggles for Truth and Justice 2017.* https://unfinishedsentences.org/the-massacre-of-el-mozote-36-years-of-struggles-for-truth-and-justice/

76. Luis Fondebrider, Soren Blau, "Personal Identification from Skeletal Remains in Human Rights Investigations: Challenges From the Field," 62nd Annual Scientific Meeting of the American Academy of Forensic Sciences, Seattle, Washington, 2010.

77. Doretti et al., *Anthropology Put to Work*, 45–64; Fondebrider, *Handbook of Forensic Anthropology*, 65–74.

78. Claire Moon, "Human Rights, Human Remains: Forensic Humanitarianism and the Human Rights of the Dead," *International Social Science Journal* 65,

250   **Book of the Disappeared**

issue 215–216 (2014): 49–63; Clyde Collins Snow, F. A. Peccerelli, J. S. Susanávar, A. G. Robinson, J. M. N. Ochoa, "Hidden in Plain Sight: X.X. Burials and the Desaparecidos in the Department of Guatemala, 1977–1986," in Jana Asher, David Banks, Fritz J. Scheuren, eds., *Statistical Methods for Human Rights* (London: Springer, 2008), 89–116; Bruce E. Anderson, Martha Katherine Spradley, "The Role of the Anthropologist in the Identification of Migrant Remains in the American Southwest," *Academic Forensic Pathology* 6, no. 3 (2016): 432–38.

79. George Wright, "40 Years On, Khmer Rouge Leaders Face Genocide Verdict," *Al Jazeera*, November 14, 2018.

80. Rupert Skilbeck, "Funding Justice: The Price of War Crimes Trials," *Human Rights Brief* 15, no. 3: 6–10.

81. Casey Grove, Mike. Dunham, "Aircraft Debris Found on Glacier 12 miles From 1952 Crash Site," *Anchorage Daily News*, June 27, 2012.

82. Jay D. Aronson, *Who Owns the Dead? The Science and Politics of Death at Ground Zero* (Cambridge: Harvard University Press, 2016).

83. Kinsella et al., *Stability: International Journal of Security and Development*, 1–14.

84. Robin Reinke, Bruce E. Anderson, "Missing in the US–México Borderlands," in Derek Congram, ed., *Missing Persons: Multidisciplinary Perspectives on the Disappeared* (Toronto: Canadian Scholars Press; 2016), 249–68.

85. Eric Klinenberg, "Bodies that Don't Matter: Death and Dereliction in Chicago," *Body and Society* 7 no. 2–3 (2001): 121–35.

86. Snow, *Annual Review of Anthropology*, 97–131; Kenna Quinet, Samuel Nunn, Alfarena Ballew, "Who Are the Unclaimed Dead?" *Journal of Forensic Sciences* 61, suppl. 1 (2016): S131–9.

87. Bartelink, *Sociopolitics of Migrant Death*, 129–41.

88. Dawn Steadman, Sarah Wagner, "Taking Stock: DNA Testing and its Complex Truths," in Henry Erlich, Eric Stover, Thomas J. White, eds., *Silent Witness: Forensic DNA Analysis in Criminal Investigations and Humanitarian Disasters* (Oxford: Oxford University Press; 2020), 268–87.

89. Alicia Gaspar de Alba, Georgiana Guzman, "*Feminicidio*: The 'Black Legend' of the Border," in Alicia Gaspar de Alba, Georgina Guzman, eds., *Making A Killing: Femicide, Free Trade and La Frontera* (Austin: University of Texas Press, 2010), 1–22.

90. Jay Levinson, "An *Halakhic* Reconsideration of Victim Identification" *Shaarei Tzedek Medical Centre* 4 no. 1 (2001): 55–7; Soren Blau, "Working for the Living and the Dead: Challenges Associated with Personal Identification from Skeletal Remains in Timor-Leste," in Lia Kent, Rui Graça Feijó, eds., *The Dead as Ancestors, Martyrs, and Heroes in Timor-Leste* (Amsterdam: Amsterdam University Presses, 2020).

91. Hannah Arendt, *The Origins of Totalitarianism* (New York: Harcourt, 1979).

92. Roberto C. Parra, Elizath Anstett, Pierre Perich, Jane E. Buikstra, "Unidentified Deceased Persons," in Roberto C. Parr, Sara C. Zapico. Douglas H. Ubelaker, eds., *Forensic Science and Humanitarian Action* (London: Wiley and Sons, 2020), 79–99.

93. Zoe Crossland, *Material Culture*, 115–31.

94. Claire Moon, "The Biohistory of Atrocity and the Social Life of Human Remains," in Christopher Stojanowski, William Duncan, eds., *Studies in Forensic*

Biohistory: Anthropological Perspectives (Cambridge: Cambridge University Press, 2017), 267–87.

95. Iosif Kovra, "Unearthing the Truth: The Politics of Exhumations in Cyprus and Spain," *History and Anthropology* 19, no. 4 (2008): 371–90.

96. Tara Brian, Frank Laczko, eds., *Fatal Journeys Tracking Lives Lost during Migration* (Geneva, Switzerland: International Organization for Migration, 2014). http://www.pensamientocritico.org/intorg1114.pdf

In Between/Underneath
(Entremedio/Por Debajo)

Jonathan Herrera Soto

In Between/Underneath (Entremedio/Por Debajo) features the faces of two-hundred male and female Mexican media workers—among them, mainstream news reporters; radio and television hosts; photographers; videographers; freelancers; journalists for small, independent outlets; and others who were murdered or made to disappear for more than a century. The exhibit explores the legacy of politically targeted violence, with its fierce hold on collective memory, and represents some of the experiences of those who were victims of a corrupt, authoritarian system. The violations continue. This exhibit questions and exposes socioeconomic forces that uphold political power. It incorporates certain printing techniques—slicing wounds with wood, burning the surface of stone with acid, and crushing onto paper under immense pressure—that reanimate acts of State-sanctioned criminal violence within the artwork.

—Jonathan Herrera Soto

Editors' Note: Targeted killings of journalists in México have existed at least since the reign of President Porfirio Díaz (r. 1884-1911) and the Mexican Revolution in 1910. The Committee to Protect Journalists (CPJ, https://cpj.org) reports that today México is among the highest-risk countries for journalists. On August 23, Fredid Román became the fifteenth journalist (the third that month) to be murdered in 2022. Worldwide, 1,405 journalists—in all aspects of the vocation—were killed from 1992 to 2021. Fifty-five were added as of September 2022. Reporters without Borders/*Reporters sans frontières* (RSF, https://rsf.org/) safeguards the right to freedom of information, in line with article 19 of the Universal Declaration of Human Rights. From January to July 2021, RSF documented 433 journalists imprisoned and 66 missing worldwide.

"First they came for the reporters. We don't know what happened next."

—2018 protest sign, anonymous

TWELVE

Retributive or Restorative Justice

Gacaca Courts' Contribution to Transitional Justice and
Reconciliation in Post-Genocide Rwanda

Hilmi M. Zawati

In the aftermath of the Rwandan genocide, which took place between April 6 and July 4, 1994, and claimed the lives of approximately eight hundred thousand Tutus and moderate Hutu,[1] national reconciliation became a high priority for the Rwandan government.[2] Being faced with an enormous caseload and compelling needs for national reconciliation, the government passed the Genocide Law in 1996 and hosted a broad spectrum of transitional justice mechanisms, including the Gacaca courts,[3] community-based judicial mechanisms designed to restore justice and mend the torn fabric of Rwanda's shattered society. In post-genocide Rwanda, truth-telling and perpetrators' public apology were deemed to be the foundation stone of transitional justice, reconciliation, and eradication of the culture of impunity.[4]

Accordingly, the Rwandan transitional government passed the law establishing the Gacaca courts in January 2001, and amended it in June 2004, as a community-based transitional dispute mechanism of restorative justice.[5] The Gacaca courts were launched to provide alternative solutions for dealing with the genocide aggravations, and to alleviate the failure of modern models of justice, namely the International Criminal Tribunal for Rwanda (ICTR),[6] to bring justice for both victims and genocide suspects.[7]

In March 2005, over 12,000 Gacaca courts had commenced processing the cases of more than 120,000 suspects awaiting trial in overfilled nationwide detention centers.[8]

However, after trying approximately two million genocide suspects, Gacaca courts were terminated on Monday, June 18, 2012,[9] by the Organic Law No.4 of 2012.[10] President Paul Kagame, who took office in April 2000, announced the termination claiming that they had achieved most of what they were created for. They left behind thousands of uncompleted cases, including the cases of suspects of heinous crimes who had been tried in absentia, as well as other cases scheduled to be transferred from the ICTR.[11] Although some commentators appreciated the Gacaca courts' speedy trials and that it alleviated tensions between Hutu and Tutsi ethnic groups,[12] this analysis argues that these courts symbolized the bleaker side of transitional justice, fell short of international legal standards, and failed to deliver restorative justice and reconciliation in post-genocide Rwanda.

In addressing the above argument, this paper begins by considering the evolution of the Gacaca courts, as a community-based judicial mechanism, then moves to underline a number of the courts' major overarching shortcomings, particularly, providing victors retributive and discriminative justice,[13] overlooking the due process obligations, falling short of adequately addressing conflict-related gender-based crimes, and failing to deliver adequate justice and sufficient reparations to genocide survivors. Finally, this inquiry concludes with an emphasis on its central legal argument that Gacaca courts utterly failed to deliver restorative justice and reconciliation in post-genocide Rwanda.

Gacaca Court: An Overview

Gacaca, in Kinyarwanda *gachacha*, is originally a traditional community-based dispute resolution forum. The word can be broadly translated to mean "justice on the grass," referring to the fact that these courts proceed their judicial process on outdoor grass.[14] Focusing on truth and reconciliation, the new Gacaca was first launched in June 2002 and spread throughout the country by January 2005.[15] By April 2009, the system comprised 12,013 courts and 169,442 judges (known as *inyangamugayo* in Kinyarwanda),[16] which completed 1,958,634 cases by the time Gacaca was terminated in 2012. On the termination date, the number of Gacaca was 12,103, subdivided into 9013 courts of the cell, 1545 courts of the sector, and 1545 courts of appeal.[17] However, the traditional—pre-colonial—form of Gacaca was based on common law and old traditions, led by wise men (experienced elders) and public figures as judges, who considered civil settlements, including inheritance, civil liability, and marital disputes.[18] The new Gacaca form was officially established by the Rwandan Patriotic Front (RPF) government, as the victor, under Organic Law 40/2000 of January 26, 2001, and passed by the Rwandan Transitional National Assembly (RTNA) to prevent the reoccurrence of the 1994 genocide and bring peace and justice to the Rwandan people.[19]

According to the National Service for Gacaca Jurisdictions, the Rwandan government pinpointed five achievements to be accomplished by Gacaca courts. The government maintained that the following goals were essential to restore justice and promote national reconciliation:[20]

First, to reveal the truth about the events of the genocide. In this respect, the government deemed that justice can't be achieved unless the truth about the genocide events was established. To make the truth public, the new Gacaca courts were instituted, where victims, suspects, and eyewitnesses could meet in open-door hearings that enable societal participation in the judicial process. Moreover, Gacaca courts considered the plea-bargaining system, which provides that Category 2 suspects can get 50 percent off their prison time if they confess during the hearings and two-thirds of their sentences reduced if they confessed prior to their hearings by giving detailed descriptions of the offenses they committed and make a public apology.[21] Nevertheless, despite the above provided advantages, none of the defendants admitted committing more than one minor crime.[22]

Second, to accelerate the trials of hundreds of thousands of genocide suspects. When setting up the Gacaca courts, the government vouched for the speed of the trials. Trying this huge number of suspects in regular courts would have required at least two hundred years and therefore would naturally violate the suspect's right to be tried within a reasonable time and without undue delay.[23]

Third, to eradicate the culture of impunity. The government, as well as many Rwandans believe that the blanket amnesty granted to the perpetrators of previous massacres played a prominent role in the occurrence of the 1994 genocide.[24] To eliminate the possibility of further genocide, the government promulgated the law of January 26, 2001, creating the Gacaca jurisdictions, and charged it with the task of eradicating the culture of impunity by investigating and prosecuting crimes committed between October 1, 1990 and December 31, 1994, and bringing all genocide perpetrators to justice. Many scholars argue that this campaign was applied selectively. While the Gacaca courts successfully prosecuted Hutu genocide suspects and brought them to justice, they completely failed to prosecute any member of the Rwandan Patriotic Army (RPA), the military arm of the RPF, which allegedly committed similar crimes against Hutu communities during the genocide. Instead, they were tried behind closed doors in a military tribunal run by RPA officials.[25] Unequal justice under the law is no justice.

Fourth, to reconcile Rwandans and reinforce their unity. As mentioned at the outset of this analysis, the Gacaca system is based on two pillars: truth and reconciliation.[26] Unfortunately, the system entirely failed to provide a truthful version of the genocide, and, accordingly, the reconciliation process was not successful.[27] Several legal case studies reveal that the reconciliation process is vague, dull, and unclear. Furthermore, Rwandans have very different understandings of reconciliation and don't agree even on minimally acceptable social relations among them.[28] Participation in the reconciliation process is not voluntary, but mandatory and thus against the will of the Rwandan people. Relying on its coercive power, the government made it clear that whoever rejects participation will face harsh consequences, including criminal sanctions.[29] In similar terms, the preamble to the Gacaca law provides that "the duty to testify is a moral obligation, nobody having the right to get out of it for whatever reasons it may be."[30] Unfortunately, reconciliation in Rwanda is still an unattainable goal.

Finally, the fifth achievement mandated by the Gacaca law was to demonstrate the capacity of Rwandan society to solve its problems through a legal system based on Rwandan custom. Although the only common factor between the traditional and new Gacacas is just the name, the government tried hard to convince Rwandans that the new Gacaca was also a societal dispute resolution mechanism based on custom and traditions and an extension of the traditional one.[31] But, as has already been pointed out, the two Gacacas are entirely different. The old system—which made participation voluntary and limited to males—considered minor problems on the basis of custom and traditions and delivered compensatory and conciliatory assessments between parties to the conflict based on the best interests of the community.[32] The new Gacaca was based on a statutory law, making participation mandatory for both males and females, and considered complex criminal cases with sentences up to life imprisonment.[33]

That being said, the government failed to convince the majority of Rwandan society that the new Gacaca was an extension of the old one, and the ideal mechanism for resolving community disputes based on custom and traditions. Moreover, it ignored the fact that Rwanda's post-war demographics are very different from those during the war, when large groups of

Hutus fled the country for fear of retaliation by Tutsis, while large groups of Tutsis have returned from exile.[34] As a result, the tendency to retaliation has overtaken the conciliatory one intended during the new Gacaca trials.

Looking into the statutory laws of the new Gacaca, the court was established by two laws: the Organic Law No. 08/96[35] and the Organic Law No. 40/2000.[36] The latter was implemented in January 2001, and then modified periodically, in June 2001,[37] June 2004,[38] June 2006,[39] March 2007,[40] and May 2008.[41] The Organic Law No. 08/96, known as Genocide Law of 1996, was drafted under the title of "Organic Law on the Organization of Prosecution for Offences Constituting the Crime of Genocide or Crimes against Humanity since October 1, 1990," by a conference on "Genocide, Impunity, and Accountability," hosted in Kigali by the Rwandan government between November 1 and 5, 1995.[42] On August 30, 1996, this law was adopted by the Rwandan National Assembly, establishing four categories of genocide suspects.[43]

The four categories of genocide suspects, incorporated in the norms of the above law[44] were echoed in the provisions of Organic Law No. 40/2000.[45] By this law, Gacaca courts were introduced at all administrative levels, including cells, sectors, districts, provinces, and the capital. Later, it was replaced by the 2004 Organic Law. The latter has reduced the four categories to three to be heard on two administrative levels; the cell and sector.[46] In June 2004, the government enacted a modified version of this law to counter and address specific challenges related to Gacaca's performance, including allowing the victims of wartime sexual violence to testify *in camera*. The law was slightly modified again in 2006 to respond to new juridical matters.[47]

Finally, the government amended the law in 2008 to transfer Category 1 crimes of gender-based crimes from the jurisdiction of the national courts to Gacaca.[48] This shift was to address the needs of wartime rape and other sexual violence victims who complained that they had waited for long periods without recognition or justice.[49]

It is worth mentioning that the new Gacaca system operated in three stages: information gathering, categorization of crimes, and judgment.[50] In the first stage, the court was required to complete several tasks, including inquiring about the number of people who were killed during the genocide, collecting information about the killers, preparing detailed lists of property crimes committed during the genocide, and verifying and examining the collected data.[51] In the second stage, the court reviewed the collected information and classified the accused persons according to the severity of their alleged wrongdoings.[52] Article 2 of the 1996 Genocide Law[53] and article 51 of the 2000 Gacaca Law[54] categorized crimes committed between October 1, 1990, and December 31, 1994, into four categories.

The first category involved those who organized and orchestrated the genocide, particularly the genocide planners, inciters, campaigners, notorious murderers, and the responsibility for using wartime rape and other forms of sexual violence as a weapon of war. The second Category includes co-perpetrators who voluntarily participated in violence with the intention to kill or cause severe injuries leading to death. The third Category comprised persons causing serious bodily injuries without intention to kill. Moreover, the fourth Category encompasses persons who committed crimes against property.[55]

The third phase of Gacaca's operations was the trial and sentencing stage, held at various administrative levels, depending on the defendant's offence category.[56] For example, trials for the first Category were held at Rwandan civil courts until 2008, while trials for other categories were held at the sector or the cell level.[57] Usually, trials took place at the suspect's home village, where judges loudly read the accusation, and heard from both the accused and accusers before delivering the verdict.[58]

Nonetheless, despite the Gacaca law's fine-sounding norms, the limitation of the Gacaca court's jurisdiction to adjudicate crimes committed between October 1990 and December 1994 has been seen as discriminative, prejudicially narrow and an open bias against Hutus, who believe that ignoring the history of discrimination and brutality[59] against them before the above dates—which had served as a catalyst for the perpetuation of the 1994 genocide—is unjust and constitutes a form of persecution.[60] Moreover, Gacaca was unable to guarantee the defendants' right to fair trial standards and fell short of meeting due process obligations under article 14 of the International Covenant on Civil and Political Rights (ICCPR).[61] Moreover, it failed to provide adequate justice and sufficient reparations to genocide survivors and fell short of adequately addressing conflict-related, gender-based crimes. These shortcomings are the subject of analysis in the second part of this inquiry.

Providing Victors Retributive and Discriminative Justice

Gacaca, as a controversial justice system, condoned different statutory and judicial problems. Its founding and terminating discriminatory provisions, which drove a wedge in the heart of the reconciliation process by granting blanket immunity to crimes committed by the RPA, the military wing of the RPF ruling dominant party, and imposed collective guilt for genocide on Hutus by accepting one single narrative of the conflict, portraying them as perpetrators and Tutsis as victims. The court's judicial system reflected conflicts of interests, extensive corruption among judges, patterns of political interference with its judiciary, and poorly trained and prejudiced judges.[62] Gacaca concluded in 2012 without providing an alternative avenue for Hutu victims to have their cases heard.[63] In the same vein, Gacaca failed to provide mechanisms to enforce sentences delivered against those who were tried in absentia.[64]

The National Service of Gacaca Jurisdictions fired more than forty-five thousand Gacaca judges after they were accused of participation in the genocide campaign.[65] Furthermore, the impartiality of Gacaca judges[66] was in question. Many of them were genocide survivors or lost one or more of their close relatives. Therefore, there was a high potentiality of conflict of interests for those judges,[67] the matter that violates the norms of different international law instruments, including the Universal Declaration of Human Rights, demanding that "Everyone is entitled in full equality to a fair and public hearing by an independent and impartial tribunal."[68] In addition, the court became a remunerative business, where judges accepted bribes from wealthy suspects in exchange for acquittals.[69] In this respect, Human Rights Watch has documented a large number of corruption-related cases.[70]

Despite the fact that the RPA committed war crimes and crimes against humanity by killing between twenty-five thousand and forty-five thousand persons between April and August 1994, Gacaca laws did not condemn these crimes although they are within the jurisdiction of the court.[71] This serious shortcoming was a result of the RPF political interference with the judiciary.[72] President Paul Kagame promoted this discriminative attitude in his June 2002 speech launching the Gacaca process, saying: "it would be a grave error to confuse genocide with acts of vengeance taken by [Tutsi] individuals."[73] The exclusion of RPA crimes from the jurisdiction of Gacaca on political grounds severely damaged the credibility of the court and its role in reconciliation and restoring justice.

The notion of victor's justice has prevailed in post-genocide Rwanda as both victims and their "elite" perpetrators, who have been granted blanket immunity by Gacaca courts, share the same land and live in the same socio-political conditions. As a result, tensions between the two warring groups became inevitable,[74] and have weakened and reduced the courts' role in the process of restoring justice and reconciliation. Indeed, the RPF government's political interference with the judiciary system put the whole

Gacaca judicial process on the horns of a dilemma and paved the way for victor's justice.[75]

A case in point is Kagame's emphasis on forcing Rwandans to testify before Gacaca courts and making it a moral obligation under the law.[76] Another case is the government's decision to prevent the trial of the RPA members in the Gacaca courts for war crimes and crimes against humanity allegedly committed by them between October 1990 and December 1994. Kagame dismissed these crimes on the claim that they were isolated cases by individuals, alleging that such crimes cannot be equated with the genocide campaign masterminded by Hutu leaders. By the same token, his government justified the dismissal of the RPA's crimes from Gacaca by emphasizing that these crimes were committed in a civil war, outside the genocide, because the RPA suspects were military personnel, not militiamen. Accordingly, Kagame and his government insisted they should be prosecuted and tried by a military court, not by a communal tribunal.[77]

It is clear that the government's manipulation of the judicial system rendered many Hutus frustrated and regarding Gacaca as a form of victor's justice, manifesting the power of the State rather than promoting accountability and restoring justice.[78] As stated above, the government's control over the judicial process has damaged the credibility of the justice system and impeded the ability of Gacaca to contribute to reconciliation.[79] Moreover, Gacaca reinforced and deepened ethnic divergence between Hutu and Tutsi by considering attacks by Hutu against Tutsi as genocide crimes while attacks by Tutsi against Hutu were seen as isolated incidents in a civil war.[80]

Lack of the Due Process Obligations

As early as the establishment of Gacaca, one of the most widely voiced concerns was the court's compromise of and failure to consider the defendant's due process rights.[81] During her visit to Rwanda in May 2007, Louise Arbour, then United Nations High Commissioner for Human Rights, criticized Gacaca for conducting unfair trials, hiring untrained judges, and imposing heavy penalties on convicted suspects. The government ignored all criticism and made it clear that compliance with international standards for fair trials was not a top priority in the Gacaca context.[82] By disregarding the norms of international human rights law, the government suppressed the court's role in giving rise to restorative justice and accountability in post-genocide Rwanda.[83]

One may wonder whether Gacaca could turn a blind eye to the defendant's right to have a fair and impartial trial in return for its efficiency, practicality, and streamlining and speeding the litigation process. An explicit response to this inquiry could be founded in deferent national, African, regional, and international legal instruments, including Rwanda's Constitution;[84] the Report of the International Panel of Eminent Personalities, Assembled by the Organization of African Unity on the 1994 Genocide in Rwanda and Surrounding Events;[85] the Dakar Declaration;[86] the African Charter on Human and Peoples' Rights;[87] the American Convention on Human Rights;[88] the European Convention for the Protection of Human Rights and Fundamental Freedoms;[89] the Universal Declaration on Human Rights;[90] and the International Covenant on Civil and Political Rights.[91] A careful examination of the provisions of the above instruments reveals that the court's efficiency and speeding up the litigation process must be accompanied by fairness and assurance of a defendant's right to a fair trial by an independent and impartial tribunal.[92]

Moreover, the court must guarantee the defendant's right to the presumption of innocence until proven guilty, equal treatment in the court, and the right to defense, including the right to be defended by counsel of his choice. This right was not adequately recognized in Gacaca trials although it is embodied in the Rwandan Constitution, the Rwandan Code of Criminal Procedure, and the African Charter on Human Rights and Peoples' Rights.[93] Unfortunately, Gacaca utterly failed to provide any of these rights according to international legal standards. Indeed, in 2000, Amnesty International documented cases of confessions obtained under duress and arbitrary arrests, violating Rwanda's obligations under international law.[94]

Furthermore, Gacaca was also criticized for the denial of the defendant's right to counsel of his/her choice and fell short of meeting due process obligations.[95] In point of fact, the court's statutory law made no explicit reference to this right, violating the norms of article 29(1) of the Rwandan Constitution,[96] as well as the International Covenant on Civil and Political Rights and other international legal instruments ratified by Rwanda. This denial resulted in a serious violation of the defendant's right to a fair trial, knowing that most of the suspects have preliminary educations, limited awareness of their rights, and could not represent themselves in a legal context.[97]

Although the defendant's right to counsel is embodied in the Rwandan and international treaties, the government politicized Gacaca and manipulated the course of justice, while many of the trials were seriously flawed. The government justified the suspension of this right, arguing that allowing lawyers for the huge number of suspects would delay the trials. It did not want Gacaca's judges to be influenced by lawyers as most judges had limited knowledge of the law. Suspending the rights of individuals to counsel was also justified by the claim that participation of the local community would be more than enough to guarantee the fairness of the trials.[98]

It is an obligation under statutory and treaty provisions that the government should provide the defendant with an avenue to appeal his sentence to a higher and competent court.[99] Contrary to this legal rule, Gacaca law lacked a clear provision on the right of the defendant to appeal his sentence.[100] The law provided a limited option to appeal without any guarantees of fair trial during the appeal stage.[101] Article 19 of the Organic Law 10/2007 provided that the defendant could appeal a judgement passed by a Gacaca court in the interest of justice. Article 20 states that a judgment can be subject to appeal if the defendant was acquitted in a judgement passed in the last resort by an ordinary court, but found guilty by a Gacaca court or vice versa; if the emergence of new evidence proving contrary to evidence on which the initial judgement of the Gacaca court was grounded, or that the defendant was sentenced in a manner contrary to the provisions relating to the charges against him.[102]

The Gacaca law permits an appeal from one Gacaca jurisdiction to a higher one for all categories except the fourth category relevant to property damages. Defendants at the level of the cell can appeal to the sector level, and those convicted at the sector level can appeal to the district level, and those tried at the district level can appeal to the province level.[103]

Falling Short of Prosecuting Sexual Violence or Providing Gender-Sensitive Justice

Various scholarly works and human rights reports reveal that Rwandan women were profoundly affected by the events and consequences of the 1994 genocide. Many were massacred, and/or endured systematic and widespread rape and other forms of sexual violence, regarded as the worst form of the Rwandan genocide. Many victims who were infected with HIV/AIDS are living a slow death. Others were widowed and forced to head their households with insufficient resources.[104] This situation made women vulnerable and affected their participation in Gacaca courts, notwithstanding the historical fact that women were excluded from the original Gacaca judicial process and continued to be prevented from speaking in the new courts.[105]

Local and international women rights' organizations have put enormous pressure on the Rwandan law-makers to recognize genocidal rape and sexual torture as Category 1 crimes, believing that this would address their desire to see these heinous crimes prosecuted and punished alongside other serious crimes of genocide.[106] Commentators split into two groups: the first argued against the inclusion of such crimes in Category 1 offenses, maintaining that sexual violations are widely considered unforgettable[107] and could lead to community ostracism, curb the reconciliation process, and aggravate tensions between Hutu and Tutsi.[108] Moreover, this group asserted that Gacaca as an open judicial arena was not the proper place to adjudicate sexual violence. Shame and stigma associated with these crimes would, they maintained, give victims a sense of re-victimization.[109] However, this argument was easily challenged. Gacaca, like the International Criminal Tribunal for Rwanda,[110] failed to deliver gender-sensitive justice. A case in point, Gacaca, like the ICTR, allowed victims of sexual torture to testify *in camera* or submit their cases in writing.[111] Although this decision was designed to fairly preserve the victims' dignity, it indicated that any woman requesting testimony in a closed chamber had been sexually assaulted and would thus maximize her feelings of shame and intimidation.

A second group argued that the exclusion of rape and sexual torture from Gacaca's jurisdiction would eliminate these serious crimes from the court's records, and consequently impede the victims' access to justice.[112] Women comprise approximately 50 percent of Rwandan society. Silencing women survivors and preventing them from seeking justice at Gacaca courts amounted to dismissing 50 percent of the truth, therefore contradicting the primary purpose of Gacaca.[113]

Apart from these opposing viewpoints, it is worthwhile to mention here that the incorporation of genocidal rape and sexual torture, as a Category 1 crime,[114] according to the 1996 Genocide Law, put it within the jurisdiction of national courts, not Gacaca. Nevertheless, the 2004 Gacaca Law had placed sexual torture under Category 1, yet excluded it from the jurisdiction of the Gacaca courts.[115] In this respect, Sarah L. Wells, a legal scholar, holds that the exclusion of sexual torture from the Gacaca jurisdiction would disparage the victims' ordeal, restrain their right to access justice, and minimize their role in the reconciliation process.[116] Echoing women's rights groups and survivors' views, Wells believes that victims could overlook the challenge of exclusion of such heinous crimes from Category 1 offenses, by speaking out either through testimonies relating to such crimes during early information-gathering stages or during their appearances in Gacaca courts as witnesses on matters not directly related to wartime sexual violence.[117] This view may collide with the idea that the primary purpose of bringing sexual crimes to Gacaca is not to reach the earshot of judges and other actors in the judicial process, but to recognize sexual assault as an aggravated crime within the jurisdiction of the court, prosecute it, and bring perpetrators to justice.

The 2008 amendment to the Gacaca law shifted Category 1 sexual torture crimes to the jurisdiction of Gacaca, and, accordingly, 6,008 cases of sexual violence were transferred from national courts to Gacaca.[118] Women victims expressed strong reluctance to bring their experiences before the court judges. Their refrain from participation in Gacaca was due to several socio-legal factors, including:

(1) Gacaca failed, like the ICTR, to deal with gender-sensitive matters at different stages of adjudication, including investigation and trial. The lack of professional female investigators, provocative questions by poorly trained investigators, judges, and prosecutors, as well as the failure of the court to recognize the sensitive nature and distinctive harms of different forms of sexual violence, resulted in the absence of many genocide rape survivors from the Gacaca judicial process.[119]

(2) The abstractness and lack of accurate description of the crimes of sexual violence in the Gacaca's statutory laws. This ambiguity led to confusion and uncertainty of the court's acceptance of the victim's cases.[120] Moreover, it increases the judicial discretion, which resulted in inadequate prosecutions of such crimes and promoted the culture of impunity. According to fair labelling, an imperative legal principle, crimes must be meaningfully defined to reflect different levels of wrongdoings through a clear structure of the offenses, and labelled in a manner that presents distinctive forms of criminality according to the gravity of each crime.[121] Theoretically speaking, Gacaca laws classified sexual violence among the most serious crimes of genocide in Category 1, but practically, the court belittled the crimes and marginalized the victims' experiences.[122]

(3) The public nature of the Gacaca process intimidated victims, causing self-blaming, shame, stigma, and re-traumatization.[123]

Additionally, the failure of Gacaca to provide adequate and effective mechanisms to protect survivors of sexual violence made them fear reprisals, threat of re-victimization, and family and community rejection.[124]

Seen through these lenses, and due to the constant failure of the Rwandan criminal justice system to address the needs of the women survivors of sexual violence, the Rwandan government should first declare those victims as wounded heroines rather than mere victims of sexual violence. This would increase their self-esteem and preserve their dignity. Moreover, the government should provide victims with sufficient healthcare, including medical treatment for HIV/AIDS and psychological counseling, as well as with economic assistance and social support. Interviews with a large number of sexual violence survivors indicate that the acute material needs of these women to meet their basic life needs are critical and underscore the urgency for reparations.[125]

Disappointingly, Gacaca demonstrated that it was doomed to failure. Gacaca's inability to adopt a policy on reparation for wartime rape and other forms of sexual violence crimes undermined the credibility of the court and violated the norms of national[126] and international law.[127] In fact, many survivors of sexual violence regarded reparations, particularly financial remedies, as an integral part of the reconciliation process.[128] However, although the government's duty to provide reparations for sexual violence crimes has been theoretically acknowledged, none of the awards made by the courts have been practically paid.[129]

Toward this end, this inquiry concludes with an emphasis on its central legal argument that Gacaca was a form of retributive criminal justice mechanism, providing victors' justice. Furthermore, it fully failed to deliver adequate justice and sufficient reparations to genocide survivors on equal basis, failed to guarantee the defendants' right to fair trial standards enshrined in international treaties ratified by Rwanda prior to the genocide; and failed to adequately address conflict-related gender-based crimes, overlooking gender-specific sensitivities, specifically the shame and stigma associated with different sexual crimes throughout the trials. By excluding crimes allegedly committed by the RPA and its allies during the genocide campaign, the Gacaca courts provided inequitable and retributive justice that would emphasize ethnic division and tensions among Rwandans and that eliminated any chances for Gacaca's contribution to transitional justice and national reconciliation. The exclusion of sexual torture from

Gacaca Jurisdiction resulted in the exclusion of victims from future Rwandan community-building, as well as from the reconciliation process.

Notes

1. Amnesty International, *Gacaca: A Question of Justice*, AI Index: AFR 47/007/2002, December 17, 2002, 201–21; Hilmi M. Zawati, *The Triumph of Ethnic Hatred and the Failure of International Political Will: Gendered Violence and Genocide in the Former Yugoslavia and Rwanda* (Lewiston, NY: The Edwin Mellen Press, 2010), 129; Stephanie Wolters, "The Gacaca Process: Eradicating the Culture of Impunity in Rwanda?" *Institute for Security Studies Situation Report* (August 5, 2005): 1.

2. Arie Wiebren Roest, *"The Road to Reconciliation in Rwanda: The Role of Gacaca Courts"* (MA thesis, Leiden University, 2016), 9; Charlotte Hulme, *"'The Truth Heals': Punishment and Reconciliation at Rwanda's Gacaca Courts"* (MA thesis, Wellesley College, 2014), 9; Cyanne E. Loyle, "Transitional Justice and Political Order in Rwanda," *Ethnic and Racial Studies* 41, no. 4 (2018): 5.

3. Charity Wibabara, *"Gacaca Courts Versus the International Criminal Tribunal for Rwanda and National Courts: Lessons to Learn from the Rwandan Justice Approaches to Genocide,"* (LLD diss., University of the Western Cape, 2013), 197.

4. Callixte Kavuro, "Gacaca Courts, Reconciliation and the Politics of Apology in Post-Genocide Rwanda," *SACJ* 1 (2017): 39; Wolters, "The Gacaca Process," 12.

5. Amaka Megwalu and Neophytos Loizides, "Dilemmas of Justice and Reconciliation: Rwandans and the Gacaca Courts," *RADIC* 18 (2010): 3; Amnesty International, *Gacaca: A Question of Justice*, 1.

6. The International Criminal Tribunal for Rwanda (ICTR) has utterly failed to provide adequate justice to genocide survivors and victims of wartime sexual violence. In the ICTR, only a few defendants have been found guilty of rape, including Akayesu, Gacumbitsi, Semanza, and Muhimana. Thus, approximately 90 percent of the ICTR's judgements are free of rape charges, while rape acquittals are double the rape convictions in number. For more information, please see Hilmi M. Zawati, *Fair Labelling and the Dilemma of Prosecuting Gender-Based Crimes at the International Criminal Tribunals* (New York: Oxford University Press, 2015), 119. See also Jean-Damascène Gasanabo, "Peace in Rwanda: Balancing the ICTR and 'Gacaca' in Postgenocide Peacebuilding," in *The Palgrave Handbook of Global Approaches to Peace*, ed. by Aigul Kulnazarova and Vesselin Popovski (Cham, Switzerland: Springer, 2019), 185; Pietro Sullo, *Beyond Genocide: Transitional Justice and Gacaca Courts in Rwanda: The Search for Truth, Justice and Reconciliation* (The Hague: T. M. C. Asser Press, 2018), 103; Tola Odubajo, "Africa's Transitional Justice System in a Changing Global Order: The 'Allure' of Rwanda's Gacaca Transitional Justice System," in *The Palgrave Handbook of Africa and the Changing Global Order*, ed. by Samuel Ojo Oloruntoba and Toyin Falola (Cham, Switzerland: Springer, 2022), 835.

7. Aneta Wierzynski, "Consolidating Democracy through Transitional Justice: Rwanda's Gacaca Courts," *New York University Law Review* 79 (2004): 1968;

Etienne Dusabeyezu, *"Closing Gacaca: Analysing Rwanda's Challenges with Regard to the End of Gacaca Courts"* (LLM thesis, University of the Western Cape, 2013), 6; Maya Sosnov, "The Adjudication of Genocide: Gacaca and the Road to Reconciliation in Rwanda," *Denver Journal of International Law and Policy* 36, no. 125 (2008): 332; Megwalu and Loizides, "Dilemmas of Justice and Reconciliation," 5; Sandesh Sivakumaran, "Courts of Armed Opposition Groups: Fair Trials or Summary Justice?," *Journal of International Criminal Justice* 7 (2009): 506; Susan Thomson, "The Darker Side of Transitional Justice: The Power Dynamics Behind Rwanda's Gacaca Courts," *Africa* 81, no. 3 (2011): 373; Susan Thomson and Rosemary Nagy, "Law, Power and Justice: What Legalism Fails to Address in the Functioning of Rwanda's Gacaca Courts," *The International Journal of Transitional Justice* 5 (2011): 13; Wibabara, "Gacaca Courts Versus the International Criminal Tribunal for Rwanda," 84; William A. Schabas, "Genocide Trials and Gacaca Courts," *Journal of International Criminal Justice* 3 (2005): 881.

8. Linda E. Carter, "Justice and Reconciliation on Trial: Gacaca Proceedings in Rwanda," *New England Journal of International and Comparative Law* 14, no. 1 (2007): 42; "Rwanda Ends Gacaca Genocide Tribunals," DW Academia. http://www.dw.com/en/rwanda-ends-gacaca-genocide-tribunals/a-16033827; Wibabara, "Gacaca Courts Versus the International Criminal Tribunal for Rwanda," 79.

9. For more information, see "Rwanda Closes 'Gacaca' Genocide Courts: Grassroots Tribunals Tried Some Two Million People Accused in 1994 Genocide, Earning Praise for Ethnic Reconciliation," *Al Jazeera*, June 18, 2012. https://www.aljazeera.com/news/africa/2012/06/201261951733409260.html; "Speech by President Paul Kagame at the Closing of the Gacaca," *Gacaca Community Justice*, June 18, 2012. http://gacaca.rw/opinion/speech-by-president-paul-kagame-at-the-closing -of-the-gacaca/

10. Organic Law No. 04/2012/OL of 15 15/06/2012, *Terminating Gacaca Courts and Determining Mechanisms for Solving Issues Which Were under Their Jurisdiction.*

11. Dusabeyezu, "Closing Gacaca," 43; Pietro Sullo, "Beyond Genocide," 8.

12. Lars Teilhet Waldorf, *"Mass Justice for Mass Atrocity: Transitional Justice and Illiberal Peace-Building in Rwanda"* (PhD Diss., National University of Ireland, Galway, 2013), 148.

13. Callixte Kavuro, "Gacaca Courts, Reconciliation and the Politics of Apology in Post-Genocide Rwanda," *South African Journal of Criminal Justice* 30, no. 1 (2017): 61; Charlotte Hulme, *"'The Truth Heals': Punishment and Reconciliation at Rwanda's Gacaca Courts"* (MA thesis, Wellesley College, 2014); Rachael Andrew, *"Hybrid Models of Justice and Rwanda's Post-Genocide Response"* (MA thesis, University of Western Ontario, 2104) 151.

14. Allison Corey and Sandra F. Joireman, "Retributive Justice: The Gacaca Courts in Rwanda," *African Affairs* 103, no. 410 (2004): 81; Jeremy Sarkin, "The Tension between Justice and Reconciliation in Rwanda: Politics, Human Rights, Due Process and the Role of the *Gacaca* Courts in Dealing with the Genocide," *Journal of African Law*, 45, no. 2 (2001): 159; Jordan Jon Nowotny, *"Local Perceptions of Justice and Identity Following Mass Participation in Rwanda's Gacaca Courts"* (PhD diss., National University of Illinois, Chicago, 2015), 30; L. Danielle Tully, "Human Rights Compliance and the Gacaca Jurisdictions in Rwanda," *Boston College International & Comparative Law Review* 26 (2003): 395; Mark A. Drumbl,

"Post-Genocide Justice in Rwanda," *Journal of International Peacekeeping* 22 (2018): 257; Sosnov, "The Adjudication of Genocide," 134.

15. Waldorf, "Mass Justice for Mass Atrocity," 128.

16. Jean-Damascene Gasanabo, Donatien Nikuze and Hollie Nyseth Brehm, "Rwanda's *Inyangamugayo*: Perspectives from Practitioners in the Gacaca Transitional Justice Mechanism," *Preventing Crimes against Humanity*, (working paper 17, June 2019): 1; Megan M. Westberg, "Rwanda's Use of Transitional Justice after Genocide: The Gacaca Courts and the ICTR," *Kansas Law Review* 59 (2011): 338; Susan Thomson and Rosemary Nagy, "Law, Power and Justice: What Legalism Fails to Address in the Functioning of Rwanda's Gacaca Courts," *International Journal of Transitional Justice* 5 (2011): 17.

17. See *Summary of the Report Presented at the Closing of Gacaca Court Activities* (Kigali, Rwanda: National Service of *Gacaca* Jurisdictions, 2012); Hollie Nyseth Brehm, Christopher Uggen, and Jean-Damascène Gasanabo "Genocide, Justice, and Rwanda's Gacaca Courts," *Journal of Contemporary Criminal Justice* 30, no. 3 (2014), 339; Roest, "The Road to Reconciliation in Rwanda," 24.

18. Bert Ingelaere, "From Model to Practice: Researching and Representing Rwanda's 'Modernized' *Gacaca* Courts," *Critique of Anthropology* 32, no. 4 (2012) 392; Dustin N. Sharp, "Addressing Dilemmas of the Global and the Local in Transitional Justice," *Emory International Law Review* 29, no. 71 (2014): 108; Emily Amick, "Trying International Crimes on Local Lawns: The Adjudication of Genocide Sexual Violence Crimes in Rwanda's Gacaca Courts," *Columbia Journal of Gender and Law* 20, no. 1 (2011): 23; Maya Goldstein Bolocan, "Rwandan Gacaca: An Experiment in Transitional Justice," *Journal on Dispute Resolution* (2005): 376–377; Tully, "Human Rights Compliance," 395–96.

19. Coel Kirkby, "Rwanda's Gacaca Courts: A Preliminary Critique," *Journal of African Law* 50, no. 2 (2006): 100; Westberg, "Rwanda's Use of Transitional Justice after Genocide," 337.

20. Anne-Marie de Brouwer and Etienne Ruvebana, "The Legacy of the *Gacaca* Courts in Rwanda: Survivors' Views," *International Criminal Law Review* 13 (2013): 940; Ariel Meyerstein, "Between Law and Culture: Rwanda's Gacaca and Postcolonial Legality," *Law & Social Inquiry* 32, no. 2 (2007): 473; *The Objectives of the Gacaca Courts* (Kigali, Rwanda: National Service of *Gacaca* Jurisdictions, 2012), cited in Sosnov, "The Adjudication of Genocide: Gacaca and the Road to Reconciliation in Rwanda," 136.

21. For more information on the prosecuted persons' categories, please see endnote 54.

22. Organic Law, No. 16/2004, *Establishing the Organisation, Competence and Functioning of Gacaca Courts Charged with Prosecuting and Trying the Perpetrators of the Crime of Genocide and Other Crimes Against Humanity, Committed Between October 1, 1990, and December 31, 1994,* June 19, 2004, arts. 54 and 73, available at www.in kiko-gacaca.gov.rw/pdf/newlawl.pdf. See also Sosnov, "The Adjudication of Genocide," 137.

23. Amnesty International, *Suspects Must not be Transferred to Rwandan Courts for Trial until it is Demonstrated that Trials Will Comply with International Standards of Justice,* AI Index: AFR 47/013/2007, November 2007, 4; Wibabara, "Gacaca Courts Versus the International Criminal Tribunal for Rwanda," 224.

24. Sosnov, "The Adjudication of Genocide," 142; Wolters, "The Gacaca Process," 2.

25. Alana Erin Tiemessen, "After Arusha: Gacaca Justice in Post-Genocide Rwanda," *African Studies Quarterly* 8, no. 1 (2004): 69–70; Nomathamsanqa Masiko-Mpaka, "Policy Brief: Traditional Transitional Justice Mechanisms—Lessons from Africa," *Centre for the Study of Violence and Reconciliation* (January 2020): 5.

26. Westberg, "Rwanda's Use of Transitional Justice after Genocide," 337.

27. Tiemessen, "After Arusha," 142.

28. Tiemessen, "After Arusha," 143–44.

29. Tiemessen, "After Arusha," 144.

30. Tiemessen, "After Arusha," 69. See also Dara Crandall, "Reconcilation, Interrupted: A Look at Post-Genocide Rwanda and the Gacaca Courts," *The Langara Student Journal of History and Political Science* 2 (2019): 23.

31. Erin Daly, "Between Punitive and Reconstructive Justice: The Gacaca Courts in Rwanda," *New York University Journal of International Law and Politics* 34 (2002) 370–71; Bolocan, "Rwandan Gacaca," 376–77; Sosnov, "The Adjudication of Genocide," 145.

32. Arthur Molenaar, *Gacaca: Grassroots Justice after Genocide: The Key to Reconciliation in Rwanda?* (Leiden: African Studies Centre, 2005), 14; Jennifer G. Riddell, *"Addressing Crimes against International Law: Rwanda's Gacaca in Practice"* (LLM thesis, University of Aberdeen, 2005), 48.

33. Molenaar, "Grassroots Justice after Genocide," 25.

34. Daly, "Between Punitive and Reconstructive Justice," 379–80.

35. Organic Law No. 08/96 of August 30, 1996, *Organization of Prosecutions for Offences Constituting the Crime of Genocide or Crimes against Humanity Committed since October 1, 1990.*

36. Organic Law No. 40/2000 of January 26, 2001, *Setting Up Gacaca Jurisdictions and Organizing Prosecutions for Offences Constituting the Crime of Genocide or Crimes against Humanity Committed between October 1, 1990 and December 31, 1994.*

37. Organic Law No. 33/2001 of June 22, 2001, *Creating Gacaca Jurisdictions and Organizing Prosecutions for Offences Constituting the Crime of Genocide or Crimes against Humanity, Committed between Oct. I, 1990 and Dec. 31, 1994.*

38. Organic Law No. 16/2004, of June 19, 2004, *Establishing the Organization, Competence and Functioning of Gacaca Courts Charged with Prosecuting and Trying the Perpetrators of the* Crime of Genocide and other ICrimes against Humanity, *Committed between Oct. 1, 1990, and Dec. 31, 1994.*

39. Organic Law No. 28/2006 of June 27, 2006, *Modifying Organic Law No. 16/2004.*

40. Organic Law No. 10/2007 of March I, 2007, *Modifying Organic Law No. 16/2004.*

41. Organic Law No. 13/2008 of May 19, 2007, *Modifying and Complementing Organic Law No. 16/2004.*

42. Jessica Raper, "The Gacaca Experiment: Rwanda's Restorative Dispute Resolution Response to the 1994 Genocide," *Pepperdine Dispute Resolution Law Journal* 5, no. 1 (2005): 31.

43. William A. Schabas, *Genocide in International Law: The Crimes of Crimes* (New York: Cambridge University Press, 2000), 389.

44. Organic Law No. 08/96 of August 30, 1996, chap. II, art. 2.

45. Organic Law No. 40/2000 of January 26, 2001, art. 51, chap. I, title III.

46. Amick, "Trying International Crimes on Local Lawns," 34; Phil Clark, "Hybridity, Holism, and Traditional Justice: The Case of the Gacaca Courts in Post-Genocide Rwanda," *George Washington International Law Review* 39 (2007): 786; Wibabara, "Gacaca Courts Versus the International Criminal Tribunal for Rwanda," 130.

47. Clark, "Hybridity, Holism, and Traditional Justice," 787; Organic Law No. 16/2004, June 19, 2004, *Establishing the Organization, Competence, and Functioning of Gacaca Courts Charged with Prosecuting and Trying the Perpetrators of the Crime of Genocide and other Crimes against Humanity, Committed between Oct. 1, 1990 and Dec. 31, 1994*, art. 38.

48. Amick, "Trying International Crimes on Local Lawns," 35.

49. Wibabara, "Gacaca Courts Versus the International Criminal Tribunal for Rwanda," 130.

50. Amick, "Trying International Crimes on Local Lawns," 33; Sarah L. Wells, "Gender, Sexual Violence, and Prospects for Justice at the Gacaca Courts in Rwanda," *Southern California Review of Law and Women's Studies* 14, no. 2 (2005): 175.

51. Organic Law, No. 16/2004, title II, chap. 1, sec. V, art. 34; Wells, "Gender, Sexual Violence and Prospects for Justice at the Gacaca Courts," 175; Westberg, "Rwanda's Use of Transitional Justice after Genocide," 338.

52. Wells, "Gender, Sexual Violence and Prospects for Justice at the Gacaca Courts," 175.

53. Organic Law No. 08/96 of August 30, 1996, chap. II, art. 2.

54. Organic Law No. 40/2000 of January 26, 2001, art. 51, chap. I, title III. This article reads:

Following acts of participation in offenses in question in Article 1 of this organic law and committed between 1 October 1990 and 31 December 1994, the prosecuted person can be classified in one of the following categories:

Category 1:
a) The person whose criminal acts or criminal participation place among planners, organisers, inciters, supervisors of the crime of genocide or crime against humanity.
b) The person who, acting in a position of authority at the national, provincial or district level, within political parties, army, religious denominations or militia, has committed these offences or encouraged others to commit them.
c) The well-known murderer who distinguished himself in the location where he lived, or wherever he passed, because of zeal which has characterised him in killings or excessive wickedness with which they were carried out.
d) The person who has committed rape or acts of torture against a person's sexual parts.

As investigations are going along, a list of persons prosecuted or convicted of having committed acts putting them in the first category is established and updated by the General Prosecutor to the Supreme Court. This list will be published in the Official Gazette of the Republic of Rwanda twice a year, in June and December.

Category 2:
a) The person whose criminal acts or criminal participation place among authors, co-authors, or accomplices of deliberate homicides or serious attacks against persons which caused death.
b) The person who, with intention of giving death, has caused injuries or committed other serious violence, but from which the victims have not died.

Category 3:
The person who has committed criminal acts or has become accomplice of serious attacks, without the intention of causing death to victims.

Category 4:
The person having committed offences against assets.

However, the author of the mentioned offenses who, on the date of this organic law enforcement, has agreed either with the victim, or before the public authority or in arbitration, for an amicable settlement, cannot be prosecuted for the same facts.

55. Brehm, "Genocide, Justice, and Rwanda's Gacaca Courts," 339–44; Cori Wielenga and Geoff Harris, "Building Peace and Security after Genocide: The Contribution of the Gacaca Courts of Rwanda," *African Security Review* 20, no. 1 (2011): 17; Karan Lahiri, "Rwanda's Gacaca Courts: A Possible Model for Local Justice in International Crime?," *International Criminal Law Review* 9 (2009): 323; Sivakumaran, "Courts of Armed Opposition Groups," 339; Wells, "Gender, Sexual Violence and Prospects for Justice at the Gacaca Courts," 172; Westberg, "Rwanda's Use of Transitional Justice after Genocide," 339; Wierzynski, "Consolidating Democracy through Transitional Justice," 1954.

56. Westberg, "Rwanda's Use of Transitional Justice after Genocide," 339.

57. Bert Ingelaere, "The Gacaca Courts in Rwanda," in *Traditional Justice and Reconciliation after Violent Conflict: Learning from African Experiences*, ed. by Luc Huyse and Mark Salter (Stockholm: International Institute for Democracy and Electoral Assistance, 2008), 42–43; Westberg, "Rwanda's Use of Transitional Justice after Genocide," 339.

58. Ingelaere, "The Gacaca Courts in Rwanda," 42; Westberg, "Rwanda's Use of Transitional Justice after Genocide," 340.

59. For more detailed information on the role of colonialism in deepening Rwanda's ethnic division, institutionalizing racism, and promoting ethnic divergence between Hutu and Tutsi ethnic groups, please see Zawati, "The Triumph of Ethnic Hatred," 35 and 63.

60. Sarkin, "The Tension between Justice and Reconciliation in Rwanda," 161–62; Wells, "Gender, Sexual Violence and Prospects for Justice at the Gacaca Courts," 179.

61. Wells, "Gender, Sexual Violence and Prospects for Justice at the Gacaca Courts," 181.

62. Human Rights Watch, *Justice Compromised: The Legacy of Rwanda's Community-Based Gacaca Courts*, May 2011, 104.

63. Dusabeyezu, "Closing Gacaca," 31.

64. Dusabeyezu, "Closing Gacaca," 58; Organic Law, No. 16/2004, chap. VI, sec. 1, art. 86; Phil Clark, "Bringing the Peasants Back in, again: State power and Local Agency in Rwanda's Gacaca Courts," *Journal of Eastern African Studies* 8, no. 2 (2014): 201; Rachel Ibreck, "Victims and Survivors from Cyangugu, Rwanda: The Politics of Testimony after Genocide," in *The Politics of Victimhood in Post-conflict Societies: Comparative and Analytical Perspectives*, ed. by Vincent Druliolle and Roddy Brett (Cham, Switzerland: Palgrave Macmillan, 2018), 308; Richard Benda, "Time to Hear the Other Side Transitional Temporalities and Transgenerational Narratives in Post-Genocide Rwanda," in *Time and Temporality in Transitional and Post-Conflict Societies*, ed. by Natascha Mueller-Hirth and Sandra Rios Oyola (New York: Routledge, 2018), 133.

65. Human Rights Watch, "Justice Compromised," 104; Wibabara, "Gacaca Courts Versus the International Criminal Tribunal for Rwanda," 148.

66. Corey and Joireman, "Retributive Justice," 85. See also Benjamin Thorne and Julia Viebach, "Human Rights Reporting on Rwanda's *Gacaca* Courts: A Story of Stagnation and Failure," in *Rwanda Since 1994: Stories of Change*, ed. by Hannah Grayson and Nicki Hitchcott (Liverpool: Liverpool University Press, 2019), 56; Jean-Damascène Gasanabo, Donatien Nikuze, Hollie Nyseth Brehm, and Hannah Parks, "Rwanda's Inyangamugayo: Perspectives from Practitioners in the Gacaca Transitional Justice Mechanism," *Genocide Studies and Prevention: An International Journal* 14, no. 2 (2020): 168; Jordan Nowotny, "The Limits of Post-Genocide Justice in Rwanda: Assessing Gacaca from the Perspective of Survivors," *Contemporary Justice Review* 23, no. 4 (2020): 411; Pietro Sullo, "Beyond Genocide," 286.

67. Human Rights Watch, "Justice Compromised," 105.

68. The Universal Declaration of Human Rights, G.A. res. 217A (III), UN Doc A/810 at 71 (1948), art. 10.

69. The Universal Declaration of Human Rights, G.A. res. 217A (III).

70. The Universal Declaration of Human Rights, G.A. res. 217A (III), 106–7. See also Jeune Marjorie Pritchard, *"Gender-Based Violence, Abortion and Sexual and Reproductive Health in Rwanda: Myth and Reality"* (MA thesis, University of Wollongong, 2021), 14.

71. Corey and Joireman, "Retributive Justice," 86; Human Rights Watch, "Justice Compromised," 119; Human Rights Watch, *Rwanda: Mixed Legacy for Community-Based Genocide Courts*, May 21, 2011. https://www.hrw.org/news/2011/05/31/rwanda-mixed-legacy-community-based-genocide-courts; Wielenga and Harris, "Building Peace and Security after Genocide," 22.

72. Human Rights Watch, *Justice Compromised*, 104.

73. Human Rights Watch, *Justice Compromised*, 119; Loyle, "Transitional Justice and Political Order in Rwanda," 2; Waldorf, "Mass Justice for Mass Atrocity," 151.

74. Tiemessen, "After Arusha," 65.

75. Clark, "Bringing the Peasants Back in, Again," 196.

76. Tiemessen, "After Arusha," 61.

77. Tiemessen, "After Arusha," 70.

78. Mwansa Ancietos, "Political Opportunism, Impunity and the Perpetuation of Victor's Justice: A Case of the Rwandan Genocide," *African Journal of Political Science and International Relations* 15, no. 2 (2021): 85; Timothy Longman, "An Assessment of Rwanda's Gacaca Courts," *Peace Review* 21, no. 3 (2009): 309.

79. Longman, "An Assessment of Rwanda's Gacaca Courts."

80. Longman, "An Assessment of Rwanda's Gacaca Courts," 310.

81. Amick, "Trying International Crimes on Local Lawns," 2; Hollie Nyseth Brehm, Christi Smith, and Evelyn Gertz, "Producing Expertise in a Transitional Justice Setting: Judges at Rwanda's Gacaca Courts," *Law & Social Inquiry* 44 no. 1(2019): 85; Loyle, "Transitional Justice and Political Order in Rwanda," 1; Raper, "The Gacaca Experiment," 47; Sarkin, "The Tension between Justice and Reconciliation in Rwanda," 164; Sosnov, "The Adjudication of Genocide," 150; Wells, "Gender, Sexual Violence and Prospects for Justice at the Gacaca Courts," 169; William R. Pruitt, *An Introduction to the Criminology of Genocide* (Cham, Switzerland: Springer, 2021), 145.

82. Human Rights Watch, *Justice Compromised*, 28.

83. Daly, "Between Punitive and Reconstructive Justice," 385.

84. Rwanda's Constitution of 2003 with Amendments through 2015, art. 29 (right to due process of law).

85. International Panel of Eminent Personalities (IPEP), "Report on the 1994 Genocide in Rwanda and Surrounding Events (Selected Sections)," *International Legal Materials* 40, no. 1 (January 2001): chapter 18, p. 49.

86. "The Right to a Fair Trial: The Dakar Declaration," *Journal of African Law* 45, no. 1 (2001): art. 4.

87. *African [Banjul] Charter on Human and Peoples' Rights*, adopted June 27, 1981, OAU Doc. CAB/LEG/67/3 rev. 5, 21 I.L.M. 58, 1982, entered into force October 21, 1986, arts. 7(1) and 26.

88. *American Convention on Human Rights*, O.A.S. Treaty Series No. 36, 1144 U.N.T.S. 123, entered into force July 18, 1978, reprinted in *Basic Documents Pertaining to Human Rights in the Inter-American System*, OEA/Ser.L.V/II.82 doc. 6 rev. 1 at 25, 1992, arts. 8(1) and 27(2).

89. *Convention for the Protection of Human Rights and Fundamental Freedoms*, 213 U.N.T.S. 222, entered into force September 3, 1953, as amended by protocols nos. 3, 5, 8, and 11 which entered into force on September 21, 1970, December 20, 1971, January 1, 1990, and November 1, 1998 respectively, art. 6(1).

90. *Universal Declaration of Human Rights*, G.A. res. 217A (III), U.N. Doc A/810 at 71, 1948, art. 10.

91. *International Covenant on Civil and Political Rights*, G.A. res. 2200A (XXI), 21 U.N. GAOR Supp., no. 16, at 52, U.N. Doc. A/6316, 1966, 999 U.N.T.S. 171, *entered into force* March 23, 1976, art. 14(1).

92. Gerald Gahima, *Transitional Justice in Rwanda: Accountability for Atrocity* (New York: Routledge, 2013), 104.

93. Human Rights Watch, "Justice Compromised," 31.

94. Amnesty International, *Gacaca: A Question of Justice*, 39; Amnesty International, *Rwanda: The Troubled Course of Justice*, Report AFR 47/10/00 (April 2000): 40.

95. Loyle, "Transitional Justice and Political Order in Rwanda," 1; Maya Goldstein-Bolocan, "Rwandan Gacaca: An Experiment in Transitional Justice," *Journal of Dispute Resolution* 2 (2004): 388.

96. Rwanda's Constitution, art. 29(1).

97. Amnesty International, *The Troubled Course of Justice*, 38.

98. Human Rights Watch, *Justice Compromised*, 28.

99. *African [Banjul] Charter on Human and Peoples' Rights*, art. 7(1)(a); Dadimos Haile, *Rwanda's Experiment in People's Courts (Gacaca) and the Tragedy of Unexamined Humanitarianism: A Normative/Ethical Perspective* (Antwerpen: Institut de Politique et de Gestion du Développement, 2008), 26; *International Covenant on Civil and Political Rights*, art. 14(5); *The Universal Declaration of Human Rights*, art. 8.

100. Sosnov, "The Adjudication of Genocide," 148.

101. Amnesty International, *The Troubled Course of Justice*, 39.

102. Goldstein-Bolocan, "Rwandan Gacaca," 389; Organic Law No. 10/2007, art. 20.

103. Corey and Joireman, "Retributive Justice," 82.

104. *Shattered Lives: Sexual Violence during the Rwandan Genocide and Its Aftermath* (New York: Human Rights Watch, 1996), 93; Usta Kaitesi, *Genocidal Gender and Sexual Violence: The Legacy of the ICTR, Rwanda's Ordinary Courts and Gacaca Courts* (Cambridge: Intersentia, 2013), 211; Wells, "Gender, Sexual Violence and Prospects for Justice at the Gacaca Courts," 183.

105. Lars Waldorf, "Mass Justice for Mass Atrocity: Rethinking Local Justice as Transitional Justice," *Temple Law Review* 79, no. 1 (2006): 48; Lori A. Nessel, "Rape and Recovery in Rwanda: The Viability of Local Justice Initiatives and the Availability of Surrogate State Protection for Women that Flee," *Michigan State Journal of International Law* 15, no. 1 (2007): 118.

106. Nessel, "Rape and Recovery in Rwanda," 120; Wells, "Gender, Sexual Violence and Prospects for Justice at the Gacaca Courts," 184.

107. Wells, "Gender, Sexual Violence and Prospects for Justice at the Gacaca Courts," 188.

108. Nessel, "Rape and Recovery in Rwanda," 122.

109. Amick, "Trying International Crimes on Local Lawns," 4.

110. Zawati, "Fair Labelling and the Dilemma of Prosecuting Gender-Based Crimes," 132–33.

111. Organic Law No. 16/2004, arts. 21 and 38.

112. Amick, "Trying International Crimes on Local Lawns," 4; Nessel, "Rape and Recovery in Rwanda," 4.

113. Waldorf, "Mass Justice for Mass Atrocity," 121; Wells, "Gender, Sexual Violence and Prospects for Justice at the Gacaca Courts," 183.

114. Organic Law No. 08/96, art. 2, category 1(d).

115. Organic Law No. 16/2004, art. 51, category 1(5).

116. Wells, "Gender, Sexual Violence and Prospects for Justice at the Gacaca Courts," 185.

117. Wells, "Gender, Sexual Violence and Prospects for Justice at the Gacaca Courts," 185–86.

118. Amick, "Trying International Crimes on Local Lawns," 3; Human Rights Watch, *Justice Compromised*, 13–14.

119. Zawati, *Fair Labelling and the Dilemma of Prosecuting Gender-Based Crimes*, 115, 132–33.

120. Amick, "Trying International Crimes on Local Lawns," 3; Human Rights Watch, *Justice Compromised*, 83.

121. Zawati, *Fair Labelling and the Dilemma of Prosecuting Gender-Based Crimes*, 115.

122. Amick, "Trying International Crimes on Local Lawns," 75; Nessel, "Rape and Recovery in Rwanda," 119; Emma M. Costello, "Justice for Whom? The Gacaca Courts and Restorative Justice for Survivors of Sexual Violence in Rwanda," (MA thesis, University of Michigan, 2016, 43).

123. Amick, "Trying International Crimes on Local Lawns," 65; Costello, "Justice for Whom?" 39; Simone Jacqueline Purdon, "*Transitional Justice failing? A Gendered Evaluation of the Transitional Justice Program in Post-Genocide Rwanda*," (MA thesis, Simon Fraser University 2008), 83; Wendy Lambourne and Vivianna Rodriguez Carreon, "Engendering Transitional Justice: A Transformative Approach to Building Peace and Attaining Human Rights for Women," *Human Rights Review* 17, no. 1 (2016): 77.

124. Costello, "Justice for Whom?" 40; Gahima, *Transitional Justice in Rwanda*, 175; Wells, "Gender, Sexual Violence and Prospects for Justice at the Gacaca Courts," 191.

125. Human Rights Watch, *Struggling to Survive: Barriers to Justice for Rape Victims in Rwanda*, September 2004, 37.

126. Law No.11/98 of November 2, 1998, "Amending and Completing the Law No. 02/98 of 22/01/98 Establishing a National Assistance Fund for the Neediest Victims of Genocide and Massacres Committed in Rwanda between October 1, 1990 and December 31, 1994," *Official Gazette of the Republic of Rwanda*, November 2, 1998, art. 1; Organic Law No. 08/96 of August 30, 1996, 32; Organic Law No. 40/2000 of January 26, 2001, art. 67(9).

127. *International Covenant on Civil and Political Rights*, Arts. 2(3) and 9(5); *Universal Declaration of Human Rights*, art. 8.

128. Gahima, *Transitional Justice in Rwanda*, 174; Kirkby, "Rwanda's Gacaca Courts," 112.

129. Heidy Rombouts, "Women and Reparations in Rwanda: A Long Path to Travel," in *What Happened to the Women?: Gender and Reparations for Human Rights Violations*, ed. by Ruth Rubio-Marín (New York: Social Science Research Council, 2006), 220; Paul Christoph Bornkamm, *Rwanda's Gacaca Courts between Retribution and Reparation* (New York: Oxford University Press, 2012), 157.

THIRTEEN

MIA

Disappearing Political Analysis in Transitional Justice

Vasuki Nesiah

Ireneo Funes, the main character in the Borges short story "Funes the Memorios," is afflicted by a prodigious memory of facts. He remembers every detail of everything he encounters— "I have more memories in myself alone than all men have had since the world was a world." Unable to forget, he accumulates memories "like a garbage disposal." In remembering all the details in their interminable infinitude, Funes finds himself unable to strive toward larger analysis. "He was not very capable of thought. To think is to forget a difference, generalize, to abstract. In the overly replete world of Funes there were nothing but details, almost contiguous details."[1]

The story offers a parable for the memory projects of the field of transitional justice and the role it has played in relation to justice struggles, including those anchored in movements against disappearances. The last three decades have seen the transitional justice field grow exponentially on many fronts—from legal and policy developments; to increased financial and institutional investment; to an expanded network of activists, practitioners, and scholars working in the field. This growth has been accompanied by its consolidation and institutionalization within the United Nations and other multilateral institutions, for instance, regional organizations, such as the European Union and African Union; donor agencies, such as the United States Agency for International Development (USAID); the United Kingdom Department of International Development (DFID) and the Swedish International Development Cooperation Agency (Sida); non-governmental agencies (NGO); and many other arenas. Most significantly, this period has seen the development and maturation of transitional justice mechanisms such as truth commissions and reparations programs alongside newly empowered prosecutorial initiatives, including special national prosecutorial units and transnational institutions such as the International Criminal Court and a number of ad hoc tribunals.

Justice struggles regarding disappearances have been one of the most pivotal catalysts in shaping the modern field of transitional justice. For instance, groups like Argentina's Center for Legal and Social Studies (CELS) and *Las Madres de la Plaza de Mayo* (Mothers of the Plaza de Mayo) advanced political analysis of the root causes of authoritarianism in Argentina, built solidarities and contributed to local and transnational social movements demanding accountability and supporting "victim" communities. While acknowledging the grievous harm they had suffered, they also refused the traditional script of "victims," who were defined by their injury alone and relegated to being passive supplicants to top-down transitional justice policies. Rather, these were political activists, who sought to shape transitional justice institutions that were established in the name of addressing legacies of disappearances and the structures, institutions, and cultures that enabled authoritarianism in Argentina. For these groups, the work of keeping these issues on the agenda is ongoing, the strategy is long-term, and their political analysis is constantly calibrated with the opportunities and constraints of the situation so that they can be responsive to changing contexts.

The struggles of these communities, and others like them in other countries, have been assimilated and absorbed into the field of transitional justice globally. They have been particularly significant to how the field conceives and operationalizes the project of historical memory. Yet, this chapter suggests some caution in celebrating this convergence and explores how justice struggles regarding disappearances can be seen as both victim of, and challenge to, that project of assimilation and absorption into the transitional justice field's approach to historical memory. I argue that the field's approach to historical memory can be described as an institutionalization of two mnemonic structures, one forensic and the other testimonial. The transitional justice field has shaped these as institutional avenues through which the disappeared can be remembered as part of a national history and, accordingly, they have been platforms that have channeled justice struggles with regard to disappearances.

In Section 1 ("Fact Finding"), I analyze the work of forensic mechanisms aimed at fact-finding the details of individual disappearances, and, in Section 2 ("Testimony"), I analyze the work of individual narrative testimony regarding victims' memories of the disappeared.[2] Both these approaches have had a number of positive, as well as negative outcomes. In each section, I first recount the reasons the approaches are valued and then highlight their negative dimensions and effects. Thus, I elaborate on the reasons for advising caution about seeing transitional justice mechanisms as the default approach to justice struggles. These reasons include the fact that these mechanisms have focused on individualized analyses of crime, perpetrator, and victim in ways that deter from larger political analyses of systems and structures. The field's privileging of immersion in the details of individual disappearances can (and often does) displace and derail efforts to bring more far-reaching change to the institutional arrangements that entrench impunity for disappearances. Relatedly, the ways in which the testimony of individual victims' experience of loss gets absorbed into narratives of closure and healing can come at the expense of analysis that accounts for the ongoing socio-political impact of disappearances, including to those families and communities immediately impacted. This, too, has implications for the form of reparations, efforts directed toward larger institutional transformation and questions of historical memory. In the concluding section, I return to the parable of Funes and explore the political dimensions of disappearances struggles that we need to revisit, even if it means rethinking the work of the institutionalized memory projects of the field of transitional justice.

Fact-Finding

There was nothing to believe in with certainty. They still didn't know what the truth was. We have never had the truth. Not even with your work on bones. . . . Most of the time in our world, truth is just opinion.

—Michael Ondaatje
Anil's Ghost[3]

[I]rrespective of any legal proceedings, victims and their families have the imprescriptible right to know the truth about the circumstances in which violations took place and, in the event of death or disappearance, the victims' fate.

—Diane Orentlicher
Principles to Combat Impunity[4]

The "right to know" has long been a central demand of those advocating for families of the missing.[5] Now enshrined in the convention on the disappeared as the "right to truth," the identification of facts regarding the circumstances of disappearance and the fate of the disappeared has been a central charge of transitional justice process.[6] The core investigative tool of transitional justice mechanisms (such as prosecutions, truth commissions, and reparation programs) is an operational methodology characterized by a case-by-case scrutiny of individual violations, and what is best described as a forensic approach to the tracking of legal responsibility and harm. To some extent the vision is that the technocratic and ethical dimensions of transitional justice institutions is a path for closing the chapter and moving on. As Monique Crettol and Anne-Marie La Rosa describe it: "The opening of mass graves, the identification of bodies, establishment of the circumstances that led to their deaths and clarification of the facts are all necessary steps for families to complete their mourning process, for victims to obtain reparation and, in the long term, for peoples and communities to come to terms with their past and move forward in peace."[7]

Disappearances are, by definition, crimes wrapped in secrecy. In this context, transitional justice institutions have been particularly invested in identifying facts through legalistic procedures predicated on due process and fair investigations. It is often asserted that the fair application of legal rules to conduct investigations, assess evidence, and pass sanctions represents the triumph of the rule of law over the abuse of power, accountability over impunity, truth over secrecy. Thus, the field advances forensic fact-finding as yielding information, but also carrying symbolic weight against regimes of covert operations that disappear evidence as they disappear bodies. It is argued that a society speaks truth to power through such fact-focused engagement that holds accountable identifiable individuals, not anonymous entities, who have conducted violations.[8] Judicial accountability is central to the field of transitional justice. Yet the goals of courts and the goals of advocates for victims of disappearances often diverge. As noted by Crettol and La Rosa in their article for the *Journal of the International Committee of the Red Cross*, "there are serious limits to the ability of criminal proceedings to comprehensively address the issue of persons unaccounted for because of armed conflict and other situations of violence. They are designed to determine the guilt or innocence of the accused, and investigations are tailored to respond to the goals of the prosecution."[9]

Even more instructive is the fact that transitional justice institutions have generally mainstreamed a judicial approach to establishing facts about what took place. The judicial system is geared toward establishing guilt and innocence under due process of law and established standards of proof. Truth commissions may also defer to this model in establishing the facts of a case through a determination of relevant criteria and procedures in ways that resemble investigations in courts and prosecutorial offices. Typically, commissions rely on a civil standard of proof and focus on the balance of probabilities rather than stricter criminal standards of proof beyond doubt. However, from South Africa to Ghana, much of the institutional resources of truth commissions have been devoted to individual case-by-case determinations of who is a victim and who is a perpetrator. The South African Truth and Reconciliation Commission (TRC) described this as the pursuit of forensic truth: "The familiar legal or scientific notion of bringing to light factual, corroborated evidence, of obtaining accurate information through reliable (impartial, objective) procedures, featured prominently in the Commission's findings process."[10] It was one of four approaches to truth that it highlighted in its report.[11] The typical institutional protocol begins with the statement-taking department developing statement-taking forms designed to procure information that will be crucial for this determination. When people come into the commission and submit their statements, truth commissions follow up with further investigations of the information provided in the statement. Commissions often have separate investigative units mandated to verify the claims made in these statements. Typically, the work of a commission's investigative unit borrows from approaches that may be used in judicial procedures; for instance, the South African commission employed ex-policemen experienced at tracking witness statements in criminal cases as principal investigators. Moreover, as was the case in South Africa and Ghana, some commissions have sought to use public hearings of testimony to perform an investigative function seeking to shed light on events, consolidate evidence and clarify the witness's story about specific incidents for the official record. Thus, commissioners may cross-examine witnesses, and even (as in the Ghanaian case) structure hearings to allow lawyers to lead the questioning of witnesses as a designated part of the process. Reparation programs often rely on the determinations made by the investigative unit of truth commissions or substitute similar processes to determine beneficiaries of reparation programs.

These institutions are oriented toward a Funes-like attention to detail within the strictures of their mandates. They operate as if transitional justice processes were a sphere of technical engagement rather than a political intervention. The mandate is translated into questions of institutional technique where the task is to ensure that these institutions function effectively according to norms grounded in best practices; that they are prop-

erly sequenced and coordinated; and that they are managed professionally, efficiently, and in accordance with due process norms. Accordingly,
an important early policy initiative of the United Nations Office of the
High Commission for Human Rights (OHCHR) was the development
of a series of reports on transitional justice mechanisms that it describes
as "Rule-of-Law Tools for Post-Conflict States."[12] These guidelines consolidate best practices on how such mechanisms should be established and
implemented and exemplify the operational preoccupations of the field.
Neil Kritz, former Director of the U.S. Institute for Peace Rule of Law
Center for almost two decades, and one of the most prominent spokesper-
sons for the field, suggests that this focus on fine tuning and coordinating
institutional strategies is the primary responsibility of transitional justice.[13]
According to this view, the substantive shape of historical work, how transitional justice institutions define their political compass, is not the issue.
The focus needs to be on the mechanics, the neutral, technical questions of
institutional pragmatics. The parameters of competence and "due process"
here are narrowly operational. Technically oriented discussion of the role
of the defense lawyers, provisions for evidence, witness protection, and so
forth are foregrounded and the role of historical context in shaping "justice" issues fade into the background—or disappear entirely. As the political histories of these terrains recede, justice issues become translated into
"knowledge"—arenas of expertise for the provision of technical analysis.

The field of transitional justice has developed through a process of
comparative learning, and international actors have played significant roles
in offering substantive support. In some cases, judges, commissioners, and
other officials involved with transitional justice processes in one context
have been called to share expertise in other contexts. Thus, the Chilean
Commissioner José Zalaquett was involved in early planning workshops for
the South African Truth Commission. Yasmin Sooka of the South African
Truth Commission was recruited to serve as an international commissioner
in the Sierra Leone Truth Commission. UN offices such as OHCHR, foreign government agencies, such as the US Institute for Peace, or international NGOs, such as the International Centre for Transitional Justice
(ICTJ) have offered technical assistance and capacity-building programs.
In many ways, the work of institutions such as ICTJ have pushed for transitional justice to become not only an arena of human rights activism but
also an area of "expertise."

The evolution of truth commission procedures is of particular interest
because these mechanisms, even more than others, are said to be quintessentially about the telling of history and inform a community's collective

memory. They are almost always mandated to study individual cases, as well as to grapple with the broader context that enabled and exacerbated human rights violations. Yet it is striking that, within the human rights community, the last decades have seen the production of an enormous truth-and-reconciliation industry focused on issues of institutional design with inadequate attention to the history those commissions will produce. An initiative on "Strategic Choices in the Design of Truth Commissions" provides a striking illustration of this operational turn. Created by the Program on Negotiation at Harvard Law School, Search for Common Ground, and the European Center for Common Ground, this initiative on truth commissions translates a commission's strategic choices into the details of institutional design.[14] Drawing from the practices of "five key truth commissions," the initiative has developed a web portal that identifies the central "design factors" commission architects may confront and consolidates lessons learned on these issues.[15] The project emerges from the premise that "Putting a Commission together is a daunting task, one that can benefit greatly from knowing what has been done elsewhere and, where evaluation has been done, seeing what impact previous efforts have had."[16] To assist with this challenge, the portal seeks to distill key issues that will enable you to design your own.[17] Strikingly, the daunting challenge referenced here is not about grappling with the history that commissions are supposed to deal with. In fact, the historical narrative is produced as self-evident, a backdrop to the operationalization of the truth commission's mandate. The authors provide the historical background of each of these commissions as a neat summary at the beginning just "to provide some historical context."[18] The portal sees the real challenge to would-be advocates as the "neutral" tasks involved in setting up the truth commission. For example, the portal describes best practices for the organization of public hearings where victims give testimony. This involves delineating its different elements, such as undertaking advance outreach, provision for translation services, determining degrees of formality, making psychological and legal support available, clarifying options for *in camera* testimony, and so on. Each of these tasks is described further through lessons learned from past practices in the five commissions that are studied in this portal. Significantly, these tasks have enormous consequences for the nature of the history that truth commissions write but the machinery that shapes the technology of truth is not unpacked for how it shapes history. In fact, unsettling those questions may interfere with the ability to manage the truth-telling process. The focus here is on "technical" matters of institutional design that can produce what British historian Timothy

Garton Ash describes as "usable knowledge" in oiling the wheels of the truth commission.[19]

Grappling with collective historical memory is central to the legitimacy and rationale of transitional justice institutions, and the details of operating procedure are central to how these institutions carry out that mandate, including the terms through which history is defined and delimited in different approaches to institutionalizing justice. In that context, it is especially striking that the different visions of history that are embodied in questions of institutional design seldom enters the frame of conversations on transitional justice policy because these are treated as matters of technical expertise.

This legalistic, technocratic approach has many implications. For instance, consider the case-by-case approach that is now part of the settled common sense of how these institutions function, from statement taking to investigations to testimonials. This approach trains an individualized telephoto lens on the crime rather than developing a broader wide-angle understanding of what circumstances enabled such serious human rights violations. As was the case for Funes, in such a world it often feels like there are "only details, almost immediate in their presence"—this person, with these characteristics, was last seen at this time, on this date, on this street. However, one of the signal characteristics of social movements fighting for accountability in response to disappearances, is that such movements have been concerned not only about the signal importance of each individual case, but also about the collective impact of a policy of disappearances. It is no accident that from Chile to Sri Lanka, Argentina to Turkey, many of the targets of disappearances were those connected to larger political goals, from minority rights to the space for dissent. The UN Working Group on Enforced Disappearances notes that "The practice of enforced disappearance is often used to repress and intimidate individuals claiming their rights."[20] The Working Group has in its docket several cases where the victims of enforced disappearance were active in exercising or promoting the enjoyment of economic, social, and cultural rights, including trade union members, environmentalists, farmers, teachers, journalists, and artists.[21] Indeed, often movements for accountability regarding disappearance are catalyzed by employing such a wide-angle lens to connect the dots between the causes for dissent and the disappearance, or between the broader solidarities and associational ties of the person and their disappearance, situating seemingly disparate individual crimes in patterns that sustain larger injustices. They organize as movements precisely because they are keenly aware that the individual focus on the facts of particular crimes is less powerful than a shared justice claim; that individual disappearances may be designed to have a collective impact. Disappearing a particularly outspoken individual, for instance, can have a chilling effect on dissent in the society as a whole, but this impact is elided when a court or commission examines it solely as an individual crime with a specific perpetrator and a specific victim.

A narrowly legalistic focus on incidents that fit the criteria of a gross human rights violation investigated by a commission may make sometimes arbitrary distinctions between an individual who was forcibly disappeared and a group of people who were forcibly transferred away from their home and community. This was the case, for instance, with how the South African Truth Commission treated the forced removal of Blacks as part of the Group Areas Act of 1950, a cornerstone of the system of apartheid. The policies enacted by this Act were relegated to the historical record included in the report and there was public testimony only from individual victims who had suffered crimes that were determined to fit the criteria of a gross human rights violation.[22] Thus given the central importance of the individual public testimony (as opposed to the written report) in defining the TRC's articulation of a collective history for the South African public, we see that the institutional design of the commission and its interpretation of its mandate also contributed to obscuring the significance of these forced removals. Foregrounding the history of apartheid was central to the commission's mandate and testimonial attention to forced removals would have revealed how targeted individual disappearances and forced collective removals worked together in sustaining apartheid.

In most contexts, there is much to be gained by examining how different dimensions of an unjust system work together or how intersecting and parallel patterns of individual and collective victimization can offer a window into issues such as racial persecution or regional marginalization. State violence can be arbitrary and capricious, but most authoritarian regimes also target dissenting and precarious groups. Indeed, those groups may be more vulnerable to arbitrary violence, so it is important to understand the underlying patterns and systems that enable mass disappearances. For instance, the story regarding enforced disappearances in Sri Lanka during the 1989–1990 period was about how the economically marginalized are more vulnerable to enforced disappearances, and that enforced disappearances can, in turn, further exacerbate economic rights violations. Many of the Sri Lankan activists who were disappeared in this period came out of struggles of rural youth regarding social justice, labor issues in free-trade zones, post-1977 structural adjustment policies, and deeper economic marginalization on a number of fronts; the indicators of that marginalization extended from dwindling employment opportunities to sharpening vulnerability to global market fluctuations.

In the case of the civil war in Peru, too, we can see how attention to collective impacts can tell a story that a focus on individual cases alone cannot. The Peruvian truth commission noted that those who suffered greater economic, social, and cultural rights violations (citing issues such as poverty, educational level, rural location, etc.) were more vulnerable to enforced disappearances. The commission found that 75 percent of those who died or disappeared during the conflict belonged to the Quechua-speaking Indigenous community. In other words, the violence was not arbitrary, and all individuals were not similarly situated in the Peruvian conflict; rather, there were systematically racist elements internal to how the violence unfolded and a fuller historical accounting would have to attend to the continuities between the history of the Peruvian conflict studied by the commission, and the longer history of colonial and genocidal violence against the Indigenous people of the Andes.

In each of the cases I have mentioned in the preceding paragraphs (South Africa, Sri Lanka, and Peru), I have very briefly highlighted significant histories that can come to light with attention to collective political subjectivity, and the ways in which a focus on individual disappearances alone can contribute to eliding these larger histories, and the systems and structures that enabled and legitimized those disappearances. In fact, I would argue that the story of disappearances in these three countries is typical of many others, including the story regarding disappearances in the Philippines during the Ferdinand Marcos years (1965–1986); Indonesia during the blood baths of 1965–1966; the Pinochet era of Chile; ongoing disappearances in Kashmir, Palestine, and elsewhere. In all these cases, an accountability process that retains a narrow focus on the injustices connected in the individual cases alone can leave intact the structures and institutions that enabled collective crimes, including ones that empowered the beneficiaries of human rights abuse, reproduced the vulnerability of human rights victims and reinforced structures of impunity.

The broader political analysis that has governed social movements active on disappearances has often been lost in translation by transitional justice institutions with their focus on forensic fact-finding within narrowly legalistic mandates. Significantly however, this is not the only register for translation problems within the transitional justice field. If forensic fact-finding practices constitute one dimension of the mnemonic structure of the transitional justice field's treatment of disappearances, the other dimension is individual victim testimonies.

Testimony

> It is true that totalitarian domination tried to establish these holes of oblivion into which all deeds, good and evil, would disappear, but just as the Nazis' feverish attempts, from June, 1942, on, to erase all traces of the massacres—through cremation, through burning in open pits, through the use of explosives and flame-throwers and bone-crushing machinery—were doomed to failure, so all efforts to let their opponents "disappear in silent anonymity" were in vain. The holes of oblivion do not exist. Nothing human is that perfect, and there are simply too many people in the world to make oblivion possible. One man will always be left alive to tell the story.
>
> —Hannah Arendt
> *Eichmann in Jerusalem*[23]

Today, public testimony that contests the historical erasure Arendt speaks of is the most prominent face of the transitional justice field's investigation into disappearances. Testimony testifies to the absent presence of the disappeared. Citing that same Arendt observation, Turkish human rights activists Ozgur Sevgi Göral, Ayhan Işık, and Ozlem Kaya produced an important report on disappearances in Turkey that includes statistics and an accounting of the larger picture.[24] However, they also emphasize that "every disappeared person means the destruction of a person who is a world in himself or herself. Here, we face something irretrievable, something that can't be brought back with figures, scientific inference, or the rankings of politics."[25]

It is against this irretrievable loss that telling the story of that person and his or her world gains such significance. Victim testimony construes victimhood as a sacrosanct icon of the human rights faith—embodying the nobility of the enterprise and underscoring its central rationale. Arguably, it is these practices of individual testimony—from the Maya activist and Nobel Peace Prize-winner Rigoberta Mechnú's testimonial to ordinary individuals speaking to their pain through the public hearings of the South African Truth and Reconciliation Commission—that have been central to how the transitional justice field captured the imagination of the international human rights community. The particular prominence attached to the voice of the victim in transitional justice processes more generally is evident in institutional contexts beyond truth commission processes as well. For instance, the architects of the Rome Statute made provision for victim participation at various stages of investigation and trial in the International Criminal Court in ways that underscored that this was not a process directed solely at determining the guilt or innocence of the alleged perpetrator, but also one where the rights of victims are vindicated. In the context of post-conflict justice, reparation policies are advanced on the rationale that their significance is not only the check in the mail, but also that they stand for the dignity of victims; thus, there is a focus on drawing on victim participation and input in shaping the contours of reparation programs. As the whole field of memorials also gets pulled into the orbit of transitional justice technocracy, practitioners underscore victim participation as central to best practice guidelines. As noted earlier, however, of the various "pillars" of transitional justice, it is truth commissions that most emphatically convey this emphasis on "victims." Resisting closure, testimonials mark that the grief and violations are ongoing: Göral, Işık, and Kaya convey this poignantly: "This loss . . . the fact that we will never fully narrate the yearning and pain of, and the gap left behind by a person who has passed away, inevitably projects the traces of melancholy upon everything that is written on this subject."[26] While a writ of habeas corpus has legal value, the narration of the survivor's loss marks the humanity of both victim and survivor; that the victim was loved and missed; that there are survivors waiting for her return, ever hopeful. As another Turkish activist, Yıldırım Türker, notes: "I would like to get to know all the disappeared, one by one. I do not want them to be collectively labeled as a social wound accompanied by a number, and placed somewhere distant from us, and for people to speak of our collective loss of memory with a pleased and smart attitude when they are remembered years from now."[27]

While disappearances may underscore the significance of testimonials in the work of truth commissions or allied transitional justice processes, today individual victim testimony has come to signify and channel the central normative anchor of the field. In most cases the greater part of a truth commission's resources in terms of staff time, monetary resources, and general institutional energy is focused on engagement with individual victim testimony through statement taking, public hearings, investigation of those individual cases, psychological support to those who give and take statements, and incorporation of the individual case record into the final report. In many truth commissions, public hearings are convened for only a small subset of the victim statements submitted; in South Africa less than

10 percent of the 21,519 statements were chosen for public hearing. However, these hearings captured the imagination of the nation and ever since the South African TRC the work of truth commissions are equated with public hearings. Commissions themselves expend an enormous amount of time and institutional resources on the public hearings and often treat this as the most central component of their work.[28] As argued previously, commissions institutionalize a range of secular and religious sacraments and rituals to create a sacred space for the testimony. Interestingly, there has been wide dissemination of traditions of feminist insights regarding the importance of voice as part of the ambient common sense regarding public hearing processes, including constructions of "safe spaces" and "experiential truths."[29] For instance, the Peruvian commission treated victim testimony as so sacred that it had to remain unsullied by the mediation of the State.[30] The Peruvian commissioners refrained from interrogating victims, and public hearings were solemn affairs that gave dignity to the pathos of the events being related. In some cases, the rituals of public hearings are explicitly religious. For instance, the Ghanaian commission's public hearings always opened and closed with prayers by Bishop Charles Palmer-Buckle or Maulvi Wahab bin Adam who were commissioners. In South Africa, Archbishop Desmond Tutu often led those assembled at public hearings in hymns and there has been much commentary on the "liturgical character" of commission proceedings and the work of the commission in creating a "civic sacrament" for a new South Africa. Commissions have not only claimed that public hearings heal victims who tell their stories of victimization, but that these victims themselves are, by virtue of their injury, healers—"wounded healers," as the archbishop described them, but healers nonetheless.[31] In undergoing the trauma of giving testimony they are said to sacrifice themselves for the nation as "citizen/survivors." If the cathartic powers attributed to talking invokes the dominant traditions of modern psychotherapy, this configuration of the wounded healer sacrificing herself for the nation's redemption invokes the Christian tradition of salvation through public spectacle of the injured body.

Mothers of the disappeared have had an exceptionally influential impact in justice struggles regarding disappearances. Partly for this reason, feminist scholars have paid particular attention to the potential of testimonials concerned that the dominance of the legalistic methodology informs not only courts but transitional justice as a whole. Feminists critical of the "forensic" approach to the tracking of injury have urged that this privileging of the juridical approach fundamentally misunderstands and excludes alternative political vocabularies. In fact, it is argued that, from the South African Truth and Reconciliation Commission to the tribunals in The Hague, transitional justice institutions have commissioned what gender studies scholar Leigh Gilmore describes as "forensic speech acts" that those institutions can traffic in as evidence, evidence that is "capable of speech."[32] In exchange for giving legal "audibility" to testimonials, Gilmore and others argue that courts and official justice exclude history, context, and affect. Moreover, in many contexts, it is women who are adversely affected by this exclusion and alienated by the reliance on the legalistic methodologies of transitional justice. Feminists have argued that for transitional justice to be more inclusive of women's voices and more appreciative of a holistic articulation of experience, it needs to be more pluralistic in the political vocabularies it entertains. For instance, Gilmore argues that literary texts such as that of Jamaica Kincaids *Autobiography of My Mother* or autobiographical speeches such as that of Rigoberta Menchú's *I, Rigoberta Menchú* may provide an alternative "testimonial archive" that is "not bound by the legalistic requirements of courts."[33] Following Gayatri Spivak, Gilmore describes these forms as producing testimony as "a wound where the blood of history does not dry."[34] These alternative testimonials can produce "the subject of historical trauma" as one "who is clearly distinct from the autonomous, rational, humanist, neoliberal, rights bearing subject that we are familiar with."[35]

Yet, as with that "original" story of sacrifice, even in truth commissions the projection of suffering from disappearances onto a public stage can become a story of individual loss alone, abstracted from social context and broader justice struggles. Thus, the models of victim subjectivity that are projected in the rituals of public testimony are quintessentially *individualized* selves. When there is questioning of the "victim" in public hearings, in commission after commission, the focus of questioning is on the individual's recollection of events, her *personal* experience of bodily violation. From South Africa to Sierra Leone, many went before the commission for a range of reasons, including the promise of monetary reparations, the fear of prosecutions, an interest in claiming their place in the history of liberation, and so on. Nevertheless, the statement-taking process and public hearings of the truth commissions focused overwhelmingly on the experience of bodily injury and detailed narratives of violence. It is the inviolability of the individual body that is the premise of victimhood, and therefore testimony about the story of that individual injury is what is solicited through the institutional procedures and rituals of a commission's public hearings. The process of making human rights violations *public* becomes, paradoxically, a *privatizing* process. Moreover, there is a particularly gendered character to the treatment of testimonials resting on the assumption that women's voices are, a priori, an articulation of injury and therefore women's testimony is always, already, testimony regarding trauma. As argued earlier, the sedimentation of "injury" as the ground from which women enter the transitional justice stage fuels the embrace of the testimonial form and experiential narratives as a project creating safe spaces for the traumatized voice.[36]

Conclusion

This paper has highlighted ways in which some of the established institutional mechanisms of the transitional justice field bend toward individualizing crimes, victims, and perpetrators in ways that distract from or deter larger political analysis. On the one hand, these institutions can be recorders of atrocity. Like Ireneo Funes, they can perform the not inconsequential work of being institutional witnesses to enforced disappearances: "Funes could continuously make out the tranquil advances of corruption, of cares, of fatigue. He noted the progress of death, of moisture. He was the solitary and lucid spectator of a multiform world, which was instantaneously and almost intolerably exact."[37]

This function of institutional witnessing is what has made transitional justice so central to the story of accountability these past decades. Yet, as a witness of a series of individual crimes, this intolerably precise record may be precisely what defeats political analysis. What I refer to here as "political analysis" is analogous perhaps to what Borges refers to when he says that Funes with his difficulties escaping the memory storm of details, "was not very capable of thought. To think is to forget a difference, to generalize, to abstract."[38] It is political analysis that can address the structure of impunity by exploring root causes, understanding the dynamics of the system and identify beneficiaries of systems of atrocity.

Central to the individualization that inheres in transitional justice processes is the positing of the human rights–wielding individual as a universal unit of measure in translating complex socio-political contests into a globally mobile blueprint for post-conflict justice.[39] The dominant field of transitional justice celebrates and seeks to perfect technologies of individuation in ways that can be better incorporated into best-practice lists and operational handbooks. This translation, this universal fungibility, may distance the work of truth commissions from questions of power in the specific contexts they address. For instance, the individualization of the harm caused by disappearances can crowd out attention to how disappearances create an atmosphere of fear, secrecy, and violence that erodes and occupies public space. The attention to the disappearance of the space to form solidarities, debate political futures, and build social movements is pivotal yet frequently neglected by the transitional justice field. In fact, the optics of individual human rights can obscure how power operates in mechanisms of global governance, and, in that obfuscation, contribute to what legal scholar Upendra Baxi has called "neoliberalism friendly human rights."[40] Funes understood the dark side of seeing the world as a continuum of individual memories. It is a perspective into the world that is simultaneously too dense, and too thin—it is dense with individual trauma and atrocity, impoverished in analyzing and acting upon the architecture of such a world.

Transitional justice institutions advance the ambitious promise of marrying ethics and expertise, acknowledging memory while creating an institutional avenue for closure. Yet the arena of disappearances underscores that closure is illusory, that yesterday's abuses reach forward into tomorrow, and that the promise of closure may be precisely how fundamental differences in interests, agendas, and ideologies are obscured. When the Mothers of the Disappeared in Argentina refused reparations without justice, calling it "blood money," they were offering a caution about that promise of closure—wary, as in Funes' world, "of multiplying superfluous gestures."[41]

Notes

1. Jorge Luis Borges, *Funes the Memorious, in Ficciones* (New York: Grove Press, 1962). 112, 115.

2. This paper draws on the author's previous work regarding the history and politics of transitional justice. In particular it relies extensively on, "Icons and Measures: (Re)presenting Victims in Truth Commission Processes," in Ashleigh Barnes ed., *Feminism of Discontent: Global Contestations* (Delhi: OUP Delhi, 2015); and "Missionary Zeal for A Secular Mission: Bringing Gender to Transitional Justice and Redemption to Feminism," in Z. Peterson and S. Kuovo, eds., *Between Resistance And Compliance* (London: Hart, 2011). Thus, there is considerable overlap in text and argument with both of these articles.

3. Michael Ondaatje, *Anil's Ghost* (New York: Alfred Knopf, 2000), 102.

4. *Updated Set of Principles for the Protection and Promotion of Human Rights Through Action to Combat Impunity*, Report submitted by Diane Orentlicher to the UN Economic and Social Council, Commission on Human Rights, 2005. Available at https://documents-dds-ny.un.org/doc/UNDOC/GEN/G05/109/00/PDF/G0510900.pdf?OpenElement

5. Monique Crettol and Anne-Marie La Rosa. "The Missing and Transitional Justice: The Right to Know and the Fight against Impunity," *International Review of the Red Cross* 88 no. 862 (June 2006).

6. As noted in article 24: 2–3 of the convention: "2. Each victim has the right to know the truth regarding the circumstances of the enforced disappearance, the progress and results of the investigation and the fate of the disappeared person. Each State Party shall take appropriate measures in this regard. And 3. Each State Party shall take all appropriate measures to search for, locate and release disappeared persons and, in the event of death, to locate, respect and return their remains."

7. Crettol and La Rosa, "The Missing and Transitional Justice," 362.

8. See, for example, A. Neier, "The Nuremberg Precedent," *New York Review of Books*, November 4, 1993.

9. Crettol and La Rosa, "The Missing and Transitional Justice," 359.

10. *South African Truth and Reconciliation Commission Report*, vol. 1, chap. 5 (1998), 110.

11. For an excerpt from the report that highlights this four-part definition of truth in its work, see https://mylearning.nps.gov/wp-content/uploads/2016/07/Excerpt-from-TRC-Report-Four-Truths.pdf

12. For instance, there is one on truth commissions, https://www.ohchr.org/Documents/Publications/RuleoflawTruthCommissionsen.pdf; another on prosecutions, https://www.ohchr.org/Documents/Publications/RuleoflawProsecutionsen.pdf; yet another on vetting procedures, https://www.ohchr.org/Documents/Publications/RuleoflawVettingen.pdf; and so on.

13. Neil Krtiz. "Where We Are and How We Got Here: An Overview of Developments in the Search for Justice and Reconciliation," in *The Legacy of Abuse: Confronting the Past, Facing the Future*, ed. by Alice H. Henkin (Washington, DC: The Aspen Institute, 2002), 21–45.

14. Program on Negotiation at Harvard Law School, *Strategic Choices in the Design of Truth Commissions*, Available at http://www.truthcommission.org/about.php?Lang=en; this initiative is a joint initiative of the Program On Negotiation at Harvard Law School (http://www.pon.harvard.edu) and Search for Common Ground, an international conflict resolution and prevention NGO based in Washington, DC, and for the European Centre for Common Ground, in Brussels (http://www.sfcg.org).

15. Harvard Law School, *Strategic Choices.*

16. Harvard Law School, *Strategic Choices.*

17. Harvard Law School, *Strategic Choices.*

18. Harvard Law School, *Strategic Choices.*

19. Timothy Garton Ash, preface to Priscilla B. Hayner, *Unspeakable Truths: Confronting State Terror and Atrocity* (New York: Routledge 1994), xiii.

20. *Report of the Working Group on Enforced or Involuntary Disappearances; Addendum: Study on Enforced or Involuntary Disappearances and Economic, Social and Cultural Rights to Human Rights Council*, A/HRC/30/38/Add.5., July 9, 2015.

21. E/CN.4/2006/56/Add.1, para. 55 (categorizing trade unions as one of the main targets of disappearance); A/HRC/13/31/Add.1, para. 18 (noting that the majority of the disappearances occurred between 1972 and 1980 and that some of

the persons disappeared were students or trade unionists, while others were journalists or members of opposition political parties); A/HRC/19/58/Add.2, para. 66 (discussing human rights defenders' disappearances); A/HRC/WGEID/103/1, para. 174; A/HRC/WGEID/102/1, paras. 81–82 and 89; and A/HRC/WGEID/101/1, para. 37.

22. For an important critical analysis of this elision, see Mahmood Mamdani, "Amnesty of Impunity? A Preliminary Critique of the Report of the Truth and Reconciliation Commission of South Africa (TRC)," *diacritics* 32, no. 3–4 (Fall–Winter 2002): 33–59.

23. Hannah Arendt, *Eichmann in Jerusalem: A Report on the Banality of Evil* (New York: Penguin, 2006), 232–33.

24. Özgür Sevgi Göral, Ayhan Işık, and Özlem Kaya, *The Unspoken Truth: Enforced Disappearances* (Truth Justice Memory Center: Hafıza Merkezi, 2013).

25. Göral, Işık, and Kaya, *The Unspoken Truth*, 78.

26. Göral, Işık, and Kaya, *The Unspoken Truth*, 78.

27. Quoted in Göral, Işık and Kaya, *The Unspoken Truth*, 78.

28. Audrey R. Chapman and Patrick Ball, "The Truth of Truth Commissions: Comparative Lessons from Haiti, South Africa, and Guatemala," *Human Rights Quarterly* 23, no. 1 (February 2001): 1–43, at 29.

29. For a more extended analysis of feminist engagements with truth commissions, see Vasuki Nesiah, "Missionary Zeal for A Secular Mission: Bringing Gender to Transitional Justice and Redemption to Feminism," in *Between Resistance and Compliance*, ed. by Zoe Peterson and Sari Kuovo (London: Hart, 2011).

30. Nesiah, "Missionary Zeal for A Secular Mission," 147.

31. Archbishop Tutu, qtd. in p. 17 of Antjie Krog, *Country of My Skull* (New York: Random House, 1998).

32. Leigh Gilmore, "Autobiography's Wounds," in W. Hesford and W. Kozol, eds., *Just Advocacy? Women's Human Rights, Transnational Feminism and the Politics of Representation* (New Brunswick, NJ: Rutgers University Press, 2005), 107.

33. Gilmore, "Autobiography's Wounds." Gilmore argues that Kincaid's oevre can be read as a serial autobiography referring to "Kincaid's ongoing self-representational project represented by *At the Bottom of the River* (1983), *Annie John* (1986), *Lucy* (1991), *Autobiography of my Mother* (1996), and, to date, *My Brother* (1997)." Gilmore, *The Limits of Autobiography: Trauma and Testimony* (Ithaca: Cornell, Cornell University Press, 2001), 97. See also Rigoberta Menchú, *I, Rigoberta Menchú* (New York: Verso 2010).

34. Gilmore, "Autobiography's Wounds."

35. Gilmore, "Autobiography's Wounds."

36. Nesiah, "Missionary Zeal for A Secular Mission," 147.

37. Borges, *Ficciones*, 114.

38. Borges, *Ficciones*, 115.

39. This dualistic structure can be seen as twin platforms of "victim" visibility where catastrophe crowds out the political from how we engage with the realms of human rights and humanitarianism—there may be an uneasy parallel with how Arendt saw the rise of the social squeeze between the private and the public spheres—but perhaps more helpfully we may see this as parallel to how Chatterjee describes the rise of civil society as crowding out political society. Partha Chatter-

jee, *Lineages of Political Society: Studies in Postcolonial Democracy* (New York: Columbia University Press, 2011).

40. Remarks made by Upendra Baxi at the Conference on "Public Differences, Private Dominations: Transcending the Public-Private Split By Gendering Legal Dichotomies," Humboldt-Universität and Wissenschaftskolleg zu Berlin, October 2011.

41. Borges, *Funes the Memorious, in Ficciones*, 115.

Stolen

Morgan C. Page

Stolen was inspired by the *Stolen* podcast, written and produced by Canadian journalist Connie Walker (see https://tinyurl.com/24xe94px). *Stolen* is dedicated to Jermain Charlo, who has been missing from Montana since 2018. The title also speaks to what has been robbed from Indigenous people throughout time.

—Morgan C. Page

Editors' note: In Canada, the 2019 *National Inquiry into Missing and Murdered Indigenous Women and Girls* found they were twelve times more likely to experience violence and seven times more likely to be killed than other women. At least 1,200 Indigenous women were killed or missing between 1980 and 2012, but the toll was likely much higher (see https://tinyurl.com/ndbwr32x). The inquiry has labeled this as genocide. Myriad women have been disappeared or murdered on a remote road in British Columbia, now called the "Highway of Tears" (see https://highwayoftearsfilm.com/watch).

In the United States, Indigenous women are up to ten times more likely to be murdered and missing than the national average, with cases consistently unsolved and unaddressed. In 2016, the U.S. Federal Bureau of Investigation tallied more than 5,712 reports of missing girls and women, including 669 unsolved cases. Throughout the Americas, since colonization, millions of Indigenous women have been victimized. The roots of this violence originate from European notions of racial superiority resulting in profound dehumanization (see https://tinyurl.com/9vr7suny).

FOURTEEN

Story as Portal

Healing, Regeneration, and Possibility after Genocide

Kayhan Irani

"When the body perishes,
all perishes,
but the threads of memory
are woven with enduring specks."

—Amrita Pritam

I can tell you the exact month and year (January 2002) that I knew, in my bones, my family was a target again. I was walking across a busy New York City street and a middle-aged man, crossing from the other side, got close to me and roared, "go back to where you came from."

A shock to the system. The heat of a stranger's rage seared onto my body. A public attack aimed at stripping away my sense of comfort and belonging. All the sensations coursing through my body brought long buried memories to the surface. Echoes of living through a similar time.

My family came to the United States at the height of the Iranian Hostage crisis in 1981. Iranians were vilified across the national media as enemies of the country and the American people. The government apparatus—international and domestic—solidified that narrative into a concrete object. One which every American could carry in her or his pocket, to hurl at the enemy. Public denouncements, discrimination, and violence were permissible, patriotic acts. While I don't have direct memories of that time, I hold the recollections of my parents. As told through their bodies. My father's voice tense, stifled; my mother's eyes diverted, shoulders resigned, when I ask about those times.

Their stories become my memory and that memory equips me with a compass that points me to a deeper understanding of what is happening as I am thrown off-kilter. I can see past the immediate confusion and victimization toward a message: the social terrain I inhabit is shifting and I will need to be careful. The counter-storytelling tradition of my parents, practices of sharing stories of racism and xenophobia that speak back to the dominant narrative of the American Dream and the model minority, becomes a mechanism of resilience to weather the Islamophobic deluge on the way. (Though our family isn't Muslim we are "Muslim looking" and of Iranian heritage which often makes us targets.)

This practice of storytelling is not only my personal coping mechanism but something that can be shared with others to build community resilience. As I tell my story I open the door to other stories—an uncle at my temple who shaved his goatee because of the unspoken intimidation he felt at work; a friend whose parents told her to stop wearing her headscarf; a student whose family member was disappeared and surfaced weeks later in an immigration detention facility hundreds of miles away. As we weave together our realities, we pull in threads of history and politics. We bear witness to the past as well as create a repository of memories that serve, in the present day, to affirm our experiences as real and as unjust within the silencing rhetoric of "with us or against us." We create a mnemonic community,[1] people willing to give and listen to testimony and personal experience that speaks back to the dehumanizing policies and cultural narratives poisoning the air. Our counter-storytelling community provides personal space for healing, feeds into movements for justice and peace, and enters into the public sphere. Injustice and grief will come, yet in sharing and storing our memories with others, they become an artifact that preserve the imprint of our lives, of our living, in the face of destruction.

> As I waited again, I became aware of something happening in the room. The black men and women were mumbling quietly among themselves; they had not known one another before they had come here, but now their timidity and shame were wearing off and they were exchanging experiences . . . their talking was enabling them to sense the collectivity of their lives, and some of their fear was passing.
>
> —Richard Wright[2]

Counter-storytelling communities emerge anywhere that people are recognizing their common experience, plotting ideas, and dreaming up new worlds to live into. These can be public or private places, intentionally or spontaneously formed, with visible or invisible membership, and that spread information in amplified, visible ways or through whispers and coded language. The shape may shift yet the purpose of counter-narratives is to recognize and preserve the experience of the oppressed, mobilize the imagination, and create cultural shifts that can build agency, heal hurts, seed claims of full personhood, and fuel movements that challenge unjust power. In essence, these counter-storytelling communities are calling forth and using modes of storytelling for social justice. In the volume of essays, *Telling Stories to Change the World: Global Voices on the Power of Narrative to Build Community and Make Social Justice Claims*, Rickie Solinger, Madeline Fox, and I highlight projects using embodied, spoken, pictorial, digital, written, archival, and ritualized storytelling methods deployed by counter-storytelling communities around the world. Part of our thinking as editors was how to present the projects: should they be arranged by region, identities of the claim makers, modes of storytelling? In the end, we decided that the best way to organize the chapters was to lift up the deeper purpose and context that each project emerged from and group them into sections. These sections provide a useful way to understand how storytelling for social justice can function in a particular context. They are

- Stories in the Service of Healing: speaking what happened, remembering, preserving tradition, aiding cultural vitality, history-making/telling;
- Stories in the Service of Protecting: defending neighbors/place, building audience and allies around urgent issues; and
- Stories in the Service of Challenging and Transforming Beliefs: envisioning futures, creating what isn't here, challenging definitions and binaries.[3]

This is not to say that a storytelling for social justice effort is exclusive to one purpose or aim, rather, that these groupings offer us a way into understanding how a particular project and/or practice developed and what it achieved. Many of the projects in the volume have overlapping and intersectional realities to contend with and goals that were stated at the outset, as well as those that emerged through their process, just as life is complex, multi-layered, and always shifting.

Of the many projects that address political violence, war, genocide, and forced disappearance, the work of Grupo Sotz'il in Guatemala offers a look at how counter-storytelling communities transform and use story, over generations, to heal from cycles of political violence and erasure—from direct killings to the elimination of a people from the historical record.[4] For the purpose of this essay, when I refer to healing, I am using the "Healing is Rhizomatic" framework created by Jennifer Lopez, which states

> When we describe something as healing (as in, *"this space was healing"*), what we are describing is that being and engaging in that space enabled us to access and channel the natural, inherent capacity to resource ourselves to be more fully and powerfully alive. . . . This capacity cannot be created or destroyed, though the ways we channel it can be blocked or fractured. It is multidimensional and multidirectional."[5]

This framework resonates with Grupo Sotz'il's idea of resistance as cyclical regeneration as well as a healing mode—where healing isn't a solitary endeavor, but a communal project tied to unlocking power and community agency through counter-storytelling.

The chapter in *Telling Stores*, "Our Ancestors Danced Like This: Maya Youth Respond to Genocide Through the Ancestral Arts," by Czarina Aggabao Thelen,[6] focuses on Indigenous youth who recreate and reclaim ancestral music, dance, and embodied storytelling as a means to not only maintain their cultural traditions, but to renew the community's struggle for political autonomy and self-determination in the twenty-first century. This group and their play, *Kaji' Imox* (currently titled *Dance of the Nawales*) created in 2006,[7] are the most recent iteration of radically healing storytelling practiced in their community and across time. The theater piece is drawn from *The Annals of the Kaqchikeles*, a colonial text documenting the Kaqchikele nation's creation, rise, governance, and eventual destruction from plagues and Spanish colonialism spanning 1300–1600 CE,[8] and is the first theater piece in the Maya language since colonization. The work, and the process of creating it, mirrors the deep, underground springs of resistance and story that the community draws from. Kaji' Imox, the main character and leader of the Kaqchikel nation's resistance to Spanish colonial forces in the late 1500s, calls out from the ancient past to mobilize the longing for freedom and self-determination in the present.[9] Speaking from a space of danger and hope in the play, as he maintained a ten-year campaign of resistance against the Spanish forces from the mountains, Kaji' Imox's words are received by the progeny of those who stayed on their land and hid in the mountains through the 1980s, when Maya villages were targeted for destruction, again. Don Anastasio, the father of one of Sotz'il's founders shared some of his experiences of that time, colloquially called "The Violence": "The military went around monitoring who were the leaders of local groups . . . I remember I had some diplomas, the ones that they give you at the recognition of an activity, I had to bury them so that the military wouldn't identify me as a member of a committee."[10] Despite this, he was targeted for "disappearance" and went into hiding. Luckily, he was already in hiding when his home was surrounded by soldiers looking for him—and who pursued him for six months. Not only is the spoken language conveying an unbroken message of strength and regeneration, it is those who have lived through genocide who can understand and receive this story, but the message of never giving up, never losing hope, highlights the links that connect with the audience's centuries-long chain of healing memory. The mnemonic tradition and storytelling networks that families and villages have deployed in order to live another day are affirmed as the hero speaks through time, mirroring the way a father, grandmother, or elder might speak about their history and heritage. The play feeds, and is fed by, a succession of memory and story as community healing practice that affirms everything that has contributed to life and living. Aggabao Thelen writes, "This is exactly what genocidal forces seek to deny and repress—because they cannot extinguish nor completely suppress a people if they are proudly proclaiming their right to exist and practicing their power of regeneration."[11]

In order to understand how young people who have grown up directly experiencing deep marginalization, witnessing violence, and erasure from educational spaces and wider social and cultural narratives can marshal the energy and resolve to generate a project like this, one has to look to the deeply nurturing and affirming communities they come from. The members of Grupo Sotz'il are products of deep counter-storytelling legacies inherited from their parents and elders who created their own storytelling strategies to survive the government sanctioned killings and dispossession of Maya peoples in the 1970s and 1980s. The grandfather of one of the group's founders was instrumental in the first potable water project in their community.[12] His son became an educator who instituted bilingual education programs in Maya communities so that the current generation could maintain a connection to their language and identity.[13] The mother of another member is a master weaver, able to create innovative weavings in order to help the group make costumes and set pieces that replicate the shapes and aesthetic of the time of Kaji' Imox.[14] The group had a relationship with a local elder, a master marimba player who carried the melodies and rhythms of Maya musicality passed down to him for generations.[15]

Each of these areas—community development, music, textile craft, language learning—contain resources, information, and knowledge needed to survive, thrive, and create anew. As importantly, the messengers and teachers are Maya elders, parents, and community members who model intelligence, dignity, authority, and love. This embodied power sits in defiance to common tropes that demean and erase Maya knowledge, expertise, and cultural contributions. In making a life, the parents and elders offer an alternative to assimilation and are proof that deep knowledge and valuable contributions have been created by Maya peoples. It is with this confidence, knowledge, and lived counter-story, that the group members are imbued with the skill, as well as the drive, to research codices in Maya, awaken the buried story of Kaji' Imox, and adapt and revive all the Maya aesthetic elements (music, costume, etc.) into a cohesive whole.

Lisandro, a founding member states, "We sought to counter the way in which we Indigenous people are represented in Guatemalan society. . . . We have our own stories. We have a history we've been prohibited from seeing and hearing."[16] By creating this tale and the play, the youth of Grupo Sotz'il are inserting a literal story into the canon of Indigenous storytelling that will serve as a counter-story for the next generation. Additionally, this story will be alive and available to wider Guatemalan audiences providing at least one complex and accurate portrayal of an Indigenous character in the performing arts. Through their contribution and creation of canon, Grupo Sotz'il mirrors the work of their elders and offers the next generation counter-storytelling resources to carry forward—modes of cultural production and research that can be extended and built upon.

The performances that Grupo Sotz'il offer are not exclusively for Maya communities. They present their work to contemporary audiences and offer their story to activate healing in all segments of Guatemalan society. Including people whose histories and legacies might be directly implicated in the repression and violence against Maya communities. The presentation of this particular work, as a window to the roots of the social fractures that pulse in the present, is what Augusto Boal, theater activist and director, calls "metaxis."[17]

Metaxis occurs when the spect-actor creates images of her real-life oppressions and transplants them on the stage. She now belongs to two worlds: the image of reality and the reality of the image.[18] As audiences travel through the story, they are asked to consider the consequences of Kaji' Imox's actions. Yet they are not only considering his actions. In a state of metaxis, they are sitting in two worlds, the world of the stage—which is also their ancestors' world—and the world in which they are living. The audience is considering how the character enacts liberation in the world of the stage as they consider the conditions of their own lives. Aggabao Thelen writes

> The multicultural audiences who watch Sotz'il's play are also implicitly invested in this story: as Mayas, Ladinos, or members of the international community that work in Guatemala, each audience member's socioeconomic position in Guatemala today is a direct result of the actions taking place in the story on stage.[19]

The stage becomes the rehearsal space for real life and what may seem impossible starts to have possibility. The healing, the regeneration at the point of fracture,[20] is activated as one confronts his or her own thoughts, imagining in which direction the character will go, and why he or she should/shouldn't go there. The actions of their ancestors and elders are mirrored, and in seeing themselves in the scenarios, living in their seats and on the stage, a portal toward healing is being opened. The story is offering a collective opportunity to choose a new direction, to grow together in a new way. Lopez describes this process as "healing-oriented knowledge" which "is a process rooted in longing, movement toward, and commitment to accessing and channeling ways of being that allow us to live more fully and powerfully."[21] Grupo Sotz'il is not only using the regenerative power of story to heal their own community, but to call all members of society into a web of healing through building new stories and changing the narrative.

> The struggle of memory against forgetting is the struggle of man against power.
>
> —Milan Kundera[22]

Where genocide, structurally sanctioned violence, and cultural erasure creates fractures, story, memory, and collective witnessing have the ability to open channels of healing and regeneration. Where communities slated for destruction by genocidal and repressive power come together, make intentional space, mark moments in time that honor, grieve, commemorate, and transmit the details of their past they are creating a mnemonic community.[23] Such formations imbue the present with particles of resistance in story form. Like the stories my parents told me of living through one version of xenophobic silencing and attack based on their presumed identity. Their stories offer me, at times, armor, tactics, lessons, or comfort so that I may survive the present with full knowledge of what is possible in the world. This simple impulse is a crucial healing practice, as seen through the context of Grupo Sotz'il's work, in awakening, sustaining, and powerfully living into a more just and connected world.

Epitaph: Amrita Pritam, "I Will Meet You Again One Day," in *The Little Magazine*, vol. IV, issue 4, trans. by Nirupama Dutt. http://www.littlemag.com/ghosts/amritapritam.html

Notes

1. Evitar Zerubavel, "Social Memories: Steps Toward a Sociology of the Past," in Jeffrey K. Olick, Vered Vinitzky Seroussi, and Daniel Levy, eds., *The Collective Memory Reader* (Oxford: Oxford University Press, 2011), 224.

2. Richard Wright, *Black Boy* (New York: Harper Collins, 1993), 300.

3. Rickie Solinger, Madeline Fox, and Kayhan Irani, eds., *Telling Stories to Change the World: Global Voices on the Power of Narrative to Build Community and Make Social Justice Claims* (Abingdon-on-Thames: Routledge, 2008), vii.

4. Czarina Aggabao Thelen, "Our Ancestors Danced Like This," *Telling Stories to Change the World*, 39.

5. Jennifer Lopez, "Healing is Rhizomatic: A Conceptual Framework and Tool," *Genealogy* 4, no. 4 (2020): 115. https://doi.org/10.3390/genealogy4040115

6. Aggabao Thelen, "Our Ancestors Danced Like This," 39.

7. Aggabao Thelen, "Our Ancestors Danced Like This," 48.

8. Aggabao Thelen, "Our Ancestors Danced Like This," 46.

9. Aggabao Thelen, "Our Ancestors Danced Like This," 48.

10. Aggabao Thelen, "Our Ancestors Danced Like This," 43.

11. Aggabao Thelen, "Our Ancestors Danced Like This," 54.

12. Aggabao Thelen, "Our Ancestors Danced Like This," 43.

13. Aggabao Thelen, "Our Ancestors Danced Like This," 43.

14. Aggabao Thelen, "Our Ancestors Danced Like This," 47.

15. Aggabao Thelen, "Our Ancestors Danced Like This," 46.

16. Aggabao Thelen, "Our Ancestors Danced Like This," 48.

17. Augusto Boal, *The Rainbow of Desire* (Abingdon-on-Thames: Routledge, 1995).

18. Boal, *The Rainbow of Desire*, 43.

19. Aggabao Thelen, "Our Ancestors Danced Like This," 49.

20. Lopez, "Healing is Rhizomatic," 115.

21. Lopez, "Healing is Rhizomatic," 115.

22. Milan Kundera, *The Book of Laughter and Forgetting* (New York: Harper Collins, 1999).

23. Zerubavel, "Social Memories," 224.

FIFTEEN

The Psychology of Bystanders, Perpetrators, and Heroic Helpers

Ervin Staub

What leads groups of people or governments to perpetrate genocide or mass killing? What are the characteristics and psychological processes of individuals and societies that contribute to such group violence? What is the nature of the evolution that leads to it: What are the motives, how do they arise and intensify, how do inhibitions decline?

A primary example in this chapter will be the Holocaust, but the social processes and instigators of violence can be applied to the Armenian genocide (1915–1916), the Cambodian genocide (1975 and 1979), as well as the Rwandan genocide (1994), among others.

In the United Nations charter on genocide, the term denotes the extermination of a racial, religious, or ethnic group. Although some scholars call it "politicide,"[1] the destruction of a whole political group is also widely regarded as genocide.[2]

This chapter focuses on the psychology and role of both perpetrators and witnesses/bystanders. Bystanders to the ongoing, usually progressively increasing mistreatment of a group of people have great potential power to influence events. However, whether individuals, groups, or nations, they frequently remain passive. This allows perpetrators to see their destructive actions as acceptable and even right. As a result of their passivity in the face of others' suffering, bystanders change: They come to accept the persecution and suffering of victims, and some even join the perpetrators.[3]

Another focus of this chapter is the psychology of those who attempt to save intended victims, endangering their own lives to do so. Bystanders, perpetrators, and heroic helpers face similar conditions and may be part of the same culture: What are the differences in their characteristics, psychological processes, and evolution?

A conception is presented in this chapter of the origins of genocide and mass killing, with a focus on how a group of people turns against another group, how the motivation for killing evolves and inhibitions against it decline. The conception identifies characteristics of a group's culture that create an enhanced potential for a group turning against others. It focuses on difficult life conditions as the primary source of the frustration of basic psychological (as well as material) needs, which demand fulfillment. Conflict between groups can be another source. The pattern of predisposing cultural characteristics intensifies basic psychological needs and inclines the group toward fulfilling them in ways that turn the group against others. As they begin to harm the victim group, the perpetrators learn by and change as a result of their own actions, in ways that make the increasing mistreatment of the victims possible and probable. The perpetrators come to see their actions as necessary. Bystanders have potential influence to inhibit the evolution of increasing destructiveness. However, they usually remain passive and themselves change as a result of their passivity, becoming less concerned about the fate of the victims, some of them joining the perpetrators.

Instigators of Group Violence

Violence against a subgroup of society is the outcome of a societal process. It requires analysis at the level of both individuals and society. Analysis of the group processes of perpetrators, an intermediate level, is also important.

Why does a government or a dominant group turn against a subgroup of society? Usually, difficult life conditions or persistent life problems in a society are important starting points. They include economic problems such as extreme inflation; depression and unemployment; political conflict and violence; war; or a decline in the power, prestige, and importance of a nation, usually with attendant economic and political problems, and the chaos and social disorganization these often entail.

Severe, persistent difficulties of life frustrate powerful, basic human needs that demand fulfillment. These include needs for security, for a positive identity, for effectiveness and control over important events in one's life, for positive connections to other people, and for a meaningful understanding of the world or comprehension of reality. Psychological processes in individuals and social processes in groups can arise that turn the group against others as they offer destructive fulfillment of these needs.

Germany was faced with serious life problems after World War I. The war and defeat were followed by a revolution; a change in the political system; hyperinflation; the occupation of the Ruhr by the French, who were dissatisfied with the rate of reparation payments; severe economic depression; conflict between political extremes; political violence; social chaos; and disorganization.

In Germany, a two-step process led to the genocide. The difficult life conditions gave rise to psychological and social processes, such as scapegoating and destructive ideologies. Such processes do not directly lead to genocide. However, they turn one group against another. In Germany, they brought an ideological movement to power and led to the beginning of an evolution, or steps along the continuum of destruction. Life conditions improved, but guided by ideology, the social processes and acts of harm-doing gave rise to continued intensification. Amid another great social upheaval, created by Germany, namely, World War II, they led to genocide.

Another instigator that frustrates basic needs and gives rise to psychological conditions in individuals and social processes in groups that may lead to genocide is conflict between groups. The conflict may revolve around essential interests, such as territory needed for living space. Even in this case, however, psychological elements tend to make the conflict intractable, such as attachment by groups to a particular territory, unhealed wounds in the group, or prior devaluation and mistrust of the other.

Cultural-Societal Characteristics

The differentiation between in-group and outgroup, us and them, tends by itself to give rise to a favoring of the in-group and relative devaluation of the out-group and discrimination against its members.[4] Devaluation of individuals and groups, whatever its source, makes it easier to harm them.[5] A history of devaluation of a group; negative stereotypes; and negative images in the products of the culture, its literature, art, and media, "preselect" this group as a potential scapegoat and enemy.[6] In Germany, there had been a long history of anti-Semitism, with periods of intense mistreatment of Jews.[7] In addition to early Christian theological anti-Semitism, the intense anti-Semitism of Martin Luther,[8] who described Jews in language similar to that later used by Hitler, was an important influence. Centuries of discrimination and persecution further enhanced anti-Semitism and made it an aspect of German culture.[9] Even though at the end of World War I German Jews were relatively assimilated. Anti-Semitism in the deep structure of German culture provided a cultural blueprint, a constant potential for renewed antagonism against them.

Overly strong respect for authority, with a predominant tendency to obey authority, is another important cultural characteristic. It leads people to turn to authorities, old or new, for guidance in difficult times.[10] It leads them to accept the authorities' definition of reality, their views of problems and solutions, and stops them from resisting authorities when they lead them to harm others. There is substantial evidence that Germans had strong respect for authority that was deeply rooted in their culture, as well as a tendency to obey those with even limited authority.[11] German families and schools were authoritarian, with restrictive and punitive child-rearing practices.[12]

A monolithic (in contrast to a pluralistic) society, with a small range of predominant values and/or limitations on the free flow of ideas, adds to the predisposition for group violence. The negative representation of a victim group and the definition of reality by authorities that justifies or even necessitates the victims' mistreatment will be more broadly accepted. Democratic societies, which tend to be more pluralistic, are unlikely to engage in genocide,[13] especially if they are "mature" democracies, with well-developed civic institutions.[14]

German culture was monolithic: It stressed obedience, order, efficiency, and loyalty to the group.[15] The evolution of the Holocaust can be divided into two phases. The first brought Hitler to power. During the second phase, Nazi rule, the totalitarian system further reduced the range of acceptable ideas and the freedom of their expression.

A belief in cultural superiority (that goes beyond the usual ethnocentrism), as well as a shaky group self-concept that requires self-defense, can also contribute to the tendency to turn against others. Frequently the two combine a belief in the superiority of one's group with an underlying sense of vulnerability and weakness. Thus, the cultural self-concept that predisposes to group violence can be complex but demonstrable through the products of the culture, its literature, its intellectual and artistic products, its media.

The Germans saw themselves as superior in character, competence, honor, loyalty, devotion to family, civic organization, and cultural achieve-ments. Superiority had expressed itself in many ways, including proclama-tions by German intellectuals of German superiority and of their belief in Germany's right to rule other nations.[16] Partly as a result of tremendous devastation in past wars, and lack of unity and statehood until 1871, there was also a deep feeling of vulnerability and shaky self-esteem. Following unification and a brief period of strength, the loss of World War I, and the intense life problems afterward were a great blow to cultural and societal self-concept.[17]

The existing conditions sharply contrasted with the glory and image of the past. Difficult life conditions threaten the belief in superiority and activate the underlying feelings of weakness and vulnerability. They inten-sify the need to defend and/or elevate the self-concept, both individual and cultural.

Another important cultural characteristic that contributes to a sense of vulnerability is a past history of victimization. Just like victimized individu-als, groups of people who have been victimized in the past are intensely affected.[18] Their sense of self is diminished. They come to see the world and people in it, especially outsiders, individuals as well as whole groups, as dangerous. They feel vulnerable, needing to defend themselves, which can lead them to strike out violently. Healing by victimized groups is essential to reduce the likelihood that they become perpetrators.[19]

A history of aggression as a way of dealing with conflict also contrib-utes to the predisposition for group violence. It makes renewed aggression more acceptable, more normal. Such a tradition, which existed in Germany before World War I, was greatly strengthened by the war and the wide-spread political violence that followed it.[20]

Turning Against Others: Scapegoating and Ideology

Scapegoating and ideologies that arise in the face of difficult life condi-tions or group conflict are means for satisfying basic needs. However, they offer destructive satisfaction of basic needs in that they are likely to lead to harmful actions against others.

In the face of persistently difficult life conditions, already devalued outgroups are further devalued and scapegoated. Diminishing others is a way to elevate the self. Scapegoating protects a positive identity by reduc-ing the feeling of responsibility for problems. By providing an explana-tion for problems, it offers the possibility of effective action or control—

unfortunately, mainly in the form of acting against the scapegoat. It can unite people against the scapegoated other, thereby fulfilling the need for positive connection and support in difficult times. Adopting nationalistic and/or "better-world" ideologies offers a new comprehension of reality and, by promising a better future, hope as well.

But usually, some group is identified as the enemy that stands in the way of the ideology's fulfillment. By joining an ideological movement, people can relinquish a burdensome self to leaders or the group. They gain connection to others and a sense of significance in working for the ideology's fulfillment. Along the way, members of the "enemy" group, usually the group that is also scapegoated for life problems, are further devaluated and, in the end, often excluded from the moral realm. The moral values that protect people from violence become inoperative in relation to them.[21]

The ideology that the Nazis and Hitler offered the German people fit German culture. Its racial principle identified Aryans, and their supposedly best representatives, the Germans, as the superior race. The material needs of the German people were to be fulfilled (and their superiority affirmed) through the conquest of additional territories or living space. The ideology identified Jews as responsible for life problems and as a primary barrier to the creation of a pure, superior race. Later, Jews were also identified as the internal enemy that joined both the other internal enemy, the communists in Germany, and the external enemy, the Soviet Union, to destroy Germany.[22] In the *Fuhrerprinzip* (the leadership principle), the ideology prescribed obedience and offered the guidance of an absolute authority.

Ideology has been important in all the other instances of genocide as well. We may differentiate between "better-world" ideologies, which offer a vision of a better future for all human beings, and nationalistic ideologies, which promise a better life for a group or nation.[23] Although the German ideology was nationalistic, it had better-world components, in that racial purity was supposed to improve all humanity—except, of course, the impure, who were to be destroyed.

Self-Selection and the Selection of Perpetrators

Those who supported Hitler at the start, by voting for him, were quite heterogeneous with regard to class and occupation.[24] Initially, those who were perpetrators of violence were the Nazi paramilitary organization, *Sturmabteilung* (SA)—in German: "Assault Division," also known as Storm Troopers or Brownshirts—and the *Schutzstaffel* (SS)—in German: "Protective Echelon," the black-uniformed, elite military corps of the Nazi Party. They were joined by others as the evolution of violence progressed, growing in numbers and influence, becoming a kind of state within the State. A by-now well-known example of this is the German auxiliary police, who were sent to kill Jews before the machinery of killing in the concentration and extermination camps was established.[25] Some people in areas occupied by the Germans, like the Ukraine, Lithuania, and Latvia, also joined in the killing,[26] probably motivated by a combination of factors, including hostility toward the Soviet Union, of which they were part, which led them to join its enemy, the Germans; deep-seated anti-Semitism; and subservience to the occupiers and conquerors and the desire to gain their favor.

The importance of ideology was also evident in the selection of ideologically devoted Nazi doctors for the euthanasia program, where they were the direct perpetrators of murder, and for the extermination camps, where they directed the killing process.[27] Given a cultural devaluation, the people who are attracted to an ideology that elevates them over others and promises them a better world need not be personally prejudiced against a devalued group that is designated as the enemy. They might have greater needs aroused in them by life problems or might carry more of the cultural predispositions that shape motivation and guide modes of dealing with them. However, in research concluded in 1933 on SS members, although not all respondents reported personal anti-Semitism, most of them were openly and intensely anti-Semitic. The SS members who expressed the most intense, vicious anti-Semitism tended to be in leadership positions.[28]

The Roles of Obedience and Leaders

Since the dramatic experiments of Stanley Milgram,[29] obedience to authority has been viewed as a crucial determinant of the behavior of perpetrators. The importance of obedience is also suggested by the training that direct perpetrators receive in fostering submission to authority.[30]

However, many of the direct perpetrators are usually not simply forced or pressured by authorities to obey. Instead, they *join* leaders and decision makers, or a movement that shapes and guides them to become perpetrators. Decision makers and direct perpetrators share a *cultural-societal tilt*. They are part of the same culture and experience the same life problems.

They probably respond with similar needs and share the inclination for the same potentially destructive modes of their fulfillment. Many who become direct perpetrators voluntarily join the movement and enter roles that in the end lead them to perpetrate mass killing.

Leaders who propagate scapegoating and destructive ideologies are often seen as acting to gain followers or consolidate their following. Gordon Allport suggested that this was the case with Hitler.[31] However, leaders are members of their group, affected by the instigators that affect the rest of the group and by cultural characteristics that predispose the group to violence. For example, in previously victimized groups, the leaders, like the rest of the population, tend to carry unhealed wounds. It is this joining of the needs and inclination of populations and leaders that creates the great danger of mass killing or genocide.

Learning by Doing, Evolution, and Steps Along the Continuum of Destruction

Mass killing or genocide is usually the outcome of an evolution that starts with discrimination and limited acts of harm-doing. Harming people changes the perpetrators (and the whole society) and prepares them for more harmful acts.

People learn and change as a result of their own actions.[32] When they harm other people, a number of consequences are likely to follow. First, they come to devalue the victims more.[33] While in the real world, devaluation normally precedes harm-doing, additional devaluation makes greater mistreatment and violence possible. Just-world thinking may be an important mechanism in this.[34] Assuming that the world is just, and that people who suffer must have brought their fate on themselves by their actions or character, ironically perpetrators are likely to devalue people they themselves have harmed. The self-perception of perpetrators is also likely to change.[35] They come to see themselves as able and willing to engage in harmful, violent acts against certain people, and for good reasons, including higher ideals embodied in an ideology.

Personal goal theory suggests moral equilibration as another mechanism of change.[36] When a conflict exists between moral value(s) and other motives, people can reduce the conflict by replacing the moral value with another value that either is less stringent or is not a moral value, but is treated like one.

Consistent with this model, in Nazi Germany there was a progression of "steps along a continuum of destruction." First, Jews were thrown out of government jobs and the military, then from other important positions. They were pressured, then forced, into selling their businesses. Marriage and sexual relations between Jews and Aryan Germans were prohibited. Having lost all their property, earning their livelihoods with menial jobs, and identified by yellow stars, the Jews were moved into ghettos. In addition to sporadic violence against them, there was organized violence (e.g., *Kristallnacht*, "The Night of Broken Glass," in 1938). Many Jews were taken to concentration camps before mass extermination.[37] Steps along a continuum of destruction often start before those who lead a society to genocide come to power.

Harm doing and violence normally expand. Even when torture was part of the legal process in Europe's Middle Ages, over time, the circle of its victims enlarged. First it was used only with lower-class defendants, later also with upper-class defendants, and then even with witnesses, in order to obtain information from them.[38] In Germany, in addition to the increasing mistreatment of Jews, other forms of violence, such as the euthanasia program and the killing of mentally retarded, mentally ill, and physically deformed Germans—who, in the Nazi's view, diminished the genetic quality of the German race—contributed to psychological and institutional change and the possibility of greater violence.[39]

In the course of this evolution, the perpetrators exclude the victims from the moral universe. Moral principles become inapplicable to them. The prohibitions that normally inhibit violence lose force.[40] The killing of the victims can become a goal in its own right. Fanatic commitment develops to the ideology and to the specific goal of eliminating the victims.

Group processes come to dominate the psychology of perpetrators. Embedded in a group, trained in submission to authority, and further indoctrinated in ideology, people give up individual decision making to the group and its leaders.[41] The "We" acquires substantial power, in place of the "I." With the boundaries of the self weakened, there will be emotional contagion, the spread of feelings among group members, and shared reactions to events.[42] The members' perception of reality will be shaped by their shared belief system and by the support they receive from each other in interpreting events. Deviation from the group becomes increasingly unlikely.[43]

As a whole society moves along the continuum of destruction, there is a resocialization in beliefs, values, and standards of conduct. New institutions emerge that serve repression, discrimination, and the mistreatment of identified victims. They represent new realities, a new status quo.

The Psychology of Bystanders

In the face of the increasing suffering of a subgroup of society, bystanders frequently remain silent, passive—both internal bystanders and external ones, other nations and outside groups.[44] Bystanders also learn and change as a result of their own action—or inaction. Passivity in the face of others' suffering makes it difficult to remain in internal opposition to the perpetrators and to feel empathy for the victims. To reduce their own feelings of empathic distress and guilt, passive bystanders will distance themselves from victims.[45]

Most Germans participated in the system, in small ways such as using the Hitler salute and through organizations and group activities.[46] Moreover, as bystanders, most Germans were not just passive: They were *semi-active participants*. They boycotted Jewish stores and broke intimate relationships and friendships with Jews. Many benefited in some way from the Jews' fate, by assuming their jobs and buying their businesses. Repeatedly, the population initiated anti-Jewish actions before government orders, such as businesses firing Jewish employees or not giving them paid vacations.[47]

The German population shared a societal tilt with perpetrators—the cultural background and difficult life conditions, and the resulting needs and the inclination to satisfy them in certain ways. This might have made the Nazi movement acceptable to many who did not actually join. Moreover, after Hitler came to power, the lives of most Germans substantially improved.[48] They had jobs and were part of a community in which there was a spirit of togetherness and shared destiny. Their passivity, semi-active participation, and connections to the system had to change the German people, in ways similar to the changes in perpetrators. Some remained passive, others accepted or supported the persecution of Jews.[49] Still others became perpetrators themselves.

Other Nations as Bystanders

Fear contributed to the passivity of internal bystanders, in Germany and elsewhere. External bystanders, other nations and organizations outside Germany, had little to fear, especially at the start of Jewish persecution, when Germany was weak. Still, there was little response.[50] In 1936, after many Nazi atrocities, the whole world went to Berlin to participate in the Olympics, thereby affirming Nazi Germany. American corporations were busy doing business in Germany during most of the 1930s.

Christian dogma was a source of anti-Semitism in the whole Western world. It designated Jews as the killers of Christ and fanned their persecution for many centuries in response to their unwillingness to convert.[51] It was a source of discrimination and often led to extreme mistreatment. In the end, profound religious-cultural devaluation of Jews characterized many Christian nations.

In addition, people outside Germany were also likely to engage in just-world thinking and to further devalue Jews in response to their suffering in Germany. The German propaganda against Jews also reached the outside world. Serge Moscovici's research suggests that even seemingly unreasonably extreme statements about attitude have influence, if initially not on behavior, then at least on underlying attitudes.[52] As a consequence of these processes, anti-Semitism increased in the Western world in the 1930s and in the United States reaching a peak around 1938.[53]

These were some of the reasons for the silence and passivity. Among other reasons for nations to remain passive in face of the mistreatment by a government of its citizens are their unwillingness to interfere in the "domestic affairs" of another country (which could be a precedent for others interfering in their internal affairs), and the economic (trade), and other benefits they can gain from positive relations with the offending nation.[54]

Silence and passivity change bystanders, whether they are individuals or whole nations. They can diminish the subsequent likelihood of protest and punitive action by them. In turn, they encourage perpetrators, who often interpret silence as support for their policies.[55] Complicity by bystanders is likely to encourage perpetrators even more.

The Power of Bystanders

Could bystanders make a difference in halting or preventing mass killing and genocide? Some lines of research and the evidence of real events indicate bystanders' potential to exert influence.

Whether or not one person verbally defines the meaning of a seeming emergency as an emergency greatly affects the response of other bystanders.[56] When bystanders remain passive, they substantially reduce the likelihood that other bystanders will respond.[57]

Real-life events also show the influence of bystanders, even on perpetrators. In Denmark, the climate of support for Jews apparently influenced some German officials. They delayed deportation orders, which gave the

Danish population the time needed to mount and complete a massive res-cue effort, taking the approximately seven thousand Danish Jews to neu-tral Sweden in small boats. In Bulgaria, the actions of varied segments of the population, including demonstrations, stopped the government from handing over the country's Jewish population to the Germans.[58] Even within Germany, in spite of the Nazi repression, the population could exert influence. When the euthanasia program became known, some segments of the population protested: the Catholic clergy, some lawyers' groups, the relatives of people killed, and those in danger. As a result, the official pro-gram of euthanasia killing was discontinued.[59] There was little response, however, to the mistreatment of Jews. Added to anti-Semitism and other cultural preconditions, the gradual increase in mistreatment would have contributed to passivity.

Hitler's attitude also indicates the potential power of bystanders. He and his fellow Nazis were greatly concerned about the reactions of the population to their early anti-Jewish actions, and they were both surprised and emboldened by the lack of adverse reactions.[60] The population even initiated actions against Jews, which further shaped Nazi views[61] and stim-ulated additional official "measures."[62]

In the French Huguenot village of Le Chambon, under the leadership of their pastor, Andre Trocme, the inhabitants saved several thousand refu-gees, a large percentage of them children.[63] The behavior of the villagers influenced members of the Vichy police. Telephone calls to the presbytery began to inform villagers of impending raids, which enabled them to send the refugees into the neighboring forest. The deeds of the village doctor, who was executed, and his words at his trial influenced a German major, who in turn persuaded a higher officer not to move against the village.[64]

By speaking out and acting, bystanders can elevate values prohibit-ing violence, which over time perpetrators had come to ignore in their treatment of the victim group. Most groups, but especially ideologically committed ones, have difficulty seeing themselves, having a perspective on their own actions and evolution.[65] They need others as mirrors. Through sanctions, bystanders can also make the perpetrators' actions costly to them and induce fear of later punitive action. The earlier bystanders speak out and act, the more likely that they can counteract prior steps along the continuum of destruction and inhibit further evolution.[66]

Once commitment to the destruction of a group has developed, and the destruction is in process, nonforceful reactions by bystanders will tend to be ineffective.

The Psychology of Heroic Helpers

In the midst of violence and passivity, some people in Germany and Nazi occupied Europe endangered their lives to save Jews. To do so, helpers of German origin had to distance themselves from their group. Some rescuers were marginal to their community: They had a different religious background, were new to the community, or had a parent of foreign birth.[67] This perhaps enabled them to maintain an independent perspective and not join the group's increasing devaluation of Jews. Many rescuers came from families with strong moral values and held strong moral and humanitarian values themselves, with an aversion to Nazism.[68] Many were "inclusive" and regarded people in groups other than their own as human beings to whom human considerations apply.[69] Interviews with rescuers and the rescued indicate that individual rescuers were characterized by one or more of the three primary motivators that have been proposed for altruistic helping: a value of caring or "prosocial orientation" with its focus on the welfare of people and a feeling of personal responsibility to help;[70] moral rules or principles, the focus on living up to or fulfilling the principle or rule; and empathy, the vicarious experience of others' suffering.[71]

Marginality in relation to the perpetrators or to the dominant group does not mean that rescuers were disconnected from people. In the largest study to date, Sam and Pearl Oliner found that rescuers were deeply connected to their families and/or other people.[72] They described a large proportion (52 percent) of rescuers as "normocentric," or norm centered, characterized by "a feeling of obligation to a special reference group with whom the actor identified and whose explicit and implicit values he feels obliged to obey." Some normocentric rescuers were guided by internalized group norms, but many followed the guidance of leaders who set a policy of rescue. Some belonged to resistance groups, church groups, or families that influenced them. In Belgium, where the queen and the government-in-exile and church leaders set the tone, most of the nation refused to cooperate with anti-Jewish policies, and the underground actively helped Jews, who, as a result, were highly active in helping themselves.[73] But normocentric influence can lead people in varied directions. In Poland, some priests and resistance groups helped Jews, while other priests encouraged their communities to support the Nazi persecution of Jews, and some resistance groups killed Jews.[74]

Many rescuers started out by helping a Jew with whom they had a past relationship. Some were asked by a Jewish friend or acquaintance to help. The personal relationship would have made it more likely that altruistic, moral motives, as well as relationship-based motives, would become active. Having once helped someone they knew, many continued to help.

Even in ordinary times a feeling of competence is usually required for the expression of motivation in action, or even for its arousal.[75] When action endangers one's life, such "supporting characteristics" become crucial.[76] Faith in their own competence and intuition, fearlessness, and high tolerance for risk are among the characteristics of rescuers derived from interviews both with rescuers and with the people they helped.[77]

Heroic helpers are not born. An analysis of two specific cases shows the roots and evolution of heroism. The many-faceted influences at work can be seen in the case of Raoul Wallenberg, who saved the lives of tens of thousands of Hungarian Jews.[78] Wallenberg was a member of a poor branch of an influential Swedish family. He had wide-ranging travel and work experience and was trained as an architect. In 1944, he was the partner of a Hungarian Jewish refugee in an import-export business but seemed restless and dissatisfied with his career. He had traveled to Hungary several times on business, where he visited his partner's relatives. Earlier, while working in a bank in Haifa, he encountered Jewish refugees arriving from Nazi Germany, which was likely to arouse his empathy.

On his partner's recommendation, Wallenberg was approached by a representative of the American War Refugee Board and asked to go to Hungary as a Swedish diplomat to attempt to save the lives of Hungarian Jews who were then being deported to and killed at Auschwitz. He agreed to go. There was no predominant motive guiding his life at the time, like a valued career, which according to personal goal theory would have reduced his openness to activators of a conflicting motive. The request probably served to focus responsibility on him,[79] his connection to his business partner, and his partner's relatives, enhancing this feeling of responsibility.

Familiarity with Hungary and a wide range of past experience in traveling, studying, and working in many places around the world must have added to his feeling of competence. In Hungary, he repeatedly risked his life, subordinating everything to the cause of saving Jewish lives.[80]

Wallenberg's commitment seemingly increased over time, although it appears that once he got involved, his motivation to help was immediately high. Another well-known rescuer, Oscar Schindler, clearly progressed along a "continuum of benevolence."[81] He was a German born in Czechoslovakia. In his youth, he raced motorcycles. As a Protestant, he left his village to marry a Catholic girl from another village. Thus, he was doubly marginal and also adventurous. Both his father and his wife were opposed to Hitler. Still, he joined the Nazi Party and followed the German troops to Poland, where he took over a confiscated factory and, using Jewish slave labor, proceeded to enrich himself.

However, in contrast to others in a similar situation, Schindler responded to the humanity of his slave laborers. From the start, he talked with them and listened to them. He celebrated birthdays with them. He began to help them in small and large ways. In some rescuers, the motivation to help followed witnessing the murder or brutal treatment of a Jew.[82] Schindler had a number of such experiences. His actions resulted in two arrests and brief imprisonments from which he freed himself by invoking real and imaginary connections to important Nazis. Both Schindler and Wallenberg possessed considerable personal power and seemed to enjoy exercising this power to save lives.

To protect his slave laborers from the murderous concentration camp, Plaszow, in Poland, Schindler persuaded the Nazis to allow him to build a camp next to his factory. As the Soviet army advanced, Schindler moved his laborers to his hometown, where he created a fake factory that produced nothing, its only purpose to protect the Jewish laborers. In the end, Schindler lost all the wealth he had accumulated in Poland, but saved about 1,200 lives.

Like perpetrators and bystanders, heroic helpers evolve. Some of them develop fanatic commitment to their goal.[83] The usual fanatics subordinate themselves to a movement that serves abstract ideals. They come to disregard the welfare and lives of at least some people as they strive to fulfill these ideals. I regard some of the rescuers as "good fanatics," who completely devoted themselves to the *concrete* aim of saving lives.

The Heroism of Survivors

The heroism of rescuers has slowly come to be known, acknowledged, and celebrated. The heroism of survivors has remained, however, largely unrecognized. Parents, often in the face of impossible odds that can immobilize people, took courageous and determined actions to save their families. Children themselves often showed initiative, judgment, courage, and maturity that greatly exceeded what we normally imagine children to be capable of.

In information I gathered, primarily from child survivors (who were less than thirteen years of age when the Holocaust began), in conversations and questionnaires, they described many amazing acts, of their own and of their parents. Parents found ways to hide children, so that they might live even if the parents were killed. Young children lived with an assumed identity, for example, as a Catholic child in a boarding school. One survivor was a seven-year-old child in a hospital. She had already recovered from scarlet fever, but to be safe, remained in the hospital. There was a raid on the hospital, so she put on clothes that were hidden under her mattress and walked out of the building, through a group of uniformed men, to the house of a friendly neighbor ten blocks away who brought her the clothes in the first place.

Their actions, which saved their own lives and the lives of others, were in turn likely to shape these survivors' personality. It was probably an important source of the capacity of many of them, in spite of the wounds inflicted by their victimization, to lead highly effective lives.

The Obligation of Bystanders

We cannot expect bystanders to sacrifice their lives for others. But we can expect individuals, groups, and nations to act early along a continuum of destruction, when the danger to themselves is limited, and the potential exists for inhibiting the evolution of increasing destructiveness. This will only happen if people—children, adults, whole societies—develop an awareness of their common humanity with other people, as well as of the psychological processes in themselves that turn them against others. Institutions and modes of functioning can develop that embody a shared humanity and make exclusion from the moral realm more difficult. Healing from past victimization,[84] building systems of positive reciprocity, creating crosscutting relations between groups,[85] and developing joint projects[86] and superordinate goals can promote the evolution of caring and nonaggressive persons and societies.[87]

Reprinted and abridged from a chapter of the same title by Ervin Staub in L. S. Newman and R. Erber, eds., *What Social Psychology Can Tell Us About the Holocaust: Understanding Perpetrator Behavior* (New York: Oxford University Press, 2002). With permission of the author and Oxford University Press. An earlier version won the Otto Klineberg Prize for Intercultural and International Relations of the Society for the Psychological Study of Social Issues.

Notes

1. Barbara Huff and Ted Robert Gurr, "Systematic Early Warning of Humanitarian Emergencies," *Journal of Peace Research* 35, no. 5 (September 1998): 551–79.

2. Leo Kuper, *Genocide: Its Political Use in the Twentieth Century* (New Haven: Yale University Press, 1981).

3. Ervin Staub, *The Roots of Evil: The Origins of Genocide and Other Group Violence* (New York: Cambridge University Press, 1989); Ervin Staub, "Steps Along the Continuum of Destruction: The Evolution of Bystanders, German Psychoanalysts and Lessons for Today," *Political Psychology* 10, no. 1 (1989): 39–53; Ervin Staub, "The Origins and Prevention of Genocide, Mass Killing, and Other Collective Violence," *Peace and Conflict: Journal of Peace Psychology* 5 (1999): 303–36; Ervin Staub "Genocide and Mass Killing: Origins, Prevention, Healing and Reconciliation," *Political Psychology* 21 (2000): 367–82.

4. Marilyn B. Brewer, "In-Group Bias in the Minimal Intergroup Situation: A Cognitive Motivational Analysis," *Psychological Bulletin* 86 (1978): 307–24; Henry Tajfel, ed., *Social Identity and Intergroup Relations* (Cambridge: Cambridge University Press, 1982); Henri Tajfel, Cedric Flamant, Michael G. Billig, and R. P. Bundy, "Societal Categorization and Intergroup Behavior," *European Journal of Social Psychology* 1 (1971): 149–77.

5. Albert Bandura, B. Underwood, and M. E. Fromson, "Disinhibition of Aggression Through Diffusion of Responsibility and Dehumanization of Victims" *Journal of Research in Personality* 9 (1976): 253–69.

6. Staub, *The Roots of Evil*.

7. Max I. Dimont, *Jews, God and History* (New York: Signet, 1962); Patrick Girard, "Historical Foundations of Anti-Semitism," in J. Dimsdale, ed., *Survivors, Victims and Perpetrators: Essays on the Nazi Holocaust* (New York: Hemisphere, 1980).

8. Raul Hilberg, *The Destruction of the European Jews* (New York: Harper and Row, 1961); Martin Luther, *Works: On the Jews and their Lies*, vol. 47 (St. Louis, MO: Muhlenberg Press, 1955–1975).

9. Girard, "Historical Foundations of Anti-Semitism."

10. Erich Fromm, *Escape from Freedom* (New York: Avon, 1965).

11. Girard, "Historical Foundations of Anti-Semitism"; Gordon A. Craig, *The Germans* (New York: New American Library, 1982).

12. Alice Miller, *For Your Own Good: Hidden Cruelty in Child-Rearing and the Roots of Violence* (New York: Farrar, Straus and Giroux, 1983); E. D. Devereux, "Authority and Moral Development among German and American Children: A Cross-National Pilot Experiment," *Journal of Comparative Family Studies* 3 (1972): 99–124.

13. Rudolph J. Rummel, *Death by Government* (New Brunswick, NJ: Transaction, 1994).

14. Staub. "The Origins and Prevention of Genocide."

15. Craig, *The Germans*; Staub, *The Roots of Evil*.

16. Craig, *The Germans*; Staub, *The Roots of Evil*; Otto Nathan and Heinz Norden, *Einstein on Peace* (New York: Avenel Books, 1960).

17. Craig, *The Germans*; Milton Mayer, *They Thought They Were Free: The Germans, 1933–45* (Chicago: University of Chicago Press, 1955).

18. Judith Herman, *Trauma and Recovery* (New York: Basic Books, 1992); Lisa McCann and Laurie Anne Pearlman, *Psychological Trauma and the Adult Survivor: Theory, Therapy, and Transformation* (New York: Bruner/Mazel 1990).

19. Staub, "The Origins and Prevention of Genocide"; Ervin Staub, "Breaking

the Cycle of Genocidal Violence: Healing and Reconciliation," In J. Harvey, ed., *Perspectives on Loss: A Source Book* (Washington, DC: Taylor and Francis, 1998).

20. George M. Kren and Leon Rappaport, *The Holocaust and the Crisis of Human Behavior* (New York: Holms and Meier, 1980).

21. Staub, *The Roots of Evil*.

22. Lucy S. Dawidowicz, *The War Against the Jews: 1933–1945* (New York: Holt, Rinehart and Winston, 1975); Hilberg, *The Destruction of the European Jews*; Kren and Rappaport, *The Holocaust and the Crisis of Human Behavior*, 1980.

23. Staub, *The Roots of Evil*.

24. David Abraham, *The Collapse of the Weimar Republic: The Political Economy in Crisis* (New York: Holmes and Meier, 1987); G. M. Platt. "Thoughts on a Theory of Collective Action: Language, Affect, and Ideology in Revolution," in M. Albin, R. J. Devlin, and G. Heeger, eds., *New Directions in Psychohistory: The Adelphi Papers in Honor of Erik H. Erikson* (Lexington, MA: Lexington Books, 1980).

25. Christopher R. Browning. *Ordinary Men: Reserve Battalion 101 and the Final Solution in Poland* (New York: HarperCollins, 1992); Daniel Goldhagen, *Hitler's Willing Executioners: Ordinary Germans and the Holocaust* (New York: Knopf, 1996).

26. Goldhagen, *Hitler's Willing Executioners*.

27. Robert J. Lifton, *The Nazi Doctors: Medical Killing and the Psychology of Genocide* (New York: Basic Books, 1986).

28. Peter H. Merkl, *The Making of a Stormtrooper* (Princeton: Princeton University Press, 1980).

29. Stanley Milgram, "Some Conditions of Obedience and Disobedience to Authority," *Human Relations* 18 (1965): 57–76; Stanley Milgram, *Obedience to Authority: An Experimental View* (New York: Harper and Row, 1974).

30. Kren and Rappaport, *The Holocaust and the Crisis of Human Behavior*.

31. Gordon Allport, *The Nature of Prejudice* (Reading, MA: Addison-Wesley, 1954).

32. Staub, *The Roots of Evil*; Ervin Staub, *Positive Social Behavior and Morality: Socialization and Development*, vol. 2 (New York, Academic Press, 1979).

33. Leonard Berkowitz, *Aggression: A Social Psychological Analysis* (New York: McGraw-Hill, 1962); Jeffrey Goldstein, Roger Davis, and Denis Herman, "Escalation of Aggression: Experimental Studies," *Journal of Personality and Social Psychology* 31 (1975): 162–70; G. M. Sykes and D. Matza, "Techniques of Neutralization: A Theory of Delinquency," *American Sociological Review* 22, no. 6 (1957): 664–70; Staub, *Positive Social Behavior and Morality*.

34. Melvin Lerner, *The Belief in a Just World: A Fundamental Delusion* (New York: Plenum, 1980); Melvin Lerner and C. H. Simmons, "Observer's Reaction to the 'Innocent Victim': Compassion or Rejection?" *Journal of Personality and Social Psychology* 4 (1966): 203–10.

35. D. L. Bem, "Self-Perception Theory," in L. Berkowitz, ed., *Advances in Experimental Social Psychology*, vol. 6 (New York: Academic Press, 1972); J. E. Grusec, L. Kuczynski, J. P. Rushton, and Z. M. Simutis, "Modeling, Direct Instruction, and Attributions: Effects on Altruism," *Developmental Psychology* 14 (1978): 51–57; Staub, *Positive Social Behavior and Morality*.

36. Ervin Staub, "Social and Prosocial Behavior," in Ervin Staub, ed., *Personality* (Englewood Cliffs, NJ: Prentice Hall, 1980); Staub, *The Roots of Evil*.

37. Dawidowicz, *The War Against the Jews*; Hilberg, *The Destruction of the European Jews*.

38. Edward Peters, *Torture* (New York: Basil Blackwell, 1985).

39. Dawidowicz, *The War Against the Jews*; Lifton, *The Nazi Doctors*.

40. Staub, *The Roots of Evil*.

41. Milgram, *Obedience to Authority*; Philip G. Zimbardo, "The Human Choice: Individuation, Reason, and Order versus Deindividuation, Impulse, and Chaos," in *Nebraska Symposium on Motivation* (Lincoln: University of Nebraska Press, 1969).

42. Stanley Milgram and Hans Toch, "Collective Behavior: Crowds and Social Movements," in G. Lindzey and E. Aronson, eds., *The Handbook of Social Psychology*, 2nd ed. (Reading, PA: Addison-Wesley, 1969); Ervin Staub, "Commentary," in N. Eisenberg and J. Strayer, eds., *Empathy and Its Development* (New York: Cambridge University Press, 1987); Ervin Staub and Lori Rosenthal, "Mob Violence: Social-Cultural Influencers, Group Process and Participants," in L. Eron and J. Gentry, eds., *Reason to Hope: A Psychological Perspective on Violence and Youth* (Washington, DC: *American Psychological Association*, 1994).

43. Staub, *The Roots of Evil*; Hans Toch, *The Social Psychology of Social Movements* (New York: Bobbs-Merrill, 1965).

44. Staub, *The Roots of Evil*; Staub, "The Origins and Prevention of Genocide."

45. Staub, *Positive Social Behavior and Morality*.

46. Bruno Bettelheim, "Remarks on the Psychological Appeal of Totalitarianism," in *Surviving and Other Essays* (New York: Vintage, 1979).

47. Hilberg, *The Destruction of the European Jews*.

48. Craig, *The Germans*.

49. Staub, *The Roots of Evil*.

50. David S. Wyman, *The Abandonment of Jews: America and the Holocaust, 1941–1945* (New York: Pantheon, 1984).

51. Girard, "Historical Foundation of Anti-Semitism"; Hilberg, *The Destruction of the European Jews*.

52. Serge Moscovici, *Social Influence and Social Change* (London: Academic Press, 1973); Serge Moscovici, "Toward a Theory of Conversion Behavior," in L. Berkowitz, ed., *Current Issues in Social Psychology* (New York: Academic Press, 1980).

53. David S. Wyman, *Paper Walls: America and the Refugee Crisis, 1938–1941* (Amherst: University of Massachusetts Press, 1968); Wyman, *The Abandonment of the Jews*.

54. Staub, "The Origins and Prevention of Genocide."

55. Staub, *The Roots of Evil*; Frederick Taylor, ed., *The Goebbels Diaries, 1939–1941* (New York: Putnam, 1983).

56. Leonard Bickman, "Social Influence and Diffusion of Responsibility in an Emergency"; Ervin Staub, "Helping a Distressed Person: Social, Personality and Stimulus Determinants," in L. Berkowitz, ed., *Advances in Experimental Social Psychology* vol. 7 (New York: Academic Press, 1974).

57. Bibb Latane and John M. Darley, *The Unresponsive Bystander: Why Doesn't He Help?* (New York: Appleton-Crofts, 1970); Staub, *Positive Social Behavior and Morality*.

58. Helen Fein, *Accounting for Genocide: Victims and Survivors of the Holocaust* (New York: Free Press, 1979).

59. Dawidowicz, *The War Against the Jews*; Lifton, *The Nazi Doctors*.

60. Dawidowicz, *The War Against the Jews*; Hilberg, *The Destruction of the European Jews*.

61. Staub, *The Roots of Evil*.

62. Hilberg, *The Destruction of the European Jews*.

63. Philip Paul Hallie, *Lest Innocent Blood be Shed: The Story of the Village of Le Chambon and How Goodness Happened There* (New York: Harper and Row, 1970).

64. Hallie, *Lest Innocent Blood be Shed*.

65. Staub, *The Roots of Evil*.

66. Staub, *The Roots of Evil*; Staub, "The Origins and Prevention of Genocide."

67. P. London, "The Rescuers: Motivational Hypotheses about Christians Who Saved Jews from the Nazis," in J. Macaulay and L. Berkowitz, eds., *Altruism and Helping Behavior* (New York: Academic Press, 1970); Nechama Tec, *When Light Pierced the Darkness: Christian Rescue of Jews in Nazi-occupied Poland* (New York: Oxford University Press, 1986).

68. London, "The Rescuers"; Samuel P. Oliner and Pearl M. Oliner, *The Altruistic Personality: Rescuers of Jews in Nazi Europe* (New York: Free Press, 1988).

69. Oliner and Oliner, *The Altruistic Personality*.

70. Staub, "Helping a Distressed Person"; Staub, *Positive Social Behavior and Morality*; Ervin Staub, "How People Learn to Care," In P. G. Schervish, V. A. Hodgkinson, M. Gates, et al., eds. *Care and Community in Modern Society: Passing on the Tradition of Service to Future Generations* (San Francisco: Jossey-Bass, 1995).

71. London, "The Rescuers"; Oliner and Oliner, *The Altruistic Personality*; Tec, *When Light Pierced the Darkness*.

72. Oliner and Oliner, *The Altruistic Personality*.

73. Fein, *Accounting for Genocide*.

74. Tec, *When Light Pierced the Darkness*.

75. Icek Ajzen, *Attitudes, Personality and Behavior* (Chicago: Dorsey Press, 1988); Bandura, "Disinhibition of Aggression"; Staub, *Positive Social Behavior and Morality*; Staub, "Social and Prosocial Behavior."

76. Staub, "Social and Prosocial Behavior."

77. London, "The Rescuers"; Oliner and Oliner, *The Altruistic Personality*; Tec, *When Light Pierced the Darkness*.

78. Kati Marton, *Wallenberg* (New York: Ballantine, 1982).

79. Staub, *Positive Social Behavior and Morality*.

80. Marton, *Wallenberg*.

81. Thomas Keneally, *Schindler's List* (New York: Penguin, 1982).

82. Oliner and Oliner, *The Altruistic Personality*.

83. Staub, *The Roots of Evil*.

84. Staub, "Breaking the Cycle of Genocidal Violence."

85. Morton Deutsch, *The Resolution of Conflict: Constructive and Destructive Processes*. (New Haven, CT: Yale University Press, 1973).

86. Thomas F. Pettigrew, "Generalized Intergroup Contact Effects on Prejudice," *Personality and Social Psychology Bulletin* 23 (1997): 173–85.

87. Staub, *The Roots of Evil*; Ervin Staub, "Transforming the Bystander: Altruism, Caring and Social Responsibility," In H. Fein, ed., *Genocide Watch* (New Haven: Yale University Press, 1992); Staub, "The Origins and Prevention of Genocide."

Contributors

Jennifer Heath is an independent scholar, teacher, award-winning activist, cultural journalist, curator, and the author and/or editor of sixteen books of fiction and nonfiction, including *A House White with Sorrow: Ballad for Afghanistan* (Boulder, CO: Roden Press, 1996), *The Scimitar and the Veil: Extraordinary Women of Islam* (Mahwah, NJ: Paulist Press, 2004), *The Veil: Women Writers on Its History, Lore, and Politics* (Berkeley: University of California Press, 2008), and *The Jewel and the Ember: Love Stories of the Ancient Middle East* (Interlink Publishing, forthcoming), She is also co-editor with Ashraf Zahedi of *Land of the Unconquerable: The Lives of Contemporary Afghan Women* (Berkeley: University of California Press, 2011) and *Children of Afghanistan: The Path to Peace* (Austin: University of Texas Press, 2014). She has written dozens of articles and chapters for periodicals, anthologies, and encyclopedias, and produced or co-produced conferences, film festivals, radio, and television presentations, and was senior academic consultant for the *BBC* feature, *Taking the Veil*. Many of her art exhibitions have traveled worldwide. She founded the Seeds for Afghanistan program on behalf of Afghans4Tomorrow and the Afghanistan Relief Organization Midwife Training and Infant Care Program, now International Midwife Association. She is a member of Costs of War; Middle East Studies Association; Association for Middle East Women's Studies; and the Association for the Study of Religion, Nature, and Culture. She was born in Melbourne, Australia, grew up in Japan, Colombia, Bolivia, Afghanistan, and Spain; and now lives in Boulder, Colorado.

Ashraf Zahedi is a sociologist and visiting scholar at the University of California, Santa Barbara. Originally from Iran, she earned her PhD from Boston University. She has extensive teaching and research experience. Her research interests include social movements, social policy, gender equality, human rights, and international justice. She has conducted research at the Beatrice Bain Research Group at the University of California, Berkeley; The Institute for Research on Women and Gender at Stanford University; and the Center for Middle Eastern Studies at the University of California, Berkeley. Zahedi has published many academic articles and is, with Jennifer Heath, the co-editor of *Land of the Unconquerable: The Lives of Contemporary of Afghan Women* (Berkeley: University of California Press, 2011)— winner of the Academic Libraries Choice 2011 Award—and *Children of Afghanistan: The Path to Peace* (Austin: University of Texas Press, 2014). She has long been involved in social justice work, and her many leadership awards include "Special Congressional Recognition" of the United States House of Representatives for Outstanding and Invaluable Service to the Community.

Dirk Adriaensens is a member of the executive committee of the BRussells Tribunal, an activist think tank and peace organization with a special focus on Iraq. This initiative of intellectuals, artists, and activists denounces the logic of permanent war promoted by the U.S. government and its allies, of which West Asia is primarily the victim. Founded around the time of the invasion in March 2003, the tribunal was largely supported by the cultural world in Brussels. Between 1992 and 2003, Adriaensens was coordinator of SOS Iraq and led several delegations there to observe the devastating consequences of the UN sanctions. He was a member of the International Organizing Committee of the World Tribunal on Iraq (2003–2005) and is co-coordinator of the Global Campaign Against the Assassination of Iraqi academics. He is coauthor of *Rendezvous in Baghdad, EPO, Antwerp (1994), Cultural Cleansing in Iraq* (London: Pluto Press, 2010); *Beyond Educide* (Ghent: Academia Press, 2012); *The Iraq War Reader* (Online Interactive I-Book Global Research, 2012); and *The Middle East: The Times They are A-changin'* (EPO, 2013). Adriaensens also regularly writes articles, in Dutch and English, for *Global Research*, where he is a research associate, *Truthout, Al Araby, Countercurrents*, the *International Journal of Contemporary Iraqi Studies, DeWereldMorgen*, and other media.

Sama Alshaibi's photographs and videos situate her own body as a site of performance in consideration of the social and gendered impacts of war

and migration. Her work complicates the coding of the Arab female figure found in the image history of photographs and moving images. Her
sculptural installations evoke the disappearance of the body and act as
counter-memorials to war and forced exile. Her monograph, *Sand Rushes
In*, was published by Aperture, New York, and features her eight-year Sil-
sila series (debuted at the 55th Venice Biennale), which probes the human
dimensions of borders, migration, and ecological demise. In 2021, Alshaibi
was named a Guggenheim Fellow in Photography. In addition to the 55th
Venice Biennale, she has participated in Bolivia's 21st International Art
Biennial of Santa Cruz de la Sierra; the 13th Cairo International Biennale;
the Honolulu Biennial; the Qalandia International Biennial; and Houston's FotoFest Biennial. She was also selected for the *State of The Art 2020*
(Crystal Bridges Museum of Art/the Momentary, Arkansas), has held solo
exhibitions at the Ayyam Gallery in Dubai, and at Artpace, where she participated as National Artist in Residence in San Antonio, Texas. Alshaibi
received the first prize Project Development Award from the Center in
Santa Fe, New Mexico, and the 2017 Visual Arts Grant from the Arab Fund
for Arts and Culture in Beirut. Other solo exhibitions include the Herbert
F. Johnson Museum of Art at Cornell University; Scottsdale Museum of
Contemporary Art, Arizona; and London's Ayyam Gallery. She has participated in 150 group exhibitions spanning the United States, Germany, the
Netherlands, México, France, and Greece. Born in Basra to an Iraqi father
and Palestinian mother, Alshaibi is professor and co-chair of Photography,
Video, and Imaging at the University of Arizona, Tucson.

Sareta Ashraph is a barrister specialized in international criminal law, with
expertise in the gendered commission and impact of international crimes.
She heads the Office of Field Investigations at the United Nations Investigative Team to promote accountability for crimes committed by Daesh/
ISIL (UNITAD). She is also a senior legal consultant with the Center
for Justice & Accountability on case-building projects concerning crimes
committed in Syria and Iraq. In 2017, Ashraph was part of the start-up
team of the International, Impartial, and Independent Mechanism (IIIM).
From May 2012 to November 2016, she served as Chief Legal Analyst on
the UN Commission of Inquiry on Syria. She is a Visiting Fellow at the
University of Oxford, and co-editor of *The Syrian War: Between Justice and
Political Reality* (Cambridge: Cambridge University Press, 2020).

Edina Bećirević is professor of Security Studies at the University of Sarajevo. She studied at the University of Sarajevo, the London School of Eco-

nomics and Political Science, and Central European University, and was a Postdoctoral Fulbright Fellow at Yale University. Her research interests are focused on topics of transitional justice, genocide, and extremism. In the 1990s, Bećirević worked as a journalist covering the war and genocide in Bosnia and Herzegovina, as well as the trials at the International Criminal Tribunal for the Former Yugoslavia (ICTY), which inspired her to pursue research in these areas. Her academic work challenges the view that the massacre at Srebrenica in July 1995 constituted the only genocide of the Bosnian War. She argues that Serbia, in collaboration with separatist Bosnian Serb forces, instigated a widespread genocidal process with the intent to exterminate Bosniaks (Bosnian Muslims). Her research has been published in her two books, *Genocide on the Drina River* (New Haven: Yale University Press, 2014) and *International Criminal Court: Between Ideals and Reality* (Sarajevo: Medunarodni centar za mir and Arka Press, 2003). Bećirević is also a cofounder of the Atlantic Initiative—Center for Security and Justice Research, where she has been involved in conducting and supervising a number of research projects related to different forms of extremism and reciprocal radicalization. Among the publications she has authored and coauthored are *Salafism vs. Moderate Islam* (Sarajevo: Atlantic Initiative) and *Left Behind: Survivors of Violent Extremism* (Sarajevo: Atlantic Initiative, 2019). She writes regularly in regional media about the dangers of nationalism, extremism, and genocide denial, as well as opinion pieces for the *Intercept*, *Euronews* and the Institute for War and Peace Reporting.

Soren Blau is the Manager of Identification Services and Senior Forensic Anthropologist at the Victorian Institute of Forensic Medicine (VIFM). She is an adjunct professor in the Department of Forensic Medicine at Monash University; and Founding Fellow Faculty of Science, The Royal College of Pathologists of Australasia (RCPA). Blau is also the Chair of the Forensic Anthropology Technical Advisory Group for the National Institute of Forensic Sciences (NIFS), and a member of the INTERPOL Disaster Victim Identification Pathology and Anthropology Sub-Working Group. Blau is the recipient of numerous awards and fellowships including a Churchill Fellowship (2013); Australian Academy of Forensic Sciences "Oscar Rivers Schmalzbach" Research Fellowship (2014); National Institute of Forensic Sciences (NIFS) Research Award (2019); and a Victorian Endowment for Science, Knowledge, and Innovation (veski) "inspiring women STEM sidebyside" program (2020). She has participated in the recovery and analysis of human remains from archaeological and forensic

contexts in numerous countries and has delivered training to forensic practitioners and related stakeholders in Australia and abroad.

Ariel E. Dulitzky is clinical professor of Law, the Director of the Human
Rights Clinic, and the Director of the Latin America Initiative at the
School of Law of the University of Texas, Austin. Among the Clinic's recent
reports is *NAMING AND SHAMING: Violations of the Human Rights of
Transgender Persons with Felonies in Texas.* Dulitzky is a leading expert in
the inter-American human rights system. In 2010, he was appointed to the
United Nations Working Group on Enforced or Involuntary Disappearances and elected as its Chair-Rapporteur in 2013 (2013–2015). Prior to
joining the University of Texas, he was Assistant Executive Secretary of
the Inter-American Commission on Human Rights (IACHR). A native of
Argentina, Dulitzky has dedicated his career to human rights—in both his
scholarly research and his legal practice. His extensive expertise is derived
from active involvement in the promotion and defense of rights, particularly in the Americas and in international human rights litigation. His
publications focus on human rights, the inter-American human rights system, enforced disappearances, afro-descendants and Indigenous collective
rights, racial discrimination, and the rule of law in Latin America.

Melvin Edwards is a pioneer in the history of contemporary African
American art and sculpture. Born in 1937 in Houston, Texas, he began his
artistic career at the University of Southern California, where he met and
was mentored by the Hungarian painter Francis de Erdely. In 1965, the
Santa Barbara Museum of Art organized his first solo exhibition, which
launched his professional career. He moved to New York City in 1967,
where his work was exhibited at the Studio Museum in Harlem, and, in
1970, he became the first African American sculptor to have a solo exhibition at the Whitney Museum of American Art. Edwards's practice reflects
his engagement with the history of race, labor, and violence, as well as with
themes of the African Diaspora. Making welding his preferred medium, his
sculptures are studies in abstraction and minimalism. Ranging from colorful painted sculptures that expand on the modernist vocabulary of artists
like Alexander Calder to barbed wire installations to tangled amalgama-
tions of agricultural and industrial elements, his work is distinguished by its
formal simplicity and powerful materiality. He is best known for his series,
Lynch Fragments, welded combinations of disparate objects that invite com-
peting narratives of oppression and creation. Edwards has a longstanding

commitment to public art having created sculptures for universities, public housing projects, and museums. His work has been widely exhibited nationally and internationally and includes retrospectives at the Neuberger, the Zimmerli, and the Columbus museums of art. He has had myriad solo exhibitions and participated in innumerable group exhibitions across the United States and Europe. His work is represented in the collections of, among others, the Albright-Knox Art Gallery, the Brooklyn Museum of Art, the Los Angeles County Museum of Art, the Metropolitan Museum of Art, Houston's Museum of Fine Arts, The Museum of Modern Art–New York, the Pennsylvania Academy of the Fine Arts, San Francisco Museum of Modern Art, Harlem's Studio Museum, and the Whitney Museum of American Art. Edwards taught at Rutgers University from 1972 to 2002, and, in 2014, received an honorary doctorate from the Massachusetts College of Art.

Chitra Ganesh is a Brooklyn-based visual artist whose work encompasses drawing, painting, comics, wall installations, video art, and animation. Through studies in literature, semiotics, social theory, science fiction, and historical and mythic texts, Ganesh attempts to reconcile representations of femininity, sexuality, and power absent from the artistic and literary canons. She often draws on Hindu and Buddhist iconography and South Asian forms such as *Kalighat* and *Madhubani* and is negotiating her relationship to these images with the rise of right-wing fundamentalism in India. Ganesh graduated *magna cum laude* from Brown University and received her MFA from Columbia University. Her work has been exhibited widely across the United States, Europe, and South Asia and held in prominent public collections such as the Philadelphia Museum of Art, San Jose Museum of Art, Baltimore Museum, the Whitney Museum, and the Museum of Modern Art.

Mariam Ghani is an artist, writer, and filmmaker. Her work looks at places, spaces, and moments where social, political, and cultural structures take on visible forms, and span multiple disciplines. Her films have screened at, among other festivals, the Berlinale, Rotterdam, CPH:DOX, DOC NYC, Sheffield Doc/Fest, SFFILM, Ann Arbor, FIDBA, and Il Cinema Ritrovato. Her work has been exhibited and screened at the Guggenheim, the Museum of Modern Art; Met Breuer; Queens Museum in New York, the National Gallery in Washington, D.C., the Saint Louis Art Museum, the Indianapolis Museum of Art; the CCCB in Barcelona; the Sharjah, Lahore, and Liverpool Biennials; the Dhaka Art Summit; and Documenta 13 in Kabul and Kassel; among others.

Yassi Golshani is an Iranian artist, born in Hamburg, Germany. She grew up in Iran before moving to Paris in 1996, where she discovered contemporary art while studying at the Sorbonne. She lives and works in Prague, Czech Republic. She has exhibited widely in Iran and France. Her work is part of the permanent collection at the Seregei Parajnov Museum in Yerevan, Armenia. In 2005, she received a UNESCO grant to work at the Fundación Civitella Ranieri in Italy. In 2019, "Yassi, The Rights of a Child: A Mixed Media Exhibition," which took inspiration from the UN Declaration of the Rights of the Child, was displayed at Amazement Square, a children's museum in Lynchburg, Virginia. Golshani's work addresses the collective memories of the Iranian people. She calls herself a "wandering woman in a labyrinth, always searching for a new path." Her use of repetition, she says, "conveys time. In repetition the heavy weight of time is felt."

Majda Halilović heads the Research Department of the Atlantic Initiative—Center for Security and Justice Research in Bosnia and Herzegovina. Her academic profile is multidisciplinary in nature—she earned a BA in Psychology at Westminster University in London, an MA in Educational Policies at the University of Cambridge, and her PhD in Sociology and Social Policy at the Open University in the United Kingdom. She is a trained family-systems psychotherapist and has been actively engaged in civil society for the past twenty years, conducting research and training about violence against women; gender; security; prejudice in enforcement of the law; social exclusion and inclusion; and radicalization and extremism. Some of her publications include: *Gender and the Judiciary: The Implications of Gender within the Judiciary of Bosnia and Herzegovina* (DCAF/Atlantic Initiative, 2014); *Survivors Speak: Reflections on Criminal Justice System Responses to Domestic Violence in Bosnia and Herzegovina* (Atlantic Initiative/ DCAF, 2015); and *Gender Bias and the Law: Legal Frameworks and Practice from Bosnia & Herzegovina and Beyond* (Atlantic Initiative/DCAF, 2017).

Jonathan Herrera Soto graduated with a BFA from the Minneapolis College in Art and Design in 2017 and is studying at Yale University. Solo exhibitions include *In Between/ Underneath* at the Minneapolis Institute of Art, *All at Once* at Brown University, and *Querida Presencia* at the Duluth Art Institute. He has participated in numerous artist residencies, such as Bemis Center for Contemporary Arts, Yaddo, Kala Art Institute, Santa Fe Art Institute, and Highpoint Center for Printmaking. Herrera Soto is a recipient of the Jerome Hill Foundation Fellowship Grant, Brown University Artists Initiative Grant, Metro Regional Arts Council Next Step

Grant, Santo Foundation Individual Artist Award, Minnesota State Arts Board Artist Initiative Grant, and is a 2021 Paul and Daisy Soros Fellow.

Kayhan Irani is an Emmy-award winning writer, a cultural activist, and a Theater of the Oppressed trainer. She creates and leads participatory theater and story-based projects to build community, grow grassroots leadership, and connect to our deepest potential for change. She works internationally and in the United States with NGOs, government agencies, and community organizations using theater and story-based strategies for organizing, engagement, and education. Her published work includes a volume of essays, *Telling Stories to Change the World: Global Voices on the Power of Narrative to Build Community and Make Social Justice Claim* (New York: Routledge, 2008); and chapters in *Culturally Relevant Arts Education for Social Justice: A Way Out of No Way* (New York: Routledge 2015) and *Storytelling for Social Justice: Connecting Narrative and the Arts in AntiRacist Teaching*, 2nd ed. (New York: Routledge, 2019). She is working on *There is a Portal*, an immersive digital story and linked pedagogy which asks: if you were to show up as your fullest self, which stories would you remember?

Amrita Kapur is a gender thematic expert with the Gender and Security Division of DCAF in Geneva. She heads a project with PRAVO Justice in the Ukraine, partnering with the National School of Judges and Academy of Prosecutors to develop curricula and training workshops to implement new laws targeting gender-based violence. In addition, she is the technical lead on a series of workshops with women leaders as part of Track II peace processes in Yemen and the Korean Peninsula; and provides gender technical and project management expertise to projects in, among others, North Macedonia, Colombia, and Honduras. Kapur was a Gender Analyst on the United Nations International Independent Fact-Finding Mission on Myanmar; consulted for UN Women; and the UN Office on Drugs and Crime, while completing her PhD at the University of New South Wales. She spent several years with the International Center for Transitional Justice as a Senior Associate for the Gender Justice Program in New York, focusing on criminal prosecutions, truth-telling initiatives, security sector reform, and reparations programs. Across her career, Kapur has practiced international and domestic criminal law, and designed and delivered gender-focused training for prosecutors, judges, police officers, parliamentarians, ministry and local government officials, truth commissioners, investigators, and civil society organizations. She holds an LLM in

International Law from NYU, as well as a Bachelor of Laws and Honors degree in Psychology from UNSW.

Nancy Maron, originally from Boston and currently living in Boulder, Colorado, began a career working with the court systems nationally in the 1970s. From there, she went to state government, eventually running the Colorado Job Training program. She received a PhD in Sociology from the University of Denver and, a few years later, with her three sons grown, painting and sculpting became her main focuses. She studied at Denver's Art Students League, the Loveland Academy of Art, the University of Colorado, and in Italy, among others. She is the author of the acclaimed *Geometry of Life: A Memoir in Painting* (Boulder, CO: Baksun Books, 2020).

Dallas Mazoori is a lawyer with a particular interest in genocide and the persecution of ethnic and religious minorities in Afghanistan and Pakistan. From 2008 to 2011, she coordinated the Afghanistan Independent Human Rights Commission's Conflict Mapping project, documenting, and analyzing eight-thousand witness testimonies on war crimes and crimes against humanity. She has also worked in Afghanistan for the International Center for Transitional Justice, Physicians for Human Rights, as a consultant for the United Nations, and is the author of several peer-reviewed publications in the field of transitional justice.

Vasuki Nesiah is professor of Human Rights and International Law at the Gallatin School, New York University. Her current projects include *International Conflict Feminism* (Philadelphia: University of Pennsylvania Press, forthcoming) and *Reading the Ruins: Slavery, Colonialism, and International Law*. She is a founding member of Third World Approaches to International Law and co-editor of *TWAIL: A Handbook*, with Anthony Anghie, Bhupinder Chimni, Michael Fakhri, and Karin Mickelson (Northampton,MA: Edward Elgar Publishing, forthcoming). Recent publications on themes related to Nesiah's chapter in this volume include "The Ambitions and Traumas of Transitional Governance: Expelling Colonialism, Replicating Colonialism," in Micha Wiebusch and Emmanuel De Groof, eds., *International Law and Transitional Governance* (New York: Routledge, 2020); "Crimes Against Humanity: Racialized Subjects and Deracialized Histories," in Immi Tallgren and Thomas Skouteris, eds., *The New Histories of International Criminal Law: Retrials*, (Oxford: Oxford University Press, 2019); and "The Escher Human Rights Elevator: Technologies of the Local," in Sally Merry and Tine Destrooper, eds., *Human Rights Transformation in an Unequal World* (Philadelphia: University of Pennsylvania Press, 2018).

Morgan C. Page is an artist, designer, and associate professor of Art at Midwestern State University in Wichita Falls, Texas. Page received a BFA from the University of Houston, Texas, and her MFA from Rutgers University. She exhibits work nationally and internationally, including at the Museum of North Texas History; Capas at Marshall Arts Gallery in Memphis, Tennessee; and Foreign Affairs Game Show at the Universidada del Claustro de Sor Joana in City, México. She is a cross-disciplinary artist working in digital illustration, textiles, photography, performance, and installation. She also regularly publishes exhibition reviews and art-related research, often on topics of immigration, cultural lineage, and abandoned pioneer towns. Her contribution to this volume is part of the *2021 Supporting Indigenous Sisters: An International Print Exchange*, initiated by Professor Catherine Prose of Midwestern State University.

Stephen Parlato Artist / Activist / Boulder Colorado.

Akila Radhakrishnan is the President of the Global Justice Center, where she leads its work to achieve gender equality and human rights. Previously at GJC, Radhakrishnan led the development of groundbreaking legal work on both abortion access in conflict and the role that gender plays in genocide. She is a globally recognized voice on issues of reproductive rights, gender-based violence, and justice and accountability. Her unique expertise as a feminist international lawyer is sought by policymakers, academics, the media, and grassroots actors around the world. She has briefed the United Nations Security Council and the United Kingdom and European parliaments, and regularly advises governments and multilateral institutions on issues of gender equality and human rights. Her expert analysis has appeared in, among others, the *New York Times*, the *Washington Post*, *BBC*, *The Atlantic*, *Foreign Policy*, and *CNN*. Prior to the Global Justice Center, she worked at the International Criminal Tribunal for the Former Yugoslavia; DPK Consulting; and Drinker, Biddle & Reath, LLP. She received her JD, with a concentration in International Law, from the University of California, Hastings, and holds a BA in Political Science and Art History from the University of California, Davis. She is a term member of the Council on Foreign Relations, serves on the Board of Directors of Reprieve U.S., is a member of the Oxford Group of Practitioners on

Fact-Finding and Accountability, and an expert on the International Bar Association Human Rights Law Committee.

Elena Sarver is a Legal Adviser at the Global Justice Center, where she has worked since 2016. During her time at GJC, Elena has contributed to a variety of legal briefs, articles, and advocacy documents. She holds a JD from Benjamin N. Cardozo School of Law, where she participated in two year-long clinics: the Innocence Project and the Human Rights and Atrocity Prevention Clinic, where she researched sexual and gender-based violence crimes for regional human rights litigation. Elena received her BA in Political Science from Macalester College and studied abroad in Egypt at the American University in Cairo.

Stefan Schmitt is the former Director of the International Forensic Program at Physicians for Human Rights, where he directs medico-legal inquiries into international human rights violations and develops education and training programs. He has twenty-five years of experience in international forensic fieldwork, including ten years in a U.S. forensic crime laboratory as a crime scene and digital image enhancement analyst. He founded the Guatemalan Forensic Anthropology Team and has worked for the International Criminal Tribunals for the Former Yugoslavia and Rwanda on archaeological excavations, exhumation, and analysis of human remains. He helped found the Afghan Forensic Science Organization in Afghanistan and has conducted forensic assessments internationally. He is a coauthor of guidelines for human identification operations and the investigation of extra-legal, arbitrary, and summary executions, as well as several academic publications.

Leang Seckon was born in Prey Veng province, Cambodia, in the early 1970s, around the time of the onset of the American bombings of Indochina. The artist grew up during the brutal reign of the Khmer Rouge and the Cambodian-Vietnamese War. His densely painted and collaged surfaces are filled with symbols that recall this traumatic past, both on a cultural and personal level. A 2002 graduate of the Royal University of Fine Arts, Phnom Penh, Seckon participated in the 2012 Shanghai Biennale. He is considered one of the foremost members of the emerging Cambodian contemporary art scene and has exhibited in numerous solo shows around the world. In 2014, he was awarded a medal from Cambodia's Queen Norodom Monineath. In 2013, he participated in a residency at the Bronx Museum of the Arts in New York, while in 2015 he was selected for the 8th

Asia Pacific Triennial of Contemporary Art in Brisbane. His work is part of the Queensland Art Gallery | Gallery of Modern Art collection.

Ervin Staub is originally from Hungary; received a PhD at Stanford; taught at Harvard; and is professor emeritus and Founding Director of the doctoral program in the Psychology of Peace and Violence Program at the University of Massachusetts, Amherst. He is past President of the International Society for Political Psychology and of the Society for the Study of Peace, Conflict, and Violence. His best-known book is *The Roots of Evil* (Cambridge: Cambridge University Press, 1989). Others include the award-winning *Overcoming Evil: Genocide, Violent Conflict and Terrorism* (Oxford: Oxford University Press, 2013); and *The Roots of Goodness and Resistance to Evil: Inclusive Caring, Moral Courage, Altruism Born of Suffering, Active Bystandership and Heroism* (Oxford: Oxford University Press, 2016). He worked with teachers, schools, and parents to promote altruism in children; and conducted projects in Rwanda, Burundi, and the Congo to promote reconciliation. In Amsterdam, amid Dutch-Muslim violence, he trained police to develop active bystandership by officers to prevent other officers from doing unnecessary harm. This work is now expanding around the United States with students to stop harmful actions by fellow students. Staub's awards include Lifetime Contributions to Peace Psychology and Political Psychology, as well as awards from the Society for Psychological Study of Social Issues, and others.

James A. Tyner is a professor in the Department of Geography at Kent State University and a Fellow of the American Association of Geographers. A graduate of the University of Southern California, he is the author of several books, including *War, Violence, and Population: Making the Body Count* (New York: Guilford Press, 2009), which won the Meridian Book Award from the American Association of Geographers, and *The Politics of Lists: Bureaucracy and Genocide Under the Khmer Rouge* (Morgantown: West Virginia University Press, 2018), which won the 2019 Julian Minghi Distinguished Book Award.

Nicolette Waldman is a Middle East North Africa Researcher for Amnesty International, based in Beirut, Lebanon. Previously, she was a researcher at the Center for Civilians in Conflict, where she led a study on civilian involvement in war and conducted fieldwork for case studies on Bosnia, Libya, Gaza, and Somalia. She has been a legal fellow at the Afghan Independent Human Rights Commission in Kabul; a program manager for

Save the Children in the West Bank and Gaza; a Fulbright Scholar in Jordan—where she worked with CARE International to coordinate resources for Iraqi refugees—and a Senior Associate in the legal and policy office at Human Rights Watch. She holds a BA in International Affairs and English Literature from Lewis & Clark College and a law degree from Harvard.

David Weissbrodt (1944–2021) was the Regents Professor and Fredrikson & Byron Professor of Law at the University of Minnesota until his death in 2021. He was a distinguished and widely published scholar of international human rights law, who represented and served as an officer or board member of the Advocates for Human Rights, Amnesty International, the Center for Victims of Torture, the International Human Rights Internship Program, Readers International, and the International League for Human Rights. He served as a member of the United Nations Sub-Commission on the Promotion and Protection of Human Rights and was elected Chairperson of the Sub-Commission for 2001–2002.

Hilmi M. Zawati is the Chair of the Centre for International Accountability and Justice in Montreal. Before joining the Centre, Zawati served as the President of the International Legal Advocacy Forum for two consecutive terms. Over the past forty years, he has taught numerous subjects at both Kuwait University and Bishop's University and been a prominent speaker and author on various hotly debated legal issues Zawati has organized, co-chaired, and participated in several international conferences; and addressed significant academic and professional gatherings in some Middle Eastern countries, Africa, Europe, and at home in Canada. He has an accomplished body of transdisciplinary scholarship and has published numerous articles in Arabic and English, as well as twenty-four books, including prizewinning volumes on international humanitarian and human rights law, such as *The Triumph of Ethnic Hatred and the Failure of International Political Will: Gendered Violence and Genocide in the Former Yugoslavia and Rwanda* (Lewistown, NY: Edwin Mellen Press, 2010). His most recent volume is *Fair Labelling and the Dilemma of Prosecuting Gender-Based Crimes at the International Criminal Tribunals* (Oxford: Oxford University Press, 2015).

Helen Zughaib was born in Beirut, Lebanon, and lived mostly in the Middle East and Europe before coming to the United States to study at Syracuse University, earning her BFA from the College of Visual and Performing Arts. She currently lives and works in Washington, DC. She paints primarily in gouache and ink on board and canvas, although has recently been using wood, shoes, and cloth. Her work has been widely exhibited in galleries and museums in the United States, Europe, and Lebanon. Her paintings are included in many private and public collections, among them the White House; the World Bank; the Library of Congress; the U.S. Consulate General, Vancouver, Canada; the American Embassy in Baghdad, Iraq; the Arab American National Museum in Detroit, Michigan; and the Minneapolis Institute of Art. Her paintings are included in the DC Art Bank Collection, and she received the DC Commission on the Arts and Humanities Fellowship award in 2015, 2016, 2017, 2018, 2019, and 2020. Her work has been included in the Art in Embassy State Department exhibitions in Brunei, Nicaragua, Mauritius, Iraq, Belgium, Lebanon, Saudi Arabia, and Sweden. She has served as Cultural Envoy to Palestine, Switzerland, and Saudi Arabia. The John F. Kennedy Center/ REACH selected Zughaib for a three-year Social Impact Residency. Her paintings were gifted to heads of state by former President Barak Obama and Secretary of State, Hillary Clinton. She is the author/illustrator with Elia Zughaib of *Stories My Father Told Me* (Seattle: Cune Press, 2020).

"As an Arab American, I hope, through my work, to encourage dialogue and bring understanding and acceptance between the people of the Arab world and the West, especially since 9/11, our wars in Iraq, Afghanistan, and the more recent revolutions and crises in the Arab world, resulting from the 2010 "Arab Spring," which lead to the current war in Syria and the massive displacement of people seeking refuge in Europe, the Middle East, and America.

"My work is about creating empathy. Making a shared space for introspection and dialogue. I ask the viewer to see through someone else's eyes, walk in another's shoes. To accept the "other." To reject divisiveness. To promote acceptance and understanding and to reject violence and subjugation of anyone anywhere. To give voice to the voiceless, to heal, to reflect in our shared humanity."

Index

Made in the USA
Middletown, DE
14 June 2023